REFLECTIONS
ON SELF PSYCHOLOGY

PSYCHOANALYTIC INQUIRY BOOK SERIES

REFLECTIONS ON SELF PSYCHOLOGY

Edited by
Joseph D. Lichtenberg, M.D.
and
Samuel Kaplan, M.D.

 THE ANALYTIC PRESS
1983

Distributed by
LAWRENCE ERLBAUM ASSOCIATES, PUBLISHERS
Hillsdale, New Jersey   London

The Analytic Press

Distributed solely by

Lawrence Erlbaum Associates, Inc., Publishers
365 Broadway
Hillsdale, New Jersey 07642

Library of Congress Cataloging in Publication Data
Main entry under title:

Reflections of self psychology.

  (Psychoanalytic inquiry book series)
  Proceedings of a symposium held Oct. 31–Nov. 2, 1980
in Boston, Mass. and sponsored by the Boston Psycho-
analytic Society and Institute.
  Includes indexes.
    1. Self—Congresses. 2. Psychoanalysis—Congresses.
3. Infant psychology—Congresses. 4. Psychotherapy—
Congresses. I. Lichtenberg, Joseph. II. Kaplan,
Samuel, 1916– . III. Boston Psychoanalytic Society
and Institute. IV. Series.
BF697.R415   1983   155.2   83-12293
  ISBN 0-88163-001-2

Printed in the United States of America
10 9 8 7 6 5 4 3 2 1

Contents

IV. *SELF PSYCHOLOGY AND PSYCHOTHERAPY: THEORETICAL AND CLINICAL CONSIDERATIONS*

V. SELF PSYCHOLOGY: IMPLICATIONS FOR PSYCHOANALYTIC THEORY

VI. THEORY

Introduction

Joseph D. Lichtenberg, M.D.

Reflections on Self Psychology is based on the Boston Symposium held at the Boston Park Plaza Hotel from October 31 through November 2, 1980. To do justice to the experience of the participants, about 1000 in all, this book must capture within its pages not only the content of what was presented, explored, and evaluated but also a sense of the people who exchanged their ideas on and off the podium and the remarkable spirit of open inquiry that invigorated the whole proceedings.

To introduce the reader to the book I first describe the animating spirit of the symposium. To claim that a book or a meeting has as its goal to "explore" a subject is conventional in the rhetoric of scientists. To accomplish it requires the most careful planning on the part of the meeting's sponsors and arrangers. The members of the Planning Committee of the Boston Psychoanalytic Society and Institute prepared the program so that the dynamic of an investigation and an evaluation would be inherent in the workings of the proceedings. It is this that the reader should keep in mind as he or she peruses each section of this book.

The reader can glean a great deal about what is to follow from the opening section of the book. It derives from postbanquet speeches and contains witty, informative, introductory remarks by Kahana, Demos, and Kohut as well as an essay by Cooper. Ralph Kahana, the President of the Boston Psychoanalytic Society and Institute, offers a charming historical survey of the contributions made by members of the Boston Psychoanalytic Society and Institute to the subject of narcissism and the self. The historian, John Demos, a former student of Heinz Kohut, notes the potential in Kohut's work to revitalize the application of psychoanalytic conceptions to historical study. Heinz Kohut, addressing the participants in a lighthearted manner, sets the tone for the whole meeting: tolerance, friendliness, and forbearance in the evaluation and exploration of a set of new ideas by individuals both informed and open-minded: "Let us be guided by . . . a feeling of comradeship as we all try to inch closer toward the, in the last analysis, unreachable truths about the essence of the depths of man. . . . [A] critic must be able to try out a new set of ideas over an extended period before he can allow himself to judge its relevance, usefulness, and its explanatory power." The essay by Arnold Cooper, president of the American Psychoanalytic Association, can serve the reader as a rich, sensitive, and impartial placing of self psychology in a historical context. Cooper surveys the development of psychoanalytic theory and its many controversies and concludes: "I think the extraordinary interest in self psychology reflects its inclusion of so many of the long-simmering ideas in the psychoanalytic scientific cauldron."

The book, like the meeting, is organized to explore four subjects: (1) The Development of the Self: Infant Research; (2) The Implications of Self Psychology for Psychoanalytic Practice; (3) Self Psychology and Psychotherapy; and (4) The Implications of Self Psychology for Psychoanalytic Theory. The final section of the book is devoted to an essay by Kohut providing an integrated response to issues and criticisms raised in the course of the symposium. This essay, although based on extemporaneous responses by Kohut during different phases of the meeting, is in its written version a cohesive, carefully revised, and edited statement prepared in the mellowing period following the meeting and before Kohut's untimely death.

The format in the sections on infant research, psychoanalytic practice, psychoanalytically oriented psychotherapy, and psychoanalytic theory follows the same basic pattern. There is a clear incisive exposition of a psychology of the self position and an evaluative exploration of that position. Presentations and discussions are balanced between participants closely identified with self psychology, others interested in applying and testing its hypotheses, and others having defined positions quite divergent from that of self psychology.

For example, the section on the Development of the Self: Infant Research is based on a panel whose function was to explore an unanswered question: What is the nature of the interplay between the findings of self psychology and infant research? The findings of self psychology had been based on empathic-introspective studies of patients undergoing psychoanalysis. The theories of a cohesive self, its bipolarity between ambitions and ideals, and its vicissitudes within a matrix of self-selfobject relationships were deduced from reconstructions in which pathognomonic transferences occurring during psychoanalysis provided the data. During roughly the same period researchers who based their formulations on data obtained from direct observations of naturalistic and experimental settings had also evolved conceptions of the development of the self and of an interactional matrix of infant and caregiver. The panel was organized to explore the following problems: Do the formulations of the two disciplines overlap, affirm, or contradict one another? Might differences in method, findings, or in metaphors chosen to explain the data sharpen issues to be studied in the future by self psychology? (The range of issues covered is breathtaking.) What overall type of organizing concepts best fit the data? How and when does "I" as compared to "we" develop? What are the different forms of "we"—that is, of the infant's being together with its caregiver? How does affect coordinate with cognitive development? What is the best method to weigh the relative significances of differing aspects of development; that is, how much weight should be given to development of competencies that are relatively independent of the caregiver activities as compared to the central importance assigned by self psychology to the empathic responsiveness of the caregiver? The reader of the material derived from this panel now has the opportunity to survey the entire dialectic of ideas as they evolved. Stechler, the chairperson, Stern and Sander, the main presenters, and V. Demos, one of the discussants, are all primarily infant researchers. M. Tolpin's discussion offers a response from the perspective of self psychology, its theory and methodology.

Self psychology's emphasis on an empathic-introspective approach to analysis is in direct continuity with a strong trend in psychoanalytic technique. But its proposals, which are based on its findings derived from this traditional mode of observation, have by their nature altered the field of study—the way the psychoanalytic situation is structured and the way the analytic material is conceptualized. In the section of the book entitled The Implications of Self Psychology for Psychoanalytic Practice, the two main contributions deal with the clinical conduct of analysis. Kohut's initial writings centered on the psychoanalysis of analysands with narcissistic personality disorders or with more general problems of narcissistic grandiosity and idealization. The present inquiry carries the method directly into technical issues that pertain to the analysis of the neuroses.

A. Ornstein, whose case material had been presented to a special meeting of psychoanalytic candidates, uses her clinical data to establish a clinical context in which to examine the relationship between self psychology and the Oedipus complex. She asks: "Where do sexual identifications and sexual conflicts fit into self psychology?" "Do parents continue to have selfobject functions during the oedipal phase and what is the nature of the transferences that arise in relationship to their failure?'' Meyers, in her discussion of Ornstein's paper, attempts to place herself in the orientation of self psychology as suggested by Ornstein. In so doing she states: ''If we define a selfobject function as meeting the child's need for affirmation, validation, and mirroring from an important, even idealized other, who offers himself for identification for the purpose of enhancing growth, then, I think, Dr. Ornstein has made a good case for such a parental function of the homogenital parent during the oedipal phase in relation to the child's oedipal strivings.'' However, Meyers objects to the narrowness and restrictiveness of this view, and she constantly offers alternatives derived from other theoretical stances. Her suggestions move toward synthesis and integration of the differing views. Lichtenberg, through psychoanalytic clinical material, demonstrates how he has applied the concepts of self psychology to his analytic work. He proposes six principles of psychoanalytic techniques starting with the fundamental centrality of the empathic vantage point for analytic observation and culminating in a comprehensive, systematic sequence for psychoanalytic interpretation. In his discussion, Treurniet uses Lichtenberg's six principles to state his general agreement with the techniques described in the case and his strong disagreement with the theory and claims of many aspects of self psychology: ''Self psychology in the narrow sense is a gain to psychoanalysis, but self psychology in the broader sense is a grave and serious loss, especially from the viewpoint of technique.'' Wolf takes a markedly different position in his discussion. He treats Lichtenberg's six principles as expositions of technical steps to achieve psychological health as viewed from the standpoint of a psychoanalytic theory of the bipolar self. Wolf considers Ornstein's case as indicating that the so-called negative Oedipus complex is a consequence of disintegration of the self, and not a part of the normally occurring oedipal phase.

The section on Self Psychology and Psychotherapy opens new clinical terrain for exploration. This section contains papers by Basch and London and discussions by Michels and Bach, each raising questions about this initial attempt to extend the application of self psychology to the practice of analytically oriented psychotherapy. Basch presents a historical survey of his personal experience with psychotherapy, emphasizing his unsatisfactory efforts to apply classical analytic formulations about psychosexual development to psychotherapy. He contends that, previously, psychotherapy lacked a suitable theoretical base, but: ''By expanding and explaining the concept of transference Kohut has laid the basis for a comprehensive theory of psychotherapy. . . .'' In his discussion Michels takes strong exception to many of Basch's assertions. Michels states that Basch: ''has chosen to caricature traditional psychoanalytic theory and along with this to ignore the various fragments of suggestions for psychoanalytic psychotherapy that had already been formulated by Bibring, Gill, and others,'' as well as several decades of developmental ego psychology. London's paper, illustrated by a case vignette of a challengingly difficult patient, is a pioneering effort to explore the relationship between confrontation and empathic techniques used by self psychology in response to selfobject transferences. London presents an unusually detailed, forthright account of a series of interactive confrontations he employed with a young patient. He states that because ''the confronting psychotherapist was not experienced as part of the self but as an independent center of initiative. This raises an interesting question for self psychology: Must the selfobject that promotes a cohesive self necessarily be experienced as part of the self?'' Bach challenges a number of points in London's formulation and approach. He suggests that the patient's central dynamic was his ''oppositional identity, the negation that he needed to feel real.'' Overall, Bach expresses skepticism that London's confrontation measures were needed in each instance. He also suggests that a confrontation selfobject transference does not seem to be ''on the same conceptual level as the mirroring and idealizing transferences.''

Stolorow, Goldberg, Wallerstein, and P. Ornstein are the principal contributors to the section on The Implications of Self Psychology for Psychoanalytic Theory. Stolorow and Goldberg each approve of the trend in self psychology toward a more phenomenological approach; that is, one that would replace experience-distant metapsychological formulations. But whereas Stolorow argues to retain a concept of psychological structure, Goldberg illustrates how even so universally accepted a construct as internalization can be replaced. Stolorow conceives of psychological structures:

> Not as contents or components of a mental apparatus, but rather as systems of ordering or organizing principles . . . through which a person's experiences assume their characteristic patterns and meanings. This concept of psychic structure provides an experience-near framework for understanding the claim that classical conflict psychology aims for the realignment of existing pathological structures, whereas self psychology is concerned with promoting tne development of structure that is missing or deficient.

Stolorow believes that ''the essential complementarity . . . between a psychology of conflict-ridden but firmly consolidated psychic structures and a psychology of missing, precarious, and disintegration-prone psychic structures'' orients the clinician to distinct experiential differences in analysis and permits an explanation of transmuting internalization. In his paper, Goldberg makes the novel suggestion that, phenomenologically, internalization refers to three inner experiences: privacy, ownership, and representability. Through a series of ingenious clinical references, Goldberg ties in ownership to such disparate psychological happenings as the child's use of a transitional object (the body), learning to read, and projection (disclaimed ownership). He states that "the concepts of things moving from one place to another, of ideas shared and feelings allowed the freedom of expression" combine to play out the privacy metaphor, "allowing us to recognize the main issue as being one of access and communicability." Representability, rather than an internal replica within the mind, refers to self-experiences that are capable of being thought about. Goldberg's main point is the need for a shift in emphasis from the discrete boundary between people to "the concept of sharing or bridging separateness by a communicative link" within the self-selfobject unit.

Wallerstein's elegantly constructed essay presents a detailed, point by point evaluation of self psychology. He believes that many of Kohut's proposals, especially "the focusing of our psychoanalytic awareness of the psychological as well as the psychopathological phenomena of narcissism," to be major contributions. Alternatively, Wallerstein finds "the specific value of Kohut's particular conceptualization of the *self* as the supraordinate unifying perspective of the personality" to be more subject to question. However, his main disagreement with self psychology lies in the ambiguous stand its theory takes on conflict, ranging from treating conflict theory as a complementary concept to replacing it, in effect, with a theory of deficit. For Wallerstein, psychoanalytic theory is so quintessentially a theory of conflict that he cannot understand or accept the either/or approach self psychology takes. I believe it is helpful to readers in their effort to follow Wallerstein's argument to recognize that in referring to conflict he is espousing "a modern and broadened psychoanalytic conceptualization of conflict" advanced by Sandler. Rejecting "the equation of the idea of 'peremptoriness' with drive impulses in one form or another in the structural theory," Sandler regards "all conflict as being a conflict of *wishes of one sort or another*." Wallerstein faults self psychology for mistakenly equating conflict, "the universal fundament of the human condition," with pathology, "its centrally untoward outcome." He believes that the concept of empathy as used by self psychology constitutes an "essential redefinition of analysis," one that he finds "idiosyncratic as well as radical." Wallerstein concludes that he is unconvinced "that the enrichment in the clinical realm requires a new theory . . . of the bipolar self." Rather, he believes that a broadened definition of conflict permits bridges between the traditional and the self psychological conceptions.

Ornstein's response to Stolorow, Goldberg, and Wallerstein constitutes in itself an evaluative essay stimulated by the three papers. Ornstein has unstinting praise for Goldberg's effort to replace internalization, with its metaphor of the spatial movement of discrete entities, by metaphors that reflect the nature of relationships. But he is more equivocal toward Stolorow. Whereas Stolorow prefers terms that retain linkages to structures, separateness, and conflict, Ornstein argues the superiority of the metaphors of self psychology—the bipolar self, a theoretical change that expands the theory of selfobjects from infantile archaic to mature sustaining relationships and a theory of secondary self-pathology. Yet it is toward Wallerstein's objection that Ornstein directs his major critical repostes. Ornstein builds up a point by point argument that self psychology rather than a subset of traditional theory or a complementary theory constitutes "a revolutionary step." Where Wallerstein argues that differences can be bridged, Ornstein answers that the vantage points from which the field is viewed are markedly disparate. Thus, in Ornstein's opinion there are "two competing basic hypotheses"—one based on a view of *primary* conflict and another in which a primal unit of rudimentary self and its empathic selfobject either weathers nontraumatic disruptions by normal structure building or defects occur leading to *secondary* conflicts. Embedded in Ornstein's complex discussion is both an attempted refutation of Wallerstein and the implications that self psychology has arrived at a rather fully developed, clinical-theoretical, separate psychoanalytic hypothesis.

The book ends, as did the symposium, with a climactic essay by Kohut. At the symposium Kohut responded first to A. Ornstein's case presentation to the candidates. He expressed great personal pleasure in his exchange with the candidates—the future of psychoanalysis as he put it. Kohut also responded to the theory panel and later to presentations made throughout the whole symposium. It was Kohut's style to speak extemporaneously in a slow, deliberate fashion in which he presented issues one at a time for comment and consideration. He would gradually build up to his conclusion, much as a symphonic composer integrates themes into one cohesive, inspirational summation. For his contribution to the book, Kohut integrates his comments made primarily at the theory panel into one flowing essay. In it he responds to questions that have been raised, reasserts positions he has already taken by reexplaining his reasons, and offers new conjectures and formulations. An overall impression he gives is that self psychology is not a theory limited to any one group of illnesses nor are its techniques designed for one group of patients; rather it aims to provide an encompassing psychoanalytic psychology. Beginning with his ironic "Three cheers for drives! Three cheers for conflicts!" Kohut makes clear that in his view "the data concerning the child's experiences do not support the old theory, but require a new one.'' In each of the five sections of his essay Kohut presents expository statements of the *new* theory of self psychology, nimbly moving from a response to criticisms of Wallerstein and others to hints and full statements of the changing and expanding nature of self psychology. He distinguishes between an oedipal stage of normal experiences and the Oedipus complex, a pathological distortion of the normal stage. He asserts the primacy of the self-selfobject relationship for determining the normal or pathological outcome of *all* developmental stages. Kohut extends the concept of selfobject relationships from archaic ones in infancy to mature ones *throughout* life. He underlines the richness of the expanding view of genetic explanations employed by self psychology, the significance of the clinical focus on empathy and introspection on self-experience, and its confirmation in self-state dreams. Kohut concludes that in his opinion there are critical and irreconcilable differences between an effort ''to identify psychological macrostructures in conflict'' and an effort to identify specific defects in the structure of the self. It would be uncharacteristic for Kohut not to include a broadly philosophic statement, and his essay includes in its final section one of his most succinct assessments of the value problems confronting our time:

> The dominant positions in the value scale of modern man are occupied by those values that further the establishment and buttress the maintenance of man's creative-productive self. The peak values of modern man . . . are those values that guide and sustain him in the attempt to reassemble his self through an increased and guilt-free ability to find appropriate selfobjects and in the attempt to liberate his innate ability to serve—and to serve joyfully—as a selfobject for others.

I hope that by providing this preview of what is to come I have stimulated the reader's interest in these reflections on self psychology. Those who attended the meeting each have their remembrances, but the impression most generally held was the excitement generated by the presentations. The written word cannot equal the drama of the personal exchanges, especially those that took place in the workshops. But even outside of the formal presentations, the debates went on. Throughout his writing and speaking, Kohut has consistently emphasized immersion—and an immersion in the pros and cons of self psychology is indeed what the Boston Symposium was. Two personal recollections may serve to convey this sense of involvement. The first is of two workshop leaders arguing the merits of self psychology at a party, stopping briefly to eat, and resuming their discussion, stopping to talk to others, and resuming their discussion—right to the door on leaving. The second is of looking at the large lecture hall late on the last day, after panels, workshops, banquet, and summary presentations. Kohut was talking and *a room full of people remained*—listening intently.

While addressing the sense of liveliness of the symposium (and the editors hope this printed version of *Reflections* as well), I believe there was also an awareness of the sense of time running out on the remarkable life and creative career of Heinz Kohut. He had been ill before the symposium. Nonetheless, he came and gave unstintingly of his time, energy, and enthusiasm. His sense of Old World courtesy—and his liking of people—had him attending meetings and responding to questions when he might otherwise have been resting. He did try to conserve his energies by not attending each panel, but he had read each presentation and would try to come and go unobtrusively so that he could hear more first hand. After the meeting, on his return to Chicago, he again fell ill. Although never fully recovered and pressed by other writing that he was determined to complete, Kohut steadfastly worked at finishing the essay for this book. In the light of his death before its publication, some of his words in his essay have a special poignant quality:

> It is not death that we fear, but the withdrawal of selfobject support in the last phase of our lives. When someone who is dying is told by a friend, "I, too, will someday have to cross the barrier that you are crossing now, and watching you and observing your courage will be an inspiration to me when I face the end of my existence," this friend functions, whether knowingly or by virtue of his spontaneous human responsiveness, as a selfobject for the dying person. And the dying person, feeling himself sustained within a functioning selfobject matrix, will end his life proudly and without undue fear, even as consciousness is fading away.

It is our hope that all of us who cared so deeply about his contribution were able to serve Dr. Kohut as part of his matrix during his lifetime and now in disseminating his work.

To conclude, *Reflections on Self Psychology* records the development of a powerful initiative to alter psychoanalytic theory and an evaluative questioning of this initiative. The dialectic that develops is between vigorous proponents of self psychology, equally energetic critics, and many participants between these polars positions. The reader can follow the interplay of ideas as they develop in response to six issues:

1. Do the developmental formulations of self psychology, based on empathic observations during psychoanalysis, confirm or contradict the findings of infant researchers based on direct observations?

2. Does the theory of self psychology provide a basis for a reconceptualization of the technique of exploratory psychotherapy as well as confrontation approaches used in psychotherapy?
3. Does self psychology provide the basis for a general reordering of
   psychoanalytic technique that applies not only to problems of narcissistic personality and behavioral disorders but also to a full, broad spectrum of all psychoanalytic cases?
4. Does self psychology now offer a new, generally applicable theory of
   oedipal phase developments and pathology based on the central significances of self-selfobject relationships rather than on the traditional
   conflict formulation?
5. Is the concept of a selfobject applicable not only to the archaic relationships of infancy but also to relationships throughout all stages of life?
6. Assuming an acceptance of many aspects of self psychology as complementary to or accommodative within traditional psychoanalytic theory,
   are its emphases on the empathic-introspective approach, its changed
   focus (the experiential states of the self), and its stand emphasizing self-
   selfobject relationships (as a basic determinant of the outcome of conflict in every stage throughout life) sufficiently radical to regard self
   psychology as a major reorganization of psychoanalysis, an historic
   move forward in the science of psychology replacing positivism and its
   lasting influence of mechanistic thought, as the proponents of self
   psychology claim?

I believe the fact that this final question could be asked underlines the significance of the symposium as reflecting a critical juncture in the development of
psychoanalysis in general and self psychology in particular. The breadth of
these issues confirms the wisdom of the organizing committee of the Boston
Society and Institute—and the stimulating experience awaiting the reader.

Acknowledgments

This book represents and reflects the atmosphere of open inquiry that characterized the symposium sponsored by the Boston Psychoanalytic Society and Institute in the fall of 1980. Many individuals contributed to the development and maintenance of that spirit. We take this opportunity to express our gratitude to the speakers, discussants, and workshop leaders who so successfully sustained this academic ambiance. In this regard, they fulfilled the wish, expressed by Heinz Kohut in an early planning meeting, that we strive to develop an opportunity for vigorous debate of the issues while maintaining a spirit of mutual respect.

To the many individuals who contributed unstintingly of their time and energy to this project, we express our sincere gratitude. Gerald Adler, David Berkowitz, Paul Myerson, and Evelyne Schwaber, the members of the Planning Committee, were vitally instrumental in helping to resolve all the problems that emerged during the actual planning of the symposium. We are cognizant of the assistance during the planning stage provided by Paul Ornstein and wish to express our appreciation to him.

We feel especially indebted to the Board of Trustees of the Boston Psychoanalytic Society and Institute for their vote of confidence in the symposium and in this book, expressed in their making available to us the funds so vitally required to convert the idea for these projects into realities. In the same vein we thank S. Joseph Nemetz, president of the Boston Psychoanalytic Society and Institute, and his successor, Ralph Kahana, for their support and encouragement from the inception to the conclusion of these enterprises. Many members and candidates of the Boston Psychoanalytic Society and Institute, provided substantial help, generously offered, in support of the symposium.

We wish to cite for our appreciation the editors and consulting editors of *Psychoanalytic Inquiry*. They have responded diligently to the confidence displayed by the symposium Planning Committee in their invitation to create this book from the proceedings of the meeting. Melvin Bornstein, Donald Silver, Sydney Smith, and Martin Mayman are responsible for carrying or helping to carry sections of the book to completion. Charlotte Lichtenberg's editorial advice and assistance helped to resolve many problems, large and small. Other editorial contributions of high order were made by David Berkowitz in editing the section on psychoanalytic technique and Arnold Goldberg in editing Kohut's taped remarks. On behalf of the Boston Psychoanalytic Society and Institute, and *Psychoanalytic Inquiry*, we are eager to express our deep feeling of indebtedness to Evelyne Schwaber, a member of the Planning Committee and a consulting editor, whose advice and counsel to both groups was invaluable to maintaining the congenial atmosphere of the meeting and throughout the preparation of the book.

We also wish to thank those authors who have had to do major revisions of their papers for publication. Anna Ornstein's presentation and Helen Meyer's discussion were originally designed for a candidate workshop discussion. They have each made extensive alterations. Paul Ornstein's discussion in response to the theory panel has been expanded to cover more adequately the breadth of the material of that complex group of presentations. To Heinz Kohut, for his encouragement to our enterprise and his careful, thoughtful conversion of his extemporaneous comments into the beautiful final essay, we are deeply indebted.

Finally, we are pleased to have this opportunity to share with you our gratitude to Mrs. Sophie Danziger, the Executive Director of this project, for her diligence and steadiness during many hectic moments. Her devoted attention to a myriad of details and her creative solutions contributed a very great deal to the smooth functioning of the entire group.

Samuel Kaplan, M.D. and Joseph D. Lichtenberg, M.D.

REFLECTIONS ON SELF PSYCHOLOGY

INTRODUCTORY SECTION

1 Reflections on Narcissism in Boston

Ralph J. Kahana, M.D.

It is testimony to the current interest in self psychology that participants in this symposium organized by the Boston Psychoanalytic
Society and Institute have assembled from across the United States,
and from Australia, Austria, Belgium, Brazil, Canada, England, Fin-
land, France, Holland, India, Italy, Mexico, New Zealand, Puerto
Rico, and West Germany. Because many visitors to Boston are unfamiliar with its traditions, I want to state at the outset that narcissism is alive and well in The Hub City. Our assumption is that
most important things began in Boston, from the American Revolution and college education to the invention of the telephone and the
spark plug. However, contrary to the prevalent belief, narcissism
did *not* originate in Boston. Yet our guests need not be entirely
disappointed, for I can state with absolute certainty that it does
have very deep roots here. In fact, its striking manifestations have
long been a subject of wonderment, envy, and amusement (Amory,
1947, 1960). All of you undoubtedly have heard that Boston is the
hub of the universe and that the Cabots of Boston talk only to God.
But you may not be aware that according to an ancient myth the
body of water in which Narcissus discovered his own irresistible face
was actually the Charles River—where it mirrors some of our great
Boston (and Cambridge) institutions of learning.

The interrelated subjects of narcissism and the self have interested and occupied mankind for a very long time. The Bible re-

peatedly enjoins us to examine ourselves while, at the same time, telling us to abjure selfishness and vanity. It attempts to overcome the difficulty of carrying out these contradictory injunctions by calling upon the aid of a higher power. Taking a leap forward through time, we find that interesting figure of the age of the enlightenment, Jean Jacques Rousseau, who wrote in 1762: " Provided that a man is not mad, he can be cured of every folly except vanity." With all his therapeutic optimism he still found narcissism a tough nut to crack. Of course, we have come a long way since then! Or have we? So much for the contributions of the prescientific era.

Freud (1899) introduced the psychoanalytic study of narcissism in a communication to his friend Fliess in which he postulated an initial autoerotic stage of libidinal development. The development of this early, primary aspect of narcissism involved transition from an autistic and self-centered phase, through symbiotic and anaclitic stages of self and object representations, to a more separate and autonomous psychological existence. During the more than 80 years since Freud's initial discoveries, the desire to find new approaches to the treatment of conditions involving disturbances of primary narcissism has provided an important reason for the continued study of narcissism and the self. The suffering and pervasive character disorder, the chronic depression and tendencies to withdrawal and to personality disorganization of many patients with narcissistic disorders, have been accessible to help only in a limited way and with great difficulty.

Until he elaborated the structural hypothesis, Freud used the term "ego" as synonymous with the "self." In comparison to the more abstract structural ego, the self as self-concept or self-directed thought, feeling, or action is closer to experience and to clinical observation. Self usually refers to the entire person, whereas the ego designates one group of functions. The vocabulary of self, from self-abandonment to self-zeal, is a rich catalog of attitudes, attributes, conditions, and behaviors. Some of these, such as self-preservation and self-knowledge, are central to our therapy and theory. Freud threw new light on self-betrayal via parapraxes, self-deception through ego defenses, self-esteem in relation to narcissism, and self-punishment as an unconscious expression of guilt. In analytic work we constantly take cognizance of our patients' and our own self-concept, self-sufficiency, and self-fulfillment. A number of self-attitudes and behaviors (e.g., self-emptiness and self-care) have become the subject of more recent studies.

Narcissism as the heightened cathexis of the self, centering upon secondary narcissism reflected from object relationships, was a lively topic in the early meetings of the Vienna Psychoanalytic Society. In those days a symposium could be held in Freud's living room. In a 1906 paper by Philipp Frey on "The Megalomania of the Normal Person," reference is made to the excessive self-assertion seen in certain minor officials, persons wearing special uniforms, actors, artists, poets, and scholars. These excessively self-assertive individuals were believed to be people whose attainments have not been equal to their own expectations or to those of others; hence they were compensating for insecure self-esteem. It was observed then, almost 75 years ago: "At no time have there been as many representatives of such semipathological existences as there are nowadays." When *did* the "culture of narcissism" begin?

In his 1913 paper on "The God Complex," Ernest Jones put forward one of the earliest psychoanalytic descriptions of the narcissistic character. Among his observations he noted that narcissistic characters who strongly identify with God the Father are often great monologuists and apt to be successful after-dinner speakers.

I have no grandiose intention of beginning with Freud's fundamental paper of 1914 "On Narcissism" and reviewing exhaustively the history of further psychoanalytic studies by Freud, Abraham, Ferenczi, Wilhelm Reich, Rado, Fenichel, Annie Reich, Edith Jacobson, and so on. Rather I want to remind you of the range of psychoanalytic contributions to studies of narcissism and the self by Bostonians. Psychoanalysts in Boston have studied narcissism clinically and theoretically from its normal to its most pathological manifestations, over the entire life cycle. They have been interested in the narcissistic character types, the narcissism of sociologically normal personalities, varieties of self-experience, the fate of narcissism embodied in the ego ideal, and the therapy of disorders of self-esteem. They have written and taught about narcissistic aspects of artistic, scientific, and political talents, children with atypical development, borderline and psychotic conditions in adolescents and adults, acting out and aggressive behavior, psychosomatic disorders, and psychological responses to physical illnesses.

Among the many Boston contributors, two, Drs. Helene Deutsch and Edward Bibring, represent part of our direct debt to the European founders of psychoanalysis. Helene Deutsch's papers on the "As-If Personality" (1934, 1942), on Joseph Conrad's tragic, romantic daydreamer, *"Lord Jim"* (1959), and her studies of narcissism in the psychology of women (1944) are representative of her researches in this area. Her autobiography is entitled *"Confrontations with Myself"* (1973). In his classic paper on "The Mechanism of Depression" (1953) Edward Bibring wrote that the early experience by the self of the infant ego's helplessness is probably the most frequent factor predisposing to depression.

A founder of the present Boston Psychoanalytic Society and Institute, Ives Hendrick, wrote that it was important to differentiate between the earliest object relationships, which are dyadic, and the triangular oedipal situation (1942, 1951). Elizabeth Zetzel described the incapacity to tolerate narcissistic injury and depressive affect seen in individuals whose self-esteem has depended on an underlying conviction of omnipotence and who have been unable to renounce this self-image or modify the self-imposed demands dictated by a grandiose ego ideal (1965). She defined the "therapeutic alliance" as an essential working relationship between patient and analyst that develops from the dyadic mother-infant relationship (1958). John M. Murray, another of our founding members, in his paper on "Narcissism and the Ego Ideal" (1964) described working conceptions of the ego ideal in clinical practice. He depicted developmental failures or regressions in the ego leading to persistence or reappearance of attitudes of narcissistic overentitlement. Through analysis, the ego ideal may be reconstituted, undergo extensive growth, and be transformed from its primitive narcissistic origins. Helen H. Tartakoff studied the (so-called) normal personality in our culture, including many talented individuals who prove to be extremely dependent on receiving recognition for achievement (1966). She described some of them as having a "Nobel prize complex." She increased our knowledge of the fantasies that underlie narcissistic expectations and transference resistances, as these phenomena unfold in the analysis of this group of patients. Elvin V. Semrad taught a generation of psychoanalytically informed therapists the art of helping people who have suffered major psychic disturbances (1969). In particular, he emphasized empathic understanding of primitive transferences and the methods needed to sustain patients who are oversensitive and fragile. Avery Weisman examined existential experience—related to self-experience (1965). Sidney Levin emphasized the importance of analyzing the affect of shame (1971) and added to our understanding of the narcissistic vulnerability of older persons (1965).

The list could be continued, but I believe that I have already established a firm connection between Boston as the setting, the Boston Psychoanalytic Society and Institute as the sponsoring organization, and the topic of narcissism and the self.

REFERENCES

Amory, C. (1947). *The Proper Bostonians*. New York: Harper and Brothers.
_____ (1960). *Who Killed Society?* New York: Harper and Brothers.
Bibring, E. (1953). The Mechanism of Depression. In: *Affective Disorders,* ed. by P. Greenacre, New York: Int. Univ. Press, Inc.
Deutsch, H. (1934). On a Type of Pseudo-Affectivity ("As-If"). *Int. Zeitschrift für Psychoanal.* 20:323–335.
_____ (1942). Some Forms of Emotional Disturbances and Their Relationship to Schizophrenia. *Psychoanal. Quart.* 11:301–321.
_____ (1944). *Psychology of Women.* New York: Grune and Stratton. 2 Vol.
_____ (1959). Lord Jim and Depression. In: *Neuroses and Character Types.* New York: Int. Univ. Press, Inc. pp. 353–357.
_____ (1973). *Confrontations with Myself.* New York: W. W. Norton.
Freud, S. (1899). Extracts from the Fliess Papers. *S.E.* 1:175–250, Letter No. 125, p. 280.
_____ (1914c). On Narcissism: An Introduction. *S.E.* 14:69–102.
Frey, P. (1906). On the Megalomania of the Normal Person. *Minutes of The Vienna Psychoanalytic Society,* ed. by H. Nunberg and E. Federn, New York: Int. Univ. Press, Inc. 1962. Vol. 1:52–61.
Hendrick, I. (1942). Instinct and the Ego During Infancy. *Psychoanal. Quart.,* 11:33–58.
_____ (1951). Early Development of the Ego: Identification in Infancy. *Psychoanal. Quart.,* 20:44–61.
Jones, E. (1913). The God Complex. In: *Essays in Applied Psychoanalysis.* International Psychoanalytic Press, London, 1923.
Levin, S. (1965). Some Comments on the Distribution of Narcissistic and Object Libido in the Aged. *Int. J. Psycho-Anal.* 46:200–208.
_____ (1971). The Psychoanalysis of Shame. *Int. J. Psycho-Anal.,* 52:355–362.
Murray, J. M. (1964). Narcissism and the Ego Ideal. *J. Am. Psychoanal. Assoc.* 12:477–511.
Rousseau, J. J. (1762). *Emile, Ou De l'Eduction.*
Semrad, E. V. (1969). *Teaching Psychotherapy of Psychotic Patients.* New York: Grune and Stratton.
Tartakoff, H. H. (1966). The Normal Personality in Our Culture and the Nobel Prize Complex. In: *Psychoanalysis—A General Psychology.* ed. by R. M. Loewenstein, L. M. Newman, M. Schur and A. J. Solnit. New York: Int. Univ. Press, Inc. pp. 222–252.
Weisman, A. (1965). *The Existential Core of Psychoanalysis.* Boston: Little, Brown and Co.
Zetzel, E. (1958). Therapeutic Alliance in the Analysis of Hysteria. In: *The Capacity for Emotional Growth.* New York: Int. Univ. Press, Inc., 1970, pp. 182–196.
_____ (1965). Depression and the Incapacity to Bear It. In: *Drives, Affects and Behavior,* Vol. 2. ed. by M. Schur, New York: Int. Univ. Press, Inc.

2 Introduction of Dr. Heinz Kohut

John Demos

I feel pleased and honored to offer a few introductory words about Dr. Kohut. Academic person though I am, I count myself a student of Dr. Kohut's. My acquaintance with him has not been particularly long in time, nor close in a personal sense, but its meaning for me has been profound. I think I can remember every one of the occasions when I have heard Dr. Kohut speak or have otherwise met and talked with him—all of them going back to a time 5 or 6 years ago when I was temporarily based in Chicago and doing course work at the Institute for Psychoanalysis there. I particularly remember the first time. A group of us at the Center for Psychosocial Studies had invited Dr. Kohut to come across Michigan Avenue from the Institute and discuss with us a paper he had just written on the psychology of leadership. (It has since been published under the title, "Creativeness, Charisma and Group Psychology.") I can clearly recall the keen sense of anticipation and excitement—mixed with just a little bit of awkwardness—that was in the air of our conference room as our guest arrived. We had all read the paper (in draft) before the meeting, and Dr. Kohut volunteered to make a few preliminary remarks, as he put it, to "break the ice." Well, such an icebreaking I have never experienced, either before or since. What he said was entirely extemporaneous, so far as I could tell. He went on for a good three-quarters of an hour, and his remarks added immeasurably to what had already been an extraordinary piece of writing. In fact—to return to the icebreaking metaphor—it was as if some vast arctic sea had been completely and dazzlingly rearranged, by the time these so-called "preliminary remarks" were finished. It's a rare privilege for most of us to observe a truly creative intelligence at work from close up, and in my own experience that has happened more with Dr. Kohut than with anyone else.

Dr. Kohut's creative achievements have, of course, won various forms of recognition over the years. I can mention only a few of them here. His current affiliations include that of Training and Supervising Analyst at the Institute for Psychoanalysis in Chicago, and Professorial Lecturer in Psychiatry at the University of Chicago. He is a past president of the American Psychoanalytic Association and a former vice-president of the International Psycho-Analytic Association. His first book, *The Analysis of the Self,* was awarded the Heinz Hartmann prize by the New York Psychoanalytic Society in 1971. He received an honorary degree from the University of Cincinnati in 1973; he was elected to the Austrian Academy of Arts and Sciences in 1979.

Some of these honors signify the spreading importance of Dr. Kohut's work—spreading, that is, beyond the analyst's couch and office into much broader fields of intellectual endeavor. And it is about those broader fields that I would like to speak for the next few minutes. There are some definite indications that the cultural soil is well prepared for, and generally receptive to, self psychology. At least two recent books, written by well-known social theorists and aimed at a general audience, have shown a considerable influence from Dr. Kohut's own writings. I refer to Christopher Lasch's *The Culture of Narcissism* and Richard Sennett's *The Fall of Public Man.* Lasch's work seems especially striking—not least because it allows for the exchange of some lively gossip. I wish, incidentally, to make it clear that I do not necessarily endorse the way Lasch has used self psychology in his narcissism book; indeed, I think he has misunderstood Kohut in various ways, and he certainly has adapted Kohut to his own rather idiosyncratic purposes. However, there are a couple of things to be said for that book. One is that it made the best-seller list—and it probably has been a long time since any work seriously attempting to incorporate psychoanalytic ideas did that. The other thing is that book was read by Jimmy Carter. As a result—so the grapevine has it—Professor Lasch was invited to Washington for an intimate supper and some heavy discussion with the President and his wife, just the three of them. I *hope* that story is true; I rather like the picture of Mr. and Mrs. Carter and Professor Lasch sitting around the table in some homey corner of the White House discussing narcissism. Actually, the story has one further twist. Having read and talked with Lasch, the President sat down with his advisors to prepare a speech on what might appropriately be called, "the psychic state of the union." You may even remember it—the famous "national malaise" speech of a couple of summers back. Actually, the President's advisors would rather you didn't remember it; in their view, it "bombed." But I, at least, thought it one of the more interesting Presidential addresses of recent years— a sort of exotic blend of self psychology, the work ethic, and southern Baptist fundamentalism. And so, from Kohut to Lasch to Carter to the American people: that is the way we historians will record the line of communication. Agreed that something may have gotten lost en route; but it is, I submit, significant that such a line should have opened up at all.

There are other lines of communication that may be worth pondering for a minute more. I refer again to the place of psychoanalysis in the world of ideas more generally. Freud himself, Dr. Kohut, and (I would guess) all the most creative figures in the psychoanalytic pantheon have worked at various projects of bridge-building toward other fields and disciplines. "Applied psychoanalysis" is the name most often given to such activity or, with special reference to my own field, "psychohistory." And I would like to conclude my stand at the podium by offering one man's view of the current state and future prospects of applied psychoanalysis.

It's a mixed view, and I'll start with the bad news. If you look over the past 20 years of interdisciplinary work in and around psychoanalysis, you see quite a ferment—a lot of hope, a lot of serious effort, and until quite recently a growing interest and receptivity on the part of scholars on the other side of all those bridges. However, I sense that this is changing now and that we are heading into a more difficult period. Two published statements during the past summer have served to herald the change: one, a book by the Yale historian, David Stannard, entitled *Shrinking History;* the other, an essay by the University of California literary scholar and critic, Frederick Crews, entitled "Analysis Terminable." (The Crews essay appeared in the July 1980 issue of *Commentary.*) Both these statements take psychoanalysis very severely to task, and both utterly reject the notion of applying psychoanalysis outside the clinical setting. To make matters worse, both authors have previously been associated with applied psychoanalysis; hence, they are speaking not ignorantly, but out of at least some direct experience. In effect, their statements amount to a recantation of views previously held. I don't know whether writings such as these are much noticed among analysts; but I can tell you that people like Stannard and Crews carry some considerable weight in the academic world and that what they now say is cause for a good deal of head-nodding, hand-rubbing, and outright "I told you so's" among people I talk to these days.

In a somewhat gentler vein a colleague of mine, himself an eminent intellectual historian and an early supporter of psychohistory, asked me not long ago how I would add up the score on psychohistorical studies over the past decade or so. He felt disappointed in the actual amount of scholarly accomplishment: There seemed to be more manifestoes, more calls to action, than solid, tangible results. And I had to confess to him some private worries of my own on that very score.

But now for the good news! Perhaps, the "disappointment" of these recent years reflects the fact that we applied psychoanalysts have been working for the most part from a too-narrow theoretical base in the classical Freudian paradigm. And, whatever the merits of that paradigm for clinical work, it is, in truth, inordinately difficult to apply to our everyday fare of historical and cultural materials. There are real problems of data, of asymmetrical issues and questions, and, indeed, of interpretive methods. So, in this context of struggles to some extent unrewarded, self psychology and Dr. Kohut's own particular achievements afford us a new opening—perhaps, I could even say, a new lease on life.

This clearly is not the time or place to spell out all the hopeful possibilities for applied self psychology, but some of them are immediately obvious. Most of the data of self psychology are, as Dr. Kohut puts it, "experience-near"—which is to say, from my standpoint, that a lot of it is in the historical record. Many of the issues to which self psychology particularly turns are immediately recognizable to historians (or to social scientists generally): grandiosity, idealization, wisdom, creativity, empathy, and so on. I could, but I won't, go on. Enough to say that self psychology is giving at least one recruit new hope and new faith in the good ship *Psychohistory*. For the coming phase of this journey psychohistorians, no less than psychoanalysts, are fortunate to have Heinz Kohut as our navigator, our teacher, and our friend.

3 Greetings[1]

Heinz Kohut, M.D.

Ladies and gentlemen, colleagues, friends,

My remarks, though serious in their ultimate intent, will be presented in a lighthearted vein, as befits this informal moment of our conference. To begin with I will tell you about two personal events, one occurring about 7 or 8 years ago, the other quite recently, about a month ago. Each has something in common with the other, and yet they are also quite different.

As I said, the first event took place about 7 or 8 years ago. To put its significance for me into a nutshell, it was the first time that I got a taste of how acerbic the reaction of a number of my colleagues would be to some of the ideas that I have expressed during the past 15 years or so. By now I have become used to the intensity with which certain critics have rejected my work. But I can still remember how much I was taken aback when somebody told me that, at a meeting in another city, an old friend of mine had said that after reading *The Analysis of the Self* he had concluded that I do not

---

*Dr. Evelyne Schwaber worked closely with Dr. Kohut during the last few months of his life, offering her editorial suggestions in the preparation of his writings for this volume. The final editing, completed posthumously, was further reviewed by her. The editors wish to express their appreciation for her invaluable assistance.

[1]Kohut's original address, which had been extemporaneous, was recorded and transcribed, and then edited by Dr. Joseph D. Lichtenberg. The version presented here was further edited by the author.

analyze transferences but that I *accept* them instead. I was puzzled. How could anyone so totally misunderstand a book in which I had extensively described a group of *analyzable* transferences which, as I thought, had formerly not been recognized? And how could any analyst misunderstand my statement that, when the first tendrils of these transferences begin to germinate, he should not interfere with their development by premature interpretations but must allow them to unfold? Had I not said clearly that to interpret them at this earliest state of development would be the same as if at the first sign of an oedipal transference the analyst would stop the patient and tell him: "Look here, I am not your father!"? I felt that, for reasons that I could not figure out, my critic had emphasized my use of the word "accept" and underplayed the context into which it was embedded. And, as I said, I felt badly misunderstood. By now I have become used to such unfriendliness (even though I continue to be puzzled by it)—but then it was still very upsetting to me.

Now the story of the experience of a month ago. We had just come back from our vacation. I went to my office for the first time, and it looked as an office usually does after one has been away for a while—it was a horror. All the glow of the vacation disappeared when I saw the mountain of mail that had accumulated during my absence. Piles of junk mail that needed to be sorted and then thrown out; semiprofessional and professional journals that had to be scanned; and, last but not least, there were the manuscripts that wanted to be read, coming largely from people who now demanded narcissistic supplies from me because they had written about my work. There was a 108-page doctoral thesis, challenging every idea I had ever put into print. It accused me of exactly the opposite of what Professor Crews had accused me of in his recent essay in *Commentary*. I could almost feel the rapid fading of the tan that I had acquired in the sun of California. But then I spied a peculiar object under this mountain of mail. It looked like a wooden box. I pushed the mail aside and, my goodness, what did I see? A whole case of Chateau Lafite of a good vintage—and I do like good wines. There was a warmly worded letter in it, from a colleague in Europe, telling me that my writings had broadened and deepened his understanding and that his patients had indirectly benefited from them. He ended with the friendly admonition that I should accept his grateful gift without misgivings. "Don't forget," he said, "that you have taught us that one must be able to accept admiration."

Now on the face of it, you might say that my benefactor was using the same words that my unfriendly critic had used some years back. But this time, of course, I was not upset about them but was deeply gratified.

What is the message that is implied in my account of these two events? It is a very simple one: A lot depends on *how* one says what one says. Some of the criticisms, certainly, that are leveled against the work done by my collaborators and me inevitably touch on pre-occupations of our own. They address yet unsolved problems and still remaining inconsistencies, such as will unavoidably be found in a set of new ideas, still in flux, which, I hope, have vitality and forward-moving potential. "Here is an error!" "Here is something unsolved!" "Here you are inconsistent!" the critics say. Fine! But why are these statements made in a challenging and harshly accusatory tone? Why is there not more tolerance, friendliness, forbearance with a set of new ideas? Why not good will as one goes about experimenting with a new point of view? As I see it, we should all be working shoulder to shoulder, trying to solve problems that are indeed difficult to solve. The world is hard to understand; people are hard to understand. Yet, little by little, we do make progress. What we need to further the momentum of the search is the ability to work side by side. We must get rid of bitterness and ill will and adopt an attitude which, for the purpose of this meeting, I suggest we call the "Chateau Lafite approach"—the generosity that one colleague who is working and striving and struggling can feel for another colleague who is doing the same. My first message, then, to the participants in this conference is this: Let us try during the forthcoming discussions to be more on the Chateau Lafite and less on the acerbic side. Let us be guided by friendliness and a feeling of comradeship as we all try to inch closer toward the, in the last analysis, unreachable truths about the essence of the depths of man.

The second point that I would like to make this evening is even simpler than the first. Although its message is directed to all of you, I like to think of it as specifically aimed at the candidates. As one grows older, it is the next generation—those who follow us and will continue our work—that becomes most important to us. To state it bluntly: People don't read. I know that they buy books. I believe even that they skim books, reading here and there, usually with a preformed idea of what they expect to find. But, in the way I understand this all-important activity, They do not read. I have often

emphasized that analysts must remain immersed in the transference of their analysands, and for a long time, in order to get at its
essence. The same is true when we try to grasp the meaning of a
complex set of new ideas through reading. It's not the mechanics of
reading that are here at stake, and Evelyn Wood won't help. What is
required is the ability for a temporary suspension of disbelief. A
reader must be able to abandon the security of traditional ways of
seeing things in order to experiment with a new point of view. And,
in our field at least, a critic must be able to try out a new set of ideas
over an extended period before he can allow himself to judge its
relevance, usefulness, and its explanatory power. He must not base
his judgment on this or that detail in isolation but must try to
apprehend newly emerging configurations, however strange and
unwieldy they might at first appear.

Ultimately all these experimentations must be undertaken in the
laboratory of our clinical practice. But before this stage is reached,
analysts must first read. Why don't they read, why are they not used
to reading—and with fascination and enjoyment—in the sense that
I outlined to you, in the only sense that deserves to be called
reading?

I have a hunch that one of the reasons why all of us have to some
extent lost our ability to read the current psychoanalytic literature
is that it is terribly boring. We open our journals, out of conscientiousness, and we force ourselves to read. But it is a real chore. I
remember that, already as a student, I would read the current literature and then rush back to Freud—to refresh myself, to participate
in the activities of an original mind at work. How exciting this was!
Even when I began to disagree with Freud's statements here and
there, even when I recognized that his outlook was slanted at times
and led to a distorted understanding of psychic life, I knew that here
was a mind at work that was exciting and uplifting to follow.

But I see that I have drifted into too much seriousness and that it
behooves me to relax a bit—in tune with the spirit of this after-
dinner occasion. Let me tell you then, at the end of my remarks, of
that pivotal moment in my life as a student of psychoanalysis when
I came to the conclusion that, in essence, my time as a reader of
current psychoanalytic literature was over. That it was over because I had reached a peak of enjoyment that could never be reached
again. This *ne plus ultra* was provided to me by a book review,
written by Edward Glover, who was and has remained one of my

favorite authors in psychoanalysis. Next to Freud (and, to a much lesser extent, to Hartmann) I learned more from Glover than from anyone else in psychoanalysis, and strange as it may sound, I consider my work to be a continuation of his. Glover's book review was about an old textbook of psychoanalysis by Nunberg that had recently been translated into English. In his short essay Glover reported Dr. Nunberg's statement that exhibitionism occurred only in men. As I read Glover's remark—as I remember it; and I refuse to check!—a little pause seemed to follow, after which Glover added: "which only admits of one conclusion, namely that Dr. Nunberg has led a very cloistered life."[2]

And now good wishes to all of us for a successful conference. May it be conducted in the spirit of Chateau Lafite and may it, after the excitement of the debate has subsided, lead us all back to our books—to study, and think, and to deepen our understanding.

---

[2]When I edited my extemporaneous remarks for publication in the sober surroundings of my study, the easy-going relaxation of the after-dinner speaker became quickly replaced by the uncompromising professional conscientiousness of the scholar. I searched for and found Glover's review of Nunberg's textbook (it was published in *The Psychoanalytic Quarterly, 25,* 586–589, 1959) and discovered that, although after 20 years my memory had indeed falsified details, it was, on the whole, not too far off the mark. This is Glover's relevant sentence about Nunberg, now given verbatim: "And his view that in our culture women never exhibit their genitals is, to say the least, a somewhat cloistered one [p. 588]."

4 Psychoanalytic Inquiry and New Knowledge

Arnold M. Cooper, M.D.

It is fitting that this conference is taking place in Boston, a cradle of American psychoanalysis. Appropriate to the city's intellectual tradition in American life, a Bostonian, J. J. Putnam, was, as much as anyone, responsible for Freud's visit to America. We not only owe to Boston a significant portion of the original spark of psychoanalysis in America, but Bostonians have also contributed their own special flavor to psychoanalysis: the equal mixture of Europeans and Americans in their institute, the predominant medical background of their early practitioners, and the successful melding of academic and hospital psychiatry with psychoanalysis and its consequent great scientific yield and powerful educational influence. Boston has been home, at one or another time, to Franz Alexander, Helene Deutsch, Erik Erikson, Karl Menninger, Grete and Edward Bibring, Erich Lindemann, M. Ralph Kaufman, Ives Hendrick, and others I could mention who have been shapers of psychoanalysis in America. Gifford, in his paper on Psychoanalysis in Boston, states: "The handful of native American analysts in the 1920's were an unusual, heterogeneous group of men and women, drawn to analysis as a new radical system of thought, as a potential answer to their dissatisfaction with conventional methods of psychiatric treatment." He goes on, referring to the period of the 1960s:

Many later applicants still resembled their forebears, seeking a radical solution in analytic theory. But, for increasing numbers of young psychiatric residents, psychoanalytic training became simply the next step in their professional education, an ultimate credential in a psychiatric career. The novelty of analysis had also diminished, as its concepts were assimilated into the prevailing *Zeitgeist* and permeated the conventional dynamic psychotherapy that was practiced by many psychiatrists [p. 340].

This conference represents the commitment of the Boston Psychoanalytic Society and Institute to explore new ideas as fully as possible, a commitment to the scientific adventure of psychoanalysis that goes well beyond simple professionalism, and perhaps represents a recrudescence of the earlier spirit of psychoanalysis in Boston. Whether we agree with, disagree with, or reserve judgment on Dr. Kohut's ideas, we have all gathered this weekend in response to his lifelong scientific adventure in psychoanalysis. His 1970 paper on "The Scientific Activities of the American Psychoanalytic Association: An Inquiry," urged that organized psychoanalysis assume the vital task of taking its research as seriously as it takes its educational and professional goals. We have not yet begun to realize this ideal, that I take as one of the important aims of organized psychoanalysis. I would be very happy with my tenure as president of the American Psychoanalytic Association if I thought I had advanced the research aim that Dr. Kohut so clearly outlined to even a small degree.

I believe that this is one of the great periods in psychoanalysis. Our scientific discourse is livelier, more informed, more diverse, and less embittered than at any other time in my memory. We are discussing ideas that not so many years ago would not have been discussed seriously within mainstream psychoanalysis; and we are doing so, and I believe will continue to do so, without further danger of split or fragmentation. I think psychoanalysis in America has reached a point of scientific health and maturity that allows for stress and change without danger and loss of our self-cohesion. We owe much of this present excitement to the work of Dr. Kohut and his followers.

The appearance of Heinz Kohut's book *The Analysis of the Self* in 1971 had an electrifying effect on our science and profession. Although there had been harbingers of what was to come in Kohut's work of the preceding decade, the book was greeted with an interest and enthusiasm previously reserved for the works of Anna Freud and Heinz Hartmann. Kohut's work was an instant topic of conversation within analytic circles. Candidates in analytic institutes were enormously excited. Because the work lay outside the curriculum, they pressed their instructors to join in their interest, an invitation that was sometimes accepted reluctantly or even declined. However, unlike the works of Anna Freud or Hartmann, Kohut's book stimulated an immediate controversy in the psychoanalytic literature. Opinions ranged from the enthusiastic belief that Kohut's ideas presented a needed and long-awaited opportunity to revitalize psychoanalysis to a view that echoed Samuel Johnson's criticism: The work is both good and original, but unfortunately what is original in it is not good and what is good is not original.

It might help us to understand the relationship of theory to the development of knowledge in psychoanalysis if we explore the reasons why Kohut's work has excited us, both positively and negatively. Other theories, some equally sweeping, some not dissimilar in their intent, have been put forth over the years, but none has engaged us as has that of Kohut and his followers. Although this may represent the merit of the work,we know from the history of ideas that merit alone does not automatically lead to interest. *The Interpretation of Dreams* did not become an immediate best seller.

Our attention to the factors that lead to acceptance and rejection of ideas in psychoanalysis, in particular Heinz Kohut's ideas, may also teach us something about the current state of psychoanalytic theory and technique and its historical development. It may also inform us about some aspects of the present state of psychoanalysis as a "movement"—an organization of people sharing important common goals, who wish to enlarge the acceptance and importance of these goals in our culture. I raise many more questions than I answer, but a consideration of these questions may provide a perspective on what is sure to be a longstanding, ongoing discussion of self psychology, which we should treat as an opportunity to reexamine ourselves.

One way to view our present interest in the self is to say that it is simply and clearly an idea whose time has come—that the theoretical infrastructure it required was put in place during previous decades. In this view the psychology of the self would be the capstone of several developmental lines in psychoanalytic theory. I would like briefly to describe some of these. First, one could trace the effort in psychoanalytic theorizing to arrive at propositions or concepts of increasingly comprehensive scope. We can follow the progression from the distinction between conscious and unconscious, through the elaboration of the drives and their vicissitudes, to an increasing focus on the ego and its adaptations, to the conceptualization of the self as a more ultimate organizer of behavior. The common theme in this developmental line is a quest for the unifying conception out of which all the elaborations of psychoanalysis would be secondary and derivative hypotheses. The concept of the self as the ultimate organizer of behavior presumably contains within it all of the concepts that previously were regarded as basic and definitional for psychoanalysis. In fact, I believe Kohut has made this claim, although not without some hesitations and extenuations. It is not entirely clear, therefore, whether Dr. Kohut regards the concepts of the self as the supraordinate hypothesis from which all other hypotheses and data are derivative, or as one of several equally important concepts, with a principle of complementarity at work to define which concept is most useful for the exploration of which particular situation. Historically, the theories of the self advanced by Mead, Sullivan, Horney, and Rado show important relationships to the work of Kohut.

A second line of development would assume that psychoanalysis has explored the psyche archeologically from the surface down. Having originally discovered the extraordinary world of the oedipal child, psychoanalysis has continued its laborious digging and has revealed a new civilization underlying it that had never been imagined by the original discoverers. Freud used this metaphor in 1931 to describe his response to the finding of the important role of pre-oedipal life for the development of the female. I think it is fair to say that Freud was both surprised and somewhat dismayed by his discovery. In his paper on "Female Sexuality," he said:

> Our insight into this early pre-oedipal phase in girls comes to us as a surprise, like the discovery, in another field, of the Minoan-Mycenean civilizations behind the civilization of Greece.
>
> Everything in the sphere of the first attachment to the mother seemed to me so difficult to grasp in analysis—so grey with age and shadowy and almost impossible to revivify—that it was as if it had succumbed to an especially inexorable repression [p. 226].

In this paper he also said:

> The pre-oedipus phase in women gains an importance which we have not attributed to it hitherto. . . .
>
> Since this phase allows room for all the fixations and repressions from which we must trace the origin of the neuroses, it would seem as though we must retract the universality of the thesis that the Oedipus complex is the nucleus of the neuroses. But if anyone feels reluctant about making this correction, there is no need for him to do so [p. 226].

Perhaps this is an indication of even Freud's difficulty in accepting the breadth of theoretical revision that data may require at times. He had maintained with consistency that the Oedipus complex was the nucleus of neurosis, and now he had data suggesting that this idea should be abandoned. Rather than give up his position, he sought a compromise that would allow the old view to stand, although modified by new discoveries. Some would hold that this compromise was inadequate and that one of the tensions in psychoanalytic thinking during the past five decades has resulted from the extraordinary unfolding of our knowledge of earlier and earlier psychologically significant events in the lives of children and the attendant uncertainty concerning Freud's dictum of the centrality of the Oedipus complex.

Some British analysts, Edmund Bergler in America, and some infant researchers have pressed for the central role of pre-oedipal events. Seen in this light, Kohut's work represents an organized and coherent statement concerning the importance and nature of the pre-oedipal world, establishing its fatefulness for later development, prior to and overriding the Oedipus complex. The development of the self is seen as both the first and the most complex lifelong task of the child. The Oedipus complex involves another but secondary task, in that the shape of the Oedipus complex, its individual vicissitudes, and its outcome will be significantly or crucially predetermined by the nature of the self with which the child enters the oedipal phase. In this perspective Kohut's view would represent one culmination and overarching conceptualization of many years of effort and research on pre-oedipal development.

A third way to view Kohut's significance would be to discuss the oscillation within psychoanalysis between the roles of nature and nurture. One may see psychic development as proceeding mainly, or most importantly, or for heuristic purposes from the nature of the biological equipment of the organism's instincts, which have a natural unfolding. Although the accidents of life create tensions that must be coped with, the natural flowering of maturation takes precedence, at least for purposes of understanding, over any social, interpersonal, or interactive events. The biology of infancy inevitably leads to frustration, to faulty fantasy because of defective reality testing, and to the emphasis on bodily experience as the defining source of ideation. The alternative view, briefly entertained by Freud but revived in more sophisticated form by the group of analysts who were then called culturalists, states that the instincts and the maturational schema have a degree of flexibility so great that the matters of interest to us involve individual difference stemming from experience, rather than the sameness conferred by instinct. Psychic development can be understood as a consequence of interpersonal impingements on the individual. From this point of view the actual relationship with the actual mother will be of greater psychoanalytic significance than the innate instinctual program of attachment. Adaptation and fitting together are of primary importance.

In this regard Kohut would seem to have come part way around the circle of dispute. He gives the actual mother and her actual successes and failures in empathic rearing of her infant a central place in understanding the fate of the infant and the adult's later behavior in psychoanalytic treatment. The dispute over the primacy of nature or nurture, of maturation or development, actually involves the hypotheses we make concerning the sources of desire and of satisfaction and their innate or social qualities. Although Kohut's view is more comprehensive and sophisticated, it is nonetheless reminiscent of Sullivan and the work of Kardiner.

A fourth longstanding debate concerns the model of discourse in psychoanalysis. Freud was concerned that psychoanalysis be based on the model of biological science as he knew it. There has always been another trend among analysts who either are inclined to deny the claim of psychoanalysis to science or who feel that Freud's scientific base is no longer appropriate. Such diverse figures as Sandor Rado, Sandler, Schafer, George Klein, and Gill have all in one way or another rejected classical metapsychology and its attendent concepts of energy and mechanism, have rejected the language of theory with its experience-remote phrasing, or have rejected the attempt at a science of cause rather than a science of meanings. Schafer has suggested that the concept of "self" is itself a transitional idea in our continuing effort to rid ourselves of an outmoded metapsychology that significantly hampers our research and our perspective. Kohut, in his most recent work, would seem to have joined those who have discarded traditional metapsychology in favor of a more existential, phenomenologic approach that acknowledges the centrality and indivisibility of the self. The empathic introspective methodology enables the participant observer to share the patient's experience which is itself ultimate and more fully describable. Kohut attempts to place the method of observation that empathy and introspection provide in the center of our scientific position and to derive all the propositions of psychoanalysis from this method. Models from other sciences are of little help because the other sciences are inspectional, exteropathic. Critics of this holistic, nonmechanistic view will complain that the phenomenologic method, although avoiding reductionism, reduces our capacity for theory formation—there are not enough parts to play with, which makes it difficult to explain complex processes. It is not clear to me where Kohut stands on the issue of hermeneutic science versus causal science, but my impression is that the empathic methodology forces a hermeneutic stance.

As self psychology has developed, in both its theoretical and clinical ambitions, we seem to be witnessing the construction of a new metapsychology. The original descriptions of self functions seemed experience-near, but the concepts of the supraordinate self, with its bipolar character and linking tension arc, and the increasing emphasis on developmentally significant self-selfobject relations throughtout the life span, appear to me to be concepts of high abstraction, no longer simply phenomenologic. We are, perhaps, witnessing the widening scope of self psychology. I have no quarrel with this development, but it does seem to be moving away from some of the earlier attempts to avoid high-level abstraction. Similarly, I believe that the connection of the concept of "self" with sets of adjectives such as "enfeebled," "firm," or "vigorous" is problematic. It may be that we are confusing levels of discourse—metapsychological and clinical—and I am not sure then of the referent of "self," "I," and "person." Just what is it that is feeble, and who is feeling feeble, and who knows about it?

These issues relate to a fifth tension in psychoanalysis—that between the traditional Freudian view of human beings as conflicted, neurotic, and guilty at the core, and the emphasis, explicit in Rado and implied in Hartmann, that unifying, synthesizing processes are central, and human beings are capable of self-actualization as creatures of joyous activity. Issues of the nature of psychopathology clearly follow from this—if the psyche is conflicted, pathology represents bad conflicts or poor defenses; if the psyche is a unit, pathology represents deficit or incapacity (a view suggested in the past by David Levy and Michael Balint, among others). There is also a historical tendency for those who are more phenomenologic and holistic to be identified as "humanistic," as opposed to the reductionistic, conflictual, and "scientific" view. This tension could be further broadened into one between an affective versus a cognitive emphasis, or even between romantic versus scientific world views. The very definition of analysis is involved. Kris and others saw psychoanalysis as the study of human beings in conflict, whereas Kohut sees psychoanalysis as the study of complex mental states.

Yet another longstanding and sometimes disguised issue that has come to the fore in the discussion of Kohut's work concerns the appropriate atmosphere of the analytic situation—the relationship of analyst and analysand. Posed against the so-called "classical" view of the analytic situation, there has always been an alternate tendency suggesting less frustration of the patient, or more reality, or greater display of the analyst's human qualities. The classical view has been set forth most cogently by Kurt Eissler, who suggested that the proper activity of the psychoanalyst is mainly interpretation. Alternate views have been suggested at one time or another including, Ferenczi's active technique, Alexander's flexible technique needed for the corrective emotional experience, Gitelson's stress on the nurturant role of the analyst, Winnicott's description of the holding function, and Greenson's and Zetzel's emphasis on the therapeutic alliance or real relationship. Freud, as many have now pointed out, seemed to describe one technique in his major technical papers, but he often did other things in practice. Self psychologists themselves seem to be unsure about whether or not they adhere to classical technique (it is refreshing to see that self psychology is not a unified movement), though it has seemed to most of us from reading Kohut that the analytic climate he describes differs significantly, at least some of the time, from that of the traditional setting—the temperature is warmer and the weather is less stormy in Dr. Kohut's office. Pathological sexual and aggressive fantasies and persistent negative transferences have lost their traditional significance and, in fact, are not, in and of themselves, of specific significance in clinical analysis; rather, they reflect defects of self-functioning or, in the case of the negative transference, failures of the analyst's empathy, which will correct themselves as the underlying self-pathology is repaired. It is my impression that Kohut is suggesting that *all* pathological manifestations of sexual and aggressive disintegration products, including those related to the oedipal period, will repair themselves without requiring special analytic attention or working through if one succeeds in repairing the disorders of the self-selfobject relationships of the specific developmental phase. If this is the claim of self psychology, does it mean that sexual and aggressive distorted fantasy productions are of analytic interest only as cues to defects of the self? Is that the meaning of the concept of "disintegration products"? Are there no defects of the self that originate in the terrors of infantile sexual and aggressive fantasy, regardless of how those bizarre and frightening products themselves originated? What are the criteria for concluding that only defects of the self-selfobject tie are pathogenic and require therapeutic attention? Perhaps Kohut's most radical idea is the suggestion that the developmental line of the self takes almost total precedence over any inherent developmental lines of sex and aggression; developmental disorders of sex and aggression are always and only disintegration products of self-disorder. It is clear, at any rate, that the presentation of self psychology has powerfully revived and influenced our discussions of technique and of the relationship of theory and practice. I would find it disturbing if theoretical revisions as sweeping as Kohut's did not have very significant implications for parallel technical innovations. Yet, as one reads the work of self psychologists, one has the impression that some say yea, others nay.

I have suggested six areas of growing scientific tension in psychoanalysis concerning: (1) the scope of our concepts; (2) the role of pre-Oedipal events; (3) the role of the real environment of adaptation; (4) the nature of our inquiry—causal or hermeneutic; (5) the nature of human beings—conflicted or unified; and (6) the therapeutic action of the psychoanalytic treatment situation. One could go on and describe other longstanding tensions in analytic theory and practice. It is a testament to the importance of Kohut's thought that so many of these currents of controversy are addressed in his formulations; and it is an index of the controversy now surrounding Kohut that his view regarding almost all these tensions would generally be considered nonclassical. I hope it is clear that my use of that phrase is in no way pejorative; in fact, an interesting discussion is just beginning on the role of the concept of "classical" in psychoanalysis.

Self psychology, in this perspective, could be seen as the most advanced, best organized attempt to synthesize newer developments in psychoanalysis that have evolved over many decades, taking account of the accumulating scientific findings and increasing discontent with our older formulation. This is the perception of many psychoanalysts and might in itself be sufficient to explain the effect that Kohut has upon us. An alternative view is that self psychology is popular precisely because it represents a coherent organization of dissident or diluting elements in psychoanalysis—the abandonment of the difficult psychoanalytic ideas of sex, aggression, the Oedipus complex, and the negative transference. In either interpretation, however, I think the extraordinary interest in self psychology reflects its inclusion of so many of the long-simmering ideas in the psychoanalytic scientific cauldron.

The Nobel prize winner Leon N. Cooper has said:

> Forty years from now—not to speak of a century in the future—physics is unlikely to have the same shape or to be founded on the same assumptions we make now. We can reasonably expect that currently fashionable assumptions will be abandoned to be replaced by unexpected new ones. It is here that our problmes with science arise, for there are many beliefs, concepts or ideas dear to us that we wish to retain even though science does not need them to construct its theories. But science, like Laplace, is strict—it makes no assumptions unless they are necessary [p. 5].

What is true for physics is true for psychoanalysis. However distressing it may be to have to change assumptions, it would be even more distressing if our assumptions did not change.

As is always the case in the history of ideas, the immediacy of our interest in Dr. Kohut did not stem only from the new synthesis he offered of some of our scientific dilemmas. Other historical factors also played a role.

Psychoanalysts, beginning at least with Edward Glover, who discussed the analytic situation in Britain in the 1930s, have been claiming that there has been a change in the human condition. They say that the classical neurotic patient seen by Freud has gradually disappeared, to be replaced by types of severe character pathology, especially the narcissistic character, with a consequent diminution of analytic effectiveness and a lengthening of the analyses. Much of our literature since that time has concerned our need to understand that change, to reconcile it with our analytic theories, and to devise effective psychoanalytic treatment techniques in response to it. In recent years everyone from Spiro Agnew to Christopher Lasch has argued that we are living in an age of narcissism, surrounded by the characterologic fallout of postindustrial society and the cultural decline of the West. The capacity for love, work, and creativity allegedly has been damaged, with a loss of idealism and humanity. The period from the mid-1960s to the mid-1970s seemed to offer powerful corroboration of this view, as America went through the Vietnam War, the Johnson and Nixon years, the student riots, the near destruction of the universities, and a sense of general despair. This period of natural discouragement and dejection was paralleled in psychoanalysis, as we seemed to go through our own bleak phase: We were threatened with the loss of the historical cultural climate required for the ideals of introspection to flourish; many had begun to feel a sense of repetitiousness about our teaching and literature; we saw the fountain of bright young candidates for analytic training drying up; some analysts were fearful of the rise of biological psychiatry with its astonishing triumphs; and some analysts felt discouraged over the prospect of carrying on long analyses with doubtful outcome while surrounded by joyous cries that psychoanalysis was dead and had been superseded by brilliant, quick therapies perfectly attuned to a hurry-up, "gimme" culture.

In this climate the appearance of *The Analysis of the Self* in 1971 seemed to be the right remedy at the right moment. Kohut's work seemed fresh, new, and hopeful. He offered therapeutic optimism and a calm sense of confidence that we would prevail. His personal literary style illuminated his understanding and his mission, and we were able to feel a resonant sense of the analytic empathy he described and to share some of his rich vision of the nature of humanity. The quality of his writing and his ideas conveyed an extraordinary optimism—not only about our immediate problems, but also about our capacity to transcend the ordinary boundaries of creativity and joy through the help of psychoanalysis. When reading Kohut one is always aware of the man whose interests are in the entire human condition rather than in psychoanalysis alone. There is an attractive quality, almost of ecstasy, in some of the writings of self psychologists. The plight of Tragic Man speaks to the existential core of the human condition and makes the problems of Guilty Man seem rather puny. Furthermore—and this was important in the 1970s—Kohut's Tragic Man could achieve joy and creativity, whereas Freud's Guilty Man was promised only ordinary human misery. These factors of cultural crisis, literary style, and personal attitude are, I believe, of great moment in helping to understand the intensity of our interest in Kohut's work at this time in the history of psychoanalysis. The history of science reveals many instances in which this confluence of theoretical issues, cultural need, and literary style was necessary for a scientific idea to come to notice.

I wish to bring up one more consideration to help us understand why Kohut has excited us, while many of his scientific antecedents left us cool. It is now four decades since Freud's death, and it may be only now that we begin to feel the strength to step out from under his massive, sheltering presence. In 1914 Freud was able to say: "I regard myself as justified in maintaining that even today no one can know better than I what psychoanalysis is, how it differs from other ways of investigating the life of the mind, and precisely what should be called psychoanalysis and what would better be described by another name [p. 7]." I think Freud always had that feeling, and probably justifiably so. It is striking that as Freud changed his views, it was often difficult for his followers to adapt; Anna Freud's "The Ego and the Mechanisms of Defense" is, in part, an exhortation to a generation of analysts to incorporate her father's more recent ideas about structural theory, the theory of anxiety, and the dual instinct theory. Today we must live without anyone who is able to tell us with complete assurance what psychoanalysis is and, perhaps more important, what it is not. Furthermore, Freud felt it was essential that a certain amount of freedom be sacrificed to the goal of retaining the identity of psychoanalysis; and his poignant correspondence with Bleuler reveals the importance he attributed to psychoanalysis as a *movement* as well as a science. Today, largely because of the successes of that movement, psychoanalysis has been disseminated far too widely in the culture for any person or group to exert authority over its directions of interest and advance, and I believe no one would want the authority that Freud could claim as the definer of psychoanalysis. This newer spirit of scientific and institutional maturity also contributes to the welcome Kohut's ideas have received and to the productivity of their discussion.

For the variety of reasons I have been suggesting and no doubt others as well, we now have powerful and competing ideas before us and grand occasions such as this one to try to adjudicate or at least to understand better the claims of the different points of view. Each theory and each theorist presents clinical evidence to support his or her position, although students cannot always agree on what has been presented. For example, Goldberg and his coauthors have presented a casebook to demonstrate self psychology in action, but readers of varying sympathies interpret it variously as proving its case, as not being different from any other analysis, or even as differing only in being bad analysis. Some discussants of the two analyses of Mr. Z conclude that Mr. Z did better in his second analysis because Dr. Kohut had become a better analyst and more empathic, regardless of his theory, and that there are no detectable differences in the two analyses that are clearly attributable to theory. If the individual case report is not persuasive, what methods have we for judging theories and their clinical consequences?

We do have some old-fashioned guidelines to help our evaluation of theory. The classical rules indicate that a theory should be elegant (i.e., parsimonious, using the fewest number of propositions and constructs required for its subject); it should be consonant with knowledge and theory in other sciences (i.e., there would have to be compelling reasons to contradict established knowledge, and the theory is strengthened if it can draw on other sciences); and a theory should be useful (i.e., it should lead to further ideas and activities that will yield new knowledge). An old Bostonian, Henry Adams, had great difficulty coping with Poincaré's idea that theories were merely useful rather than true. Various attempts have been made to subject analytic theory to these tests, most prominently by Rappaport, who felt that only a few of our propositions were essential. This is another good time to subject our theories to this kind of philosophical scrutiny. We may be more willing now to alter conceptions that no longer stand up to such examination. The positivist philosophers of science have suggested that a good hypothesis would yield the disconfirming experiment, and we know that analytic hypotheses are not likely to yield that possibility. More modern philosophers of science, including Ricouer, Rubenstein, Simpson, Polanyi, and others, have demonstrated that many of the complex sciences cannot yield such methods of confirmation and must rely on the weight of evidence, on affirming predictions (which are available to psychoanalysis), and on postdiction. These are the methods with which we are familiar. There is clearly a need, however, for the planned experiment, for sophisticated outcome research, for the greater use of a shared data base through recorded analyses, and for bringing the knowledge of extra-analytic fields to bear in our psychoanalytic thinking. We do all these things, but too seldom, with insufficient intensity, and without the cadre of trained full-time researchers that psychoanalysis must eventually develop. These "harder" research methods will, of course, always be supplementary to research done directly through the psychoanalytic method of discovery, that is, clinical psychoanalysis.

Whether or not self psychology represents a new paradigm in psychoanalysis as some have suggested, Kohut's work has led us to nothing less than a reassessment of our basic theories. The same historical processes that bring Kohut's work to the forefront also permit a new level of discussion of our scientific activities—more open and more tolerant of uncertainty than has sometimes been the case in the past. All science requires acts of faith. Arno Penzias, in his Nobel laureate address, described how the development of modern cosmology depended on the development of the faith that certain conditions *must* obtain in the universe, although there were then no data for it. But with faith the data were sought and eventually found. Psychoanalysis has progressed through the faith of its researchers; at times, however, that faith of the inquirer has become the tradition of the conserver. A dialectic of these trends is necessary in science. It seems to me that the current climate of bolder reexamination of our present ideas and fearless exploration of new ideas can be a source of anxiety that should be respected. We should not lightly give up any tradition, and we should take full cognizance of the anxiety engendered by any change of belief—an issue that, as I mentioned earlier, even Freud confronted with his followers when he changed his views. However, it is the essence of our Freudian tradition that we have the courage to use the best of the scientific method of our era in the effort to add to our knowledge, to correct errors, and to improve our theories. Penzias quotes Eddington as saying: "Never fully trust an observational result until you have at least one theory to explain it." In psychoanalysis we rarely lack theories, but we rarely subject either our data or our assumptions to the most rigorous tests possible.

The issue of whether or not psychoanalysis is scientific is, I think, irrelevant in the light of our current views of science—that quivering, imaginative, uncertain enterprise of the human observer en-twined with the observed in a pursuit of new knowledge that can be validated. I believe that Kohut, in developing self psychology as boldly as he has and in paying such close attention to methodologi-cal issues, has been a main source of energy invigorating psycho-analytic science. This Boston conference is the exemplar of this sci-entific renewal, and I hope it will be the inspiration for continued deepening of our humanistic scientific commitment. Whatever the ultimate fate of Kohut's psychology will be, the theory of the self has already fulfilled at least one of the criteria of a good theory: It has led to an explosion of scientific activity, new ideas, and new investi-gations. It will be a test of our scientific maturity to maintain our discourse as we look for still better ways to add to our knowledge, to test our theories, and to improve our clinical capacity. I am greatly encouraged concerning our ability to do just that by the knowledge that Kohut has attracted some of our most gifted and creative people and that self psychology is developing as a genuine field of inquiry, with questions and disagreements, rather than with a unified belief system.

REFERENCES

Bergler, E. (1969). *Selected Papers of Edmund Bergler, M.D. 1933–1961*. New York: Grune & Stratton.

Cooper, L. N. (1980). Source and limits of human intellect. *Daedalus,* Spring, pp. 1–18.

Eissler, K. R. (1953). The effect of the structure of the ego on psychoanalytic tech-nique. *J. Amer. Psychoanal. Assn.* 1: 104–143.

Freud, A. (1946). *The Ego and the Mechanisms of Defense*. New York: Int. Univ. Press.

——— (1931). Female sexuality. *S.E.* 225–246.

Freud, S. (1914). On the history of the psychoanalytic movement. *S.E.* 14.

Gifford, S. (1978). Psychoanalysis in Boston: Innocence and experience. In *Psycho-analysis, Psychotherapy and the New England Medical Scene, 1894–1944,* ed. G. E. Gifford. New York: Science History Publications.

Glover, E. (1955). *The Technique of Psychoanalysis*. New York: Int. Univ. Press.

Goldberg, A., ed. (1978). *The Psychology of the Self: A Casebook*. New York: Int. Univ. Press.

Hartmann, H. (1958). *Ego Psychology and the Problem of Adaptation*. New York: Int. Univ. Press.

Kardiner, A. (1945). *The Psychological Frontiers of Society*. New York: Columbia Univ. Press.

Kohut, H. (1970). Scientific activities of the American Psychoanalytic Association. *This Journal* 18: 462–484.

_____ (1971). *The Analysis of the Self.* New York: Int. Univ. Press.

_____ (1977). *The Restoration of the Self.* New York: Int. Univ. Press.

Lasch, C. (1978). *The Culture of Narcissism: American Life in an Age of Diminishing Expectations.* New York: Norton.

Penzias, A. (1979. The origin of the elements. *Science* 205: 549–554.

Rado, S. (1962). From the metapsychological ego to the bio-cultural action self (1958). *Psychoanalysis of Behavior* 2: 142–48.

Rappaport, D. (1960). The structure of psychoanalytic theory: A systematizing attempt. *Psychol. Issue,* New York: International Universities Press.

Schafer, R. (1973). Action: Its place in psychoanalytic interpretation and theory. *Annual of Psychoanal.* 1: 159–196.

_____ (1973). Concepts of self and identity and the experience of separation—individuation in adolescence. *The Psychoanalytic Quarterly* XLII: 42–59.

Sullivan, H. S. (1953). *The Collected Works of Harry Stack Sullivan,* eds., H. S. Perry & M. L. Gawel. New York: Norton.

Wallerstein, R. (1981). The bipolar self: Discussion of alternative perspectives. *J. Amer. Psychoanal. Assn.* 29: 377–394.

THE DEVELOPMENT OF
THE SELF: INFANT
RESEARCH

5 Prologue

Donald Silver, M.D.

In reflecting on the past history of collaborative efforts to establish a theory of infant development and of the evolution of the self, we are reminded of ships passing unseen at night. In one of his major papers on development, Freud (1905) anticipated the dilemma we are faced with today:

> Psychoanalytic investigation, reaching back into childhood from a later time, and contemporary observation of children combine to indicate to us still other regularly active sources of sexual excitation. The direct observation of children has the disadvantage of working upon data which are easily misunderstandable; psychoanalysis is made difficult by the fact that it can only reach its data, as well as its conclusions, after long detours. But by cooperation the two methods can attain a satisfactory degree of certainty in their findings [p. 201].

The position of self psychology with respect to the developing field of infant research has been equivocal. M. Tolpin (1971), in her oft-quoted paper on the beginnings of a cohesive self, and Basch (1976, 1977, 1982), in a series of major contributions, have utilized the findings of infant research and enriched the field with their own conceptualizations. Alternatively, Kohut (1971) has emphasized the differences in conceptualization between two different basic observational attitudes: infant research "observes the behavior of small children; I reconstruct their inner life on the basis of transference

37

reactivations [p. 219]." At the same time the two approaches inevitably come together in that each attempts to evolve a developmental conception of the self, as distinguished from a preoccupation with drives or with experience-distant concepts of macrostructures (id., ego, and superego). The reader will find that with a spirit of cooperation the presentations in this section represent a collaborative effort to reconsider the issue of the ontogeny of the self. This provides an opportunity to compare the developmental model proposed by self psychology with others derived from infant research. Self psychology traces the development of a cohesive self, which it regards as forming in response to the empathic support derived from the interaction of the infant and a caregiver called a selfobject. This model is not based on direct observation but comes from empathic introspection and reconstruction derived from the analytic situation. Other theories with similar focus on the ontogeny of self have been formulated from data obtained by direct observation by a group of infant researchers composed of psychoanalysts, psychologists, and pediatricians. Representing the group of researchers in this section are Gerald Stechler, Daniel Stern, Louis Sander, and Virginia Demos. Marian Tolpin's comments derive from self psychology.

Stechler's introduction addresses two central dilemmas within psychoanalytic developmental theory. The first, a concern of both Freud and Kohut, is the compatibility of the reconstructive versus the contemporaneous view of infancy. Stechler argues that there are actually satisfying cross-validations between these two methods. He cites that Stern, Sander, and proponents of self psychology believe that the developmental thrust for the infant occurs during quiet moments rather than primarily as outgrowths of drive and drive discharge. Stechler also notes that the dichotomy between the "objective" direct observations of infant research and the empathic-introspective subjectivity of clinical self psychology is a false delineation in that infant researchers clearly use an empathic mode of observation as one of their research methods. The second controversy Stechler notes is the conflict basis of psychic development versus nonconflicted psychic development evolving from an infant-caregiving unit or as a self-selfobject unit. In a brief, tightly reasoned portion of his remarks Stechler attempts a resolution of this controversy by offering a "broader concept of incompatibilities, within which the more narrowly defined psychoanalytic concept of conflict forms an important subset." Incompatibilities "function as the dialectical tensions from which future structures could emerge, with those evolving structures in turn serving as the framework within which true intrapsychic conflict could arise." The reader might want to consider these suggestions about pathological development from two perspectives: (1) to relate them to the presentations of Stern and Sander that focus on means by which normal development occurs as a result of compatibilities; and (2) to compare Stechler's position with the discussions of the importance, definition, and role of conflict as it appears repeatedly in later sections of the book.

In Stern's paper the reader should be prepared for an approach to the early development of schemata of self that is at marked variance with other psychoanalytic formulations, both traditional and current. Stern presents clinical data that place him in opposition to widely accepted formulations of a narcissistic stage, a symbiotic stage, and timetables of selfobject differentiation. He espouses a theory that places normal development as a sequence entirely independent of presumptions based on abnormal developments being continuations or permutations of early archaic stages. Stern argues "that beginning at birth the infant starts perceptually and cognitively to differentiate self and others and self from others successfully. Infants appear to be predesigned by nature . . . such that salient natural categories such as self and other are not left to be slowly and painstakingly learned from scratch." Stern then applies his findings to the categorization of schemas of affective experience of "self with other" into three groupings: self–other complementing, state sharing, and state transforming. He challenges the view that during moments of state sharing the infant is merging or fusing or slowly experiencing self through a mirroring process: "Instead, we propose that he is engaged in the slow and momentous discovery that his experience which he already senses is distinctly his own is not unique and unparalleled but is part of shared human experience." Arguing against assumptions based on pathological outcomes, Stern states "it is not clear why experiences of being with have to disrupt self and other representations or schemata. Rather, the inherent conflicts in the two kinds of schemata will act constructively to sharpen differences and thereby solidify the formation and integration of both the affective and cognitive components of the experiences of being with another."

Louis Sander (Sander & Condon, 1974) made the observation that newborns move their heads and limbs in rhythm with the voices they hear around them. This response is specific for human speech, and the neonate does not respond in a similar way to music or other auditory rhythms. It is through wonderful observations of this type that Sander has helped us to understand how babies become part of the human family. Sander's thinking about the origins of the self as outlined in his paper, "To Begin with—Reflections on Ontogeny," is reminiscent of the richness and depth of intellectual mastery that Freud brought to his project for a scientific psychology in the 1890s. This is true because Sander's background includes training in neurology, physiology, pediatrics, as well as psychiatry and psychoanalysis, and because he studies the infant and the caregiving environment together as a living biological system. He employs a language that is difficult and unusual for psychoanalysis. For example, he uses terms such as "biorhythmicity": the cycling of life's patterns; and "trajectory": the course of a developmental pattern over time. He follows a line of reasoning employing a systems-theory method to achieve understanding of the evolving complexity embodied in the dawning of awareness in the neonate. In contrast, he rejects such terms as "tension reduction" and "undifferentiation" because the ideas they express are contradicted by the burgeoning body of infant research.

Sander studies the factors that cause the infant to synchronize with the rhythms and cycles of those around him or to oppose them, and he is able to see from the very beginning either normal lines of development unfold as the infant and environment fit together or pathology evolve as the regulation offered by the caregiver fails to harmonize with the specific needs of the newborn. In addition to his insight into the achieving of synchrony and thus engagement with the environment, he is interested in the patterns of disengagement. Through the alternating rhythms of engagement and disengagement, Sander feels he can discover the dawning of awareness of the infant. For him the first beginnings of self-awareness occur in periods when infants can temporarily remove themselves from synchrony with the caregiver's rhythms and pursue their uniqueness. He explains that during these "open periods," when infants are temporarily free of inner need or external intrusion, they are able to begin to discover themselves.

Through his essay Sander offers the reader a new and different approach to development that, although sometimes difficult to follow, is nonetheless highly rewarding. His novel ideas provide a basis for understanding the paradox of how neonates become integrated with their environment and simultaneously, while maintaining synchrony with their caregivers, begin to develop their own individuality.

Just as Stern and Sander argue that there are inborn perceptual and cognitive capabilities that allow infants to learn about and differentiate themselves from their objects, Demos argues for the idea that affects as instruments of communication and motivation should be recognized as important means through which infants and caregivers come to know each other. To Demos, affect becomes the medium of mutual and reciprocal modulation through which harmony and equilibrium are achieved.

After stressing the importance of affect in psychic development, Demos discusses the relative importance of the "we" and "I" experiences for development. She notes that Kohut emphasizes the "we" experience, that is, the interplay of the self-selfobject unit, as the basis for the internalization of psychic structure and the creation of the self. Alternatively, Sander and Stern give greater relative emphasis to the infant's contribution, the "I" experience, in terms of the infant's own complex organizational capacities and changing initiatives. Though feeling that both "I" and "we" experiences are involved and essential, Demos favors a swing of the pendulum toward more emphasis on the "I" experience.

Tolpin, responding to Stern's rejection of the concept of merger in an undifferentiated state as the earliest form of infant psychic existence, agrees with him and spells out what self psychology calls merger, broadening the concept markedly from its usual usage: "By merger of self and selfobject we mean psychological connectedness—for instance, between delighted child and mirroring audience; between cranky, tired child and idealized, uplifting pillars of strength and support; between children who want company and their lively partners who lend their presence." Using a delightful clinical vignette, she illustrates the self psychological definition of merger. Tolpin regards the basic psychological constituents of the nuclear self to be the grandiose exhibitionistic self, the idealizing self, and the partnering self, each operating in harmony with the responsive selfobject. Tolpin thus indicates that for self psychology the emphasis is on the "we" experience as the source of the epigenesis of a consolidated self, and she would move the pendulum away from the infant and its own "I" experience as emphasized by Stern, Sander, and Demos.

Each of the papers in this section portrays the infant's development in experience-near concepts. Each gives somewhat different weight to differing aspects of the experiences. For example, the reader may wish to compare Stern's depictions of self and other and self with other to Sander's open space developments, to Demos' emphasis on affects, and to Tolpin's basic constituents of the nuclear self.

REFERENCES

Basch, M. (1976). The concept of affect: A re-examination. *J. Amer. Psychoanal. Assn. 2412* 759–777.

———— (1977). Developmental psychology and explanatory theory in psychoanalysis. *Ann. Psychoanal.* 5: 229–263.

———— (1982). Empathic understanding: A review of the concept and some theoretical considerations. *J. Amer. Psychoanal. Assn.*

Condon, W. & Sander, L. (1974). Neonatal movement is synchronized with adult speech. *Science* 183: 99–101.

Freud, S. (1905). Three essays on the theory of sexuality. *S.E.* 7, 125–248.

Kohut, H. (1971). *The Analysis of the Self.* New York: Int. Univ. Press.

Tolpin, M. (1971). On the beginnings of a cohesive self: An application of the concept of transmuting internalization to the study of the transitional object and signal anxiety. *Psychoanal. Study Child* 26: 316–354.

6 Infancy Research: A Contribution to Self Psychology

Gerald Stechler, Ph.D.

One of the less productive controversies within psychoanalysis concerns the compatibility of the reconstructive versus the contemporaneous view of infancy. That the two views are different is undeniable. But that difference should be the goad for further inquiry, not the basis for discarding one view or the other. Both are relevant to psychoanalysis. The task is to bridge the two domains so that a unified understanding becomes possible. Relativistic thinking tells us that we should expect our view to be determined in part by our viewing platform. Nevertheless, scientific advancement comes when we can triangulate on a common problem using a range of methods and thereby transcend the parochial view that is tied to a particular method.

Coupled with the reconstructive-contemporaneous distinction is the dichotomy between the subjective and the objective position. Kohut (1977) refers to the latter dichotomy as the difference between the empathic stance and the so-called psychobiological perspective. Although he acknowledges the value of the latter approach, he believes it is premature to attempt to compare the methods, findings, and formulations. However, others have found

*Faculty, Boston Psychoanalytic Society and Institute; Professor and Chairman, Department of Child Psychiatry and Child Development, Boston University Medical Center.

themselves "floundering in a morass of conflicting, poorly based, and often vague theoretical speculation," and like Kohut (1977) have "decided that there was only one way that would lead to progress: the way back to the direct observation of clinical phenomena and construction of new formulations that would accommodate [the] observations [pp. xx–xxi]."

To bring the two perspectives—that of the analyst and that of the baby watcher—into closer approximation so that some comparisons and even syntheses become possible, it may be useful to point out that similar critiques and similar reformulations of certain aspects of psychoanalytic theory have arisen independently from each of the perspectives. Paramount among these similarities has been the difficulty encountered by some analysts and some infant investigators in fitting their respective clinical observations into the drive theory. The return to the data within an essential psychoanalytic framework has been the common attribute of the two groups. The more rarified, speculative, and metapsychological aspects of psychoanalytic theory have been found to be most problematic. Thus, when Kohut (1977) finds "that the primary psychological configurations in the child's experiential world are not drives, that the drive experiences occur as disintegration products when the self is unsupported [p. 171]," he is expressing, from his vantage point, a position very similar to that of both Sander and Stern who, along with other investigators, see the developmental thrust for the infant occurring during quiet moments.

The portrayal of the neonate and young infant within mainstream psychoanalytic theory emphasizes the disorganized, amorphous nature of the baby, with what little organization is to be found being based on drive and drive discharge. Recent reformulations focus on the multitude of calmer, more resonant exchanges between the baby and the caregiver. These are as much the states from which regulation and self-organization emerge as are the biological need states, and they most frequently are the states within which one sees and senses complex affective and cognitive functioning. There is a satisfying cross-validation when analysts, operating on the basis of their empathy with adult patients, and infant investigators using their tools zero in on the same problem and come up with highly compatible answers.

Cohler (1980) has attempted to lessen the magnitude of the crib-couch gap by pointing out how infant research itself encompasses a wide range of methods. Some of them are objective, observing the infant from the outside; others attempt a more empathic approach, viewing the events in infants' lives from the perspective of what might be subjectively experienced by the babies themselves. Cohler believes that the relevance of baby research for psychoanalysis and self psychology in particular hinges on the specific methodological question of whether the baby watcher is operating as the empathic analyst does and not on whether the subject is a baby or a patient in analysis.

To be sure, as one engages in developmental research with infants, particularly in studies that involve intensive longitudinal contact with a small number of families in which the investigators are themselves analytically trained, the empathic tuning can become very sensitive. That empathy, which is the central core of healthy parenting, can be the stance of the developmental investigator and psychoanalyst alike. As can be seen in the presentations of Sander and Stern and in the discussions by Demos and Tolpin, the baby comes to life as a feeling person, which leaves little doubt about the empathic stance of the reporter.

If the possibility and utility of building bridges are accepted, it may be worthwhile to address some other important theoretical questions of contemporary psychoanalysis and to inquire what, if anything, from the realm of developmental research can be brought to bear on those questions. One such question that is raised in the clinical sections of this symposium concerns the relationship between deficit and conflict and their respective contributions to psychopathology. Deficit, as defined by Kohut, results from a mother's repeated failure to empathize with her infant. The outcome of this process is a self-organization that is fragmented rather than cohesive, leading (after further development) to the line of narcissistic disorder. These disorders are seen as having a different etiology and a different outcome, and they require a modified analytic approach as compared with the conflict-based neuroses.

Tolpin (1980), elaborating on this distinction, notes that the part of psychoanalytic conflict theory which has proven its utility concerns "late," that is, oedipal conflicts, found in individuals who have shown prior normal ego development. ". . . [T]he problem of massive anxiety, depression, rage, psychic pain, etc., associated with ego abnormality is beyond the explanatory limits of any and all theories of psychic conflict [p. 51]."

The debate is difficult to resolve for a number of reasons. One is that within structural psychoanalytic theory, conflict by definition arrives late on the scene, stemming as it does from the battle among the tripartite agencies. Thus, the idea of conflict found within the earliest periods of development becomes almost a contradiction of terms.

Second, even if one accepts a dialectical model of structure building, as is found in George Klein's (1976) model of the development of the self, there remains a chicken-and-egg problem. Intrapsychic conflict can exist only if internal structures are in opposition to each other, and conversely, the internal structures come into being out of the resolution of the dialectical tension of the conflictual polarities. A partial resolution of this dilemma (Stechler & Kaplan, 1980) is based on Klein's broader concept of incompatibilities, within which the more narrowly defined psychoanalytic concept of conflict forms an important subset. Thus, a person at any stage of development can be confronted by and experience incompatibilities such as the simultaneous urges to perform two incompatible behaviors or, more directly on the point in question, to reach a mother who at that moment is not there, either physically or psychologically. The reaching out to an unresponsive or unempathic parent would, in Klein's terms, result in an experience of incompatibility on the infant's part. The incompatibilities could then function as the dialectical tensions from which future structures could emerge, with those evolving structures in turn serving as the framework within which true intrapsychic conflict could arise. What, then, can the students of early development contribute to this question of the origins of psychopathology?

For one, they, along with psychoanalysts, can attempt to specify terms such as "conflict" and "deficit" so that they relate to some clinical observables, rather than being deduced from some a priori set of metapsychological propositions. Once the concepts become tied to something clinical, whether from a patient or a parent-infant pair, the questions can be looked at empirically, rather than as theoretical abstractions. If we accept Klein's clinically based definition of conflict and view it as a member of the broader class of incompatibilities, we can see both deficits and conflicts as arising from early interactions, and we can propose a hypothesis about the relationship between the two.

By virtue of the sheer nature of existence, infants encounter a large number of incompatibilities in their day-to-day life. These may be typified by situations in which the affect, plan, expectancy, need state, communication, or other function of the baby is unmet or mismet by the parent or caregiver. It may lead the baby to a distress state, to a withdrawal of interest, to an increased effort to communicate, or to some other self-regulatory maneuver.

The outcome, and by implication the internal sensation of the baby, is not predictable in purely theoretical terms. But as an empirical question it can be investigated. Thus, investigations such as those of Sander, Stern, and my own indicate that parents by virtue of their empathic understanding of the baby can regulate the interaction so that the incompatibilities experienced by the infant are kept within some manageable range and the resolutions facilitated.

Klein's model and our observations support the idea that the cumulative outcomes of encounters with incompatibilities determine whether the self is strengthened or weakened, whether it becomes more cohesive or more fragmented. If the outcome has been the creation, by the infant, of a new regulatory process, of a new, more complex problem solution, or of more articulated affective expression, then the self has been added to, and it becomes more cohesive or resilient, and over time self-esteem has been increased. If, on the other hand, the challenge is beyond the integrative capacities of the infant, then in Klein's terms repression or defense is employed, and the self is shrunken or enfeebled. In this view infants themselves construct, or fail to construct, cohesive selves. The parent is vital in regulating the magnitude and frequency of the challenges, their timing, their quality, and most important, via empathic exchanges, facilitating the integrative solution to a particular incompatibility.

Returning now to the question of structural deficit versus unresolved conflict as the basis of psychopathology, a new formulation becomes possible. The details of the infant's life embedded in the family milieu inform us that there is not an either/or distinction between deficit and conflict. Rather, the issue becomes one of quantity and, to some extent, of timing. How often does the baby encounter an overwhelming circumstance? If it reappears over and over, unmitigated by a comparable set of "successful" integrative encounters, the condition of structural deficit is likely to prevail. Not only have creative solutions to incompatibilities not been found, but the tools for finding them, the very expectation of finding or creating them, are themselves diminished.

As development continues, the more familiar sequences occur whereby the early structural deficits warp and fragment the self so that later conflict, in the bona fide psychoanalytic sense, cannot evolve. Thus, deficits can be seen as part of the process whereby early failures in the dialectic process become structuralized and through that structural failure exert lasting influence on the later dialectic defined as conflict. Further elaboration of this model differentiates between "I" and "we" encounters and addresses the process of internalizing the "I" and the "we" transactions (Stechler & Kaplan, 1980). That, however, is not the central point of this discussion.

The central point is that one can retain the clarity of the psychoanalytic definition of conflict and still, via the broader concept of incompatibility, introduce a dialectic process starting from birth. That dialectic process is akin to conflict and conflict resolution. It is to some extent regulated and facilitated by the parent, but it is accomplished inside the infant. With this hypothesis, deficit and conflict are both subsumed under a single superordinate concept, and they have a plausible and logical relationship to each other.

Whether this formulation will prove useful in future inquiries remains to be seen. It is, however, another example of how convergence of a patient-centered clinical reformulation, together with infant research, can address and possibly resolve an apparently unyielding problem in theory and practice.

REFERENCES

Cohler, B. J. (1980). Developmental perspectives on the Psychology of the Self in Early Childhood. In *Advances in Self Psychology*, A. Goldberg, ed. New York: Int. Univ. Press, pp. 69–116.

Klein, G. S. (1976). *Psychoanalytic Theory*. New York: Int. Univ. Press.

Kohut, H. (1977). *The Restoration of the Self*. New York: Int. Univ. Press.

Stechler, G. & Kaplan, S. (1980). The development of the self. *Psychoanal. Study Child* 35: 85–105.

Tolpin, M. (1980). Discussion of "Psychoanalytic Developmental Theories of the Self." In *Advances in Self-Psychology*, A. Goldberg, ed. New York: Int. Univ. Press, pp. 47–68.

7 The Early Development of
Schemas of Self, Other, and
"Self with Other"

Daniel N. Stern, M.D.

INTRODUCTION

The impetus for this paper is the advances in our understanding of
infants and the nature of their knowledge of the world. I attempt to
integrate recently available knowledge as it applies to the persistent questions about the infant's earliest development of inner
mental constructs or schemas[1] of self, of others,[2] and of various
self–other experiences.

---

[1]For the purpose of clarity I use the term "schemas" to refer to inner mental
constructs that are elaborated during the presymbolic period of sensorimotor intelligence (ending roughly some months after the first birthday) and reserve the term
"representations" for inner constructs elaborated during the period of symbolic functioning and capable of symbolic transformations as defined by Piaget (1953). This is
the general convention observed, although not rigorously (partly for historical reasons), in psychoanalytic literature. Though I strongly believe that the distinction
between schemas and representations becomes blurred when one addresses inner
constructs about interpersonal experience and that much more thought and observation is needed regarding this distinction and its developmental timing, I adhere to the
convention because it helps clarify at which points current findings and established
theory are truly at odds or are simply addressing the same material from different
perspectives.

[2]I use the term "other" to refer to a significant (cathected) other person rather
than the more usual psychoanalytic term "object." Because I do not in this paper use
libido theory with its energic assumptions, the term "object" should not be used, as it
loses its meaning and even becomes confusing outside the context of libido theory.
However, because the major theories that I wish to address do use the terms "object"
or "selfobject" (with or without their energic connotations), I employ that terminology when referring to the concepts of those theories.

A view of the infant's inner world is described on the basis of recent findings about infants' perceptual organization, action tendencies, and cognitive competencies. This view presents the following major conclusions:

1. From the point of view of sensorimotor intelligence, infants probably never experience an undifferentiated phase of life—that is, the infant is predesigned to discriminate and to begin to form distinct schemas of self and of other from the earliest months of life.
2. Accordingly, clinical entities observed after infancy, such as "part objects," "symbiotic objects," and "selfobjects," need not be seen as reactivated residua or breakdown products of the dissolution of an undifferentiated phase, but rather may be viewed as normal or abnormal ongoing developmental constructions.
3. We need a new descriptive typology of the different affective infantile experiences of "being with" another and a more elaborated way of understanding how infants schematize or represent "being with" a particular other. This becomes a necessity if we assume the interaction between some separate sense of self and of other from the beginning of life.

It is immediately clear that this viewpoint has significant implications for current theories of infancy and perhaps for clinical practice. For that reason I wish to make clear the intent and scope of this paper.

There has always been, in all dynamic psychologies, a continuing dialogue about the nature of infants' inner sense of self and other during the first year of life. Currently in psychoanalysis, this dialogue has been couched in the form of a particular and perhaps too narrow question: Which "baby" best fits our descriptive and clinical notions—the "baby" of classical analysis, that of object relations theorists, or that of Heinz Kohut and his colleagues? It is not the intent of this paper to support one "side" or to challenge any theory per se; rather it addresses some crucial issues common to all such theories in light of newly accumulated information.

It is often stated that formulations of infants' inner mental life derived from direct observation of infants and those derived from reconstruction exist in different domains of discourse, which are impervious to translation, or that they are like two lines coming from different directions and never meeting because of the discontinuous nature of development. Even if both of these statements were true, it would not matter because our conception of what happens inside the infant's mind will probably always remain in part an issue of the "goodness of fit" of our notions to the available knowledge. It matters little where that knowledge comes from, as long as it influences our appreciation of what may make sense and produces new observations. The knowledge that is presented in this paper comes largely from experimental and observational approaches to the infant.

It is artificial to divide the experience of self and other into cognitive and affective aspects. Yet the major advances in knowledge about infants concerns their perceptions and cognitions, not their emotions. This has resulted in a picture of "two infants": the *cognitive knower* of the experimental psychologists and the *affective experiencer* of the psychoanalyst. The two views lead to different conclusions about the infant's sense of self and other, yet there is only one infant. Perhaps the greatest unknown in this clash of views is whether the affective and cognitive experiences of self and other are truly at odds, and if so, which predominates in organizing experience at which times.

The first part of this paper concerns findings indicating that cognitive differentiation of self and other takes place very early in the infant's development. The second part concerns the affective experiences that may occur between these two distinct entities—that is, the nature of early experiences of self "being with" the other.

PART 1: EARLY ORIGINS
OF A DIFFERENTIATED SELF AND OTHER:
COGNITIVE ASPECTS

I argue that the infant has clearly separated experiences and schemata of self and other by the first half-year of life, when the phase of normal symbiosis is thought to be at its height. Also, there exists no systematic or pervasive confusion between the self and other stimuli and agents in the world, or between the other and the world at large. And finally, the experiences and schemas of self and other never were systematically or pervasively fused or confused by the infant in the course of early development, but rather formed separately, as emergent sensorimotor-affective and cognitive constructs. Before presenting the evidence suggesting such a view, it is necessary to review briefly the current understanding of and timetable for self differentiation, other differentiation, and self–other differentiation during the first year of life.

The Prevailing View of the Differentiation of Self and Other

The prevailing view of the process and timetable of self–other differentiation in infancy is briefly as follows. Infants are born unable to distinguish their own acts from those of the caregiver ministering to them. Throughout the first half of the first year, at least, infants are generally assumed not to make the distinctions that would separate them as entities or agents from the caregiver as an entity or agent. According to Mahler, Pine, and Bergman (1975) the infant is thought to exist in a "state of undifferentiation, of fusion with the mother, in which the 'I' is not yet differentiated from the 'not-I' and in which inside and outside are only gradually coming to be sensed as 'different' [p. 44]." This view of the infant as not differentiating self from other is generally shared by developmental psychologists as well as psychoanalysts. Most psychoanalysts (see Mahler, 1975) argue for a state of fusion on the basis of the infant's affective experience. This position is not directly arguable, but its implication for the infant's cognitive view of self and other must somehow be brought into line with recent knowledge of infants' cognitive abilities.

The developmental psychologists, on the other hand, adhere to the notion that the infant occupies a state of self–other nondifferentiation on cognitive grounds alone. Each of the entities (self and other), on its own, is thought to undergo a lengthy process of differentiation from the stimuli of the world at large. The developmental psychological literature does not stress, as does the psychoanalytic literature, the need for the specific differentiation of self from other out of a fused self–other entity. Mahler and her colleagues, however, carry the picture of the infant a step further (Mahler, Pine, & Bergman, 1975). They state that "the essential feature of symbiosis [2–7 months] is hallucinatory or delusional somatopsychic *omnipotent* fusion with the representation of the mother and, in particular, the delusion of a common boundary between two physically separate individuals [p. 45]." The additional step taken in this statement is quite significant. It is one thing for the infant to be unable to differ-entiate and therefore unable to conceptualize in any form the sources of various stimuli in the world, some emanating from the self, some from others, and some from the inanimate world. It is quite another thing to generate and elaborate a "representation" of an entity that is in fact two different entities fused. The "delusions" (a schema?) of a fused selfobject is a fairly high-order cognition, well beyond simply not discriminating the two. The reasons why psycho-analytic thinkers, of whom Mahler is the most influential example, have added this elaboration to the undifferentiated phase, are dis-cussed later. At present I am attempting only to describe the in-fant's presumed state of self–other differentiation early on.

The difference in the infant's cognitions about self and other as seen from the psychoanalytic view and that of most developmental psychologists is akin to the difference between confused knowledge and ignorance. In both views, however, the infant is left without schemas of self or of other during a prolonged phase of nondifferen-tiation.

This initial phase of nondifferentiation is generally thought to come to a close toward the end of the first year with psychic develop-ments of which the appearance of the separation reaction is a land-mark. The advent of the separation reaction is generally held to imply that the infant has made a differentiation between self and caregivers, and the infant now regards mother as a separate indi-vidual from self. Separation reactions have been interpreted as providing the evidence for the emergence of object constancy—the formation of a stable internal *representation* of the caregiver. It is stable in the sense that the infant does not simply recognize the caregiver when present but can evoke or retrieve her image when she is absent. Both psychoanalysts and developmental psychologists have refined this important distinction. The psychoanalysts call the form of memory necessary for this phenomenon "evocative" memory (Fraiberg, 1969), and the experimental psychologists call it "re-trieval" memory (as opposed to simple "recognition" memory).

Attachment theory (Ainsworth and Bell, 1978; Bowlby, 1969) is concerned mainly with the formation of observable behavioral ties rather than the process of developing phases of internal representa-tions. Nonetheless, it also makes the assumption that some internal "working model" (representation or schema?) of the caregiver must be present toward the last quarter of the first year of life, when attachment behaviors become so manifest. Attachment theorists imply that before the age of 6–7 months a state of nondifferentiation is assumed with regard to infants' sense of the other or of self, and that only after 6–7 months does an effective working model of mother begin to form (Ainsworth, personal communication; Bowlby, 1960).

From the point of view of attachment theory as well as traditional developmental theories, the onset of separation and/or reunion reactions is thought to mark the passage of the developmental phase of nondifferentiation of self, of other, and of self from other. Several features and assumptions contained in these views of the infant require explication before proceeding with a critique of this view and suggesting an alternative one.

Assumptions Implicit in the Traditional Views

There are at least five assumptions implicit in the prevaling view of the infant's early state of nondifferentiation with regard to self and others. Some of these assumptions are no longer held when applied to the infant's relationships to things and events or even to human behavior as stimuli, but they are still prevalent when applied to the entities of self and other. These assumptions are:

1. The infant must differentiate self from other through the laborious, piecemeal process of building up a schema and then representation of self and other from "nothing," that is, from the homogenous array of stimulus events that the world presents the infant. Furthermore, the process of building up the schemas must occur through the gradual processes of associative learning (e.g., progressively establishing the relationship between each element belonging to the mother's behavior and each element of the self's behavior) and through the gradual process of assimilation, accommodation, and then integration of separate sensorimotor schemata related to self and others.

2. The infant has no special predesigned or innate perceptual tendencies or biases to detect specially marked or salient features of human behavior that would dichotomize the supposedly homogenous world of stimuli into categories of self and other. The infant has no innate organization of perceptual and response systems that would make inevitable or even easier the early discrimination of the entities of self and of other.

3. The long process of acquiring and coalescing "islands of consistency" in the formation of stable schemas and representations of others or of self awaits the maturation of sufficient evocative or retrieval memory before object (or self) "constancy" or "permanence" can exist. The schedule assumed for the maturation of this memory operation is largely modeled after that observed infants' memory of inanimate objects. The crucial developmental landmark is assumed to be at about 8–9 months, when inanimate object permanence, as defined by Piagetian (1954) criteria, and person constancy, as defined by separation reaction (Bowlby, 1960), both appear.

4. Many psychoanalysts, most notably Mahler and M. Klein, assume that even if infants could distinguish self from other very early in life on perceptual grounds, they would not do so for protective or defensive reasons. A main reason for the theoretical establishment of a "delusion of a common boundary" between two physically separate individuals is Mahler's assumption that the infant's ego must be protected from stress (Mahler, Pine, & Bergman, 1975).

5. Psychoanalysts and developmental psychologists differ as to the nature of the earliest schemas or representations of others that they consider important or even researchable. The psychoanalysts assume that it is mainly the schemas or representations of *affective experiences* with another that are crucial. The developmental psychologists (with notable exceptions) have found the affective experience to be intractable to experimental observation and have mainly considered the other as a perceptual or cognitive category, implicitly assuming it to be such in the infant's mind.

Critique of Assumptions

Assumptions 1 and 2

1. The infant is a slow, traditional learner.
2. The infant has no predesigned perceptual tendencies to help distinguish self from other.

These two assumptions are most easily discussed together. The central issue is: How does the infant come to "know," "learn," or "sense" that certain stimulus events do or do not belong together, forming separate natural categories, entities, and events? There has been a revolution in our thinking about infants in the past several decades that affects this issue. As has often been said, the infant was previously seen as passive, as a "tabula rasa," and confused by the welter of world stimuli because he or she had no innate perceptual or cognitive competencies. Now the infant is seen as an avid learner from birth (Lipsitt, 1969; Papousek, 1959); as highly competent, in the sense of being predesigned to perceive the world in a highly structured fashion; and as mentally active in organizing these pre-structured perceptions. New infant capabilities are being revealed at an astounding rate. Wherever in the research one looks, the infant is found to be less naive than previously thought (see Kagan, Kearsley, & Selano, 1978).

Of the many experiments on early infant competencies, several can be singled out to illustrate the main points. Bornstein (1975) has demonstrated that by 3 months of age infants show categorical perception of color. Infants perceive the perceptual (not linguistic) categories of blue, green, and yellow (just as adults do), without ever having to learn where the boundaries between each color ought to be placed. Infants thus appear to be predesigned so that innate perceptual biases and organization preclude the need for them to discover through learning the existence of certain separate categories. (Imagine the enormity of the task of learning to discriminate the category of blue from the category of green, without an innate perceptual boundary or zone between the two!)

The work of Eimas, Sigueland, Jusczyk, and Vigorito (1971) revealed, even earlier, that the infant was predesigned to categorize human speech sounds into the appropriate sound units that constitute the building blocks (phonemes) for the sounds from which known languages are constructed. Once again, certain categories—in this case, units of human behavior—did not have to be learned; rather, the emergent knowledge was prestructured in the organization of perception.

Meltzoff and Borton (1979) have provided another dramatic example of the same principle, one that extends the amount of pre-structured knowledge available to infants even further. In their experiment a 2–3-week-old infant was permitted to mouth a cube placed in his mouth while wearning a blindfold so he could not see it. The cube was then removed and placed next to a sphere of the same size. The blindfold was taken off. The infant spent more time looking at the cube. (If the infant had mouthed the sphere, the results would have been reversed.) In other words, the infant could, without prior learning, recognize in one modality (vision) an object he had only experienced in another modality (tactile, through the mouth). This demonstration of early "cross-modal equivalence" represents a challenge to our traditional views of how infants construct their knowledge of the world. No learning-theory explanations of how the infant could accomplish this feat without prior practice are tenable, and a Piagetian explanation would require that two separate sensorimotor schemas ("cube in mouth" and "cube as seen") be slowly integrated through experiences that the infant had never had. We are forced to conclude from this situation the existence of prestructuralism.

The work of Spelke (1976, 1979) and others adds yet another area in which infants appear to have considerable knowledge of the world. (Spelke and her colleagues do not rely on prestructural or nativist explanation; rather their position derives from the theory that perceiving depends on the detection of *invariants* in stimulation. (See Gibson, 1969.) Spelke (1976) has reported that infants are responsive to temporal congruity between auditory and visual stimuli, tending to match events that are synchronous in time across modality. She presented 4-month-old infants with two films projected side by side, with the sound track appropriate to only one of the films emanating from a speaker placed midway between the two images. The infants looked at the film that was appropriate to the accompanying sound track. From a variety of similar experiments, researchers have argued that the infant can recognize the common temporal structure of auditory and visual events that are synchronous (Lawson, 1980; Lyons-Ruth, 1977; Spelke, 1979).

To summarize the implications of these experiments, it now appears that nature has designed infants to give them a considerable head start in perceiving and recognizing the world as it is (as perceived and defined by adults of the species). The categories and dimensions of many (perhaps most) of the salient perceptual phenomenon that make up the human world are not left to be slowly and painstakingly learned "from scratch." Rather, perception is largely prestructured so that cognitive categories of these salient phenomena will more readily—in fact, inevitably—be formed in the course of normal life experience. Learning will then build upon these predesigned or emergent structures.

If infants are thus predesigned to perceive from very early in life and subsequently to recognize natural categories of events important to humans, why are infants not predesigned to perceive early on the categories of self, other, and inanimate objects? These certainly qualify as important "natural" categories. I argue that the infant is, in fact, so designed. I do not mean by this that infants have prestructured categories of self, other, and inanimate objects (as they have for colors or certain sounds). No such mechanism is conceivable (or even adaptive). "Self" and "other" are categories and experiences of enormous complexity, requiring redefinition at each point in development. I argue, rather, that the infant has various inborn perceptual and cognitive biases and capabilities that would make the early discrimination and differentiation of self from other not only likely but inevitable.

A form of prestructuring analogous to what I propose for self and other has been found in the infant's perception and recognition of human faces. It is now widely accepted that the infant does not have an innate schema of the human face. Instead, the infant is born with a set of visual biases and visual-motor tendencies, such as visual preference for certain amounts of light–dark contrast, pattern complexity, curvilinearity,and angularity, as well as for symmetricality around the vertical axis and certain shapes. In addition, after about 4–6 weeks, infants tend to scan objects located within a boundary. Most of these perceptual biases and response tendencies "happen" to be ideally satisfied by the stimulus parameters of the human face. Infants' prestructuring thus leads them, almost inexorably, to be in an optimal position to prefer, to discriminate, and later to recognize (i.e., to abstract) the invariant features of the face—in other words, to form a generalized schema of it. The "face schema" can thus be conceptualized as a predesigned *emergent structure* in that it necessarily emerges through the interaction of the infant's predesigned perceptual and cognitive apparatus with an expectable environment.

Using this example of the face schema, if self and other are to be conceptualized as predesigned emergent structures, what predesigned perceptual biases, sensorimotor tendencies, and cognitive abilities would an infant have to be equipped with in order to be lead by his or her own nature and that of the world to the earliest possible discrimination and differentiation of self and other? The following predesigned emergent operations or structures would be essential:

1. The infant must have some way(s) of determining that the array of diverse stimuli (sounds, sights, touches, etc.) resulting from the infant's own or another's behavior actually emanate from a single source and that the separate stimuli are parts of an organized whole sharing certain structures, rather than existing as unrelated, disorganized events from a variety of sources.
2. The infant must have some way(s) of being able to maintain the integrity of the perception of the structure of the stimuli emanating from one person in the face of interfering stimuli emanating from the dyadic partner (self or other).
3. The infant must have some way(s) of maintaining the identity of self or other as the perception of them alters by virtue of changes in their position and expression (internal changes as opposed to external interferences).
4. The infant must be able to recognize causal relationships between the structured and separated behaviors of these two participants.

What evidence exists that the infant is so equipped? Each of the four points may be addressed in turn.

1. Another person's behavior (particularly social behavior) is made up of several behaviors, many of which are normally performed simultaneously (vocalizing, moving hands, shifting body, making facial displays, touching, etc.). The same is true of one's own behavior, with the important additions of proprioception. These simultaneous behaviors share several organizing structures.

First, the physical locus of origin for each piece of behavior or behavioral modality is fixed within certain limits, as are the relationships of each locus of origin to each other and to the person as a whole, space-occupying entity. It has long been known that infants orient visually to the source of a sound (Butterworth & Castillo, 1976; Mendelson & Haith, 1976; Worthheimer, 1961). Part of the problem is thus already accounted for. By the age of 3 months the infant has come to expect that the sounds of a voice from a moving mouth should come from the same direction as the visual location of the face. Through the use of a microphone and two widely separated loudspeakers, which can "throw" the voice of a speaker from a different direction, Aronson and Rosenbloom (1971) demonstrated that by the age of 3 months infants become upset if there is more than a small angle of discrepancy between the locus of face and voice. Because infants' reflexes and expectations assure that they will be watching what they are listening to, and vice versa (under most natural conditions), they are in a better position to perceive any organization specific to the behaviors of another as a separate entity, not just as the locus of origin of the behaviors.

A second organizing structure pertaining to the behavior of a separate and distinct individual is time. The many behaviors that are invariably performed simultaneously by one person share a temporal structure. Condon and Ogston (1966) have labeled this "self-synchrony," which refers to the fact that separate movements of limbs, torso, face, etc. tend to—in fact, probably must—move together synchronously, to a split second. Starts, stops, and changes in direction or speed in one muscle group occur synchronously with starts, stops, and changes in other muscle groups. This does not mean that the two arms must be doing the same thing at the same time, or that the face and leg, for example, start and stop moving together. Each body part can trace its own pattern and start and stop independently, but all adhere to a basic temporal structure in which changes in one body part occur only in synchrony with changes in other parts. In addition, these changes in movement occur synchronously with natural speech boundaries at the phonemic level. The temporal structure of self-synchronous behavior is like an orchestra in which the body is the conductor and the voice the music. In short, all of the stimuli (auditory, visual, tactile, proprioceptive) emanating from the self or other share a common temporal structure. Stern (1977) has remarked that all features of infant-directed maternal self-synchronous behavior are highlighted or exaggerated, and Beebe and Gertsman (1980) have observed that the "packaging" of maternal behaviors into synchronous bursts or units is especially tight.

If the infant were equipped with the ability to perceive a common temporal structure in what is seen and heard, the task of differentiating self from other or of differentiating this other from that other would be greatly facilitated. The work of Spelke (1976) and others, already referred to, may provide a key. They have found cross-modal integration in 4-month-old infants, that is, perception of the temporal structure shared by events in two modalities, so that the infant acts as if two events sharing the same temporal structure belong together. Taking the step from experimental stimuli to the stimuli provided by natural human behavior, it seems more than likely that the infant should readily perceive that the sound and sights (voice, movements, and expressions) which share a common temporal structure belong to an entity (self or other) that is distinct by virtue of its unique temporal organization. Although no experiments have as yet extended these findings to the proprioceptive or tactile senses, the weight of evidence is increasing that infants inhabit a sensory world in which the integration of cross-modal experience permits—in fact, insists—that to avoid distress they recognize the sounds, sights, and touches that come from themselves or from another as separate phenomena, each with its own singular temporal structure.

A third organizing structure pertaining to the behavior of a separate and distinct person is that the behaviors emanating from one person also share a common "intensity contour structure." This refers to a state of events in which the modulations in the intensity gradient of one behavior or modality generally match the gradations in the intensity of another behavior or different modality. For example, the loudness of a vocalization and the speed or forcefulness of an accompanying movement will generally be matched, not only absolutely, but as their intensity varies during the performance of the behaviors. This state of events also holds true for the infant's own behavior as the infant perceives it. For example, if an infant's distress builds and a cry crescendoes, as the cry builds in intensity (as an auditory event) so will the proprioceptive sensations in the chest and vocal chords, the sight and proprioception of a forcefully flailing arm, and so forth. In short, all of the stimuli (auditory, visual, tactile, proprioceptive) emanating from the self or from the other share a common intensity contour structure.

Is it possible that the infant utilizes the perception of this form of intrapersonal organization to discriminate self and others? Recent experimental work provides a clue that infants may be able to perceive the intrapersonal organization of a common intensity contour and utilize that form of cross-modal integration to distinguish interpersonal events, just as they may use the temporal form of cross-modal integration. Evidence now suggests that infants are capable of matching the intensity of a stimulus experienced in one modality with the intensity of a stimulus experienced in another. For instance, a light of a given brightness is perceived by infants as be-longing with a sound of a given loudness (Lewkowicz & Turkewitz, 1980). Matching of intensity across modalities and the seeking of cross-modal equivalence is thus another way in which infants would be aided in distinguishing one agent (self or other) from another. Several authors have recently stressed the relatively greater impor-tance for infants, compared to adults, of gradient or dimensional information, such as brightness or loudness, as compared to cate-gorical information, such as pattern or phonemic structure (Emde, Lingman, Reich, & Wade, 1978; Stern, Barnett, & Spieker, 1980). Given that young infants may be particularly attentive to the quan-titative variations in stimulation in preference to or even to the exclusion of qualitative variations, the ability to match intensities across modalities would be most helpful in discriminating whether a particular stimulus (e.g., the loudness of a vocalization, or the speed or forcefulness of a movement) belonged to one or the other member of the dyad in which the infant was participating.

In light of these findings, it is difficult to imagine that, in the absence of motivational conflict, the infant by the age of 3–4 months should have trouble in recognizing each participant's behavior as differentially structured and separate.

2. A second predesigned emergent operation that would be essen-tial for the early perception of self and other as distinct entities would be some form of selective visual and auditory attention or inattention. This would mean that the infant can attend to and follow in time and intensity contour the stimuli emanating from one participant (which we now assume the infant can structure) without disorganizing interference from the sights and sounds of the other participant's behavior. A recent experiment by Walker, Bahrick and Neisser (1980) bears on this problem. They have demonstrated the ability of 4-month-old infants to be selectively inattentive to com-peting visual events. The infants were placed in front of a rear projection screen. Two films of different events were projected on the same area of the screen, one superimposed on the other. The appro-priate (i.e., time synchronous) sound track of only one of the films was heard. The images of the two films were gradually separated so that the two images were then seen separately on different parts of the screen. The infants acted as if the film not accompanied by the sound track was a novel event and the film with the sound track was

a familiar event. The authors concluded that "perceptual selection is not accomplished through special mechanisms constructed in the course of cognitive development but is a feature of the art of perceiving early on [p. 9]." In light of this evidence, it becomes reasonable to assume that the infant would be capable of attending the behavior of the mother and remaining inattentive to his or her own behavior, or vice versa. The problem of interference and thus confusion of assigning a source to stimuli may be a theoretical problem for us, but it is not a problem for infants in real life.

3. So far, we have an infant who can perceive that the behavior of each individual (self or other) is located distinctively and is organized uniquely with regard to time and intensity contour, and who can maintain those perceptions in the face of external interfering stimuli. We would also wish the infant to be capable of maintaining the identity of such perceptions in the face of internal interfering stimuli, that is, those arising from changes in the behavior of the "person" (entity) whose parts are perceived as having common structures. For instance, we would not wish changes in facial expression or position of presentation to override the infant's ability to maintain a perception of the structures of location, timing, and intensity contour. Otherwise, the other, in spite of the continuity of his or her structures, would continually shift identity and become something different each time he or she changed position or expression, even though the "new entity" shared in common with the "previous entity" structures such as location, timing, and intensity contour.

Recent evidence on the infant's early ability to maintain the identity of a three-dimensional object, regardless of its presentation from a novel perspective, partially responds to this issue. Fagan's (1977) finding that 7-month-old infants can recognize the never-before-seen profile of a face after a short familiarization with the full face or, even better, to a three-quarters view, addresses this issue of the effects of certain changes in position of the other. In our laboratory, Spieker (1981) has preliminary results indicating that infants conserve the identity of a particular face across the various transformations of that face involving different facial expressions. Recall that many previous formulations suggested that the smiling mother and frowning mother were experienced as two different objects, even when the behaviors were adjacent in time.

In summary, the evidence suggests that changes in position and expression, which normally accompany the interactive behavior of an other, need not be seen as problematic for the infant's conservation of the other as a single entity. In fact, this evidence suggests that individual facial configuration is yet another obvious "structure" that from very early in life permits discrimination of one other from all others (Fagan, 1976).

4. The final predesigned emergent operation that would be essential for the early perception of self and others as distinct entities would be the ability to recognize causal relations between the separated and differently structured entities that make up a dyad. It has been amply demonstrated that infants, beginning on the first day of life, can be successfully conditioned (Papousek, 1959). Watson (1979), among others, has commented that although infants are readily conditionable before 2 months of age, they appear to be relatively passive learners compared to older infants, who engage experimental learning tasks with activity and avidity. In itself the "knowledge" of causation implicit in the ability to learn would be of no help in self–other differentiation. After all, the infant can learn that certain acts of his own or of his mother have predictable consequences without ascribing a different source to acts of his own versus acts of his mother. However, recent demonstrations of infants' considerable abilities to discriminate different schedules of reinforcement provides more leverage to the problem (Watson, 1979, 1980). Using a paradigm in which the infant must turn his head against a pressurized pillow to get a mobile to turn, Watson has demonstrated that by the age of 3 months infants can distinguish between schedules of constant reinforcement (each head turn is rewarded), a fixed-ratio of reinforcement (e.g., every third head turn is reinforced), and a variable schedule (where head turns are rewarded on a less predictable basis). The implications for self–other differentiation are clear. Of necessity most classes of action of the self on the self have a constant reinforcement schedule. (The lip and tongue action of a sucking movement always results in increased pressure upon the thumb that is in the mouth, etc.) Actions of the self on others are usually variably rewarded.

In examining the basis of causal inference in infancy, Watson (1980) suggests that there are three features of causal structure available to infants by 3–4 months of age: an appreciation of temporal relationships between events; an appreciation of sensory relations (i.e., the ability to correlate intensity or duration of a behavior and its effect); and an appreciation of spatial relations (i.e., taking into account the spatial laws of a behavior and the laws of its effects). These three dimensions of information about causal structure presumably act additively or interactively in providing the infant with rudimentary knowledge of different occasions or conditions of causality, which should readily separate the world into self-caused and other-caused effects.

A remaining problem concerns whose organization belongs to whom. How, for instance, does an infant "know" that his organization of behaviors is the one that belongs to him? The two most ready ways out of this quandry are to assume that only "his" organization is attended by the sensation of proprioception. (This obvious reality probably predates all other self–other distinctions.) An interesting addition or elaboration involves the will or motive, in that only behaviors belonging to the infant's own organization are preceded or accompanied by some psychic phenomenon akin to will or motive, which come to be known through proprioception. Further discussion on this point is beyond the scope of this paper.

Assumption 3. Separation reaction is the criterion of object permanence. The third assumption supporting the traditional view of gradual self–other differentiation concerns the infant's presumed inability to establish object constancy or permanence prior to the onset of separation reactions during the first 8 months. There are two problems with this assumption: (1) the interpretation placed on the separation reaction; (2) the belief that the infant has inadequate memory capabilities prior to 8–9 months to form stable internal schemata. Schaffer, Greenwood, and Parry (1972), Kagan, Kearsley, and Selano (1978), and McCall (1979), among others, have criticized the more traditional view of separation distress as coming about solely because of the maturation of memory processes permitting an internal representation of mother such that at her departure the memory of her can be evoked, compared to the condition of her absence, and the infant forced to deal with aloneness which is done with distress. Kagan, Kearsley, and Selano (1978), most notably, have pointed out various problems with this formulation: Why, for example, does the infant cry as the mother is moving away but is still in sight? Why does the phenomenon vary so little depending on cultural and social variables such as day care, which provides the infant with very diverse experiences of separation? Why does an unfamiliar setting so strongly enhance the effect? For instance, if the mother leaves from a familiar exit in the home, the infant shows less distress than if she leaves from an atypical exit such as a closet (Littenberg, Tulkin, & Kagan, 1971).

An alternate interpretation of separation distress, similar to that proposed by Schaffer, Greenwood, and Parry (1972), suggests that two processes must come to maturation in order to produce separation distress. The first is the necessary but not sufficient condition that the infant has an enhanced ability to retrieve and hold a schema of past experience (i.e., to evoke an internal representation of the other). The traditional explanation stops here. The second and necessary maturational ability to emerge at this age is the "ability to generate anticipations of the future-representations of possible events." Kagan, Kearsley, and Selano (1978) describe this new capacity as the "disposition to attempt to predict future events and to generate responses to deal with discrepant situations. If the child cannot generate a prediction or instrumental response he is vulnerable to uncertainty and distress [p. 110]."

It may prove more helpful to break these two processes necessary for the separation reactions into three distinct processes: an improved retrieval (evocative) *memory;* an ability to generate *future-representations* of possible events; and the ability to generate communicative or instrumental *responses* to deal with uncertainty or distress caused by uncongruities between present events and future representations of events.

It is generally agreed that memory improves greatly toward the end of the first year of life. It is also clear, however, that some memory functions spanning days and weeks are present long before the advent of separation distress at 8–9 months. It has been demonstrated that 3-month-olds and possibly even 1-month-olds can activate with minimal cues, including context, the memory of an event that occurred days before (Rover-Collier, Sullivan, Enright, Lucas, & Fagen, 1980; Ungerer, Brody, & Selano, 1977; Watson, 1980). The distinction of when we are dealing with evocative memory and when with recognition memory depends in large part on how minimal a cue is required to recall an entire memory and what the relationship is between the cue and some attribute of the memory. These experiments show that minimal cues, even context, retrieve memories as measured by responses, at early ages. These examples of early memory all relate to schemata of experimental stimuli. There has been inadequate experimentation or observations of memory function for familiar caregivers during the first half year of life. Without such evidence, however, it seems likely that if infants manifest delayed recognition memory (Fagan, 1973) and something akin to retrieval memory of nonsalient experimental stimuli with which they have had relatively little familiarization, they would be very likely to perform similar feats of memory for schemata or representations of their mothers. In other words, relevant memory functions may operate earlier than we have as yet had evidence for.

In a similar vein the developmental course of the ability to generate anticipations of the representations of possible future events is far from clear. It is equally unclear when this ability has reached what would constitute a critical "level" to permit separation reactions. The naturalistic data of Brazelton, Koslowski, and Main (1974) and of Tronick, Als, Adamson, Wise, and Brazelton (1978) used the "still face" procedure, in which a mother violates the infant's interactive expectancies by keeping her face still during their interaction. These data suggest, but do not prove, that infants have expectations of particular social events given a certain context by 3 months of age. There is much more anecdotal information supporting such a view (see, e.g., Stern, 1974, 1977).

We know that infnat responses to separations have been described from as early as 2 months of age (Fogel, 1980). The particular developmental course of the form and repertoire of these responses, whether viewed as instrumental or communicative, has also not been adequately studied. However, it is important to point out that some of the changes in response occurring at around 8–9 months have to do with developments in physical and coordination abilities not directly related to psychic developments. Mahler was perhaps the first to point out that infants' ability to move about not only permits them to create a new danger but also gives them a new response category whereby the potential to deal with a discrepancy between current events, a memory, and a representation of a possible future event, could be resolved or frustrated by way of locomotion as a response. That is to say, she squarely placed the major developmental event on a motor landmark.

Accordingly, it is equally reasonable to suggest that of the three requisite conditions for separation distress—adequate retrievable memory of mother with minimal cues, the ability to anticipate future events, and new instrumental responses to deal with uncertainties (locomotion)—the first two have been present for months, waiting for the emergence of the latter to produce separation distress. If this is in fact the case, then separation reactions are a poor developmental landmark for the onset of object permanence or for dating the generation of representation of the future, but they may be an important landmark for the emergence of putting into effect certain coping mechanisms for certain kinds of uncertainties.

Assumption 4. Non-differentiation on defensive grounds. The fourth assumption supporting the view of gradual self–other differentiation is perhaps closest to the heart of psychoanalytic formulations. The first three assumptions have largely concerned the infnat's perceptual and cognitive abilities. The fourth assumption is motivational in nature and posits that even if the infants could tell self from other, they would not do so for defensive reasons, that is, to ward off anxiety or stress. Mahler postulates that from birth until 2 months, the infant's ego is protected by the postulated stimulus barrier. After that barrier is gone, the infant would be left with all the stresses and threats of being on its own, unless the reality of separateness and aloneness is replaced with the delusion of a state of fusion with mother and thus protected state. According to Mahler, Pine, and Bergman (1975): "The libidual cathexis vested in the symbiotic orbit replaces the inborn instinctual stimulus barrier and protects the rudimentary ego from premature phase-unspecific strain, from stress traumata [p. 45]." These formulations also are mainly concerned with representations of affectively laden experiences rather than of persons per se. The theories of M. Klein are a partial exception in that she implies that the infant can indeed tell self from other but out of protective needs utilizes defensive maneuvers, such as projection, to distort a reality-based appreciation of self and other. M. Klein is almost exclusively concerned with affectively laden experiences of tension reduction or buildup. Mahler, too, is largely concerned with the representations of object-related experiences involving shifts in energy and also with the object as a cognitive representation. The distinction, however, is not always clear.

There are thus two issues here: Is the infants' early sense of self and other necessarily distorted for defensive reasons? What distinctions between representations of affectively laden experiences and purely cognitive representations of others must be made in contemplating the problems of differentiating self and other? These two issues, though highly intertwined, are discussed separately.

The argument that the infant needs to be protected from internal and external trauma and does so by way of the symbiotic "delusion" as proposed by Mahler or the schizoid or paranoid mechanisms proposed by Klein is a theoretical construct supported by no experimental or observational findings during the period of development in question. These theoretical positions result in part from the need to postulate anlage for, and points of fixation toward which, psychopathological phenomena, seen later in life, can regress (see Klein, 1980; Peterfreund, 1978, for further discussion on this point) and for the need to consider the role of traditional conflict in these issues.

Assumption 5.   This concerns the nature of early representations and posits that those of crucial importance for psychic and interpersonal development "consist" of *affectively laden experience*. This assumption reintroduces the important distinction mentioned in the introduction. Is the interpersonal world of the infant that of the "affective experiencer," the "cognitive knower," or both? This issue is taken up in Part 2.

Summary of Part 1

Evidence has been gathered to argue that beginning at birth the infant starts perceptually and cognitively to differentiate self and others and self from others successfully. Infants appear to be predesigned by nature, in the form of perceptual and cognitive preorganization, such that salient natural categories such as self and other are not left to be slowly and painstakingly learned "from scratch"; rather, they are prestructured emergent entities that result from the interaction between a prestructured perceptual and cognitive organism and natural events in a predictable external world.

This picture of the infant deeply questions the notion of an initial, let alone a protracted, 9-month phase of undifferentiation with regard to self and other, and replaces it with an infant, who on perceptual and cognitive grounds at least, begins the process of forming relationships with distinct and separate notions of self and other. It is important to reiterate here that we are speaking of sensorimotor schemata and not of representations capable of symbolic transformations.

PART 2: SCHEMAS OF AFFECTIVE
EXPERIENCE OF "SELF WITH OTHER"

In Part 1 of this paper I concluded that the infant, as viewed from a cognitive point of view, would most certainly "know" that self and other were quite discrete entities and agents, not likely to be confused or "fused." In this second part I consider the infant's experience with the other from an affective point of view, integrated with the previously considered cognitive viewpoint. (Once again I view the infant prospectively and normatively. Normal developmental construct need not take into account, let alone be based on, pathological phenomena which are seen clinically at later points in development; Klein, 1980; Peterfreund, 1978.)

Psychoanalytic theories have always assumed that affect and motivation organize experience, that the perceptions and cognitions of self and other take their central orientation from the affective experience occasioned by the other. Early formulations were concerned almost exclusively with the infant's experience of tension and gratification (unpleasure and pleasure). Hunger and feeding played the central role in these formulations because, among other things, they exemplified so prototypically the workings of Freud's energic model. "Good" and "bad" experiences, deriving from the status of internal tension, defined "good" and "bad" mothers and selves. With the realization of the importance of autonomous ego functions, many forms of stimulus-seeking and playful (i.e., nonphysiological, need-gratifying) experiences received greater attention. It is important to note that these activities are not necessarily more cognitive in nature and of lesser emotional impact than activities involving hunger and satiety. It is only during interpersonal play that one sees active joy in the sense of exuberance. Similarly, only in play, first directly with caregivers and then indirectly, does one see the strong emotions associated with curiosity and exploration, including enthusiasm, awe, surprise, and feelings of mastery. In addition to the foregoing, there are the many affective experiences associated with the successful and unsuccessful performance of attachment behaviors:

gazing, grasping for, reaching toward, holding, cuddling, and later, following. In short, after the infant's sixth or eighth week, in a mother-infant pair that is normally well regulated physiologically, the major and most frequent passions and emotions are interpersonal, not physiological. (Of course, the feeding period can become the organizing event in which episodes of play and food intake are made adjacent in time. Nonetheless, the important affective "action" is progressively more in the play portion and does not require adjacency to feeding to acquire its affective importance.) In the absence of any theory of cognitive development, psychoanalytic theory has made the infant's cognitions about experience with another almost entirely subservient or epiphenomenological to assumptions about the likely nature of the infant's affective experience. Concepts such as "selfobjects," "symbiotic-objects," "part-objects," and other similar clinical phenomena are derived from later emotional experiences occurring in states of pathology. This is not to diminish their true clinical importance, but to urge that they not be borrowed to be retrospectively installed as normal parts of the infant's affective-cognitive experience.

A prospective viewpoint is now needed in which schemas of the experience of self with other include both affective and cognitive components. (Some affective processes may occur in the absence of cognition, Zajonc, 1980, but if they remained outside cognition, these would be of little interest for understanding the formation of clinically important schemas and representations even in the youngest infant. Similarly, cognitions that are not affectively toned or incited are equally of little interest for this purpose.) Accordingly, I attempt to distinguish three general ways of "being with" another in terms of the affects and cognitions that might be schematized with such a particular experience.

One major problem to conceptualizing schemas of being with another concerns the nature of human, and in particular infant, memory. A schema of being with involves a memory of some dynamic series of events, that is, a microplot which is characteristic and frequently repeated, or even a "moment," but a dynamic moment that has duration. This involves a form of event knowledge, and there has been a recent surge of interest in the representation of event knowledge. Studies of "social scripts" (Nelson & Greundel, 1979), "frame analysis" (Goffman, 1974), "scripts" (Schank & Abelson, 1977), and "episodic memory" (Tulving, 1972) all fall into the general category of representations of memory for events. It is recognized that event knowledge or its memory is different in process and structure from knowledge of categories or unrelated information. Another major problem arises because one of the events of central importance in schemas of being with another is emotion. So far, prior work on the nature of event knowledge and its schemas has not been concerned with emotion as one of the attributes of remembered events. This is an area greatly in need of more research before further progress can be made. The dichotomy between schemas of emotionally laden events as against other information is the essence of the problem posed by Assumption 5. Psychoanalysis has claimed primacy in early infancy for schemas of emotional experience (emotional event knowledge) in comparison to schemas of categories, agents, or identities. The following typology of being with another assumes that the infant uses both types of knowledge in schematizing human interactions.

The three types of being with another are described as actions because I am postulating that the experience of being with someone and the schemas and representations of such experiences consist of dynamic events, not static entities. In the first, *self–other complementing,* each member provides the needed and different action so as to complete or fulfill the interpersonal experience. The relation between the self and object is most closely akin to that described by the British Object Relations School in the sense that the behavior with the other is itself the aim. Physiological satisfaction of needs is not the aim; the aim is rather an interpersonal behavior between self and object in which the object complements the self behavior and vice versa. In *mental state sharing and state tuning,* the self or other provides for or induces the opposite member into a similar state of experience. During state sharing the central focus of the relation between self and other is on the similarity of experience that each is having. Empathy in the affective domain, interintentionality in the domain of motives, or intersubjectivity in the domain of cognition capture the essence of state sharing with a similar other. In *state transforming,* a major change in neurophysiological state and state of consciousness occurs by virtue of the action of another. The relation between self and other is most clearly akin to the traditional psychoanalytic view of being with an anaclytic object during need gratification. These three different views of the self–other relationship have often been associated with rival theories. Rather than treat them as such, each seems to capture the nature of different interpersonal moments or ways of being with.

The distinction between the three types of self–other experience cannot always be determined by overt behavior. In any given experience, the "center of gravity" of the encounter can at times shift from self–other complementing to state sharing and back, from state transforming to sharing, and so forth.

Self–Other Complementing

There are four essential features of self–other complementing: (1) each member's actions are the complement of the partners; one person performs the action, another receives it; (2) because each partner is acting quite differently from the other, the intactness of self and other is readily maintained; the perceptual cues of the other as having a separate temporal and intensity contour organization and being involved in a causal relationship are not interrupted by the complementary activity; (3) experiencing the other *directly* is the aim of the activity; (4) the self-experience involves an affective, sensorimotor, and cognitive part of the self that cannot be experienced without a concomitant complementary experience of the other; it cannot be experienced alone.

Some simple examples are cuddling or moulding to a warm, contoured, soft body; having a "greeting response" (seen by 2 months of age) plus the sensations that accompany this response when a known human face appears; vocalizing or babbling back and forth with another, who is alternately "listening" and vocalizing; rolling a ball back and forth between partners and other give and take routines; the "holding environment" (Winnicott, 1965) or "secure base of operation" (Ainsworth & Bell, 1978) of a toy play session for a 7–12-month-old, in which the mother is game-observer/infant-watcher and the infant is game-player/mother-observer; and attachment behaviors such as grasping, holding, or following the caregiver.

The experience of the self can never become free from experiencing the complementary aspect of the other. Experiencing the self and experiencing the other are irrevocably "bound." Cuddling, holding onto, or following the caregiver are good examples. There is no way to have such experiences without an actual or fantasized other. The only issue, developmentally and clinically, is how readily the actual complementary experience can be "reproduced" internally. A far more advanced activity, such as talking, may also fall into this category in that talking, even when done alone, may not occur without the presence of a fantasized listener. These kinds of self-experiences are perhaps the most totally "social" of our experiences in the sense that they can never even occur unless elicited or maintained by the actions of another and would never exist as a part of known self-experience without another.

Self–other complementing can be contrasted with the "selfobject" concept of Kohut (1977) as it applies to pathological transference phenomena. They both imply a self–other experience in which the self-experience is inseparable from experiencing the other. The self-object concept, however, implies some lack of differentiation between self and object. The self-experience in self–other complementing does not imply any confusion or lack of differentiation concerning the distinctness of self from other. In fact, the opposite is the case. For self–other complementing to occur, there must be a distinction between self and other. Both self and other must also be present, mentally if not literally, or else the phenomena will not be encountered. To further highlight the difference between self–other complementing and concepts related to the selfobject, consider that within the context of a differentiated self and a differentiated other, the experience of "merging" (a form of complementing) with someone during a pleasurable moment should be an extraordinary event. However, within the context of the self–other fusion of "normal" symbiosis and self–other undifferentiation, it should be an ordinary event that is only noticeable because it is pleasurable, not because of the sense of merging, which is already the assumed state of things. In other words, only if one postulates a fair degree of self and of other differentiation can complementing experiences (of which merging can be one) have high impact and attain the enhanced position of figure against background. This requires that the schemas of self and other remain intact during self–other complementing.

Experiences and schemas of self–other complementing develop as normal enduring parts of our psychobiology rather than as the residual products of a phase-specific nondifferentiation of self and other that remains unfinished. They are inevitable, biologically ordained representations of self with other, which remain through life; in fact, they grow in number and complexity and can never be dissolved.

Most occasions of self–other complementing are such that the self-experience can, with development, exist without actual experiencing of the other. Presumably, playing with a toy soon becomes a self-experience that can occur without an actual or consciously or unconsciously fantasized complementary other. It is in this area that the work of "separation-individuation" takes on such importance. What changes developmentally, however, is not the discrimination of self from other, but the locus (in the mind vs. in external reality) and strength of action of the experience of the other.

The major clinical issues related to self–other complementing representations are those of attachment and the degree to which thought, action, and feeling are ultimately socially based (i.e., object related). Issues of dependence and autonomy depend on the developmental history of the internalization and strength of the experienced complementing other.

Mental State Sharing and Tuning

There are two essential features of state sharing: (1) the activities of the two partners are sufficiently similar in the sense of being isomorphic, synchronous, and similarly contoured so that infants' perceptual cues, which permit distinguishing self from other on grounds of locus, timing, intensity, contouring, or causality, are largely obliterated (but the proprioceptive component can never be obliterated); (2) there is some sense of commonality of experience or sharing of similar external or internal experiences. "Mental state" is meant to include a broad array of experiences; "state sharing" and "experience sharing" are identical notions as used.

Some simple examples are simultaneous imitative events; vocalizing together (i.e., not in alternation) and other forms of "co-action," such as pat-a-cake; interactional synchrony as described by Condon and Sander (1974);[3] the transmission of gradient features of affect signals (e.g., loudness) such that the responder or receiver has his or her nervous system partially "taken over" by the sender and other such forms of protoempathy; temporal pace setting, in which

---

[3]It is most important to state that this finding of interactional synchrony between a newborn and an adult is still highly controversial. It is my impression (Stern, 1971, 1977) that this kind of interpersonal temporal interlocking can and does occur for short moments of high arousal, but is not the ubiquitous background condition claimed.

the tempo of one member's behavior comes to set the pace for the others; mutual gazing; and affect intensity "contagion" between mother and infant, where the affect (e.g., smiling) keeps eliciting an increase in the level of the display by increments, by one partner eliciting a bigger smile from the second partner, and the "response" increment in return eliciting another increment in the first partner, thus producing a positive feedback loop.

These experiences, unlike self–other complementing, are experiences of self–other similarity. They can theoretically obliterate temporarily and partially the infant's sense of self–other distinction and potentially create a conflict for the integrity of the self. The nature of experiences of state sharing or self–other similarity is such that terms like "mirroring," forms of "merging," and certain "selfobject" phenomena appear to capture it.

These moments are clearly of great importance. So many have argued that our view and sense of ourselves can only develop from the ways others behave to and with us, and that we can evaluate ourselves only through the ways in which we perceive others to perceive us. However, even more basic is that during these moments of sharing experience the infant gets a first glimpse of having something like a similar experience with another. This crucial phenomenon, particularly as it applies to shared intentions, has been called "intersubjectivity" (Trevarthan, 1980). The affective aspects of it might be called a form of protoempoathy. I use the more inclusive term *mental state sharing,* which is not limited to shared feeling as are all sym-em-co-pathy words, or to shared cognitions and motives as has become true of "intersubjectivity" or "interintentionality." State sharing refers to the sense—in or out of awareness, surmised or known for sure—that some aspect of your actions, perceptions, sensations, feelings, motives, intentions, thought, or beliefs is being shared by another. This shared aspect can be limited in the young infant to level of arousal, overt behavior, or the prevailing emotion. With development, the shared aspect can become a joint focus of attention; later, it can become mutual intentions and, later stil, shared symbols and thoughts. It is the existence of the interpersonal phenomenon of sharing a state that is being isolated and proposed as an affective-cognitive entity for the infant. The nature of the state is a secondary issue. Exactly what gets matched and shared changes with development. The fact of possible sharing is the issue at stake.

State sharing, by its very nature, creates subjective intimacy. Perhaps more accurately, subjective intimacy, as against physical intimacy, consists largely of sharing experience on many levels—that is, of many mental states.

Moments of state sharing are clearly of the greatest importance. Current assumptions about the infant during those moments of being with another similarly hold that the infant is fusing or merging (or already is fused and merged) with the other (i.e., experiencing dual unity) or he is slowly experiencing self through a "mirroring process." Instead, I propose that he is engaged in the slow and momentous discovery that his experience, which he already senses is distinctly his own, is not unique and unparalleled but is part of shared human experience. In other words he is establishing subjective intimacy. In order to do that the infant must maintain the separate entities of self and other, because the power of state sharing lies in the sense of what is happening between two separate persons.

Mirroring, an invaluable concept, is in fact predicated on a more basic concept such as state sharing. Mirroring as a process would have no way of working if it did not assume some capacity in the infant to sense similarity of experience between people. In this sense we see "mirroring," or that form of modeling self-experience implied in the term, as an elaboration of the more basic concept of mental state sharing.

The work on language acquisition, such as that of Bruner (1975), Bates (1976), and others, clearly indicates that by about 7 months infants match and expect the mutual sharing of intentions between self and caregiver (Trevarthan's "intersubjectivity"). Our observations of even younger infants strongly suggest that infants have some sense of the extent to which affect and intensity of affect or arousal are "inter-experienced" (i.e., shared mental states).

Episodes of self–other similarity provide the essence of this encounter with experience or state sharing. State sharing—whether at the level of sensing it, surmises it, or knowing it for certain—is generally of high positive emotional valence as well as of great intimacy. However, encountering state sharing through an episode of self–other similarily can also be negative. Mutual gazing and mimicry, either by face or "shadow talking," are good examples. Gazing, facial or postural mimicking, and shadow talking are all used by children to infuriate their peers or adults. There is some-

thing intolerably invasive in the sense of negative intimacy to be
the recipient of these particular experiences of self–other similarity.
On the other hand, in different circumstances, such as between
lovers or between mothers and infants, these same behaviors appear
to be the very vehicle of positive intimacy as well as self-definition. I
am suggesting, then, that occurrences of self–other similarity in
which mental state sharing is encountered play an important role in
the development of self-esteem and the capacity for *subjective
intimacy.*

In state tuning as opposed to sharing there is some mismatch in
the roughly similar behaviors, and there is the motive to match,
that is, to create a commonality of experience. Much of a mother's
activity is spent doing this. In many, though not all, of the activities
that fall into this general category, there may be a temporal lag
between the behaviors of each partner, a momentary mismatch in
intensity contouring, and so forth. The infant's temporal processing
abilities are accurate enough to detect split second violations of
"similarity" (synchronicity, isomorphism, etc.). In other words, the
infant will experience the difference between moments of full similarity in which most self versus other cues are eclipsed and moments in which the cues for self–other discrimination reappear, but
in a context in which there is something like the "intent" (sometimes mutual) to obliterate these cues and "get together"—to state
share more fully.

State Transforming

These are the experiences that have originally and traditionally
preoccupied psychoanalysis, namely, gratifying the hungry infants
and causing the shift in state from hunger to sleep. Even recently,
such moments have been considered the cardinal "magic moments,"
against which all else in early infancy is background (Pine, 1980).
Another dramatic and frequent example is the physical soothing of
the distressed or crying infant. Once again, a dramatic transformation in neurophysiological state is involved (in this case arousal
level rather than hunger level is reduced). The reasons that these
events received such attention, which for a long while eclipsed the
ability to discern the importance of the other ways of being with
another, have already been touched on. Nonetheless, this way of
being with is clearly of great importance. These experiences and

their representation have been thought to most closely approximate the feeling of total merging, of obliterating selfobject boundaries and fusing into a "dual unity." There has now certainly been enough experiences with well-fed institutionalized infants and babies in the kibbutz, as well as experimental primate evidence to make it clear that powerful relationships are not forged by feeding in comparison to experience sharing and complementing. It is perhaps time to suggest that the experience of being hungry, getting fed, and going blissfully to sleep does not, even when associated with a particular person, lead to subjective intimacy with the feeding person, unless accompanied by self–other complementing and state sharing. Rather, it involves an experience of the self with dramatic self-transformations that requires the physical mediation of an other. The essential experience is not, however, with the other. It is truly anaclitic, and the major experience is with transformation of the self and human physical events (natural forces of a kind) effecting self-state. In line with this point of view, the experiences and representations of state transformations via another can be thought of as playing a crucial role in the development of *physical* but not *subjective* intimacy.

It is important to stress that the three forms of self–other experiences—complementing, sharing, and transforming—can all occur in the course of a single activity (e.g., in making love all three certainly occur). Furthermore, one cannot always predict the likely form of experience from the overt behaviors. For instance, when a 7–8-month-old reaches his arm toward mother, opening and closing his hand, looking from her face to a cookie she is holding, vocalizing "eh! eh!" and mother hands him the cookie, there are two different self–other experiences occurring, either of which could be predominant: a simple complementing experience of give and take or a state sharing event in which the sensing of an intention match between self and other is central.

Summary of Part 2

We are left, then, with a background of distinct schemas of self and other and, in addition, several different kinds of experiences and schemas of "self with other." These are: (1) *self–other complementing:* I tentatively suggest that disturbances in complementing schemata affect the attachment process and global capacities to be social; (2) *state sharing:* I suggest that disturbances in these schemata have a major impact on developing subjective intimacy and self-esteem; (3) *state transforming:* I suggest that disturbances in these schemata relate to developing physical intimacy and trust.

The suggestions concerning which experiences of being with another most influence which developing process is to be taken as preliminary and tentative. At this point it represents an attempt to point in the clinical direction that a developing typology of schemas of self with other might lead.

There remains one final issue to be taken up again, which concerns whether the schemas of self and of other described in Part 1 are in conflict or cooperation with the schemata of self with other described in Part 2. In particular, do the experiences of sharing or transforming eclipse the cohesive experience of self and of other and force a conflict between experiences or schemas? An essential feature of the traditional view of the undifferentiated infant was that most experiences of self with other that were gratifying confounded differentiation of self and of other. In the case of later pathology involving borderline or psychotic phenomena, the most intense being with experiences are conceived of as fusions in the sense of boundary dissolution and ego (or self) diffusion. If we do not take such a pathomorphic view (Emde & Robinson, 1979) and consider the developing infant from the viewpoint of normal rather than abnormal behavior, then it is not clear why experiences of being with have to disrupt self and other representations or schemas. Rather, the inherent conflicts in the two kinds of schemas will act constructively to sharpen differences and thereby solidify the formation and integration of both the affective and cognitive components of the experiences of being with another.

We have too long put ourselves at a disadvantage by viewing normal stages in terms of later pathological mistakes or delusions about the nature of reality, as potential threats to the establishment of a once differentiated self and other in older children, or as wished-for states whose activation involves some assumed regression to an early point of postulated nondifferentiation. The problem with these views is that being with experiences are also the stuff that human connectedness, as well as normal intimacy and basic trust, are made of at all points in development. The ability to engage in them is among the most needed and healthy of capacities. The point of view I am taking proposes to take the being with experiences (in normally developing infants) beyond their primarily problematic role in the differentiation of self and other and establish them as positive human capacities, the development of which is best understood against a background of intact schemata of self and other. From this point of view, later pathological phenomena need not be byproducts of the breakup of a normal undifferentiated phase that get reactivated. Rather, they can be seen as failures of the normally developing process of the capacity to be with another person in various ways. Further insights into the problems of pathogenesis must await our further understanding of normal development.

ACKNOWLEDGMENTS

I wish to acknowledge the support of the Jane Hilder Harris Foundation. I also wish to acknowledge the many contributions of Roanne Barnett, Lynne Hofer, Kristine MacKain, Pat Nachman, Susan Spieker, and John Dore in helping to conceptualize this paper.

REFERENCES

Ainsworth, M. D. S. & Bell, S. M. (1978). Attachment, exploration and separation illustrated by the behavior of one year olds in a strange situation. *Child Dev.* 41: 49–67.

Ainsworth, M. D. S. et al. (1978). *The Strange Situation: Observing Patterns of Attachment.* Hillsdale, N.J.: Lawrence Erlbaum Associates.

Aronson, E. & Rosenbloom, S. (1971). Space perception in early infancy. Perception within a common auditory-visual space. *Science* 172: 1161–63.

Bates, E. (1976). *Language and Context: The Acquisition of Pragmatics.* New York: Academic Press.

Beebe, B. & Gerstman, L. J. (1981). The "packaging" of maternal stimulation in relation to infant facial-visual engagement: A case study at four months. Paper presented at the Ann. meeting Soc. for Res. in Child Dev., Boston, 1981.

Bornstein, M. H. (1975). Qualities of color vision in infancy. *J. Exp. Child Psychol.* 19: 401–419.

Bowlby, J. (1960). Separation anxiety. *Intl. J. of Psychoanal.* 41: 89–113.

———— (1969). *Attachment and Loss,* vol. 1. New York: Basic Books.

Brazelton, T. B., Koslowski, B., & Main, M. (1974). The early mother-infant interaction. In *The Effect of the Infant on Its Caregiver,* M. Lewis & L. Rosenblum, eds. New York: Wiley, pp. 49–77.

Bruner, J. S. (1975). The ontogenesis of speech acts. *J. of Child Language* 2: 1–20.

Butterworth, G. & Castillo, M. (1976). Coordination of auditory and visual space in newborn human infants. *Perception* 5: 155–160.

Condon, W. S. & Ogston, W. D. (1967). A segmentation of behavior. *J. Psychiat. Res.* 5: 221–235.

Condon, W. S. & Sander, L. S. (1974). Neonate movement is synchronized with adult speech. *Science* 183: 99–101.

Emde, R. N. et al. (1978). Emotional expression in infancy: I. Initial studies of social signaling and an emergent model. In *The development of affect,* M. Lewis & L. Rosenblum, eds. New York: Plenum Press.

Emde, R. N. & Robinson, J. (1979). The first two months: Recent research in developmental psychobiology. In *Basic Handbook of Child Psychiatry,* vol. 1, J. D. Noshpitz, ed. New York: Basic Books, pp. 72–105.

Emias, P. D. et al. (1971). Speech perception in infants. *Science* 171: 303–306.

Fagan, J. F. (1973). Infants' delayed recognition memory and forgetting. *J. of Exp. Child Psychol.* 16: 424–450.

——— (1976). Infants' recognition of invariant features of faces. *Child Dev.* 47: 627–638.

——— (1977). Infants' recognition of invariant features of faces. *Child Dev.* 48: 68–78.

Fogel, A. (1977). Temporal organization in mother-infant face-to-face interaction. In *Studies in Mother-Infant Interaction,* H. R. Schaffer, ed. New York: Academic Press.

——— (1979). The effect of brief separations on two-month-old infants. Paper presented at the Soc. for Res. in Child Dev. San Francisco, 1979.

Fraiberg, S. (1969). Libidinal object constancy and mental representation. *Psychoanal. Study Child* 24: 9–47.

Gibson, E. J. (1969). *Principles of Perceptual Learning and Development.* New York: Appleton-Century-Crofts.

Goffman, E. (1974). *Frame Analysis.* New York: Harper Colophon Books.

Kagan, J., Kearsley, R. B., & Selano, P. R. (1978). *Infancy: Its Place in Human Development.* Cambridge: Harvard University Press.

Klein, M. (1980). Mahler's autistic and symbiotic phases: An exposition and evaluation. Paper submitted for publication.

Kohut, H. (1977). *The Restoration of the Self.* New York: Int. Univ. Press.

Lawson, K. R. (1980). Spatial and temporal congruity and auditory-visual integration in infants. *Dev. Psych.* 16: 185–192.

Lewkowicz, D. J. & Turkewitz, G. (1981). Intersensory interaction in newborns. *Child Dev.* 52: 827–832.

Lipsitt, L. P. (1969). Learning capacities of the human infant. In *Brain and Early Behavior,* R. J. Bobinson, ed. New York: Academic Press.

Littenberg, R., Tulkin, S., & Kagan, J. (1971). Cognitive components of separation anxiety. *Dev. Psych.* 4: 387–388.

Lyons-Ruth, K. (1977). Biomodal perception in infancy: Response to audio-visual incongruity. *Child Dev.* 48: 820–827.

Mahler, M. S. & Furer, M. (1968). *On Human Symbiosis and the Vicissitudes of Individuation.* New York: Int. Univ. Press.

Mahler, M. S., Pine, F., & Bergman, A. (1975). *The Psychological Birth of the Human Infant: Symbiosis and Individuation.* New York: Basic Books.

McCall, R. B. (1979). Qualitative transitions in behavioral development in the first three years of life. In *Psychological Developments from Infancy,* M. H. Bornstein & W. Kassen, eds. Hillsdale, N.J.: Lawrence Erlbaum Associates.

Meltzoff, A. N. & Borton, W. (1979). Intermodal Matching by Human Neonates. *Nature* 282: 403–404.

Mendelson, M. H. & Haith, M. M. (1976). The relation between audition and vision in the human newborn. *Monographs of the Society for Research in Child Development* 41: (Serial No. 167).

Nelson, K. & Greundel, J. M. (1979). *From Personal Episode to Social Script.* Paper presented at the Biennial Meeting of the Society for Research in Child Development, March 1979, San Francisco.

Papousek, H. (1959). A method of studying conditioned flood reflexes in young children up to the age of six months. *Pavlov J. of Higher Nervous Activity* 9: 136–140.

Peterfreund, E. (1978). Some critical comments on psychoanalytic conceptualizations of infancy. *Int. J. Psychoanal.* 59: 427–441.

Piaget, J. (1954). *The Construction of Reality in the Child,* trans. M. Cook. New York: Basic Books.

Pine, F. (1980). In the beginning: Contributions to a psychoanalytic developmental psychology. Paper presented at the New York Psychoanalytic Society.

Rover-Collier, C. K. et al. (1980). Reactivation of infant memory. *Science* 208: 1159–1161.

Ruff, H. A. (1980). The development of perception and recognition of objects. *Child Dev.* 51: 981–992.

Schaffer, H. R., Greenwood, A., & Parry, M. H. (1972). The onset of wariness. *Child Dev.* 43: 165–175.

Schank, R. & Abelson, R. (1977). *Scripts, Plans, Goals and Understanding.* Hillsdale, N.J.: Lawrence Erlbaum Associates.

Spelke, E. (1976). Infants' intermodal perception of events. *Cognitive Psych.* 8: 553–560.

Spelke, E. S. (1979). Perceiving bimodally specified events in infancy. *Dev. Psych.* 15: 626–636.

Spieker, S. (1982). Infant Recognition of Invariant Categories of faces: person identity and facial expression. Ph.D. Thesis, Cornell Univ.

Stern, D. N. (1971). A micro-analysis of mother-infant interaction: Behaviors regulating social contact between a mother and her 3½ month old twins. *J. Amer. Acad. Child Psychiatr.* 10: 501–517.

—— (1974). Mother and infant at play: The dyadic interaction involving facial, vocal and gaze behaviors. In *The Effect of the Infant on Its Caregiver,* M. Lewis & L. Rosenblum, eds. New York: Wiley.

—— (1977). *The First Relationship: Infant and Mother.* Cambridge: Harvard University Press.

Stern, D. N., Barnett, R. K., & Spieker, S. (1980). *Early Transmission of Affect: Some Research Issues.* Paper presented at the First World Congress on Infant Psychiatry, April 1980, Portugal.

Trevarthan, C. (1980). The foundations of intersubjectivity: Development of interpersonal and cooperative understanding in infants. In *The Social Foundation of Language and Thought: Essays in Honor of Jerome S. Bruner,* D. R. Olson, ed. New York: W. W. Norton & Co. pp. 316–341.

—— (1977). Descriptive analysis of infant communicative behavior. In *Studies in Mother-Infant Interaction,* H. S. Schaffer, ed. New York: Academic Press, pp. 227–270.

Tronick, E., Als, H., Adamson, L., Wise, S., & Brazelton, T. (1978). The infant's response to entrapment between contradictory messages in face-to-face interaction. *J. Amer. Acad. Child Psychiatr.* 17: 1–13.

Tulving, E. (1972). Episodic and semantic memory. In *Organization of Memory,* E. Tulving & W. Donaldson, eds. New York: Academic Press.

Ungerer, J. A., Brody, L. R., & Selano, P. (1978). Longterm memory for speech in 2 to 4 week old infants. *Infant Behavior and Dev.* 1: 177–186.

Walker, A. S., Bahrick, L. E., & Neisser, U. (1980). Selective looking to multimodal events by infants. Paper presented at the International Conference on Infancy Studies, New Haven, April 1980.

Watson, J. S. (1979). Perception of contingency as a determinant of social responsiveness. In *The Origins of Social Responsiveness,* E. Thoman, ed. Hillsdale, N.J.: Lawrence Erlbaum Associates.

84   STERN

———— (1980). *Bases of Causal Inference in Infancy: Time, Space, and Sensory Relations*. Paper presented at the International Conference on Infant Studies, New Haven.

Winnicott, D. W. (1965). *The Maturational Processes and the Facilitating Environment*. New York: Int. Univ. Press.

Worthimer, M. (1961). Psychomotor coordination of auditory visual space at birth. *Science* 134: 1692.

Zajonc, R. B. (1980). Feeling and thinking: Preferences need no inferences. *Am. Psych.* 35: 2, 151–175.

8 To Begin with—Reflections on Ontogeny

Louis W. Sander, M.D.

When Dr. Kaplan invited me to participate in this symposium, I understood his request as wanting me to respond to the question: In what ways can early developmental research contribute to a discussion of "a psychology of the self within psychoanalysis"? (to use Dr. Kohut's familiar designation of the topic). I would like to convey in this presentation the point that one of the chief contributions developmental research can make is that of stimulating a basic shift in the way we view the organization of behavior. I am now talking about "organization," not about the behavioral elements themselves, moving from the view that the organization of behavior is the property of the individual to the perspective that it is the property of the system of which the individual is a part. In order to make this point I have to illustrate what we mean by "system." Then I need to address the next question of how we can understand the way organization in the system contributes to an understanding of an ontogeny of self.

We are at a moment, in the history of human effort to comprehend the human condition, at which new integrations of diverse and complex information are unavoidable. Information is beginning to coalesce. Our own integrations of experience and insight are built on a foundation of others' integrations and insights, and soon our contribution will be swept into another's even more fruitful comprehension. We need each individual's integration. Each new view-point adds a facet. This presents us with the paradox of integration leading to diversity! The excitement of the present moment lies in the glimpse of new commonalities to be found among diversity. In general, I think this symposium must, of necessity, confront the matter of complexity and the paradoxical relation between complex-ity and unity, the relation of each part to the whole and the ordering influence of the whole on the function of each part—namely, the matter of organization, an essential characteristic of all living sub-stance. To look, at this time, for reduction to simplistic answers is to look in the wrong direction. To search for broader perspectives is to encounter *generalizing principles* of a higher order governing orga-nization, ones that may cross disciplinary lines and suggest insights that connect these wider realms of data and relate one level of obser-vation to another. This is the task of integration, an essential ele-ment of the life process, of development, and of "the self."

This task of integration requires us to assimilate into our think-ing and conceptual formulations a wide range of new findings and ideas useful to other biological disciplines such as neuropsychology, neurophysiology, neurochemistry, advances in open systems theory, cybernetics, information-processing theory, and then to consider the possible relevance of these diverse domains to a conceptualization of development and of the self. This is a remarkable challenge for integrative creativity.

There are truly exciting advances in the biological concepts at hand that we have not yet begun to think of incorporating into our ideas of personality organization. For example, how do you fit Roger Sperry's (1976) conclusion—based on his work with patients who had surgical section of the corpus callosum—into your thinking? Sperry holds that consciousness is an *emergent property* of the com-plex function of brain components and, at the same time, is also *causal* in ordering those functions and the relationships between them. Acceptance of his concept of the way that consciousness is causal in regulating brain physiology and function has the most far-reaching implications, namely, the way our consciousness,—our awareness,—is organized, organizes us. We are here at the doorstep of the self.

Spitz (1957) wrote: "The self is the product of awareness, the subject's awareness that he is a sentient and acting entity separate and distinct from objects in the environment. But awareness—goes through a number of developmental stages [p. 119]." In other words, self-awareness has an ontogeny by which it achieves its organization—a production of self-regulating, interactive processes—going on between individual and caregiving environment, and in turn affecting that interaction. We must know what these interactive processes are and what principles govern the characteristics of organization involved. The idea of development as a creative process seems obvious, but how the creation takes place is not so obvious. It is only now that we are realizing that we must approach its investigation in new ways—different from the traditional reductionist search for first causes carried out in the hope that ultimately first causes will be related by some linear-causal logic to the organization of the whole. The alternative approach to investigation is the organismic viewpoint, which views both the whole and the parts, with the parts affecting the structure and function of the whole and the whole concurrently affecting the structure and function of the parts. The idea of "emergent-properties" of the whole is part and parcel of this alternative viewpoint—properties that cannot be inferred from a knowledge of properties of the parts separately or summed and, if we follow Sperry's view of consciousness, that also exert an ordering effect on the parts.

There is not time here to pursue this fascinating subject of integration further. In this presentation we can only consider some of the implications of viewing the organization of behavior from the perspective of the system rather than as the property of individual. What do I mean by system? There are precise and useful definitions by Ross Ashby (1952) and Paul Weiss (1969) but here, very simply, we can think of the infant always in exchange with a caregiving environment: infant–exchange–environment, with all three constituting the system. To bridge to development we consider the system itself as having a life span trajectory of changing organization within which the ontogeny of self is proceeding via an active organizing process operating within, and perhaps because of, the curious features of the system. These features are those of the system's characteristics of polarity and of paradox, of opposing processes going on concurrently, such as opposing tendencies of affiliation and separation, of integration and differentiation, of the child's goals of positive reinforcement and of taking a contrary position. There is *both* conflict and the integration related to it. Nature's basic mechanisms by which regulation, adaptation, and integration are accomplished within the *biological system* shed light on the way the natural polarity that characterizes the biological system provides necessary conditions for life's active organizing process.

Early developmental research can now describe the characteristics of the system at its outset in a way that begins to illuminate what I have been saying. We are becoming aware that the newborn arrives as a relatively sophisticated, highly organized creature, for example, having, almost from the delivery room, visual preference for facial pattern, auditory preference for speech sounds, a capacity for operant learning, and a capacity at microsecond levels for finely tuned interpersonal exchanges. Investigation of early postpartum contact makes clear that it is a highly organized infant and a highly organized environment that can "meet" in the moments after birth, in patterned spatiotemporal exchange. If the situation is optimal, each partner is in a state of being "ready" for the other. "Meeting," "state," and "readiness" are not adequately comprehended in the conceptual world of stimulus and response or in that of "an undifferentiated phase" or "drive reduction." Conceptually, one needs at least a "system" that is complexly organized for specific multimodal, spatiotemporal exchange between partners, each participant having both an endowment of organized functions and the capacity for modifying these in adaptive encounters to achieve a coordination or a "fitting together." From the work of Klaus and his colleagues (1972), and from the work of many others since then, we observe during that first hour or two after birth something that we cannot define as belonging to the infant, or to the mother, or to the father. We now recognize a certain "state" in the group involving each of the participants *and* what is going on between them. This state is an example of an emergent property of the system for a fleeting moment in time, in the trajectory of the system's life span. But the wonder of it is that it exerts influence on the *subsequent* organization of the system, even at this early point influencing its trajectory. We must surely ask: Why were we not aware of all this before? The phenomena have been there; it is our *consciousness* of their significance that is changing the impact of the system's emergent properties as causal in ordering its subsequent history.

The traditional viewpoint that the infant starts from the simple and builds to the complex has gone along with the notion that it is "organization" that develops. It is now clear that we begin with complexity and with the organization of this complexity. We must now grasp how coherence and unity can be achieved and maintained in the individual despite rapid morphological and functional shifts in this organization of both individual and system over the course of development. We look for explanations of coherence in terms of mechanisms of synthesis—of creative integrative mechanisms that are evolutionary solutions for the inherent polarities, and often paradoxical opposing tendencies that characterize the living systems of nature. They pose the discontinuities and tensions that mechanisms of synthesis in the developing organism must resolve. The paradoxical relationship between complexity and unity characterizes organic life at its every level, and each level has its mechanisms of integration that insure a harmonious solution for the inherent paradoxes of the system at that level. Many have asked: What function does "the self" serve? I am convinced that at the evolutionary level of "person," the "self" belongs to this array of vital and ingenious mechanisms of integration.

However, we must return to the constraints of the paper and see if we can illustrate some of these points by the data obtained from the two major areas of research we have worked in: a continuous, noninvasive bassinet monitoring of neonate activity and interaction with caregivers over the first 2 months of life; and a naturalistic, longitudinal study of infant-mother interaction over the first 3 years of life.

The bassinet monitor is a window of noninvasive observation on the infant-caregiver system, recording events in both the infant and the mother in real time, around the clock. From the *record,* we can read the sequence of states in the baby, such as the transition from waking to sleeping, the cycling of substages of sleep, the transition then to waking, the occurrence of crying, the approach of caregiver to the bassinet, the time of removal of infant from bassinet, the duration of removal, the time of return to the bassinet, the state of the baby on return, whether or not it is then asleep or how long it takes to fall asleep, or whether it must be picked up again, or even again, before sleep can resume.

From the 24-hour monitoring data we have learned how sleep, waking, and feeding become organized in 24-hour time around the clock, how a daytime and a nighttime pattern become established over the first month of life as an interaction between the idiosyncratic characteristics of state regulation of a particular infant, and the interventions of its particular caregiving environment. We found that the particular course of this initial adaptation over the first 2 months of life has an impact on the organization of specific infant functions, such as feeding and visual behavior and how these functions are employed in the exchanges with the caregiving environment to reach adaptive coordination or fitting together (Sander et al., 1979).

Continuous 24-hour data immediately introduce phenomena related to biorhythmicity which characterize not only the infant and caregiver as a system and not only the infant as an organism in its own right, but also the different component functions and physiological subsystems of the infant, each having semi-independence in temporal organization. Most of us are familiar with jet lag and its related desynchronization of functions. The achievement of coherence in the complex array of component physiological subsystems or the lack of it, as the individual progresses through the basic rest/activity cycle or the longer ultradian and circadian rhythms of the 24 hours, distinguishes the normal well-organized infant from the infant at risk, just as the temporal disorganization of certain high-risk families distinguishes them from their healthier counterparts. From the system's viewpoint of biorhythmic functions, both adaptation and integration are resolved as matters of phase synchronization, dependent on mechanisms of entrainment and of phase shifting of the periods of the component functional subsystems.

The paradox in the biological system posed by the coexistence of both its unity and its extraordinary complexity are harmonized in the dimension of time and timing by mechanisms representing the characteristics of endogenous biorhythmicity. This endogenous "primary activity" of the organism is in endless fluctuation; physiology from cell to system is constantly varying and is only brought into order by the interaction of part with part and part with whole. Coordination is achieved *through* interaction between these fluctuating elements by mechanisms that relate the phase position of one rhythmic function to that of another, much like an ensemble of musicians each playing quite a different instrument, who may be tuned up and in harmony, or in varying degrees out of harmony.

Let me illustrate what I mean by two figures that depict the development of 24-hour sleep and awake patterns of two infants over the first month of life. The first (Fig. 8.1) shows the pattern of a baby very difficult to regulate, fostered first by one caregiver then another; the second (Fig. 8.2) shows the pattern of a well-organized,

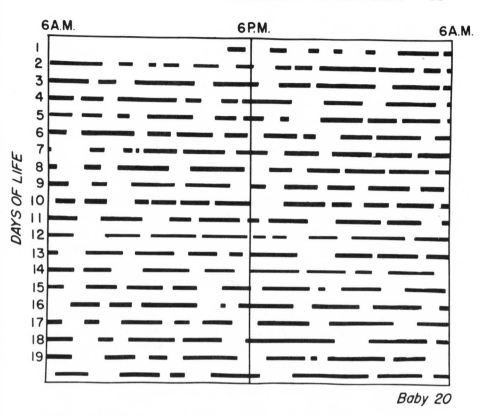

FIG. 8.1.   Twenty four hour sleep-awake organization over first 20 days of life—Baby one. Each day is represented by a line on the chart numbered from 1 to 20 that depicts the occurrence and duration of sleep (black bars) and awake periods (open spaces) in relation to clock time each 24 hours between 6 AM and 6 PM and between 6 PM and 6AM.

second-born infant of an experienced mother, roomed-in with that mother from birth and provided with an infant-demand feeding regimen.

Each awakening is a recurrent situation, an adaptive trial. For the first baby one can see that from one day to the next there is little predictability regarding the time of day of the occurrence of awakenings, nap length, or day-night differential in occurrence of sleeping or awakening. This means, in addition, the *center* of household organization will be diverse and difficult from one awakening to another and not provide the mothers or the infants the experience of a regular occurrence of a stable household situation at the same

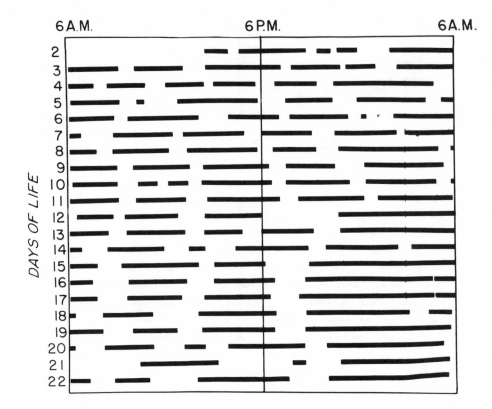

FIG. 8.2. Twenty four hour sleep-awake organization over first 20 days of life—Baby two. (See Fig. 8.1.) Note that by 7 days of life the time of occurrence of awakenings begins to become relatively stable as does nap length. By 12 days the duration and occurrence of sleep periods gains a distinct day-night difference.

times of day as is likely for baby two. For the second baby, by the seventh day the entire 24 hours begins to have an organization.—As time goes on each awakening begins to fit into a particular context in relation to the recurrent events that characterize that family's environment in morning, midday, evening, and night. The context becomes common to, or shared by, both infant and mother when such a background becomes established. Thus, the significance of variations, or of new events or details in the foreground, can serve first to signal, then, if recurrent, come to have meaning in relation to the background context.

On the basis of our data over the first 2 months of life on the interaction of infant effects and caregiver effects in terms of 24-hour regulation of sleep and awake states, and of change in infant and caregiver behavior in the feeding interaction, we have constructed a model illustrating these various features of fitting together. The model is for a normal, well-organized infant at about 3 weeks of life and a mother, when an initial coordination has been achieved. This is the point at which a mother often says that she now thinks she "knows" her new baby.

In the usual instance, by 3 weeks of life there is a basic time structure to the day, with a longest awake period occurring late in the day or early evening, and a number of earlier briefer awakenings; the major part of a longest sleep period occurs in the 12 night hours, with briefer naps during the day and perhaps some predictability as to their duration and occurrence in morning and afternoon. Thus, there is a broad background of 24-hour temporal organization in the system that is starting to be shared by caregiver and infant; the organization of caregiver expectancy is beginning to match the periodicity of recurrent states of the infant. Taking the complete awake period as the basic unit of observation, a characteristic course or sequence of events during this period also begins to gel (see Fig 8.3) so that by the third postnatal week in the adapted system there is a familiar order and sequence to the course of events.

The time course of the awakening is represented in Fig. 8.3 by the line, the shape of which is determined by the interaction between maternal influences (above) and infant influence (below) the line. This can be segmented into subunits of regulatory interactions, each with its own aims, goals, and specific exchange patterns. In the diagram seven such segments are labeled: initial, preparation 1, feed, social, open space, preparation 2, and final. Dyads can be compared in regard to these segments, their boundaries, content, duration, and variability from observation to observation and from day to day.

A first criterion for match or mismatch in the regulatory exchanges is constituted by the direction and timing of infant state change. Change toward arousal or drowsiness is indicated by the upward or downward direction of the arrows in Fig. 8.3. This is the infant's first level of initiative in the system and requires the caregiver to read the "direction" of change. Direction of change can be viewed as an initial inference of the infant's aim or intention, for example, "I think the baby *wants* to go to sleep now." In Fig. 8.3,

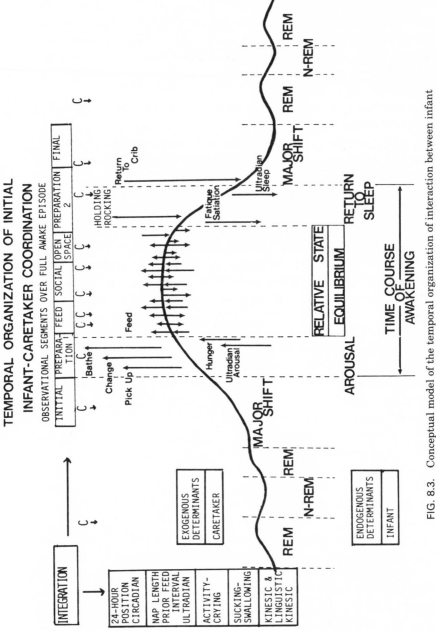

FIG. 8.3. Conceptual model of the temporal organization of interaction between infant behavior and caregiver behavior over the complete course of one awake period at approximately 3 weeks of age. See text for complete explanation.

94

coordination in "direction" or lack of it is represented by the correspondence in the direction of the arrows on the infant's and on the caregiver's side of the time line. The interaction, then, is itself a first-order determinant of events over the awake period—a sequence which, when established, constitutes a first syntax for the dyadic conversation. I would like to call your attention here to the significance of a recent paper by Chappell (1980) of Boston University entitled, "The Ordering Function of Time and Context in Caregiver-Newborn Interaction."

In Fig. 8.3, integration is depicted on both the horizontal and vertical axes. The horizontal axis concerns the integration of the sequence of events up to any point in the awakening as described by the seven segments; the vertical axis represents the integration of the array of rhythms, which also must bear on the exchange at any point. At each point over the sequence of the awake period, the mother is organizing her decision-making process and her actions in an integration of these two axes. The C in Fig. 8.3 represents the points at which crying may occur, the "meaning" of the crying is "read" by where in the now familiar sequence it occurs; "appropriate" intervention on the basis of correct reading insures coordination of mother's and infant's "direction."

The system's perspective of regulation, however, sheds light on a third set of considerations, namely, those features that provide the conditions for differentiation. The concept of phase synchrony, emerging from biorhythm research, gives empirical substance to the notion of *equilibrium* in the regulative system.

First a word about equilibrium. As you may know, the notion of equilibrium in the system is basic to Piaget's (1964) adaptive model of cognitive development and to Ross Ashby's (1952) model of differentiation of function in the adapting system. These represent two somewhat different uses of the concept. Its importance here is that it refers to a condition in the system—to a "state" of the system— temporary perhaps, but a condition that provides a very special context for the *initiation of the voluntary act,* that is, for volition. Action is always organized in relation to salient features of context. Action must incorporate or assimilate these features of context in its organization if the action is to be adaptive. For example, a toddler must take account of the fact that the edge of the table is at the same height as his head if he wants to stop bumping into it everytime he goes by.

However, Ashby points out that when the system is in this state of balance (i.e., in equilibrium), the components or subsystems of the larger system can reveal a temporary and partial independence of the constraints of the whole. This is what Ashby calls "disjoin" or loose coupling. Each subsystem must still operate within its region of stability but shows a partial independence in that it can be stimulated and respond within its region of stability without the excitation spreading to involve the whole system. i.e., The subsystem is "disjoined" temporarily from the rest of the system. This temporary and partial independence of subsystems reduces the time it takes for adaptation of a highly complex organism, and it is an optimal condition for the finer differentiation of the functions of a subsystem in interaction with its surround. On the other hand, if the system as a whole is *not* in a state of balance, is out of kilter, regulation of the individual's state will also be out of kilter, and the organization of action will be preempted by basic regulatory mechanisms governing the organization of those behaviors that must now restore balance.

Ashley's concept of equilibrium and "disjoin" or loose coupling of subsystems is useful in conceptualizing how an active "integrative core" (e.g., Weil 1970) might underly the initiation of action. The "core would be a subsystem constructed of a set of higher brain functions, related to the organization of consciousness and perception. The set would consist of the following at least: the awake alert state of the infant, the orienting response with the focusing of attention, the related capacities of habituation of repetitive input and representation of pattern of stimulus input upon which both the functions of habituation and novelty detection depend. Finally an essential part of the "core" are the neural networks that activate both attentive organization and the volition to initiate the action that further scans and explores details of the stimulus or novelty being encountered. Epigenetically this constellation of higher brain functions soon becomes part of the more extended networks that organize and initiate voluntary action to produce operant contigent *effects* on novelties so focussed. Almost from the outset of postnatal life the infant can be demonstrated to be an operant "contingency detector".

In investigations of the neurophysiology of attention, especially the activation of visual saccades which shift gaze to focus on a point of interest or meaning, the command function is beginning to be empirically explored by single-unit recordings that account for the endogenously arising volition that initiates an act (Mountcastle, 1978). A basic assumption underlying our work is that active self-regulation and the individual's "active organization of his world" depend critically on the *integrative* neural *mechanisms* by which synthesis of a multiplicity of endogenous determinants selects the program initiated in "the act." Constrained by time, the act is the final common path by which the paradoxical co-occurrence of great complexity with final unity becomes harmonized in the living system.

Studies of operant contingency examine the effects on attention when the infant produces an effect by an act he or she initiates. This research connects the domains of initiation of action, detection of operant effects, organization of attention, learning, problem solving, and the infant's joyful affect concomitant with a predictable operant outcome. It is important to recognize that in the normal infant a tight integration of all these functions exists almost from the outset, at least by 3 months postnatally. In the high-risk infant such a functional subsystem lacks coherence. One can see also that this coherent cluster of functions has to do with awareness and its relation to the state of the system and to conditions necessary for the infant to be the endogenously motivated agent in the initiation of his own action. Again we are at the doorstep of the self.

Let us see how this might be illustrated in our model of the normal infant-caregiver system at 3 weeks postnatally. In the figure, coordination or synchrony of caregiving behavior and infant state course over the awake span are indicated as being in relative equilibrium. At least by 3 weeks of life, this makes possible a span of time in the sequence in which the caregiver and infant can experience a relative disengagement—the segment designated in the figure as "open space." The mother places the infant in the reclining baby seat to "entertain" himself where mother can be seen as she goes about her other duties. At this point regulation of the infant, the caregiver, and their exchange has provided a state in the system of relative equilibrium in which the infant is fed, dry, and comfortable, but not ready to return to sleep.

Here, infant behavior is optimally disengaged ("disjoined") from both endogenous and exogenous control. This provides a condition allowing for options in the infant's exercise of an individually idiosyncratic and selective volitional initiative. This is an equilibrium in which neither basic endogenous infant regulation (e.g., infant state) preempts infant behavior, nor does the caregiver's initiative capture infant response contingencies. The infant's own interests, his active selective exploration of himself, or the low-intensity stimuli or discrepancies in the surround between habituated patterns and new variations in them provide differentiating self-regulatory feedbacks that now can become more specifically assimilated to the infant's own more specific goals. The infant can begin to organize his world actively with a freedom of option that can reflect small idiosyncracies of his experience, his interests, and his preferences giving a particular pattern to the organization of his attention and the organization of his action in relation to it.

Here then, in the open-space segment of the awake period, there is documentation for Winnicott's (1958) paradox: "The basis of the capacity to be alone is a paradox; it is the experience of being alone while someone else is present [p. 30]." Further: "It is only when alone (that is to say in the presence of someone) that the infant can discover his own personal life. The pathological alternative is a false life built on reactions to external stimuli [p. 34]." The open-space segment can be thought of as a first level of Winnicott's (1958) intermediate area, a condition describing the system rather than the infant, but in which:

> the infant is able to become unintegrated, to flounder, to be in a state in which there is no orientation, to be able to exist for a time without being either a reactor to an external impingement, or an active person with a direction of interest or movement. The stage is set for an id experience. In the course of time there arrives a sensation or an impulse. In this setting the sensation or impulse will feel real and be truly a personal experience [p. 34].

Winnicott (1963) identifies this as a private core, an integrative core, the basis for the initiation of experience. We describe it here as an "emergent property" of a system in a state of adapted coordination. This is one reason why the current fascination with bonding or attachment of infant and mother must be enriched by a concept of regulation of exchange, in which the pattern of disengagement has a place of equal importance with patterns of engagement and attachment.

In the open-space segment of the adapted system, the conditions are optimal for infants to differentiate effects contingent on their own initiation. The experience of contingent effects has a profound impact on the alerting and focusing of infant attention. The perception of the direction and focus of attention is one of the most primitive and basic perceptions one human makes of another, but its directions can also be completely private and hidden.

In his description of the experience of, the place for, and the function of this "isolated core," we understand Winnicott as identifying the essential inviolability within the individual of this source necessary for endogenous governance of initiation, basic to the understanding of all aspects of development (e.g., learning, defense, adaptive organization, etc.). Winnicott (1963) adds: "The traumatic experiences that lead to the organization of primitive defenses belong to the threat to this isolated core, the threat of its being found, altered, communicated with [p. 187]."

In sum, then, the optimal conditions for increasing differentiation of percepts of both inner and outer worlds reside in the open-space condition of equilibrium in the system and, during this condition, in the relative disengagement of (or disjoin of) the self-regulatory core in its integrative function from preemption by imperative endogenous or exogenous determinants. At such equilibrium the richness of selectivity or option would be maximal, a site of personal integration from which the initiation of new behavioral organizations originate, and which have the qualities of "real" and of "own."

Having identified these conditions of regulation in the system, we can trace during the next months of life a sequence of levels of such adaptive equilibria. The necessity for new adaptation is introduced into the infant-caregiver interaction by *new* activity that the infant becomes able to initiate. The infant's new initiatives become the center of struggle and mutual adjustment until areas of approval and reinforcement for the behavior are negotiated along with the limits. The strategies for achieving and maintaining these new levels of fitting together represent unique solutions for each family system. In analogy to Piaget's (1936) developmental epistemology of the inanimate world—the sequence of interpersonal coordinations, that I am proposing are achieved in a sequence of adaptations with the caregivers, can be discussed as an epistemology of people—by this is established each individual's own schemata or repertoire of interpersonal knowledge, which obviously can only be constructed on the basis of adaptation with those particular individuals the infant actually encounters. These schemata then organize the infant's "own" idiosyncratic strategies for interpersonal adaptation, later to underlie those interpersonal predispositions that we would recognize as "archaic" transferences.

This perspective has emerged from the second area of our research that was mentioned earlier, namely, the longitudinal study of early personality development, which was primarily based on the observation of mother-infant interaction over the first 3 years of life. It was our task to compare the longitudinal sequence of changes in this interaction over the first 3 years across a sample of mothers selected to represent a spectrum of character formation from the best organized to the most poorly organized in a general hospital prenatal clinic. In carrying out this comparison the observational material suggested that the interactional data could be arranged as the negotiation of a sequence of issues of interpersonal adaptation between the growing infant and its caregivers. By following the thread of the actions the infant initiated, we could see the changing arenas of perturbation and the negotiation of a sequence of solutions between infant and caregiving environment as the infant grew. This connecting thread, namely, the following of new capabilities to initiate action, suggested a way to trace negotiations over the first 18 months to those of the second 18 months, particularly if we considered the concurrent progress of opposing tendencies as they became integrated in achieving the sequence of adaptive solutions. The sequence of issues to be negotiated are summarized in Table 8.1.

Psychoanalysis has long been aware of the simultaneous existence of opposing tendencies that constitute elementary characteristics of the system and part of its natural polarity. In 1957 Spitz wrote: "The simultaneous presence of diametrically opposed tendencies in the child *beginning with birth* cannot be sufficiently emphasized. The tendency to separateness counteracts from the beginning that child's more obvious tendency of clinging to the mother [p. 123]." I have tried to illustrate that there are biological mechanisms actually carrying out integration of the system's polarities at each level of complexity from living cell to living system. The accomplishment of integration is not a hidden mystery. Pathogenesis can be approached from the viewpoint of the opposing tendencies (i.e., conflict, which has been traditional) or from the viewpoint of the integrative mechanisms (as a psychology of the self emphasizes), but both must be included for understanding because it is an *interaction* between them that gives the unique organization of the individual

TABLE 8.1
Adaptive Issues Negotiated in Interaction Between Infant
and Caregiver

Issue	Title	Span of Months	*Prominent Infant Behavior that Become Coordinated with Maternal Activities*
I	Initial regulation	1–3	Basic infant activities concerned with biological processes related to feeding, sleeping, elimination, postural maintenance, etc., including stimulus needs for quieting and arousal.
II	Reciprocal exchange	4–6	Smiling behavior that extends to full motor and vocal involvement in sequences of affectively spontaneous back-and-forth exchanges, activities of spoon feeding, dressing, etc., become reciprocally coordinated.
III	Initiative	7–9	Activities initiated by infant to secure a reciprocal social exchange with mother or to manipulate environment on his own selection.
IV	Focalization	10–13	Activities by which infant determines the availability of mother on his specific initiative, tends to focalize need-meeting demands on the mother.
V	Self-assertion	14–20	Activities in which infant widens the determination of his own behavior, often in the face of maternal opposition.
VI	Recognition	18–36	Activities (including language) that express perceptions of own state, intentions, and thought content.
VII	Reversal (continuity or conservation of self as active organizer)	18–36	Activities rupturing and restoring coordination on an intentional level (intended and directed aggressive behavior in equilibrium with directed initiations aimed at facilitating restoration of interactional concordance).

and the particular trajectory of change in organization that represents the developmental course of the individual.

In describing this trajectory of changing organization, as suggested by our model, we are interested in identifying the levels of engagement between infant and caregiver that achieve temporary levels of coordination or equilibrium and the activities the infant initiates that accomplish differentiation when an interactive equilibrium is achieved, which permits disengagement. Paradoxically, both the processes of engagement and disengagement go along together from the outset. This paradox becomes understandable if one recognizes that it is by a specific spatiotemporal *pattern* of exchange in the system that processes of engagement and disengagement can be reconciled. Once they are reconciled the open space for new integrations can be temporarily achieved in the harmony that results from the reconciliation. One must include in our description of the trajectory of changing organization the domains of time, of space, and of modality. One also needs to appreciate epigenesis, the contribution of each advance of integrative resolution to the particular configuration of subsequent advances.

As one observes this epigenesis in describing the empirical features of the longitudinal trajectory, it becomes evident that if the system permits, the disengagement becomes obviously and actually *initiated* by the infant at later levels. In the second year of life in well-coordinated systems, infants begin to initiate the taking of a contrary position in a way that can become directly provocative to their caregivers.

The option to take a contrary position is an elementary aspect of the early developmental sequence that any formulation of an ontogeny of self must take into consideration. It has been described by Spitz (1957) in pointing to the significance of the toddler's head-shaking gesture and the use of the word "no," both in play and vis-à-vis caregivers. The same principle is described by Winnicott (1963) in emphasizing the significance of the option to "not communicate." We have formulated an adaptive issue of "reversal" in the infant-caregiver interactions of the second 18 months to allow description of the extent to which the taking of a contrary position can be negotiated between infant and caregiver to establish a new level of "fitting together" in the system. This new coordination defines the extent to which, and the circumstances under which, this option of a new level of "being alone in the presence of someone" may be employed by the child in that particular system.

This negotiation has a particular significance when we approach development from the standpoint of regulation by organizing processes in the biological system—a significance that is not captured by understanding such action only in terms of aggressive drive. In our formulation it relates to an essential temporary and partial disembedding or uncoupling of this core subsystem of self-regulatory integrative functions that is connected to awareness and, in turn, governed by self-awareness, referred to earlier. In Ashby's (1952) model, the "disjoin" of such a self-subsystem would have key significance for subsequent adaptive competence. This viewpoint establishes this early consolidation of an integrating, self-organizing subsystem as a necessary mechanism of adaptation, if adaptation is to be achieved at a high level of complexity. Obviously, the extent to which the system provides toddlers with the option to take a contrary position, and the actual configuration of regulatory functions that such a self-regulatory subsystem is *allowed* to serve in the system, represents what Erikson (1959) has designated as the key developmental issue at this age, namely, that of relative autonomy. Erikson made it clear in his discussion of mutuality that the toddler's relative autonomy says something about the system as well as about the toddler within that system. Here we are only reemphasizing Erikson's point that emerging autonomy must also be viewed epigenetically in relation to initial organizing processes necessary for later consolidation of the self of the toddler.

The relative stability over the longer term of strategies of interpersonal regulation characteristic of the system at the family level (see Ziegler & Musliner, 1977) suggests the conditions under which these same processes subsequently tend to function. This bears importantly on our inclusion of developments during latency and especially adolescence in a discussion of the ontogeny of the self.

The domain of time itself now limits me to indicating that the sequence of the seven issues of adaptation between the infant and its caregivers over the first 3 years of life, which we have studied in our observational data, and the *ways* these issues are negotiated have an impact on the characteristics of interpersonal adaptation, integration, self-regulation, self-awareness, and the self.

I would like to conclude by expressing the hope that this viewpoint, coming from empirical data of early developmental research does indeed contribute to our thinking of an ontogeny of self and the steps in its construction. The perspective suggests that the necessary clues lie in the regulatory-adaptive mechanisms that preserve coherence of the individual in the presence of the changing and increasingly complex organization of infant-caregiver interrelationship when this is considered in the light of biological systems concepts.

REFERENCES

Ashby, R. (1952). *Design for a Brain*. London: Chapman & Hall.
Chappell, P. (1980). The ordering function of time and context in caregiver-newborn interaction. In preparation.
Erikson, E. H. (1959). *Identity and the Life Cycle. Psychol. Issues,* Mongr. Vol. 1, No. 1, New York: Int. Univ. Press.
Klaus, M. H. et al. (1972). Maternal attachment: The importance of the first postpartum days. *New Eng. J. Medicine* 286: 46–63.
Mountcastle, V. B. (1978). Brain mechanism for directed attention. *J. Royal Soc. of Medicine* 21:14–28.
Piaget, J. (1936). *The Origins of Intelligence in Children* (2nd ed.). New York: Int. Univ. Press, 1952.
_____ (1964). The role of the concept of equilibrium in psychological explication. In *Six Psychological Studies*. New York: Random House, 1967, pp. 100–116.
Sander, L. W. (1976). Infant and caretaking environment: Investigation and conceptualization of adaptive behavior in a system of increasing complexity. In *Explorations in Child Psychiatry,* E. J. Anthony, ed. New York: Plenum Press, pp. 129–166.
Sander, L. W. et al. (1979). Changes in infant and caregiver variables over the first two months of life: Integration of action in early development. In *Origins of the Infants' Social Responsiveness,* E. Thoman, ed. Hillsdale, N.J.: Lawrence Erlbaum Associates.
Sperry, R. W. (1976). A unifying approach to mind and brain: Ten year Perspective. In *Perspectives in Brain Research,* Vol. 45 pp. 464–69 M. A. Corner & D. F. Swaab, eds. New York: Elsevier.
_____ (1970). An objective approach to subjective experience. *Psychol. Rev.* 77: 585–590.
Spitz, R. (1957). *No and Yes on the Genesis of Human Communication*. New York: Int. Univ. Press.
Weil, A. (1970). The basic core. *Psychoanal. Study Child* 25: 442–460.
Weiss, P. (1969). The living system—Determinism stratified. In *Beyond Reductionism* A. Koestler & J. R. Smythies eds. Boston: Beacon Press.
Winnicott, D. W. (1958). The capacity to be alone. In *The Maturational Processes and the Facilitating Environment*. New York: Int. Univ. Press, 1965.
_____ (1963). On communicating and not communicating leading to a study of certain opposites. In *The Maturational Process and the Facilitating Environment*. New York: Int. Univ. Press, 1965.
Zeigler, R. & Musliner, P. J. (1977). Persistent themes: A naturalistic study of personality development in the family. *Family Process* 16: 3, 293–305.

9 Discussion of Papers by Drs. Sander and Stern

Virginia Demos, Ed.D.

The contributions of Dr. Stern and Dr. Sander are extraordinarily rich and challenging clarifications of our understanding of the developmental process. Specifically, both Stern and Sander have provided a complex framework within which we can begin to trace the ontogeny of the self. I would like to highlight some of the issues they have raised and try to integrate the ideas expressed in the two papers. I believe these papers complement each other and together articulate what hopefully is becoming a predominant view in developmental psychology.

Let me begin with the issues of self–other differentiation in early infancy as presented by Stern. I should say at the outset that I am in essential agreement with the arguments he has marshaled and with his view of the young infant as possessing a variety of preadapted, prestructured perceptual and integrative capabilities. He argues that this built-in organization biases the newborn's early interactions with the environment and makes inevitable the construction of distinct schemata of self and other right from the beginning. Thus, development is described as the interaction of two simultaneous processes: (1) the emergence of distinct schemata and representations of self and other; (2) the emergence of schemata and representations of "being with" another. I would only add to this account that the infant possesses prestructured affective programs as well, and these play an important role in the emerging schemata and representations of this dual developmental process. I return to this point later.

Sander makes a similar statement about development, but at a different theoretical level, when he argues that the traditional view of the infant as starting from the simple and building to the complex is no longer tenable. He advocates a systems approach that accepts as given a complex organization that includes both what goes on within the infant and what goes on between the infant and the caregiver. Our task must be to describe how the organism achieves and maintains a coherence despite rapid shifts in this complex organization. He speaks of looking for creative, integrative mechanisms and, at the psychological level, sees the self as one such mechanism.

Sander has also provided an organizational framework for locating the occasions when the emerging schemata and representations in Stern's model and the integrative processes in his own system can take place. He described the successful mutual regulation of the infant's states and bodily needs as producing what he calls "open spaces" when the infant's adaptive capacities are neither preempted by internal needs, nor by the external influences of the caregiver. At such times the infant is able to pursue her own interests. Here we can begin to see how the built-in perceptual capacities described by Stern tend to direct the infant's attention to particular kinds of stimuli, such as parts of her own body or nearby objects; how, left to herself, her own actions result in a constant reinforcement schedule, as opposed to a variable one when the caregiver is involved; and how these moments or "open spaces" allow the infant the opportunity to integrate her experience and to construct sensorimotor representations of self and selfobject interactions.

I would expand this description to include the affective component. Silvan Tomkins, a psychologist, has provided a useful model. He postulates the existence of innate affect programs that are attuned to the gradient and intensity properties of stimuli. Thus, moderately increasing stimulation evokes the affect interest, rapidly increasing stimulation evokes fear, and a sudden increase in stimulation, the steepest gradient, evokes a startle, whereas relatively high levels evoke distress or anger, and decreasing levels evoke enjoyment. He also postulates that the function of affect is to amplify the stimulus, thereby making good things better, making bad things worse, and creating an urgency that is experienced as motivating. In this model the organism is biased to prolong and maximize positive affect and to try to change and minimize negative affect. Now, equipped with this formulation, if we return to our infant, left to her own resources in one of Sander's "open spaces," we can see that it is not only the perceptual characteristics of the stimulus, such as its contours or color, but also its intensity or gradient features that matter. When these are at a moderate or optimal level, they evoke the affect interest, and it is the infant's interest that sustains her involvement in the situation. As the infant's perceptual and integrative capacities, sustained by interest, begin to produce expectable events, enjoyment is evoked, and because the infant is biased to prolong such positive experiences, she seeks or is motivated to repeat them. There are many variations on this paradigm, but the point is that the prestructured affective responses and the prestructured perceptual capacities appear to be integrated and inseparable from the start and represent another facet of the complex organization of the young infant.

In pursuing this line of thought a little further, I would like to emphasize the importance of the contribution Stern has made in articulating three ways of being with the other, namely, self–other complementing, mental state sharing or state tuning, and state transforming. He insists that these three ways presuppose on the part of the infant some kind of "event knowledge" that includes both affect categories and categories for remembering dynamic events. The issue of how the infant experiences and remembers these interpersonal events is central for both clinical and developmental psychology, and yet as Stern points out, we have no theoretical models to guide us. The only work I know of that tries to integrate the affective component into the process of remembering events is, once again, that by Silvan Tomkins (1979) in his article on script theory. Tomkins describes an essentially analogic process by which the affect in an affectively laden experience can, over time, become magnified, and the other components of the experience (e.g., agents, setting, etc.) can be generalized to other people, settings, and so on so that eventually a nuclear script evolves, which may come to dominate the person's psychic organization.

Stern's three ways of being with another may prove to be a useful beginning in sorting out both clinical and observational data on interpersonal experiences in infancy. However, I must voice some disagreement with his treatment of the state-transforming way of being with another. I believe Stern is correct in pointing out the overemphasis in traditional psychoanalysis on the model of gratifying the hungry infant. He is also probably correct in saying that when a distressed or crying infant is soothed, it represents an anaclitic experience for the infant—a transformation of the self via another. However, I believe he is in error when he lumps drive states with affect states and discounts them both as essentially physical transformations, important in the development of physical intimacy. Drives and affects represent separate systems in the personality, and there exists a growing body of data and theory which argues that affects are the primary motivating system in the personality and that drive states, except in life-threatening situations, only acquire urgency by recruiting affects, which serve to amplify their messages.

This is an extremely important, complex, and controversial issue which I can only touch on here. It is also an issue that by and large separates psychologists from psychoanalysts, for psychologists have essentially given up on drive theory as an adequate explanatory model of human motivation. Stern, too, was relegating drives to a mere physical status, but in failing to distinguish drives from affects he was also, I believe, seriously underestimating the importance of affective state transformations in providing the infant with the emotional capacity to engage in moments of subjective intimacy.

I would place the emphasis more on modulation of affective states than on transformation, although both are probably involved, and would argue, as I have elsewhere, that affective states, even in early infancy, have a psychological-motivational component as well as a physical one. Thus, if one accepts the possibility that infants are born with prestructured affective programs, but possess only limited capacities for modulating these affective states, then the infant is highly dependent on the caregiver as a soothing, modulating agent. And it seems likely that it is the successful, mutual modulation of affective states (e.g., the experience for the infant of building up and coming down from states of excitement, joy, distress, and anger, without experiencing a loss of control) that leads to a sense of basic trust, a trust of one's own inner states as well as of the caregiver's skill in protecting one from overloading and becoming disorganized. These repeated experiences, in which one remains in control even as one's affective state intensifies, gradually enable the infant to tolerate moderately intense affective states. This growing tolerance is an important psychological component of the infant's capacity to engage in moments of self–other complementing and mental state sharing. For only as infants learn to feel comfortable about their inner states will they be free to risk becoming affectively aroused in complementing or state sharing encounters.

I would like to shift the focus slightly now to a related issue, namely, the dual process of development that both Stern and Sander have described, although each uses a somewhat different language. Stern speaks of the polarity between the child's emerging representations of self and other, and the representations of "being with" the other. And Sander describes the necessity for intermediate areas, or open spaces, free of direct pressure for adaptation, as well as the ongoing negotiations of a "fitting together" with the caregiving environment. Others, such as George Klein (1976) and more recently Stechler and Kaplan (1980), have also talked of the "I" and "we" aspects of the self and their simultaneous development. What I would like to call attention to in these formulations is the importance placed on the I part of this simultaneous process for the creation and integration of psychic structure. This emphasis represents a departure from current psychoanalytic views of development. Kohut has suggested that the infant gradually internalizes the psychic functions of the mother on those occasions when small, inevitable, empathic breaks occur. In this model psychic structure is created when there is a brief loss of the usually sufficient we. However, if we accept the observations from infant research as articulated by Stern and Sander, the Kohutian view would have to be broadened to incorporate all those I experiences when the infant is not stressed by either internal or external pressures and seems to be busy integrating and constructing his or her world. Indeed, I would be tempted to extend this reasoning (and at this point I absolve Stern and Sander from all responsibility for these ideas) and suggest that the bulk of psychic structure is created when both the I and the we experiences of the infant are going well. For example, the developmental literature is replete with descriptions of how the infant's behavior is enhanced in smooth interactions with a caregiver—interest is prolonged, variations on a theme and imitations of new behaviors occur, and the infant's repertoire is expanded. Ainsworth (1974) has described how, at slightly later ages, the securely attached infant explores and plays more freely in the presence of the attachment figure. Thus, structure building is going on during good, empathic, we experiences as well. What happens, then, during an empathic break? Well, I would speculate that there is an intensification of already existing adaptive structures, produced by the increase in negative affect that occurs when the infant's expectations of a generally empathic mother are violated. Whether or not this intensification leads to a creative reorganization and integration probably depends on the infant's already established capacity for tolerating an intensification of negative affect and her particular repertoire of adaptive capabilities. In other words I am suggesting that the empathic break could be seen as presenting the infant with a challenge to her adaptive capacities, which by and large have been developed in more optimal situations.

Now I would like to turn to the problem of how to conceptualize the ontogeny of the self. The problem is really which formulations will be the most promising in our mutual search for an understanding of this developmental process. The current psychoanalytic formulations, influenced heavily by Mahler's work, assume that the infant starts out in an undifferentiated, symbiotic bond with the mother. By contrast, Kohut's position does not assume this undifferentiated state, but stresses instead a self-selfobject matrix in which the beginnings of the self are in the eyes of the beholder. (I believe Stern is mistaken when he lumps Mahler and Kohut together as representing similar positions on this issue.) The propositions offered here today, however, argue that there is coherence *within the infant* from the beginning that goes through transformations and organizational shifts.

Stern presents data from a variety of sources to demonstrate the infant's perceptual, cognitive, and psychological capacities for early, differentiated experience. And Sander proposes a sequence of seven developmental issues that are negotiated between the infant and caregiver. Throughout, these issues reflect the infant's active role and the preservation and changing focus of the infant's initiative. Other researchers, namely, Stechler and Kaplan, have proposed a similar progression that also emphasizes the infant's capacity to actively organize and integrate experience, first at the perceptual, sensorimotor, affective level, then as an agent with goals and plans, and in the second year of life, as a self-aware agent capable of monitoring one's actions and intentions. If we were to try to integrate the Kohutian view with the observations from infant research, we would have to say that Kohut tends to emphasize the role of the caregiver, partly, I would assume, from lack of expertise in the field of infant development and partly because the experiences of early infancy are not directly accessible to the psychoanalytic method. On the other hand, the description of early development articulated by infant researchers acknowledges the interpersonal matrix and at the same time stresses the infant's contribution in terms of the infant's complex organizational capacities and changing initiatives. There is no question in my mind that the latter view is a far more accurate representation of infancy.

However, the two views come together in the second year of life, when an important new organizational shift seems to occur. Kohut has described it as the emergence of a cohesive self. Sander has described this shift as involving the toddler's capacity to "experience that another is aware of what he is aware of within himself." Both views point to the infant's new capacity for representation of the self and inner experience. Perhaps because he studies normal infants and mothers, Sander chooses to stress the gain in adaptive resources that this shift represents. And Kohut, perhaps because he works with a clinical population of adults, tends to stress the vulnerabilities, the risks in not being empathically recognized or validated when new structures emerge. Needless to say, both points of view are required in order to enrich our understanding.

And this brings us to the final issue I would like to address— namely, what can infant research and psychoanalytic theory do for each other? I have just suggested that the two disciplines can enrich each other as long as they acknowledge and respect each other's territorial superiorities. Infant researchers are in a better position than analysts to observe what actually goes on between infants and caregivers, to infer, at least, the contemporaneous meaning of those events, and to develop theoretical models to describe the processes we observe. We are not, however, in a good position to predict how those events successively become organized and related to a variety of other events and eventually emerge as memories of childhood or as psychic reality in adulthood. Analysts, on the other hand, are in a prime position to observe the subtle workings of the psyche, the motivational dynamics, and the distilled representations of early childhood events. Hopefully, a well-articulated and accurate developmental theory will aid the clinician in trying to make sense of these childhood memories just as advances in psychoanalytic theory, and here I refer specifically to the seminal work of Heinz Kohut, will aid the researcher in conceptualizing observable behavior. This is a round about way of saying: We need each other.

REFERENCES

Ainsworth, M. (1974). Infant-mother attachment and social development: Socialization as a product of reciprocal responsiveness to signals. In *The Integration of the Child into the Social World*, M. Richards, ed. Cambridge, England: Cambridge University Press, pp. 99–135.

Demos, E. V. (1982). Affect in early infancy: Physiology or psychology. *Psychoanal. Inq.* 1: 533–574.

Klein, G. S. (1976). *Psychoanalytic Theory: An Exploration of Essentials*. New York: Int. Univ. Press.

Kohut, H. (1971). *The Analysis of the Self*. New York: Int. Univ. Press.

——— (1977). *The Restoration of the Self*. New York: Int. Univ. Press.

——— (1980). Reflections on Advances in Self Psychology. In *Advances in Self Psychology*, A. Goldberg, ed. New York: I.U.P. Inc. pp. 473–554.

Stechler, G. & Kaplan, S. (1980). The development of the self: A psychoanalytic perspective. *Psychoanal. Study Child* 35: 85–105.

Tomkins, S. (1962). *Affect, Imagery, Consciousness, Vol. I: The Positive Affects*. New York: Springer.

——— (1963). *Affect, Imagery, Consciousness, Vol. 2: The Negative Affects*. New York: Springer.

——— (1979). Script theory: Differential magnification of affects. In *Nebraska Symposium on Motivation. Vol. 26*, H. E. Howe, Jr. & R. A. Dienstbier, eds. Lincoln, NE: Univ. of Nebraska Press, pp. 201–236.

10 Discussion of Papers by Drs. Stern and Sander

Marian Tolpin, M.D.

I agree with Dr. Demos that psychoanalysis and developmental psychology need each other. In certain respects I also agree that direct observation of infants is superior to analytic reconstructions from adults' psychopathology. For example, take Kohut's (1971) early idea about the formation of the self, namely, that "self nuclei" gradually coalesce to establish a cohesive whole, an idea influenced by Glover's (1943) notion of separate ego nuclei and by much prevailing analytic theory. The theory of a normal stage of fragmented, separate body-mind parts and separate body-mind functions simply does not fit the developmental data, nor does it fit "what every mother knows" about a healthy infant. Consequently, Kohut revised his experience-distant version of the beginnings of a cohesive self. We no longer start with the prevailing analytic view that the infant is normally fragmented into separate autoerotic zones, split-up by archaic (pre-oedipal) conflict, objectless, psychologically fused with its caregiver, and so forth. This view, indeed, arose from failing to recognize that adults' mental-disintegration products are not remnants of a normal stage of nondifferentiation of self and object, lack of a cohesive organization, etc. Instead we start out our developmental-clinical theorizing with an entirely different view of normal and abnormal early childhood development. We think the evidence points to a baby with an inherent organization (provided that his or her endowment is normal), from the very start a baby with an integrated, differentiated, in-phase nuclear self in partnership with its expectable human world (its selfobjects). In my view, then, "The Competent Baby" (Bruner, 1973; Stone, Smith, & Murphy, 1972) described by the developmental psychologists, including Stern and Sander, and "Kohut's (Cohesive) Baby" are made for each other. Our respective babies are two different sides of the same coin (the "outside" observable reality and the "inside" psychic reality). Both conceive of a differentiated, organized, in-phase nuclear self in a selfobject unit. However, the competent baby has both feet planted in the observable reality of attachment of child and parent. The cohesive baby, on the other hand, has one foot in the vicissitudes of attachment, including *etiological* faults and failures of attachment, whereas the other foot is in the child's inner psychological experience, including the *pathogenetic* features of faulty attachment. Perhaps the most significant result of seeing the baby as normally cohesive, rather than fragmented, is this: As far as psychic reality is concerned, babies who are adequately cared for experience themselves and their parents as strong, competent, effective, and powerful. The consequence of faulty attachment, first and foremost, is that this experience of their own and their parents' greatness and power—the nucleus of health—is traumatically shattered.

For the main part of my discussion, I want to respond with an indirect answer to the questions of theoretical framework raised by Sander and Stern and to some of their other questions by describing a developmental-clinical vignette. The vignette concerns the self observed and reconstructed. It could be entitled, "On Becoming a Man." It consists of a two-part dialogue—one part is a belated developmental dialogue between the analyst and her patient; the other part is an ongoing, expectable, developmental dialogue between the patient and his small son. Without knowing it, the patient put into "people language" what we mean by the self-selfobject unit, by the twinship, partnership, side by side self-selfobject psychological tie or merger (terms that all mean one and the same thing).

Psychoanalysts of different theoretical persuasions use the term "merger" to mean very different kinds of psychological states. By merger of self and selfobject we mean psychological connectedness—for instance, between delighted child and mirroring audience; between cranky, tired child and idealized, uplifting pillars of strength and support; between the child who wants company and the lively partners who lend their presence. Selfobject in ego psychology and object relations theory denotes an undifferentiated, psychologically fused state. Thus, we mean something quite different by merger than Stern thinks. In fact, self-selfobject merger includes many of the kinds of experiences Sander, Stern, and Demos describe. The tie or merger between self and selfobject I am going to describe is between the nuclear "grandiose exhibitionistic self" of Ted, a 3-year-old (a competent, cohesive baby, if you will), and his father, Ted's ordinary, tuned-in, turned-on, idealized, mirroring, partnering selfobject, all rolled into one.

Their merger meeting took place in the wee hours of the morning while Ted used the "potty" and his sleepy father presided. One parent had to preside because, although Ted had been proudly "going potty" for some time now, he still needed company and he still needed help to wipe himself. Ted's father, Mr. G, was a successful attorney whose life work was devoted to child welfare. His own father had been an unreliable alcoholic and a tremendous source of embarrassment to him. His long-suffering and plodding mother was the reliable breadwinner, although he thought in retrospect that she was probably chronically depressed. However, she could always be counted on to go to work during his father's periodic binges and hangovers. Mr. G had been in analysis for 2 years. He suffered from a chronic low-grade feeling of depression, and he lacked zest and enthusiasm, except for his work and for the little son who was his pride and joy. In spite of his depression, he was an indefatigable worker, and he took comfort in the fact that he had a great deal of drive and ambition. He thought his intelligence and his ability to achieve had saved him from a far worse disturbance.

Prior to the 3:30 A.M. encounter of father and son, the analyst had offered an interpretation and genetic reconstruction of a pervasive, frustrating character resistance. The resistance in question was an amalgam of caution, coolness, distancing, and impersonalness. A complex and habitual form of self-protection, these traits were motivated by shame over his reactivated transference needs for parental participation with him and by his fear and dread of reencountering the indifference of the reinstated parental selfobject (the analyst). Long ago in his childhood, he began to live in the frozen universe of one of his first dreams in analysis—a universe he was terrified to leave because he might get lost and not find his way back. The transference hopes—to find the undepressed mother who could be enthusiastic, to find the nondisheveled father of whom he could be proud—exposed him to this very danger. In effect, the analyst told him that he continued to carefully guard himself from showing what he wanted and hoped he would get from her, that he guarded himself from showing his hope that he himself would be able to respond with a depth of feeling, and that he evidently also guarded himself out of shame and his fear of rebuff.

A weekend interruption intervened. In the session following the weekend, the patient returned immediately to the analyst's comments on Friday and said, "That was a good hour. You made a good point. I won't think of how I'm going to say goodbye to you yet." He reminded her of what he meant by the latter remark. At the very beginning of the analysis, he had wondered about termination and whether he would terminate and leave the last analytic hour by giving the anlayst a kiss or a businesslike handshake. He remembered that now. (The patient had thus alluded, in the opening phase of the treatment, to his characterological coolness, guardedness, and distancing and to his goal for himself—to be able to "warm up.") He continued, "I won't think about how I'm going to say goodbye to you. I'll stick around for a while. I know I'm not open, but maybe it's not hopeless." Feeling that she was on the right track, the analyst began to amplify with a variation on the interpretation and beginning genetic reconstruction of the transference and resistance, and she said, "You guard yourself but you're still watching and listening out of the corner of your eye [the mixed metaphor in the clinical situation was intended] for the kind of responses you originally hoped for so much. For example, you're listening to see if I chuckle at one of your jokes; or if I show some recognition and appreciation of your latest work."[1] Then, as an afterthought, she added a speculation about the nature of the selfobject transference, "I don't know the specifics of exactly what you wanted originally from your mother or from your father. You let so little of that show with me. [Subsequently the analyst realized she was partially in error. The patient

---

[1]Like most provisional analytic interpretations, this one was incomplete until considerably later. The patient was listening and looking to see if the analyst-selfobject was lively and undepressed and could enjoy him so that he could come to fully enjoy himself; he was looking to see if she was enthusiastic and animated so that he himself could come to feel animated and express enthusiasm. He listened at other times to see if the analyst-father was together, effectual, instead of dilapidated and disorganized, in order to look up enthusiastically to a self-esteem–enhancing ideal that would uplift him and cure his depression.

did not defensively guard himself from remembering. He "enacted" his childhood needs, in a new version, precisely because *he actually did not and could not remember.*] I wonder if what you specifically wanted from your mother was for her to play with you, to think you were cute and funny. Perhaps when you were a little boy you wanted her to react to your manliness."

There was a silence. In the pause that followed (i.e., in what Sander calls the "open space"), a single tear rolled down the patient's cheek. In a choked voice he said, "I didn't know I was a man till I was 20." It was at this point in the reestablished developmental dialogue that his thoughts turned to his son Ted. For a moment he griped about having to get up with him. In a still choked voice, which little by little began to loosen up and get warmer, louder, and firmer, he said, "I say to Ted, 'Ted, you're so squeezable; this cute little ass, it's so perfect.' [This is people language for the merger between the child's grandiose exhibitionistic self and the parent as mirroring selfobject.] And then when I pee he has to run in there and pee with me." [The latter is people language for the merger between the self and the selfobject as twin, alter ego, and/or partner.] He continued with pride, "And he runs up to Liz [Ted's mother] and says to her, 'Do squeezes.'" The patient spread out his arms to show how Ted hugs his mother and is hugged by her. [Finally, this is people language for the mutual joy of parents and child engaged in an expectable oedipal phase.] Then Mr. G sobered. His thoughts had wandered to a pregnant teen-ager he saw in Family Court. "At 8," he said, "she ran up to her new stepfather after he married her mother and said, 'Dad, Dad!' [He imitated a child's exuberance.] He turned on her angrily and said, 'Don't call me Dad—I'm your stepfather.'" Sounding depressed, he added, "Now she falls madly in love with older boys who take her to bed . . ."

I think that the concept of the selfobject and the idea of the self-selfobject merger between the child and the parents as expectable psychological environment is the concept of the child-parent relationship Stern is looking for. I hope that the encounter between analyst and patient, father and son, begins to demonstrate that the self-selfobject tie or merger is a multifaceted, complex mental configuration in depth and that the psychic reality of the tie can be the child's own feeling of his cuteness, manliness, lovableness, capacity for loving, and so forth. Although the relationship between the young infant and the parents differs in *contents,* their psychological (nonverbal, preverbal) dialogue is not dissimilar. Their tie does not start with an experience of infantile self and object fused, undifferentiated, without boundaries. Further, an expectable tie does not involve isolated libidinal and aggressive drives (e.g., an isolated anal-sadistic drive) seeking peremptory discharge on parents as split-up (body-part) drive objects. The normal tie involves the totality of the child's self, a child who offers himself to the participating parent. The drive and drive experience is normally part of the totality: From early on the child offers himself to his parents, and from early on he expects them to be an alive, appreciative, participating audience to his display. Similarly, he looks up to and reaches up to the parents on high, and in short order he expects them to lift him up, to lend him their calmness and strength. From early on he wants to be side by side with them. The parents' pride and pleasure in response to his display, their comforting care, their company, and their participation with him in an infinite number of ways produce the firming, strengthening, confirming, approving capacities that the child needs to acquire for himself in order to be a reasonably together, self-affirming self. These are the capacities the patient was referring to when he said he did not know he was a man until 20, and which he needed to acquire to feel he was a real man.

The clinical vignette of the dialogue between analyst and patient, father and son, touches on almost every aspect of psychoanalytic theory which bears on the normality and pathology of the self and on the psychoanalytic treatment and psychotherapy of self-disorders. In particular, the patient's in-depth response to the analyst's guess that he needed to be enjoyed as a little boy and his joyous response to his son's "becoming a man" touches on our thinking about the classical view of phase-specific psychosexual development and normative psychosexual conflict. It seems to me that it would be fair to say that there is considerable agreement between the developmental psychologists and the self psychologists on the critical and central feature of early childhood development, namely, the fitting together, mutual empathy, and reciprocal regulations of child and parents. Where prevailing conflict theories assign a central role to a series of nuclear conflicts, including an anal-sadistic conflict, our findings point instead to the centrality of the shared pride and pleasure in phase-specific developmental steps and proudly undertaken achievements such as sphincter control. From this perspective the anal-sadistic conflict of classical theory is a disintegration or breakup of the normal self-selfobject configuration of the second and third year of life. Its persistence is the result of a chronic, continuing breakup of the kinds of in-phase experiences the patient was vicariously sharing with his small son and the analyst, his own reactivated selfobject audience.

The clinical vignette also touches on important questions about the normality and pathology of the oedipal stage and the typical oedipal conflict postulated by classical psychoanalytic theory. The phallic-sadistic conflict that has been regarded as central in the child's psychic reality is also a breakup of the normal connectedness of child and parents, and it is in marked contrast to the child's expectable in-phase feeling that he is adequately equipped, that he has what it takes. Fitted together with reasonably responsive self-objects, he can take inevitable, phase-specific disappointments and injuries including oedipal disappointments and injuries; and he can negotiate the stages of his development, from the beginning on, with the psychological experience of competence and effectiveness developmental psychologists describe, and with the inner experience we describe as his feeling that he is a power to be reckoned with, that he has the wherewithal to get where he wants to go, to reach what he is going after. (Again, it needs to be borne in mind that the child's experience of feeling that he himself is adequately equipped and that he is equipped to deal with his universe depends largely on his having phase-adequate control over his selfobjects.) Further, the clinical vignette on the patient's selfobject transference and "becoming a man" touches broadly on the normality and pathology of the small child's protosocial capacities (Emde, 1981), that is, on the capacity for "warmth," mutuality, sociability, affection, friendliness, and so forth. In my view the genesis and pathogenesis of these capacities, as well as of capacities to be self-righting, to reorganize, to recover from injury, are to be found in the vicissitudes of self and selfobjects rather than in the vicissitudes of instincts and their objects and/or in the so-called autonomous conflict-free sectors of the personality. (Very little is truly autonomous in infants—their "autonomy," initiative, organized center, etc. depends on the intactness of the unit established by the reciprocal psychological tie with the parents.)

All of the foregoing topics need to be pursued further, and they all call attention to the need for a changing metapsychology which actually accords with our emphasis on the centrality of self-cohesion and of threatened self-cohesion. Freud's (1914) "bad witch" of metapsychology is out of favor presently, in my opinion, because Freud and others like Hartmann (1939) called on theory to take the place of clinical and developmental discoveries that were needed to understand and treat disorders of the self. I illustrated this point briefly in connection with Kohut's earlier erroneous idea of isolated self-nuclei. This idea proved to be no more than the superstructure, the scaffolding, of self psychology in its own beginnings. The theory of a normal stage of self-fragmentation, of isolated nuclei later undergoing coalescence into a whole, was influenced by the prevailing idea of an undifferentiated, autoerotic, objectless baby. Thus, like Freud in 1914, Kohut started out with the theory that the baby is at first in (autoerotic) bits and pieces and that developmental "progression" consists of the bits and pieces coming together. The idea of a normal stage of isolated parts and part functions is not consistent with his own views on the function of the selfobject, even as he first elaborated these views in *The Analysis of the Self*. This is a good example of how "bad" metapsychology can influence clinical-developmental theory. It should be the other way around: "Good" metapsychology should be an outgrowth of clinical-developmental findings and theory. For the future, then, we need an updated metapsychology of the self-selfobject unit, of threatened self-cohesion, of reorganization and recovery. This metapsychology has to start by taking the psychic relationship of self-selfobject as a unit in its own right, a unit with its own course of normal and abnormal development over the life cycle, its own functions and fate. (For example, cf. Tolpin, 1971, for the eventual fate of the early childhood selfobjects as soothing, organizing, anxiety-regulating *endopsychic structures*.)

What I really want to say is that the competent baby and Kohut's cohesive baby are made for each other. I think that analysts like Sander and Stern, and an entire generation of developmental psychologists like Demos who have described the competent baby, are mapping out the gross anatomy, histology, and embryology, as it were, of the normal self-selfobject unit of infancy and the early years in the dimension of its observable interpersonal reality. During the past decade and a half, Kohut and his collaborators have been exploring the chemistry, physiology, and pathophysiology, as it were, of this unit in its new transference editions (i.e., in its depth-psychological dimensions as these are revived in a reengaged developmental process). The past decade and a half actually comes close to being an analytic era, long enough to begin to test out a new theory and to begin the inevitable analytic work of theory revision and correction. In my view this has been an analytic era in decisive transition from id and ego psychology to psychoanalytic self psychology (cf. Tolpin, 1980 for a discussion of the earlier self-theories which remained theories of archaic psychic conflicts). Ego psychology with its emphasis on the vicissitudes of instincts and their early objects, ego autonomy, and ego defect left the clinical field of psychoanalysis with the unsolved problem of anxiety, depression, and rage, which went beyond the explanatory limits of structural conflict theory. Self psychology with its emphasis on the intrapsychic vicissitudes of the self and childhood selfobjects has made headway with precisely this problem by recognizing the pathogenetic origins of chronic *disintegration anxiety,* depletion-depression, and rage in faulty and/or failing self-selfobject units. Our further analytic investigations of the problem of disintegration anxiety face us with more problems for investigation, such as the problem of self-organization and reorganization, of disintegration and capacities for reintegration, of injury and capacities for recovery.

In point of fact, self psychology and developmental psychology are concerned with the problem of the "mysterious knot" of the personality that binds isolated parts into a whole unit (cf. Eissler, 1953; Tolpin, 1971). Analysts have been able to learn a great deal more about this knot or organizing-organized center (Emde, 1981) by conceptualizing the locking into place of the nuclear self with all of its species-specific, constitutional, genetic givens and its basic *psychological* constituents. The basic psychological constituents of the nuclear self are: (1) the grandiose exhibitionistic self—the child saying, as it were, "Look ma, no hands!" and looking to his parents for their "gleam" and return smile; (2) the idealizing self—the child looking up to and reaching up to the parents, to be lifted up, calmed down, and perked up so that he can recover and begin again with some enthusiasm to look around to see where the action is; (3) the "partnering" self—the child who wants to hold hands with the parents, be with them, be like them (like the patient's small son who "peed" when he did).

The striking resemblance between the brainchildren of our two fields is due to a very simple fact: The starting point of developmental psychology and self psychology is the smallest, indivisible psychological unit—the unit of child and expectable parental environment. Both fields have taken Hartmann's (1939) idea of "fitting together" seriously, the fitting together of the child with his or her givens and the parents with their givens. The starting point of developmental-clinical theory thus makes a psychological world of difference. If we start with the drives and their archaic objects as the smallest unit, psychoanalysis ends up with a totally different vision of psychic reality (Schafer, 1970) than if we start with the child-parent unit. The reality of the one is the "split-up" baby, the small child and later the adult patient split by archaic, pre-oedipal conflict who "progresses" via conflict resolution to the construction of a whole object and whole self. The reality of the other is the child and later the adult patient (with treatable self-pathology) who starts out with a whole (cohesive) self and whole (self)objects and "progresses" in two interrelated ways: through the maintenance and restoration of the cohesive state; and through the lengthy process of gradually taking over for oneself where the selfobjects inevitably begin to leave off.

Clearly, both fields have a great deal more to map out, explore, and discover. In the meantime, there is an impressive coming together of the work of developmental psychology and psychoanalytic self psychology, with the concept of the self-selfobject unit serving as a theoretical bridge between the interpersonal reality of the attachment and reciprocal exchanges that make for the competent baby, and the inner psychic reality of psychological connectedness that makes for the organized-organizing center, which is the nuclear self of Kohut's baby. There is every reason to anticipate the continued coming together of our respective baby's futures, as well as our coming together again for further advances and further reflections on the self and its psychology.

REFERENCES

Bowlby, J. (1969). *Attachment and Loss, Vol. 1: Attachment.* New York: Basic Books.
Bruner, J. S. (1973). *Beyond the Information Given.* New York: Norton.
Eissler, K. R. (1953). The effect of the structure of the ego on psychoanalytic technique. *J. Amer. Psychoanal. Assn.* 1: 104–143.
Emde, R. N. (1981). Changing models of infancy and the nature of early development: Remodeling the foundation. *J. Amer. Psychoanal. Assn.* 29: 179–219.
Freud, S. (1914). On narcissism. *S.E.* 14: 69–102. London: Hogarth, 1957.
Glover, E. (1943). The concept of dissociation. In *On the Early Development of the Mind,* New York: Int. Univ. Press, 1956, pp. 307–327.

Hartmann, H. (1939). *Ego Psychology and the Problem of Adaptation*. New York: Int. Univ. Press, 1958.

Kohut, H. (1971). *The Analysis of the Self*. New York: Int. Univ. Press.

_____ (1977). *The Restoration of the Self*. New York: Int. Univ. Press.

_____ (1978). Remarks about the formation of the self. In *The Search for the Self, Vol. 2*, P. H. Ornstein, ed. pp. 737–770. New York: Int. Univ. Press.

Schafer, R. (1970). The psychoanalytic vision of reality. *Int. J. Psychoanal.* 51: 279–298.

Spitz, R. A. (1965). *The First Year of Life*. New York: Int. Univ. Press.

Stone, J. L., Smith, H. T., & Murphy, L. B., eds. (1972). *The Competent Infant*. New York: Basic Books.

Tolpin, M. (1971). On the beginnings of a cohesive self. *Psychoanal. Study Child* 26: 316–352.

_____ (1977). Self-objects and Oedipal objects—A crucial developmental distinction. *Psychoanal. Study Child* 33: 167–184.

_____ (1980). Discussion of "Psychoanalytic Developmental Theories of the Self: An Integration" by Morton Shane and Estelle Shane. In *Advances in Self Psychology*, A. Goldberg, ed., pp. 47–68. New York: Int. Univ. Press.

_____ & Kohut, H. (1980). The disorders of the self: The psychopathology of the first years of life. In *The Course of Life, Vol. 1: Infancy and Early Childhood*, S. I. Greenspan & G. H. Pollock, eds. pp. 425–442. Washington, D.C.: U.S. Government Printing Office.

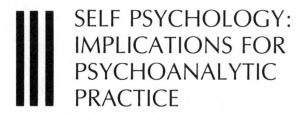

III SELF PSYCHOLOGY: IMPLICATIONS FOR PSYCHOANALYTIC PRACTICE

11 Self Psychology: Clinical Considerations

David A. Berkowitz, M.D.

Still in the process of evolution, the conceptual contributions of self psychology have already exerted a major influence on psychoanalysis. The proliferation of related literature since Heinz Kohut's early work attests to the widespread interest in and relevance of this work to clinical practice. I mention only a few of those writings, which provide a broader context for the papers in this section. The evolution of the theoretical and clinical contributions of self psychology has been traced in detail by Paul Ornstein in his introduction to Kohut's *The Search for the Self* (1978). Some of the basic concepts of self psychology have been briefly summarized by Kohut and Wolf (1978). There are numerous presentations of clinical material throughout Kohut's own writings, including, especially, the now well-known case of Mr. Z (1979). Finally, the *Casebook* edited by Arnold Goldberg (1978) presents comprehensive, detailed case reports of analyses conducted from the vantage point of self psychology.

In this section the implications of self psychology for clinical practice are taken even further. In an illuminating paper Joseph Lichtenberg utilizes cross-sectional fragments of an analysis to present a clinical application of the self psychological viewpoint. In a clear and concise manner he spells out six principles of psychoanalytic technique, starting with the fundamental centrality of the empathic vantage point for analytic observation and culminating in a comprehensive, systematic sequence for psychoanalytic interpretation. Anna Ornstein's contribution demonstrates the continuing evolution of self psychology. She attempts to move beyond earlier firm distinctions between the classical transference neuroses and the analyzable narcissistic disorders by presenting a case report of an analysis of a patient whose oedipal psychopathology is viewed as related to selfobject failures. Each paper is followed by thoughtful, searching, challenging, and at times critical discussion from the standpoints of ego psychology, object relations theory, and classical drive conflict psychology. As background for these papers and the discussion and debate that follow them, I would like to review briefly some central concepts of self psychology relevant to clinical psychoanalysis along with some of the issues they have raised for clinical practice.

The pivotal concept in self psychology is the "selfobject," an object that is psychologically experienced as part of the self rather than being perceived as separate and independent and/or used in the service of the self and the maintenance of self-esteem (Kohut, 1971). The self thus expects to exercise control over selfobjects as over a body part. The notion of the self-selfobject unit refers to the manner in which the infant and small child whose self is not yet fully cohesive and self-regulating utilizes parental figures in his or her environment to provide externally certain functions that cannot yet be performed endopsychically. Provision of these functions, including soothing, anxiety reduction, and self-esteem regulation, enable children through the gradual internalization of psychic structure to progressively provide these for themselves from internal sources.

With average expectable care, during the second year of life a nuclear "bipolar self" emerges consisting of rudimentary ambitions and rudimentary ideals. In Kohut's (1977) view the child has two chances to establish the firmness of this early bipolar self. The first opportunity is through an approving, confirming, mirroring relationship with a maternal selfobject; the second opportunity is through a relationship with an admired, idealized, usually paternal selfobject.

The responsiveness of selfobjects is viewed as important throughout childhood, and self psychology's view of the oedipal phase is of particular relevance to Anna Ornstein's paper. Briefly, Kohut (1977) suggested that the child's oedipal experience is colored by the empathic or unempathic responses from his selfobjects. He described the optimal parental reaction to the assertive-competitive rivalry of the oedipal child as one of pleasure and pride in the child's vigor, assertiveness, and developmental achievement. In her paper Anna Ornstein challenges the traditional view of the negative Oedipus complex, that idealizing needs coupled with sexualization represent a retreat from the infantile sexual longing for the mother and competitive, murderous wishes toward the father. She suggests that rather than representing a defensive regression, combined idealized and erotized transference phenomena may be reconceptualized as a revival of intense, thwarted developmental needs to be merged with and admired by the same-sexed parent. In her discussion Helen Meyers raises cogent questions about these formulations and reviews alternative possibilities for understanding the clinical material.

Self psychology thus emphasizes a conceptual shift toward a focus on maturational failure with a developmental deficit arising from thwarted growth. "Missing psychic structure" refers to missing capacities of the self arising from less than adequate early developmental experiences with primary selfobjects. According to self psychology the specific needs that had remained unresponded to due to specific faulty interactions between the early self and its selfobjects are reactivated in the selfobject transferences. This may take the predominant form of wishing for mirroring confirmation or of an idealizing transference in which the patient needs to merge with or maintain continuous attachment to an idealized, omnipotent object in order to support his or her self-esteem. Thus, where the early self-selfobject relationships have been traumatically disillusioning or disappointing, the selfobject transference that is formed in the later therapeutic relationship appears to glue a vulnerable and fragmentation-prone self together.

Once the selfobject transference is established, minute failures of empathy and/or failures to perform the therapist's assigned function—be that mirroring confirmation or serving as an idealizable object—lead to significant disruptions in the transference, with outbursts of narcissistic rage, distrust of the therapist that may border on paranoia, or withdrawal from the therapist into a haughty, cold isolation. The correct understanding and clarification of the matrix in which these disruptions arise, the detailed pinpointing of the events that lead to each disruption, and the acknowledgment of the legitimacy of such feelings within the archaic level of the patient's felt experience result in the reestablishment of the selfobject transference and the dissolution of the patient's narcissistic rage.

The early needs that are revived in the unfolding transferences are not gratified, but are analyzed and interpreted. Contrary to a frequent misunderstanding, self psychology espouses an interpretive psychoanalytic technique. However, the focus of interpretation is not on intersystemic or intrasystemic conflict, but on the effects on the developing childhood self, self-esteem, and psychopathology of the often inevitable failures of the early selfobject environment to meet certain developmental needs of the child optimally. As the child's needs for either an affirming, approving, mirroring selfobject or an idealizable selfobject are revived in the selfobject transferences, the groundwork is laid for a possible construction of the ways in which, for example, the early maternal selfobject failed to support the development of the patient's self-esteem and a cohesive self by failing to fulfill a mirroring function, and/or the ways in which the later paternal selfobject was too disillusioning to provide a strong, idealizable selfobject that might have supported the patient's self-esteem and development of a cohesive self during a later phase of development. Because the patient's original complaint, now reinstated in the transference, is understood as valid within that early context, concepts such as "narcissistic entitlement" (Murray, 1964) and some forms of "acting out" may no longer be as meaningful given this frame of reference (Berkowitz, 1977).

It should be emphasized that responses to perceived failures in empathy are interpreted. Empathic failure does not necessarily mean that an actual mistake has been made by the analyst that needs to be confessed or rectified. It means that something the patient perceived or experienced within the therapeutic relationship, in the analyst's activity or nonactivity, contributed to evoking the patient's response or transference manifestation. Through pursuing the reactions to felt empathic failures, the analyst gains further insight into the patient's psychological experience of his or her early milieu.

An important implication of such an understanding is that what was formerly often relegated to "resistance" no longer can be classified as such without a careful scrutiny and exhaustive search of the patient-analyst interaction for possible precipitants. If the patient's activity, such as silences or outbursts of rage, is viewed outside the context of the patient-analyst relationship, it may not be appreciated as an appropriate reaction to failures of the analyst's empathy. In a related vein the concept of the "negative therapeutic reaction," a therapeutic impasse usually attributed to an unconscious sense of guilt in the patient, has been questioned in light of self psychology (Bacal, 1979; Brandchaft, 1979; Stolorow, Atwood, & Lachmann, 1981). The issues of resistance and the negative therapeutic reaction both call attention to an extremely important differential diagnosis in stalemated treatments.

A reexamination of the traditional view of the therapeutic alliance in light of these newer conceptual developments is implicit in some recent literature (Adler, 1979, 1980; Gutheil & Havens, 1979). Adler has suggested that Kohut's concept of the selfobject transference may be the element that supports the successful engagement of a patient in the therapeutic process. He questions whether a therapeutic alliance exists with more disturbed patients or whether primitive stable selfobject transferences themselves allow the patient to be sustained in the treatment. If the patient at some level or early in the treatment needs the therapist to function as an extension of himself—as a stabilizing, self-soothing psychic structure that he needs to have under his control in order to provide cohesion to his self—then at that level the patient may be unable to feel sufficiently whole and separate to join forces spontaneously with the therapist in what would be regarded, in Sterba's (1934) sense, as a "rational" therapeutic alliance. To expect the patient to manifest an observing ego stance or the capacity for a rational therapeutic alliance at the beginning of treatment may be felt as critical and may further damage the patient's already precarious self-esteem and therefore be destructive to the gradual emergence of a true alliance (Berkowitz, 1982).

Finally, it may be readily apparent from the foregoing that self psychology places a special emphasis on empathy or vicarious introspection (Kohut, 1971) for data gathering in the psychoanalytic process. Empathy does not mean sympathy or support. Rather, it refers to a specific vantage point for listening. As a mode of listening, the empathic position has been recently elaborated by Schwaber (1979) and is further developed here by Lichtenberg. In brief, such a position requires that analysts place themselves in the patient's shoes, as it were, and try to see events and feelings through the eyes of the patient at however regressed the level the patient may be perceiving and experiencing. The listener seeks to hear from the perspective of the subject. In the view of self psychology the subjective-empathic position stands in significant contrast to the objective-observational position in which behavior is observed from the outside, as it were, and inferences made from these observations are interpreted. Seen from this vantage point, original traumatic empathic failures may be repeated when the analyst superimposes from an objective position theoretical preconceptions on the patient's material. For example, interpreting the patient's anxiety over a tentative, forward developmental step as a regressive retreat from oedipal conflict and the transference neurosis may result in the patient's superficial compliance. However, closer examination of the patient's response may reveal a deeper upset, which rather than representing a confirmation of a correct interpretation, may indicate that the patient felt misunderstood. As a mode of listening, the empathic vantage point would therefore seem to provide an important stance for listening to all the patient's material, be it self-selfobject relationships and "self-states"[1] or object-related instinctual conflict, or be it selfobject transference or transference neurosis. In his discussion, Ernest Wolf further elaborates Lichtenberg's technical principles and relates Lichtenberg's central position of empathy to Kohut's view of psychological health and the curative process in analysis. In his discussion of Lichtenberg's paper, N. Treurniet raises important questions regarding the role of both the subjective and objective vantage points in analysis as well as the limitations of empathy.

REFERENCES

Adler, G. (1979). The myth of the alliance with borderline patients. *Amer. J. Psychiat.* 136: 642–645.

———— (1980). Transference, real relationship and alliance. *Int. J. Psychoanal.* 61: 547–558.

Bacal, H. (1979). *Empathic lag in the analyst and its relation to 'negative therapeutic reaction.'* Unpublished manuscript.

Berkowitz, D. (1977). The vulnerability of the grandiose self and the psychotherapy of acting out patients. *Int. Rev. Psychoanal.* 4: 13–22.

———— (1982). Implications of the selfobject concept for the therapeutic alliance. *Hillside J. Clinical Psychiat.* 4: 15–24.

---

[1]See Kohut's concluding remarks in this volume for a discussion of the self-state dream in Anna Ornstein's case report.

Brandchaft, B. (1979). Negativism, the negative therapeutic reaction and self psy-
    chology. In A. Goldberg, ed. *The Future of Psychoanalysis*. New York: Int. Univ.
    Press.
Goldberg, A., ed. (1978). *Self Psychology: A Casebook*. New York: Int. Univ. Press.
Gutheil, T. & Havens, L. (1979). The therapeutic alliance: Contemporary meanings
    and confusions. *Int. Rev. Psychoanal*. 6: 467–481.
Kohut, H. (1971). *The Analysis of the Self*. New York: Int. Univ. Press.
—————— (1977). *The Restoration of the Self*. New York: Int. Univ. Press.
—————— (1978). *The Search for the Self*, P. Ornstein, ed. New York: Int. Univ. Press.
—————— (1979). The two analyses of Mr. Z. *Int. J. Psychoanal*. 60: 3–27.
—————— & Wolf, E. (1978). Disorders of the self: An outline. *Int. J. Psychoanal*. 60:
    413–425.
Murray, J. (1964). Narcissism and the ego ideal. *J. Amer. Psychoanal. Assn*. 12:
    477–511.
Schwaber, E. (1979). On the 'self' within the matrix of analytic theory—Some clini-
    cal reflections and reconsiderations. *Int. J. Psychoanal*. 60: 467–479.
Sterba, R. (1934). The fate of the ego in analytic therapy. *Int. J. Psychoanal*. 15:
    117–126.
Stolorow, R., Atwood, G., & Lachmann, F. (1981). Transference and coun-
    tertransference in the analysis of developmental arrests. *Bull. Menning. Clin*. 45:
    20–28.

12 An Idealizing Transference of the Oedipal Phase

Anna Ornstein, M.D.

INTRODUCTION

The development of psychoanalysis as a science of depth psychology depends on the continued interaction between clinical observation and the development of new theories that provide, at a particular time in the history of psychoanalysis, optimal tools for the explanation of what can be empathically understood about our patients. Once we are committed to a particular theory, that theory helps us in the organization of our clinical data in a fairly consistent manner.

The change in Kohut's conceptualization from the self as a content of the mental apparatus (1971) to the concept of the bipolar self as a supraordinate constellation (1977) has made it necessary for us to rethink and reformulate various theoretical and technical aspects of psychoanalysis. A similar reformulation was made necessary by Freud himself when he advanced the structural-tripartite model of the mind over the topographic model.

In terms of the theory of the bipolar self, this need to reexamine well-accepted propositions of classical theory becomes particularly obvious when questions are raised regarding the position of the Oedipus complex in self psychology. Examples of such questions are: Where do sexual identifications and sexual conflicts fit into self psychology? Because self psychology emphasizes the self-selfobject matrix in development, do parents continue to have selfobject func-

tions during the oedipal phase and what is the nature of the transferences that arise in relationship to their failure?

These questions require thorough and careful answers, answers
that will come from the contributions of analysts who are willing to
examine and reexamine the clinical and theoretical implications of
all forms of transferences, be these oedipal or pre-oedipal in their
origin and manifestations. My task in this paper has to be limited in
scope, but I hope it represents a modest attempt to establish a clinical context in which the aforementioned questions can be more felic-
itously examined.

The emphasis here on the clinical context has to be emphasized
because, I believe, that efforts at "integrating" the findings of self
psychology with those of classical theory may not be as readily possible as appears desirable. In relation to the Oedipus complex, for
example, we have to consider that the understanding and explanation of the Oedipus complex has been traditionally derived from a
theoretical frame of reference that differs from self psychology in its
basic assumptions. Every aspect of the oedipal experience, the
child's readiness to enter this phase, the actual experiencing of the
oedipal passions themselves, and the resolution of the conflicts associated with them have been theoretically tied to the appearance of
phase-specific unconscious *fantasies,* which are related to the maturation of the sexual and aggressive drives. In classical theory the
developmental significance of the parents' personalities has been
limited to the last subphase of the Oedipus complex, namely, to the
identification with the homogenital parent. During the oedipal engagement itself, when oedipal passions run high, the homogenital
parent is expected to be experienced only in terms of conflicts emanating from drive-determined rivalrous and hostile feelings. In relationship to Little Hans, for example, Freud (1909) comments that
though Hans loved his father whom "he had always loved and was
bound to go on loving, who had been his model, had been his first
playmate, and had looked after him from his earliest infancy, it was
this father whom he could not help hating as a rival. . . . For Hans'
nature had so developed that for the moment his love could not keep
the upper hand and suppress his hate [p. 134]." The parents' *actual*
attitude and behavior toward the child during this phase of development is expected to become negated under the impact of the drive-
dominated fantasies.

Viewing the Oedipus complex in light of the theory of the bipolar self, on the other hand, we would have to say that the oedipal phase, similar to other developmental experiences, can only be fully understood when viewed within the context of the child's emotional milieu. According to Kohut (1977): "As was true with regard to earlier phases of development, the child's experiences during the oedipal phase become understandable only when they are considered within the matrix of the empathic, partially empathic or unempathic responses from the side of the selfobject aspects of the environment [p. 230]." In terms of the task in this presentation, Kohut's proposition means that in order to begin a meaningful integration of the two theoretical positions we first have to reexamine the nature of the oedipal transferences themselves. Should we be able to demonstrate the presence of oedipal selfobject transferences (transferences that arise in relation to parental failure to have optimally responded to the oedipal-age child), we would have established the clinical context in which we can more meaningfully examine the theoretical questions raised regarding the relation between self psychology and the Oedipus complex.

In the following, I describe a particular feature of a transference in which a male patient had developed a persistent wish to experience his female analyst as if she were a strong man. The patient felt that without being able to idealize the analyst as if she were a man, who in turn, would respect and admire him, his analysis would not be complete.

THE EMERGENCE OF THE IDEALIZING TRANSFERENCE

The wish to idealize the analyst as if she were a man emerged after a pathognomonic regression had established itself, and many of the conflicts related to his mother have been worked through. This occurred in the second phase of the analysis in which there was an "overlap" of the working through of the conflicts related to the mother and an increased intensity in the longing for a strong father.

The transference affects related to his father emerged against a great deal more resistance than those related to his mother. The anger and disappointment not only threatened the patient's tender and loving feelings toward the man who was his primary caregiver, but more importantly, it threatened a vital connection with his father that has been established through a massive and gross identification with him. The content of this identification was a chronic, "futureless" depression and a deep conviction that in every way, he will repeat his father's life. With the development of the father-related transference, it had become clear that this identification (a gross identification that was not "depersonalized") had been warding off a deficit in the self, a deficit related to the failure on the part of the father to have recognized and empathically responded to the selfobject needs of the oedipal-age child.[1]

The patient had now regretted having chosen a female analyst. The anger at himself for this choice alternated with anger at the therapist for being a woman. At about the same time, the patient's dreams and associations began to concern themselves with homosexuality. He dreamt about "pretty boys," blond and smooth-skinned, "the kind homosexuals find attractive." The patient felt that these boys represented a part of himself; the part that he wanted to get rid of. He was scared of the implications of the dreams and that he still enjoyed the company of his male friends, and that he felt more enhanced by them than when he spent time with his female friends.

---

[1]The important difference between identification and the building up of psychic structures as this occurs through transmuting internalization when the growing child's selfobject needs are met phase appropriately cannot be detailed in this paper. The reader is only reminded that historically the building up of psychic structures has always been conceptualized in psychoanalysis as a form of internalization, and that identification is one way in which the psychological characteristics of one person are "taken in" and become part of another. When this form of internalization does not become transmuted but the features of "the other" remain grossly unaltered in the self, then, I believe, they constitute defensive rather than primary psychological structures (Kohut, 1977). These defensive psychological structures in the form of gross identifications serve the function of securing a bond, a reliable connection between the child and the parent who, because of his preoccupations, is unable to perceive and respond empathically to the growing child's legitimate developmental selfobject needs. I am here referring to what Winnicott (1967) described as a defensive identification or "impingement" that occurs when the mother, because of her preoccupations, is unable "to mirror" the infant. The infant, under these circumstances, joins the mother in her internal state rather than risk losing the mother all together. Putting it another way, we would say that a parent's inability to tune empathically into the growing child's internal state represents a challenge for the infant or child to tune into that of the parent in order to avoid the severance of the all-important selfobject tie.

The analyst's theoretical outlook, which guided her interpretations, viewed the sexual elements in the dreams as well as the patient's associations that being with his male friends had enhanced him more than being with his girlfriend as the expression of the erotized longing to be enhanced by the strength and power that he had attributed to his (idealized) male friends. Contemptuous of the effeminate features in his own personality, he expected to be cured of these by being close to and admired by his male friends. This was the essence of his wish to experience his female analyst as if she were a strong male.

Putting the need to be merged with and admired by his idealized male friends and the erotization of the longing to be close to them into self-psychological perspective, I considered this phenomenon to be related to the disappointments he suffered in his father during the oedipal phase of his development. Kohut (1971), in his discussion of the idealizing transferences, distinguished between oedipal and pre-oedipal forms of idealization:

> The internalization of the narcissistic aspects of the child's relationship to the oedipal parent[2] leads to the narcissistic dimensions of the superego . . . ; the internalization of the narcissistic aspects account for *the exalted position* which these contents and functions have vis-à-vis the ego. It is from their idealization—that the specific and characteristic aura of absolute perfection of the values and standards of the superego are derived; and the omniscience and might of the whole structure are also due to the fact that it is partly invested with narcissistic, idealizing libido [pp. 41–42; italics added].

I believe that the idealization of the superego as this occurs during the oedipal phase of development is better conceptualized in terms of the selfobject functions that the parents of a child of this developmental phase are expected to provide, than when the idealization is viewed as a defense against oedipal competition and hostility. This statement can only be substantiated with clinical data, specifically, by demonstrating that traumatic disappointments in the homogenital parent during the oedipal phase of development have pathogenic significance and that the pathology that develops under these circumstances is that of a discrete deficit in the pole of

---

[2]Today Kohut would refer to this relationship as the oedipal selfobject tie.

ideals in the bipolar self. The disappointments in the homogenital parent have special pathogenic significance because it is at this phase of development that the ideals of the bipolar self become "the carriers" of gender-linked values and standards such as "masculine" strength and self-assertiveness and "feminine" beauty and the capacity to nurture.

It could be argued that the appearance of idealizing needs that are coupled with sexualization represent the negative Oedipus complex in the transference, a retreat from the infantile sexual longing for the mother and competition and murderous wishes toward the father. The negative Oedipus complex has been viewed traditionally as a pathological constellation when it becomes manifest in the transference. In contrast, in the course of normal development, this phenomenon has been linked to the fate of archaic narcissism. (Blos, 1979: "The negative oedipal attachment is a narcissistic object tie.") I believe that this contradiction between the interpretations of the meaning of the transference phenomenon in which idealization and erotization are combined can now be understood as an intense (therefore, sexualized) need to be merged with and to be admired by the parent of the same sex. I am suggesting that what has traditionally been described as "the negative Oedipus complex" in the transference can now be recognized as an effort to resume psychological development at that phase when the child through phase-appropriate mirroring by the idealized homogenital parent acquires pride and pleasure in his own masculine strength or her own feminine beauty and nurturance. Therefore, when, in the transference, the experiential content is either a longing for sexual closeness with the homogenital parent or when the longing appears as "latent homosexuality" in dreams and associations, or when these affects are defended against with an exaggerated emphasis of the positive oedipal affects, the erotization under these circumstances represents *the intensity* of the longing to be united with and to be mirrored by the idealized homogenital parent.

The interpretation and working through of the fear of homosexuality produced further memories about his father most of which represented disappointment in him; the most traumatic disappointments related to his father's inability to stand up to his mother who would berate and belittle him.

The transference wish that the analyst be a strong man who could help him become a man different from his father, was particularly well expressed in a dream in which he wanted to fly but the airplane wasn't perfect. The pilot was brilliant but physically unable to handle the plane. Associating to the dream made him sad and irritated with himself: "But it isn't you but me who is the inadequate one. The inability to look up to you is my flaw, not yours." He stopped and added: "Still I would kill you, not me."

Just as in relation to the idealization and sexualization the analyst's theoretical outlook affected her interpretations, so was her understanding relative to the source of the patient's anger at her affected by her self-psychological frame of reference. In relationship to the anger, the question that had to be raised was this: Was the patient's wish to kill the analyst a revival of the oedipal wish to kill the father because he was big and possessed the mother sexually? Or was the anger related to the child's traumatic disappointment in the father for not being able to look up to him and for not encouraging him for his efforts to be a self-assertive boy?

Here, too, the difference in theoretical views affects the analyst's interventions. If she considered the anger to be the expression of an inadequately sublimated aggressive drive that has been reactivated in relationship to the boy's oedipal struggle with his father, she would have to interpret the memory of the father as a man whom he could not idealize and at times actively humiliated him as the child's *distortion*. She would have to help the patient face his murderous affects of childhood, which would promote the process of identification with the father and the ultimate repression of his incestuous wishes toward his mother. When such murderous wishes expectedly create unconscious conflicts because the child also loves his father, the interpretations would still have to be directed toward the drive-related fantasies that underlie this conflict, so that these can be fully exposed and worked through.

Whether or not the wish to idealize the analyst as if she were a strong male was a defense against oedipal rivalry and hostility or a legitimate developmental need that has been traumatically interfered with, and whether or not the anger at the father was related to this disappointment or represented the poorly sublimated aggressive drive, holds the key to our original question, namely, whether or not we could—on the clinical-theoretical level—recognize the presence of selfobject transferences that relate to the oedipal phase of development. Considering the reactivation of the anger as related to the disappointment in the father focuses our attention more specifically on the pathogenic aspects of the father's responses to the oedipal-age boy's emotional needs. The patient was particularly distressed whenever he witnessed his father's fearful, almost cowardly, response to his mother's demands of him. These disillusioning experiences in his father's masculinity were coupled with the father's inability to be enthusiastically responsive to the patient's interests in matters masculine.

RESOLUTION OF THE IDEALIZING TRANSFERENCE

The successful working through of this phase of the analysis slowly diminished the patient's disappointment that his analyst was not a male. His new perception of her was contained in a fantasy in which he saw her as someone he could "spar" with. He thought that she could not only withstand his challenges but that she would delight in his assertiveness and competitiveness. This change in his perception of her was again represented in a dream in which he engaged the analyst in a boxing match. In the dream he felt free to hit hard and enjoyed the vigor of the interaction. The analyst considered this to be the essence of an idealizing transference related to the oedipal phase: the strong and able father who is delighted with and welcomes his son's oedipal assertiveness and competitiveness.

Now that the patient was more consistently able to experience himself in relationship to his female analyst as "if she were a man," he still had to continue the process of disengagement from his mother. He now had the analytic task to maintain the image of himself as a strong man in light of the expectable swings in his self-perception when the analyst would be transformed in his experience from a strong father into a potentially humiliating or controlling mother.

Whenever he was able to maintain the image of himself in relationship to the analyst as if she were a strong man, the patient experienced a new dimension to his analysis. He always had been a prolific dreamer, but now his dreams (and fantasies) became more colorful, more exciting to him. He also experienced greater freedom in making love and greater joy in a "good argument" with a friend. He had now obviously more fully experienced the developmentally crucial oedipal affects, sexual passion, and rivalry.

The patient began to feel cautiously optimistic that he may be able to overcome his fear that his female analyst won't be able to help him experience himself as a strong and sexually competent male.

There were additional changes in his life outside of the analysis that made him feel hopeful: He stopped smoking, which he had tried to do many times before, and began to exercise more regularly. In the past he had interpreted his inability to stop smoking and live a potentially physically damaging life (such as not eating the right food and not sleeping enough) as his compulsion to relive his father's life by acquiring his illness and dying young.

A further indication of his wish (and increasing ability) to idealize his analyst "as if she were a man" was expressed in a dream in which the analyst was represented as the captain of a ship. The dream also indicated the beginning of a specific concern that he had about termination:

> I was a mate on a ship. The captain wanted to rebuild the inner workings of the ship. We took the boat to a lagoon and undid all the screws holding the hull, the ship together. That made the ship turn over, but it still kept floating—the screws were rusty, some were missing. The boat began to drift. There were two other boats on a collision course. The waves from that affected our ship. But we were able to get the boat back to shore.

The patient associated to the various aspects of the dream separately: The drifting away from the shore made him think of his fear that he may be "stripping" himself away from the analysis prematurely. "Now that I began to idealize you, made you the captain, I don't want to leave. It would feel as if I am drifting without the screws being put back in place. . . ." That all the screws were removed made him think that the analysis for him was an "overhaul"—but for the moment, instead of this making him feel stronger, it made him feel more vulnerable; he needed the analyst (the captain) to help him (the mate) put all the screws back again. The analyst added that his concern that termination may be premature might be related to the premature death of his parents. There was fear of leaving the safety of the analysis (the shore); the waters of the ocean, away from the safety of the shore, still looked forboding and dangerous to him.

In the course of a relatively calm period during which he felt well connected to a now idealized analyst, the patient displayed considerable self-analytic skills. He made keen observations about himself, his friends, and their families that had facilitated his efforts to reconstruct his early childhood experiences with both of his parents. At one time he spoke of the interactions he observed in a young family that he thought faithfully represented what his relationship with his mother must have been like and what it was he longed to experience with his father. The patient was observing a 2½-year-old boy as he was pulling away from his mother's embraces who, he felt, was imposing her hugs and kisses on the child: "I can't stand watching her kiss him. The kisses are not for him, they are for her. . . ." He also sensed that, at the same time, the child had "a desperate longing to be with her" as the boy, while pulling himself away from the mother, "was constantly checking back with her." The fear, however, which he himself felt to be "almost biological," made the move away from mother an absolute necessity.

The patient once observed the same child being caught by his father as he was about to fall off a swing. "What perfect timing!" he said. He thought that the child must have experienced two marvelous affects simultaneously: He could feel *the exhilaration* of swinging all by himself and *the safety* of his father's firm arms as he was caught in midair just in time. "What rejoicing!" referring to the joy that he observed on the face of the father and the son when the child safely landed in his father's arms after accomplishing the feat of swinging all by himself. He thought that he may have experienced something of this sort in his analysis when he analyzed his own dreams with the secure knowledge of the analyst's presence: "But I can also catch myself when you are not there." This made him reflect on his parents in a new way: "I must have been caught by them many times that I can do this now for myself." In terms of the analysis, he thought that the analyst was most helpful when she understood his rage and ambivalence early in the analysis in relationship to his mother, and maybe it was that experience that made him feel that she could now spar with him "as if she were a man."

The patient appreciated anew his choice of a female analyst; the working through of his conflicts related to his mother had made it possible for him not to feel a sense of gratitude and obligation at a time of termination. But now that unexpected affects in relationship to his father were activated in the analysis, termination had taken on an added significance: Leaving the analysis appeared as a final separation from his father as well.

In the past the patient had frequently indicated that to be suffering in small ways (not buying himself proper warm clothing for the winter and not allowing himself small pleasures in other ways) had kept him close to his father: "I have to hold on to my sadness as if this was all I had left of him." Now that he was feeling more active and vigorous (he delighted in his new well-fitting clothes and the prospect of some travels), this change in himself threatened the connection with his father in its least obvious but psychologically most meaningful level, namely, on the level of identification. Feeling better constituted the biggest threat to his connection with his father; being different from him represented the final separation.

As is so frequently the case, it was during the termination phase that the patient was able to recall pleasant memories from his early childhood. He had seen home movies of himself as a child many times, but now he was struck with his own vivaciousness and friendly, outgoing nature as a child of 4 and 5. He thought that he was both girlish and exhibitionistic in these pictures. The "girlish," showoff qualities disturbed him at first, but he could also appreciate that those must have secured him a great deal of attention from his father. This freely exhibitionist, gregarious behavior that characterized his early childhood changed as he was growing older into a withdrawn, depressed adult. The change, as it could now be understood, was related to a massive identification with his father because of traumatic disappointments in him during and after his oedipal phase of development. When the analyst made an interpretation to this effect, the patient cried (this had occurred only once before in the analysis and was also related to his father) and said that this was so painful to him because his father was "so good in so many ways." He wondered what kind of a father he would make and was pleased that his thoughts now turned to the future in a positive way.

DISCUSSION

In my discussion of this clinical vignette I return to the original objective of this presentation, which was to establish a clinical context in which the question of the relationship between self psychology and the Oedipus complex could be meaningfully examined. Not all questions that have to be answered in this respect can be taken up in relationship to a single clinical vignette, especially because in this case, only one aspect of a complex transference constellation was examined. However, I hope I was able to demonstrate that the transference that this patient developed in the second half of the analysis can most productively be viewed as an oedipal selfobject transference. I consider this to have been a selfobject transference because the transference arose in relationship to a deficit in the self, a deficit created by the father's failure to have optimally responded to the developmental needs of the oedipal-age boy.

The objection could be raised that there is no need to postulate the presence of an oedipal selfobject transference, that the patient's need to experience himself as a strong, freely competitive man vis-à-vis his female analyst as if she were a strong male could just as well be related to a wish "to exchange" a pathological identification with his passive and depressed father to a healthy one. However, I do not believe that this was a question of a difference between a "healthy" and a "pathological" identification. Rather, the difference has to be conceptualized as one between structure building as it occurs through the transmuting internalization of phase-appropriate selfobject responses and structure building as it occurs through identification—be this identification "healthy" or "pathological." Psychological structures that develop in relationship to phase-appropriate selfobject responses facilitate the transformation of archaic narcissistic structures because they are in harmony with the child's developmental needs and are specifically "tailored" to that child's unique skills and talents. Identifications, on the other hand, represent a particular form of internalization in which the psychological characteristics of one person are "taken in" and become part of another. In many instances, therefore, identifications may have to be considered either as defensive or as compensatory, rather than as primary psychological structures. In the case of this patient, his depressive mood, his futureless attitude were manifestations of gross identification with his father. This identification "filled in" the deficit in the pole of ideals of the bipolar self and assured a sense of connectedness between himself and his father. I believe his wish to be merged with an idealized man and to be mirrored by such a man was specifically related to the oedipal phase of development because it is during this phase that the growing child's ideals become more specifically gender-linked.

This emphasis on the oedipal-age child's need to be merged with the idealized homogenital parent and to be validated by him raises the question of whether or not patricidal wishes and castration anxiety are part of the *normal* Oedipus complex or whether these phenomena appear in the transference in response to failures in paren-

tal empathy, spacifically related to the oedipal-age child's developmental need to be affirmed in his self-assertiveness, competition,
and growing sexuality. Viewing psychological development as occurring throughout life within the context of a selfobject environment and recognizing that empathic failures of this environment
remain pathogenic not only prior to but during the oedipal phase as
well, we would have to consider that the appearance of patricidal
wishes and castration anxiety are "breakdown products" (Kohut,
1977) as much as are other drive manifestations that appear when
the self is threatened in its cohesion or in its vigor and vitality
(Tolpin, 1979).

In terms of this particular case a further point has to be made. I
believe it was crucial that the analyst recognized the patient's need
to complete a specific developmental task in his analysis. I would
suggest that such a need may not be recognized and responded to by
interpretation if the analyst expects the nature of the transference
to be determined by his or her own gender rather than evolve in
keeping with the patient's intrapsychic, unconscious developmental
needs. In other words when the pathognomonic regression has been
established in relationship to the Oedipus complex, a male patient's
transferences toward a woman analyst do not necessarily evolve in
relationship to his unconscious heterosexual conflicts or in the case
of a male analyst in terms of competition and hostility. This patient's conviction that his analysis could not be complete unless he
experienced himself in relationship to his female analyst as if she
were a strong man expressed "a thwarted need to grow." It was the
recognition of this need and its systematic interpretation that exposed the "father identification" as a defensive psychological structure, an effort to "fill in" the specific deficit in the pole of ideals in
the bipolar self. The improvements in the analysis were signaled by
the patient's increased vigor and aliveness, a fuller and freer experience of his sexual passions, and his anger as well as his competitiveness, all of which were indicative of the increased capacity for joyful
and vigorous experiences with both men and women.

REFERENCES

Blos, P. (1979). Modifications in the classical psychoanalytic model of adolescence. In
    Adolescent Psychiatry, S. Sherman & P. Giovacchini, eds. Chicago: Univ. of Chi-
    cago Press.
Freud, S. (1979). Analysis of a phobia in a five-year old boy. *S.E.V.* X: 3–149.

Kohut, H. (1971). *The Analysis of the Self.* New York: Int. Univ. Press.
———— (1977). *The Restoration of the Self.* New York: Int. Univ. Press.
Tolpin, M. (1978). Self-object and Oedipal object: A crucial developmental distinction. *Psychoanal. Study Child* 33: 167–184.
Winnicott, D. W. (1956). Primary maternal preoccupation. In *Through Pediatrics to Psychoanalysis,* New York: Basic Books, Inc.

13 The Oedipal Complex and Self Psychology: A Discussion of Paper by Dr. Ornstein

Helen Meyers, M.D.

Dr. Ornstein's paper invites us to join her in the exploration of another major step in the development of self psychology. Until now, self psychology concepts seemed to have been offered for understanding the development of self-structure and pathology involving defects in the self prior to the oedipal period with its conflictual pathology. Now self psychology has turned its attention to a reexamination of the Oedipus complex itself, a logical progression. In *The Restoration of the Self* Kohut (1977) asks:

> Could it not be . . . that it is only the self of the child whose self objects are severely out of touch with his newly forward-moving oedipal self, that begins to break apart? . . . That . . . the dramatic, conflict-ridden Oedipus Complex . . . is not a primarily maturational necessity but only the frequent result of frequently occurring failures from the side of narcissistically disturbed parents [p. 247].

And later in his "Reflections" in *Advances in Self Psychology,* Kohut (1980) tentatively asks whether instead of oedipal neurosis and disorders of the self, one might not talk of oedipal and non-oedipal self-pathology. These are heavy questions indeed, and Kohut (1980) suggests that to answer them analysts must take a fresh look at these experiences of their patients in the oedipal transference. Dr. Ornstein has done so, and we are grateful to her.

149

Dr. Ornstein points out that one's listening is guided by one's theoretical outlook and asks us to suspend our own outlook as we join her. This is no easy task for me, coming as I do from a different frame of reference that has served me well. Yet, committed to the necessity and value of new ideas and invigorated by the possibility of new horizons, I would like to understand what Dr. Ornstein puts before us. My preference would be to synthesize and integrate concepts from self psychology with other concepts, rather than discard one or the other. Thus, it would be a matter not of one theory or the other exclusively, but a basic framework utilizing aspects of various theories, perhaps at different points. This would mean adding what one finds new and useful and discarding what one finds not so, whether old or new, and transposing or translating from one "language" to another what one finds similar or familiar. It would also mean clarifying differences to define what is incompatible, though perhaps applicable for different pathologies or stages of treatment.

The clinical self object transferences, for example, might be considered in the new and useful category to be added or perhaps to be translated. Empathic listening might be more similar or familiar, though its emphasis and stress might almost make it new. The concept of the supraordinate bipolar self would be more at variance with other concepts of the self as content of the mental apparatus, though related to Hartmann's (1950) total self. Finally, most incompatible with classical conflict theory is the conceptualization of a defect only theory that would include the proposed view of the oedipal conflict as a disintegration product of the threatened self only. In contrast, concepts of defect and developmental arrest used to understand early pathology, as additions to conflict theory, have been quite possible to integrate into a larger framework.

There are, of course, obvious problems in attempts to integrate theories: the danger of blurring concepts and reducing their efficacy, the lack of clarity, and the chance of confusion. It is tempting to follow one model to its ultimate conclusion, not only for the appeal of clarity but to test its limits and give a chance for new understanding. That is, so we are told, the nature of scientific revolution. Perhaps revolutions are necessary to bring issues into focus, stir the imagination, and fight lethargy, but evolution may be the necessary road for implementation. There is merit in both. But even following up the notion of keeping different frames of reference or models intact and separate, one might even then propose an umbrella concept, such as "developmental" or "normative crises"—nodal points in normal development, as the child moves from phase to phase. This concept includes both the notion of positive forward thrust of development and the concept of conflict. The healthy or pathological outcome of a developmental crisis depends on both inner maturational programs, equipment, needs, and pressures, as well as the child-parent interaction (external pressures as internally experienced). Could we not organize within this one framework of normative crises such very different constellations as the Oedipus complex, the rapprochement crisis, and the stages of establishment of the bipolar self as well? Would there be an advantage for us in the use of such a framework, or would we indeed be only squeezing incompatible partners into one Procrustean bed?

At any rate, differently structured pathologies, such as neurotic, narcissistic, and structural defect pathologies, might require different models of conceptualization and correspondingly different technical considerations (as pointed out by theorists from various schools of thought, e.g., Cooper, 1978; Kernberg, 1980; Tolpin, 1978). I would like to extend this notion of differently structured pathologies in different people to the idea of a mixture of pathologies within the same person, with different aspects dominant at different times, requiring shifting, different models at different times. This is in general agreement with Gedo and Goldberg's (1973) hierarchical scheme of *Models of the Mind,* except I would add other models such as separation-individuation and object relations, or with Stolorow and Lachmann's (1980) propositions in *Psychoanalysis of Developmental Arrests.* The idea of that kind of "mixture" occurring frequently in our patients is, I think, in agreement with Dr. Ornstein's (1980a) thesis in a previous paper "Fantasy or Reality." It is perhaps even in agreement with Kohut's (1980) "Reflections": "as we observe the transferences of our analysands we are able to focus our attention not only on the structural conflicts (on drives and defenses or anxiety and guilt) but also on structural defects (on the stunted self and its need for a selfobject in order to complete its development) [p. 518]," even though I am not sure whether he is referring to conflicts and defects in different people or in one and the same person. Our conclusions, however, differ in emphasis. For Dr. Ornstein, as demonstrated in her case, this "mixture" of defects along with the conflict seems to confirm the universality of self-pathology, the supraordinate explanatory power of the psychology of the self, the dominance of selfobject transferences, and the value of exclusive use of the empathic stance—all of which seem to work for her most impressively. For me it suggests the valuable *contributions* of self-theory *in addition* to other explanatory concepts and analytic tools. Certainly, we all have had experience with a patient's wish and need for affirmation and validation from the analyst and wish for mirroring and merger with the idealized other in the transference, as well as the convincing effect of empathic interventions.

It should be understood, of course, that the point of reference for comparing theories today is not Freud of 1909 (Little Hans) or even Freud of 1923 and 1926 when Little Hans was revisited and structural theory was born. Rather the starting point would be modern ego psychology which, though essentially an internal conflict theory (as opposed to an interpersonal or defect theory), does not rest solely on internal instinctual vicissitudes, unaffected by perceptions of the outer world, as I think Dr. Ornstein suggested. Instead, modern ego psychology involves the understanding of development of all the psychic structures (ego, id, and superego) in their autonomous, cognitive, identificatory, defensive, and adaptive aspects. Modern ego psychology uses concepts of self and object representations, the self in relation to the object world (Hartmann, 1939–56; Jacobson, 1954–64; Piaget, 1952–69). However, these concepts of self as content of the psychic structures clearly differ from the supraordinate concept of the bipolar self of current self psychology. Within this framework of ego psychology, one already differentiates oedipal and pre-oedipal pathology as well as recognizes the complexity of their relationship. Pre-oedipal conflictual problems, fixation, and trauma will affect the nature of the resolution of the Oedipus complex, and oedipal pathology will have pre-oedipal precursors (except possibly in rare cases of pure oedipal trauma). Furthermore, oedipal pathology can be expressed regressively in pre-oedipal manifestations and vice versa.

It was from the vantage point of modern ego psychology, not early Freud, that we had to view contributions such as Mahler's (1963–75) separation-individuation concepts and Kernberg's (1970–76) object relations theory (both conflict theories), as well as Kohut's early (1966–71) self-structure defect formulation. Insofar as these theories now added to the understanding of the prestructural pathology that precedes the formation of the cohesive self and object constancy and of narcissistic pathology, these different concepts could be compared and related to each other as well as to ego psychology. One difficulty is, of course, that these theories, like all theories, have not arisen de novo, like Venus from the sea, but have evolved from previous concepts of classical psychoanalysis already familiar to us, so that assignment of the origin of ideas becomes most problematic. At the same time we have already become so thoroughly familiar with some of these new contributions that they have imperceptibly been absorbed into our work, a fact we sometimes forget.

From this point of view, then, by careful diagnosis and observation of transferences, we would be able to differentiate the early prestructural and narcissistic pathologies from the neurotic oedipal and pre-oedipal conflictual pathologies, in which structures are established, although they can "mask" each other. For instance, patients with self or selfobject pathology may manifest a neuroticlike superstructure, or there may be defensive regression from oedipal conflicts even to the point of fragmentation (Kernberg, 1980; Tolpin, 1978).

In the new theory of the supraordinate bipolar self—a now all inclusive psychology—we are asked to consider something very different; namely, that it is not a matter of differentiating between later conflictual and earlier structural pathology, but rather that there is a continuum of pathology of the self. Even the dramatic manifestations of the oedipal conflict, it is suggested, might be only disintegration products of a threatened self not adequately mirrored in the oedipal phase, rather than evidence of a universal Oedipus complex. This, I think, is Dr. Ornstein's tentative answer to her question: "Where do sexual identifications and sexual conflicts fit into self psychology?"

Now let us look at what Dr. Ornstein presents to us. It is unrealistic, I think, to try and second guess someone else's case. Dr. Ornstein was there; I was not. In addition, the material presented is, by needs, preselected—for the sake of brevity, for relevance to the issues, and by the fact that, as Dr. Ornstein points out, the original listening to the patient must be informed by the analyst's theoretical base. All one can really do, therefore, is speculate on some issues, raise some questions, and be grateful for a view into someone else's world.

I am sorry Dr. Ornstein had to delete her discussion of Little Hans, which was originally intended for inclusion in her presentation. At least then we would have had equal access to the same data

to indulge our speculations on equal footing. It would have been fun
to compare Dr. Ornstein's conceptualization of the case with that of
Freud, with my own, and with others based on separation-individuation issues.

In both Little Hans and in Dr. Ornstein's case, she wishes to
demonstrate the continued selfobject function of parents in the oedipal phase by elucidating, in the analysis, oedipal selfobject transferences related to the failure of these parental selfobject functions.
Thus, her main theme relates to the second proposition she poses at
the beginning of her paper. For this purpose she selected a case she
judged to have predominantly oedipal pathology; a case where there
would be no doubt that the discrete self-structure deficit arose from
failure of the selfobject function during the oedipal phase. She did
not choose a "mixed" case, by which she would mean a case with
both narcissistic and oedipal features where the self-pathology
might be related to earlier selfobject failures. Thus, there would be
no doubt about selfobject functions being specifically relevant to the
oedipal period. This is a most fascinating proposition, as I said in the
beginning, and one that took some getting used to.

Actually, I rather suspect that this patient had a good deal of
earlier pathology. This is suggested by the peculiar quality of the
symptom (intolerable aversion to the analyst and her voice), the
marked fear of invasion and fusion, the rapid alterations of state
into intense rages, the quality of object relations, and depersonaliza-
tion feelings on the couch (reported in a longer version of the case).
But again this may be a matter of emphasis. For practical purposes I
can use this patient who does demonstrate oedipal pathology (whatever else he also demonstrates) to discuss Dr. Ornstein's proposition.

Let me summarize the way I understand Dr. Ornstein would
formulate her case. The patient entered the oedipal period intact;
that is, there had been adequate mirroring by the pre-oedipal selfobjects to permit adequate transmuting internalization, with the re-
sultant formation of adequate self-structures or a cohesive bipolar
self. This healthy structure formation, despite inadequate empathic
response from his mother, is posited as having been due to his father
who performed adequate maternal selfobject functions pre-
oedipally. This permitted, I presume, the formation of strong compensatory structures (or were they primary structures?). As the boy
entered the oedipal phase, however, both parents failed in their

phase-appropriate oedipal selfobject functions, and discrete structural deficits, manifest as oedipal pathology, resulted. The oedipal
selfobject failure included the mother's seductive and intrusive responses. But more importantly, the weak, ill father did not provide
the idealized selfobject who could joyfully mirror the oedipal strivings of the youngster. These two empathic failures then emerged in
the two transference periods, first in reference to the maternal selfobject (reported elsewhere), then in reference to the more deeply
buried failure of the paternal selfobject. Dr. Ornstein is careful to
point out that the conflicts in relation to the oedipal passions toward
mother also emerged in that first phase of maternal transference.
That phase, however, proved to be "an introduction" to the more
important second phase when attention to the paternal selfobject
failure took center stage, as presented in Dr. Ornstein's clinical
material. Without the focus of the second stage the analysis would
not have been complete. Empathic interpretation and working
through of these transferences led to transmuting internalizations,
firming structure formation appropriate to the oedipal phase and a
satisfactory conclusion.

This, of course, is not the way I would have formulated the case
myself, the language of self psychology not being my mother tongue.
I would, instead, have talked of unconscious fantasy, conflict, and
defense on both oedipal and pre-oedipal levels; of a positive and
negative Oedipus complex; of sexual and aggressive impulses and
superego guilt and fear of punishment; of castration and separation
anxiety and inhibitions and symptoms; of sadistic and masochistic
fantasy solutions; perhaps of primitive wishes for and fears of merger; of the quality of object relations; and of many other things. But
that is not the issue at hand. Instead, using this different language,
let us consider the concept of a parental selfobject function in the
oedipal phase, the existence and meaning of such a function, and its
role and importance in traversing the oedipal phase and in the resolution of the Oedipus complex. What does this concept add to our
understanding and what is its clinical usefulness?

If we define a selfobject function as meeting the child's need for
affirmation, validation, and mirroring from an important, even idealized other, who offers himself for identification for the purpose of
enhancing growth, then, I think, Dr. Ornstein has made a good case
for such a parental function of the homogenital parent during the

oedipal phase in relation to the child's oedipal strivings. I not only agree with her, but I thank her for explicating this important aspect of this phase.

I question, however, the importance implicitly placed on the self-object function of the homogenital parent, both theoretically and clinically in Dr. Ornstein's case, as the primary determinant of successful progress through the oedipal phase. I see it as one factor, an important factor perhaps, but the healthy or pathological resolution of the Oedipus complex seems to me to rest on many factors, described and explained by ego psychological concepts. Such factors would include the intensity of conflict, strength of drives, nature of unconscious fantasy, negative oedipal issues, and pre-oedipal arrests and conflicts related to relationships and identifications with the pre-oedipal mother and father. The outcome would depend on the self and object representations and the quality of interal object relations from earlier phases, as well as on traumatic and supportive experiences in the oedipal phase itself. These all influence the degree and quality of repression of the oedipal conflict and the nature of superego internalizations. Within these conceptualizations there clearly is room for the impact of the homogenital parent's response to the child's oedipal strivings (as perceived by the child), as well as the kind of identificatory image offered in terms of whether it leads to success or to difficulty in the dissolution of the Oedipus complex. Although not the same, these ideas, if translated, can be related to the concept of a paternal selfobject function, as defined earlier. This concept then would not only be compatible but, I think, adds to and emphasizes an important aspect of this phase, which may often be neglected.

To emphasize a need for a new concept, Dr. Ornstein perhaps overstresses the growth-enhancing selfobject function of the oedipal father, posing it almost as his exclusive role. This she places in contrast to the classical position in which she describes the oedipal father as exclusively experienced as the hated rival, as the result of drive-dominated fantasy, *negating* all other internalizations of the father. Both are oversimplifications. In this connection it is interesting to review the quote from Freud's case of Little Hans (1909):

> But his father, whom he could not help hating as a rival, was the same father whom he had always loved and was bound to go on loving, who had been his model, had been his first playmate and had looked after him

from earliest infancy . . . and this it was that gave rise to the first conflict—For Hans' nature had so developed that for the moment his love
could not but keep the upper hand and suppress his hate, though it could
not kill it [p. 134].

Freud (1909) thus stressed both hateful rivalry and idealization and
need for the father, although in conflict with each other. Continuing
with the case of Little Hans, but trying out the concept of the father's oedipal selfobject function, would it be too fanciful to suggest
that although failure in this function might have added to the development of the phobia in the first place, the father's ability to then
accept, applaud, and mirror the boy's oedipal strivings in the analysis facilitated Little Hans' resolution of the Oedipus complex and
speeded his recovery (in addition to the treatment's other therapeutic actions)?

What about the "evidence" for the oedipal selfobject transference,
the "need to experience the analyst as if she were a strong man"
that is, the need for an idealized father in the transference, so
important to Dr. Ornstein's constructions? Any patient's, and particularly this patient's, expressed yearning for a strong supportive
father in the analysis can, and usually does, serve several functions,
have several meanings at the same time, and lend itself to a number
of different interpretations, in addition to the one chosen by Dr.
Ornstein. It could be a direct need for validation, for support, to fill
in a defect, as postulated by Dr. Ornstein. Depending on the underlying unconscious fantasies, it could also be a devaluation of the
analyst as a defense against oedipal wishes or a narcissistic need to
devalue, or an idealization of a strong father image as a resistance
against exploring underlying conflict with a rival, a defense against
guilt over the oedipal wish to kill (father had died) and the fear of
retaliatory castration by father. It could be a negative oedipal desire
for father, possibly even to defend against the unacceptable wish for
mother (mother was experienced at times as seductive, and the patient was reported as close to father prior to the oedipal period). It
might be a defense against the wish for and fear of engulfment and
intrusion by or against the wish for and fear of merger or identification with mother. Or the insistence of the need for, and therefore the
complaint of having been deprived of, a strong father can be in the
service of justification out of guilt for the patient's continued rage at
father and mother for other reasons. Dr. Ornstein is aware of these

various interpretations and gives us suggestive evidence for all of them. Yet she chooses to pursue one exclusively, apparently without exploring the others. The answer, I am sure, would be that it is dictated by the clinical material. Yet, as she herself put it, her listening and her interventions are informed by her theoretical base. And although I do find merit in her argument, it is a problem.

I particularly want to support Dr. Ornstein's comments on recognizing a father transference with a female analyst (Meyers, 1981). It would indeed be a serious error, as Ornstein points out, "if the analyst expected the nature of the transference to be determined by his or her own gender rather than evolved in keeping with the patient's intrapsychic, unconscious, and developmental needs." Specifically in relation to the Oedipus complex, as stated by Dr. Ornstein "a male patient's transferences toward a woman analyst do not necessarily evolve in relationship to his unconscious heterosexual conflicts [only], . . . or in the case of a male analyst in terms of competition and hostility" only. Indeed this would appear self-evident, unrelated to one's theoretical frame of reference, except that it is all too often neglected. Fleming, for instance, has pointed out (in verbal communication) how often the pre-oedipal mother transference is overlooked in analyses with male analysts, and female analysts have more difficulty in recognizing themselves as male, competitive, oedipal-transference figures.

Let us continue with another related question about the patient's identification with his father, whom he perceived as weak, deserted by the woman through death, and dead himself. In a thought-provoking formulation, Dr. Ornstein sees this as a defensive identification to fill a self-defect, created because the absence of the idealized oedipal parent led to the failure of a more positive transmuting internalization. No doubt this identification served the purpose of maintaining a connectedness with the father and undoing the loss of a lost object. At the same time this vulnerable self-image made it too frightening to relate to women. But identifications may serve many purposes simultaneously. I hear disappointment and anger at the father in Ornstein's material. At the very least, I could not exclude a defensive guilt identification with father, a sense of weakness and impending death as superego punishment for oedipal competition and other death wishes. The ineffective, inhibited self-representation and inability to relate to women could also be a denial of the patient's own strength, a withdrawal from oedipal competition

with a father who was sick and whom he needed and loved, as well
as a host of identifications and conflicts in relation to mother, which
Dr. Ornstein suggests she dealt with in the earlier part of the analysis. As Schafer (1968) points out in his *Aspects of Internalization,* the
processes of identification and the resulting identifications themselves are not simple. Identifications can be with one or more characteristics of the object, total or partial; they can achieve different
levels of autonomy and involve various motives. These motives may
be viewed in terms of many variables such as content, genetic level,
complexity, conceptual level of abstraction, and point of view. According to Schafer, identifications "cannot be created out of nothing,
but involve selective reorganization of already existing wishes, behavior patterns, capacities, viewpoints and emphases—quite possibly earlier identifications, too [p. 147]." A discussion of this view of
identification in relation to the concept of transmuting internalization has to be left for another time.

Now Dr. Ornstein points out that it makes a great deal of difference how one conceptualizes a particular phenomenon, that one's
understanding affects one's intervention. And so it does. A provocative question then comes to mind: How can we understand relatively
comparable good results in analyses by competent analysts using
different theories exclusively? Is there indeed such discrepancy between theory and practice (as Kohut suggests) that we all do more or
less the same thing without knowing it? Perhaps one modifies one's
technique as one goes along, using what is effective, having already
absorbed aspects of many theories unconsciously (as I mentioned
earlier). Or do we consciously or unconsciously select the appropriate case for our approach? Or is it possible that each approach indeed addresses only one sector of pathology, be it oedipal conflicts, a
defect in the self, or the threat of destructive rage and envy by
internal objects. That sector of pathology, then, having been re-
dressed, the person is in a stronger state to deal with the remaining
sectors of pathology on his or her own—whether this improvement
is conceptualized as freed energy, increased ego strength (due to
maximum beneficial alteration of the patient's conflict), improved
internal object relations, or restoration of the self (Meyers, 1980).

There is a final theoretical question: Does the stress on the oedipal selfobject function of the parent imply that without this affirmation the oedipal child's self would fragment? Apparently, Dr. Ornstein assures us that self-disintegration is not the central issue at

this stage, not unless there was self-structure defect before. However, oedipal conflicts are conceptualized as "breakdown products" of the threatened self at the oedipal phase, sexual problems as "discrete deficits in the self." Perhaps these discrete deficits with oedipal selfobject function failure should be considered more in the area of self-esteem only. This follows Stolorow's proposal (personal communication) that the parental selfobject function varies with the level of structural development, beginning with meeting the child's self-needs for cohesion, then for continuity, and finally for esteem at higher levels (e.g., oedipal). If this is so, I have no problem with it. But why not call it a separate object with various functions? Calling it selfobject function implies a need for merger, a lack of separateness, a lack of boundaries. If so, I have serious questions about its place as late as the oedipal period. In this connection it has puzzled me why some authors interested in attachment (Ainsworth, 1981; Kohut 1980) have regarded the aim of Mahler's separation-individuation process as the opposite of attachment, as if object relations theory advocated detachment as a developmental goal. In object relations theory there is no self-representation without a link to an object representation; the goal of development is an integrated, cohesive, separate self related to and able to depend on an integrated, separate, constant object, internal or external, without danger of merger. In fact the ability to relate in depth to objects is one major criterion for the diagnosis of higher level functioning.

I have raised many questions, more perhaps than I have answered. Many more topics come to mind, stimulated by Dr. Ornstein's intriguing presentation. These questions concern termination—classical versus self psychology criteria; reconstruction—internal versus external realities; considerations in respect to the superego—the role of the superego in monitoring the stability of self-representations versus continued selfobject functions for self-structure maintenance after the oedipal period. They will have to wait for future discussion. In the meantime I want to thank Dr. Ornstein for her thought-provoking presentation and beautiful case material.

REFERENCES

Ainsworth, M. (1981). Infant attachment and maternal care: Some implications for psychoanalytic concepts of development. *Bull. Assoc. for Psychoanal. Med.*, 20.

Cooper, A. (1978). Clinical psychoanalysis: One method or more? *Bull. Assoc. for Psychoanal. Med.* 17.

Freud, S. (1909). Analysis of a phobia in a five-year old boy. *S.E. 10.*, London: Hogarth Press, 1955.

———— (1923). The ego and the id. *S.E. 19.* London: Hogarth Press, 1961.

———— (1924). The dissolution of the Oedipus complex. *S.E. 19.* London: Hogarth Press, 1961.

———— (1926). Inhibitions, symptoms and anxiety. *S.E. 20.* London: Hogarth Press, 1961.

Gedo, J. & Goldberg, A. (1973). *Models of the Mind.* Chicago: Univ. of Chicago Press.

Hartmann, H. (1939). *Ego Psychology and the Problem of Adaptation.* New York: Int. Univ. Press, 1958.

———— (1950). Comments on the psychoanalytic theory of the ego. *Psychoanal. Study Child* 5:74–96.

Jacobson, E. (1964). *The Self and the Object World.* New York: Int. Univ. Press.

Kernberg, O. (1976). *Object Relations Theory and Clinical Psychoanalysis.* New York: Jason Aronson.

———— (1980). Character structure and analyzability. *Bull. Assoc. for Psychoanal. Med.* 19.

Kohut, H. (1971). *The Analysis of the Self.* New York: Int. Univ. Press.

———— (1977). *The Restoration of the Self.* New York: Int. Univ. Press.

———— (1980). Reflections. In *Advances in Self Psychology,* A. Goldberg, ed. New York: Int. Univ. Press.

Mahler, M., Pine, F. & Bergman, A. (1975). *The Psychological Birth of the Human Infant.* New York: Basic Books.

Meyers, H. (1978). Current perspectives in psychoanalytic technique: A hierarchy of techniques. *Bull. Assoc. Psychoanal. Med.* 18.

———— (1981). Transference and countertransference in analytic work by and with women: The complexity and challenge. *Bull. Assoc. Psychoanal. Med.* 21.

Ornstein, A. (1980a). Fantasy or reality: The unsettled question—pathogenesis and reconstruction in psychoanalysis. Unpublished.

———— (1980b). Little Hans Revisited. Unpublished paper.

Piaget, J. (1963). *The Psychology of Intelligence.* Totowa, N.J.: Littlefield, Adams.

Schafer, R. (1968). *Aspects of Internalization.* New York: Int. Univ. Press.

Stolorow, R. & Lachmann, F. (1980). *Psychoanalysis of Development Arrests.* New York: Int. Univ. Press.

Tolpin, M. (1978). Self-object and Oedipal object: A crucial developmental distinction. *Psychoanal. Study Child* 33: 167–183.

14 An Application of the Self Psychological Viewpoint to Psychoanalytic Technique

Joseph D. Lichtenberg, M.D.

The task requested of me is to illustrate the clinical applications of the self psychological viewpoint as I utilize it. Unlike many of the other presenters I have not had the opportunity to work and consult directly with Dr. Kohut. My personal utilization derives from my careful study of the published work of Kohut and others, plus thought-provoking discussions with many colleagues and friends. Most of all, my application is based on taking the ideas from these sources and testing them in the crucible of the everyday experience of my clinical work as a psychoanalyst.

My plan is to present six principles of technique that illustrate the manner in which my exploration of the self-psychological viewpoint has influenced the current state of my thinking as a clinical psychoanalyst. I illustrate each principle with material from a single case. I must ask the reader to make the creative effort to piece together from clinical fragments, interrupted by statements of principles, the sense of two people at work—myself and my analysand— and the sense of a whole person, Mr. N, and a whole analysis. To assist you in this integrative effort I begin by sketching the broad outlines of the analysis.

Mr. N, a Jewish accountant in his late twenties, sought analysis because he felt unable to achieve his potential and because he desperately wanted to marry. He had sought psychiatric help in his hometown of Richmond during a moderately severe depression after the breakup of his second engagement. He was referred for analysis by the therapist after he became involved with a woman who had paranoid tendencies similar to Mr. N's mother. His nuclear family consisted of his father, mother, and brother, Jay, older by 3 years. His father was a largely ineffectual litiginous businessman who was now physically failing. His mother was a bossy, controlling school-teacher who had attacks of hysterical anxiety and persecutory fears. Jay, whose personality was remarkably phlegmatic, had recently married and, like Mr. N, was an accountant. The illness of others was to play an important part in Mr. N's life. When Mr. N was 3, Jay had been seriously ill with nephritis. During Mr. N's first few years, his mother had had a series of deaths in her family, and during his adolescence she had survived a cancer operation. In the beginning of the analysis, Mr. N was restrictively attached to his family; he returned to Richmond each weekend and called daily. Gradually, he reduced his involvement with them and cultivated a social life in Washington. As a manifestation of an idealizing transference, he developed a strong interest in art, and in a specific painter whose work hung in my office. At the end of the fourth year of analysis he married an attractive, intelligent Jewish girl. Prior to his marriage material dealing with his extreme ambivalence toward both his parents alternated with material specifically related to his phallic-oedipal strivings. His ambivalence marked his continuous struggle to free himself from a sense of being controlled, and his phallic strivings were blunted or turned to sadistic aggressiveness because of his fears of dominance by women and of bodily danger from injury and disease. After his marriage he associated directly to triangular oedipal rivalry wishes and fears centering on his father-in-law. He terminated his analysis after $6\frac{1}{4}$ years.

Dr. Kohut (1977) and I (1972) have appreciated the descriptive power of Eugene O'Neill's autobiographical statement: "Man is born broken. He lives by mending. The grace of God is glue!" Mr. N to my mind was not broken. He was intact but constricted, inhibited, and without ease or joy. Throughout the analysis he struck me as a man who required not glue but something that lubricates and effer-vesces.

1. The first technical principle is the centrality of the empathic vantage point for analytic observation.   Perceiving the analysand's state of mind, his immediate and general way of experiencing himself and others, his range of feelings and thoughts is, of course, the critical task of analysis, but to do it requires the greatest discipline. We are all trained and skilled as natural science observers, and we all have mastery of the language of the evaluator from the outside. Consequently, it requires the wrenching of a major mental set to alter and adjust our perceptual vantage point, whether we are thinking of our overview of the analysand or the comprehension of any specific communication within an hour. In a series of papers (Lichtenberg, 1981; Schwaber, 1979, 1980a, 1980b, 1981a, 1981b) an effort has been made to describe the empathic mode of perception and to provide clinical illustrations of its use. Dr. Schwaber has stressed the differences between observing from inside or outside the analysand's state of mind and the differences between a focus on the analysand's subjective (psychic) reality and an attempt at objectivity (see Malin, 1981). Because I regard the empathic vantage point to be central to the technical principles I describe in this paper, aspects of it are found in each of the other five principles of technique and clinical illustrations.

If we assume the position of an outside observer, then Mr. N is easily recognizable as a man whose symptomatology is obsessional, with reaction-formation adherences to rituals of servicing his parents and of barely disguised obstinancy, argumentativeness, and sarcasm. Indeed Mr. N could easily describe himself in such words using the diagnostic label and formulation. Were he to do so, he would feel that this "clinical" description fit in with his view that his world is one in which he received critical, unappreciative, negative evaluations and that it missed entirely a view of what he feels and what he strives for in his inner world. To indicate the particular character of my experience with Mr. N's analysis, I must say that I found Mr. N to be unusually difficult for me to sense from within his own state of mind. This difficulty arose, I believe, from his extreme resistance to introspection about the nuances of any of the interactional aspects of the analysis. Because this deprived me of a familiar point of entry into the empathic mode until the analysis of this resistance rather late in the treatment, I am appreciative of the discipline emphasized by the psychology of the self to try continuously to maintain the empathic vantage point.

Mr. N began his analysis with a series of revelations of embarrassing transgressions—climbing under the piano to defecate until age 6 or 7, stealing, cheating in school, changing prices on books, masturbating as an adult, and craving "forbidden" women. In an early hour I asked this conservative, religiously observant man if these memories that he said he had "kept in" him for years weighed heavily on him and distressed him. In his response he resolutely negated and denied my effort to enter into his feelings. A few hours later he complained that since starting analysis, thoughts about episodes of stealing, of masturbating thinking of black girls, and the like stayed in his mind until he told them to me. I responded sympathetically that talking here probably had increased his awareness of distressing thoughts, which previously he could have more easily put out of his mind. He answered that they weren't distressing thoughts. I asked about his objection considering that he had said he couldn't get out of his mind thoughts about stealing and masturbating. Within a few minutes after this expression of gentle persistence on my part, he expressed himself in a manner that, for the first time, seemed *meant* to allow me to share his inner feelings. With a flow of tears he described his feelings of loss when he was 13 and his beloved dog Connie died. This brief sequence provided the basis for two significant entries into his state of mind. It led me to sense that my persistence was important in raising his trust in me for reasons that would be important to analyze. Second, I could appreciate that his affectionate feelings were strong, but that they were displaced from what must have seemed to him an unloveworthy human environment.

2. The second technical principle is that analysts form constructions by having their perception shift between what the analysand is experiencing in what I term the "foreground" and the "background." This principle derives from a full realization of the significance of relationships with selfobjects[1] as revealed by transference phenomena. Transference-derived aspects of the relationships with selfobjects invariably constitute background ex-

---

[1]Selfobjects refer to aspects of caregivers—mothers, father, teachers, etc.—who are experienced at providing something necessary for the maintenance of a stable, positively toned sense of self. The mother of an 18-month-old who at about the same time as the child recognizes his hunger functions as a selfobject (close to self as an empathic perceiver of his need, close to an object in her providing of the food). The sum total of these experiences in the foreground form, in the background, an ambiance of mother as feeder who has set the whole regulatory balance (pleasurable or troubled, compatible or conflicted) that forms the background experience.

periences in all analyses. Previous attempts to define these background experiences have used concepts such as the basic dyadic relationship, the therapeutic relationship, the working alliance, the analytic ambiance, and so on. Self psychology, as I understand it, has emphasized how specific manifestations of the selfobject transferences that occupy the background may enter the foreground—the immediate associative sequence. This occurs more commonly in those patients for whom empathic failures have been particularly significant. The success of the analytic work in the foreground will affect the background experience. A general appreciation by the analysand of the analyst's empathic skills constitutes a background experience that is, I believe, a significant determinant of the carrying power of the analysis as a whole through difficult resistances and slow, laborious, working-through periods.

By foreground I mean the immediate content and meaning of the associations the patient is relating. In the foreground, at a specific moment, as a separate, distinct, outside person, I might be the recipient of his well-organized feelings; or I might be a selfobject needed to serve some suspended, unavailable, or underdeveloped function. For example, when Mr. N would comply with his conception of the basic working principle of free association by telling me all about his transgressions and reject as wrong the comments I made, he may have been establishing the immediacy of transference of a judgmental disputatious nature directed to a specific, separate, outside person. Alternatively or additionally, he may have been establishing a transference calling forth a response from a selfobject based on his need for regulation of his irritability and distrust. His response to my gentle persistence pointed to the latter.

By background I mean the more general status of the receptivity that the patient presumes he will receive from the analyst as a transference person, persons, or milieu. At any given moment the patient may or may not have an awareness of the psychic reality he perceives to color his background. By and large the transferences that characterize the background communications in analysis tend to be centered on one aspect of selfobjects in that they commonly speak to the broadened sense of "support systems" that form and sustain self-cohesion and basic trust, optimism, and a capacity for joy. Looked at another way the analyst's empathic perception of the background transference may tell more about the analyzability of a patient in general and the receptivity of the analysand for interpretive help at any given moment than the immediate foreground communication.[2]

Mr. N's first dream and his associations to it (ninth hour) can serve to illustrate the relationship of foreground and background. After relating another stealing episode from his past, he stated he had had dinner at his parents and awoke at night with cramps. In his dream he was going to take an English exam in college or high school. He went to pick up his blue books. Mrs. Nash, a nervous black secretary in the office where he now works, was handing them out. He was 15 minutes late and nervous. Mrs. Nash told him not to worry, he could take the exam anywhere. He went to the back of Mr. Brown's class, but he couldn't concentrate because of the noise. He was very frustrated. His associations were to the terrible pressure he felt at different times in school. His mother had worked and worked with him until he became one of the best students. He skipped a grade but in the new class became one of the worst students. During one of the bad years, he had held a knife to his throat. When he would tell his mother about his upset, she would give him one of her Valiums. Mr. Brown was a teacher who had said something wrong. When Mr. N brought it up to him, Mr. Brown, the asshole, asked: What are you, a smart aleck?

With the wisdom of hindsight, Mr. N's dream can be seen to present issues that would occupy the foreground and background of

---

[2]The recommendation to permit one's empathic perception to oscillate between foreground and background is an attempt to deal with problems of basic orientation in space and time that make the analytic situation so complex. Analogous recommendations have been offered with respect to infant development and to painting. Sander (1980) has stated: "We traditionally rely on a linear cause–effect model—one thing leading to another. . . . This we need to replace with . . . a model . . . where there can be a background and a foreground, both being the site of synchronies and asynchronies in varying degrees [p. 195]." Sander illustrated the use of the concepts of background and foreground to explain the fitting together of mother and infant in the domain of time. Building up a basic regulatory equilibrium out of low-frequency rhythms such as sleep and circadian rhythm, mother and infant construct a background of shared expectancies in time. Foreground events, such as high-frequency bursts of sucking and making and breaking eye contact are given meaning in the framework of the background of a shared temporal organization. Shared expectancies in time provide the background for recognizing who is initiating what in the foreground. This in turn provides the necessary condition for the self to become more distinct and separate.

John Ruskin, in *Letters on Landscape Painting* (1855), advised: "When you have acquired some proficiency in foreground material, your next step should be the study of atmosphere—the power which defines and measures space."

his analysis in the years ahead. He experienced himself as being under examination in so pressured a way as to provoke the cramping of his mind and bowels. Whichever way he turned there were problems. He was 15 years late in getting the help he needed at the time he had felt desperate and suicidal. These issues represent an important way in which Mr. N sensed himself—as a person constantly under duress to prove his worth. This might be available as an issue in the foreground on those occasions when specific transference references could be elicited and examined. Often throughout the analysis, this troubled aspect of himself in relation to his environment as a whole existed as a background experience of generalized discontent, distrust, and feeling of being overtaxed and underappreciated.[3] In terms of his selfobject transferential world it meant a background in the analysis in which the easy ebb and flow of affection and anger, joy and sadness, was replaced by the dragging tempo of the sum total of school without play, of "blue" books without end. The analyst's appreciation of this background ambiance is, I believe, crucial to alert him to appreciate those moments in which directly related material comes into the foreground, opening up the possibility of its analysis and working through over time.

If the setting of the dream, an examination in a school with blue books, constituted a significant reference to the self as pressured, cramped, and delinquent in seeking help, what constitutes the relationships with objects that contributed to these difficulties? Using the imagery of the associations to this initial dream, but from the vantage point of the completed analysis, his mother is represented as Mrs. Nash the "teacher," whose nervousness and despondency he shared. She tried to be reassuring but could offer no real help other than her own means to regulate her anxiousness and depression—Valium. When these means failed, she resorted to projection with consequent paranoid ideation, a danger that terrified him lest he fall prey to it. His father, represented in the dream as Mr. Brown, under whose wing he tried to learn and work, was involved in the "noisy" chaos of an ineptly run business and nonproductive law-

---

[3]I have described (Lichtenberg, 1979) the manner in which the individual in his experiencing of himself and others shifts between a tendency to generalize and a tendency to particularize. The tendency to generalize builds up the background; the tendency to particularize leads to a foreground focus. The tendency to shift back and forth between the two constitutes perceptual and conceptual roots for the associative sequencing in analysis.

suits. A further determinant to a feeling of hopelessness in mastering life's examination was his recurrent experience that neither parent would listen to his criticisms without an explosive backlash. These relationships presaged an analytic encounter replete with negative transferences in both foreground and background. This was an especially puzzling problem in the background during the early period of the analysis. In the foreground each parent emerged at times as rather distinct individuals with a mix of positively and negatively experienced attributes. But in the background I came to appreciate that neither seemed to emerge as an effective selfobject helping to regulate the negative effects of the other. The background transference was as though empty of an advocate whose support of his needs could permit his or her idealization when it counted. As these issues appeared one by one in the foreground with respect to each parent (and his brother), Mr. N's generalized pessimism and disillusion in others gradually lifted. What made this particularly difficult to deal with was Mr. N's resistance to spontaneously or secondarily recognizing linkages between, for example, a question I had asked in response to his telling me that I was wrong and the figure of Mr. Brown in the dream. This was to make analytic work in the foreground unusually ponderous and awkward.

I was able to draw optimism from a number of sources in this early material. He represented himself in the dream as trying, a characteristic about himself that was to prove crucial during difficult periods. The reference in the dream to his believing himself free to take the exam anywhere was indicative that he regarded himself as free to seek a selfobject away from his parents, especially his mother. This indicated that no matter how intense the passive-aggressive interdependence between them remained, he did not regard himself as hopelessly enmeshed (narcissistically merged) with her. That he could feel an independent current of affection was clear from the love he expressed for his dog in the earlier hour.

3. The third technical principle involves the recognition of symptomatic alterations in the sense of self. These may be restricted to states of depletion and enfeeblement (as in the case of Mr. N) or progress to states of fragmentation (where the pathological self-disturbance is more severe). By his attention to the impairments of the functioning of the self as a vital cohesive unit, the analyst is able to focus on significant aspects of disturbances in self-regulation:

What facilitates or what impairs the analysand's ability to be flexibly active-assertive or passive-restorative? Is a disturbed sense of self the result of an immediate foreground problem being dealt with (e.g., an ascendant, unresolved, intrapsychic conflict, and/or a specific empathic failure in the analytic interaction)? Is a disturbed sense of self the result of prolonged disturbance (resistance state) in a background relationship with a selfobject that has lost its sustaining positive "carrying" power?

In the middle phase of his analysis Mr. N went through a 3-month period of an apathetic, depressive slump in all areas of his life and in the analysis. The immediate stimulus was his failure to obtain a promotion, which he felt he had been promised and had earned. Efforts on my part to acknowledge and explore his disappointment at his work brought agreement, but no deepening of our understanding. My efforts to pick up and explore transparently clear transference displacements in dreams and associations led to symptomatic worsening. I acknowledged to him that I recognized that, when I tried to help him to explore feelings of disappointment with *me*, he perceived me as being out of touch with what he found helpful. This interpretation served to lessen his regressive distancing and permitted a more effective focus on the symptomatic depletion state, its origins, and meaning.

Interspersed with his repetitious complaints were occasional, fragmented references to similar emotional "collapses" in the past. One occurred when, after being a top student, he was skipped in religious school and then had become unable to work at all. Another occurred during the summer after his Bar Mitzvah when he had cramps, nausea, and vomiting for several months. When in the seventh grade, he would sit and stare at his books unable to work. As each of these earlier depletion experiences followed periods of success, I conjectured that they might represent an overexcitement stimulated by exhibitionist expansiveness. Although this seemed logical, I could sense no support for it in my contact with Mr. N. Rather, I could feel that he blamed me and wanted something from me. At first it seemed clear from his provocativeness that he wanted me to fight with him. We came to recognize that this was a repetition of his efforts as a pushy little boy to penetrate the invisible shield of unemotionality of his older brother Jay. We gradually understood the fighting to be a stopgap effort to gain temporary relief from his feeling of depletion and ennui. His deeper wish lay elsewhere. I pieced together that the key element was that he regarded his successes more as the result of the input of his mother and tutor than of his own. After the push to produce the success ended and he was left on his own, he felt abandoned and would collapse. Finally, his mother would recognize his state and take him in hand. Thus, his disappointment in me was twofold. First, I had not provided the push to get him his promotion. Second, I had not responded as he wished after his slump; that is, I had not revitalized him through a persistent, encompassing, educational stewardship.

The recognition of Mr. N's symptomatic alteration in his sense of self led to a focus on a significant disturbance in his self-regulation. This required a series of steps. A direct foreground approach through transference references in dreams led to a worsening of the state and had to be acknowledged as such. Then, material dealing with similar states in the past had to be analyzed accurately from the standpoint of Mr. N's inner state of experience. His provocativeness was a self-assertive effort to enliven his dreary, sickly state. Behind it was the anger at me for failures in providing those measures of compensatory stewardship that he felt were responsible for his past successes and recoveries. What empathic disturbance and/or unresolved conflict led to his diminished confidence in his own capacity, and in his deeply felt requirement for a compensatory stewardship, remained to be analyzed.

4. The fourth technical principle is the need to follow patterns in each hour and in each sequence of hours that indicate subtle and gross fluctuations of the patient's way of sensing his state of self in relation to his way of sensing the analyst and the analytic milieu. This principle places an emphasis on the transitions that occur in experiential states and in communicative modes. Its focus leads to the recognition and interpretation of continuities and discontinuities that reflect vicissitudes of transference strivings.

Mr. N's pattern of speech in most hours was to talk in a tense forced you-told-me-I-am-to-do-this-so-I'm-doing-it style. Occasionally there was some easing, but more often there was an increase in overt irritability and sarcasm. At times he would become more tense and constrained, lapsing into prolonged silences. He would hold his chin and have a look of intense, strained concentration—the pose of Rodin's *The Thinker* or of a child straining on the toilet.

Efforts to encourage him to describe his feelings at these times failed to help. I became convinced he did not have sufficient self-awareness to be more revealing. Asking him, rather than being helpful, was experienced by him as drawing attention to his inadequacy in introspection. I resolved to "listen" to the gap in his speech to try to help identify his inner state of self. After various periods of this "concentration" silence, he began to describe fantasies he was having. Generally, these were of some kind of blatant aggressive action toward someone in his present or past. Examples are having a conversation with his boss in which Mr. N is devastatingly sarcastic or having a group of people under his power hold a young girl while he sexually assaults her in a humiliating fashion. I could take up successfully with Mr. N that the rage that appeared in his fantasy arose in response to a specifiable narcissistic slight he had experienced. He would be responsive to these interpretations, but this analytic work shed no light on the meaning of his silences. In addition, there were no easily comprehensible bridges between the fantasies and prior associations in the particular hour. Gradually I began to conceptualize that the silences were gaps in which he might have a direct feeling toward me were he not so constrained defensively to fragment his inward attentional focus. I had long recognized that he avoided having and acknowledging a direct feeling or wish toward me as though his very being would be threatened. His conscious fixed placement of me was as a calm successful man who had it all together and who would use his professional skills to help him get himself all together. He was terrified lest he respond to some action or inaction of mine with rage. If he were to experience an anger outburst toward me, he feared he would destroy the equanimity he strove to achieve in the reciprocal envelope of a calm but rigidly formal interaction with me. By focusing on his discontinuities in speech and by using the contents of his fantasies as indicators of the defended-against transference feelings, I was able very gradually to enter into the state of mind he tried so desperately to shut me out of and, at the same time, help him to appreciate the need he felt to exclude me.

For example, in an hour late in his analysis, he began by stating with pride that as a result of the analysis he had continued to work despite a desire he had felt to follow his prior pattern of letting down when he felt resentful. Yet he was disappointed that he still fretted over a minor criticism from his boss. Then, after a typical constrained silence, he reported a fantasy of saying goodbye to a woman colleague whose response was cold and perfunctory. He took a gun and killed her husband. After a further silence, he stated he'd like to ignore his fantasy. I noted his wish to treat it as a waste product of his mind to be discarded and ignored as shameful. He agreed and said his action in the fantasy of killing the husband reminded him of his resentment toward his father for not being able to prevent his mother from her cold, cutting ways. I asked him about having the fantasy at the particular time during the hour, and he answered that he knew it probably had a meaning but he couldn't make the connection. I reminded him that, after telling me with pride of what he had accomplished, he had said that he was disappointed at *still* being upset by a small criticism. "Oh," he said, "I'm angry at you that after all this analysis I still get upset." From this beginning he was able to widen his exploration into his feelings, ending by saying that when I wasn't responsive to him, like the woman in the fantasy, he gets distant and "irritating." I noted his saying "irritating." After a denial he acknowledged that he has long known, but felt too much spite to admit, that his silences, his ignoring me, must be frustrating and irritating to me.

It is my belief that only through a careful focus on this highly individualistic form of discontinuity, repeated in many analytic hours, could Mr. N and I obtain introspective and empathic entry into his state of mind. He was later to label this state as one of "self-anesthesia" to the potential of a certain-to-be-painful emotional connectedness with me.

5. *The fifth principle of technique is that the analyst's perception is directed toward an appreciation of the analysand's intentions as the analysand would himself perceive them.* In this mode of perceptual focus the analyst carefully attends the analysand's conscious and able-to-be-made conscious aims, ambitions, and ideals. The analyst attempts to identify what the analysand may experience consciously or unconsciously as an impelling pressure and then interprets the self-directed goals that derive from it when the analysand is able to sense and acknowledge the intention as his own (either directly or defensively). In following this technical principle the analyst's perception of the analysand's aims, ambitions, and ideals, and his interpretation of them remains experience-near (preconcious and con-

scious). The premis that guides this work is that with each recognition and successful interpretation of the analysand's available-to-consciousness intention, a deepening of his introspective entry into his own state of mind will occur. As a result, what is from the standpoint of an outside observer a deeply buried (unconscious) urge at one point in the analysis will become gradually accessible to the analysand's introspective appreciation through correct interpretation at a later point in the analytic work.

By focusing on intentions as the analysand would himself perceive them, the analyst can recognize both contradictory intentions (conflict) and regulatory failures. This focus allows what psychoanalysis has identified as manifestations of competing pressures between drives, defenses, and prohibitions to be understood and appreciated from inside the patient's self-perception. With this focus the analysand's associations reveal the struggles he is having to carry out an intention that he believes will lead to satisfaction, mastery, and/or the preservation or enhancement of self-esteem, ideals, and/or cohesion. The analyst is often severely challenged to form an empathic conceptualization of the analysand's intentions when, from the standpoint of the external observer, goals intensely pursued seem maladaptive, and others strongly defended against seem harmless or beneficial.

Mr. N's conscious intentions were clear to him. He wished to observe the religious practices his father valued. He had wished to be chaste until marriage and to marry a virgin whom his mother would approve of and who would honor and respect his mother. He had altered his intention to remain chaste during his brief period of psychotherapy, but he was deadly serious about his intentions to perform all the other actions of a dutiful son. The attendant turmoil this caused him, and the ambivalence he felt, did not alter his determination to pursue his ideals. His goal was to produce harmony, and from his point of view, his outbursts of rage occurred when either parent behaved in such a way as to frustrate his carrying out his intentions to make them comfortable and happy. He regarded the proudest moment of his life to have been when he got the family together and, without screaming or provoking, persuaded his father that he had done marvelously well but, because of changing times and failing health, he should give up his business. Father agreed, and the chaotic, often unproductive, business efforts were brought to an organized, systematic end. From the point of view of an outside observer, Mr. N's dutiful son adaptation would appear as a patently obvious reaction formation. The murderous wishes that appeared in his fantasies were contained (defended against) in this way. By replacing his father and older brother, he could be seen as achieving an oedipal victory of sorts. With Mr. N I found that if I offered an interpretation based on these deductions formed from the viewpoint of the external observer, he responded in ways that clearly indicated the interpretation struck him as insensitive to his goals and ideals. These interpretive efforts seemed to worsen the deflation of his self-esteem caused by his failure to marry and his inability to win the appreciation of his parents.

It was possible to approach these impelling pressures through an appreciation of Mr. N's intentions as he himself perceived them. An alternative group of self-aims and ideals came to notice through persistent dream images of and associations about his parents' little dog Freddy. Freddy frisked about, greeted everyone with eagerness, and showed his happiness with undisguised joy. At first, when Mr. N associated to Freddy, I regarded it as his attempt to cheer himself up and soothe away his anxiety and depression. Then I realized that Freddy represented a latent unconscious self-image of Mr. N when as a very little boy he had been spontaneous, affectionate, and lively, before he became the superserious child who was somewhat cruelly nicknamed "the Judge." In an early dream Freddy was pictured to be in danger from snakes as he romped in the yard. I suggested that Mr. N may have enjoyed similar romping but had become frightened. He quickly assured me that although he enormously enjoyed watching Freddy, he could not imagine himself ever doing that because his mother always made him wear shoes. This was, he added, a protection he regarded as quite sensible, giving an indication of the distance (repression) between his intentions as he knew them and this latent self-image.

With this beginning we were gradually able to use the image of Freddy to identify an alternate current of intentions to be a freer, looser person. Much analytic work needed to be done with respect to his fears before he could even acknowledge that to be looser was a desirable change. After his acceptance of the current of intentions identified through Freddy as his own, the conflictual nature of his previously accepted intentions to pursue a rigid formal "goodness" was recognizable by him. The problems he had in sustaining a spirit of assertive playfulness indicated a regulatory disturbance that underlay and accentuated the intrapsychic conflict. Focusing on these difficulties as they were reflected in his self-directed goals as he perceived them provided a thread that linked the early work with the Freddy image to the work with his fears that was to come later and to the whole working-through process of his conflicts and regulatory disturbances associated with selfobject empathic failures.

6. *The sixth technical principle describes a sequence for the interpretive effort of the analyst. Regarded overall, the aim of this sequence is to enable the analyst to construct for himself and the analysand an "observation platform" on which both can stand and perceive the data of the analyst's empathy and the analysand's introspection.*

1. When the analyst through his empathic perception is able to construct a verbally communicable understanding of the patient's state of mind, he offers this initial bridging interpretation as a way to affirm and confirm the shared state of emotion-laden comprehension. The sense of efficacy or mastery that the analysand experiences as a result of this accurate emotional in-tuneness or mirroring is *not* that of the resolution of conflict. Rather it is the success the patient is having in communicating his state of mind to the analyst and thereby making himself understood. This is the first way station on the path to mastery of an underlying problem, but it is not an end in itself. It is a point where the analyst can often best gauge the success or failure of his empathic perception. Small discrepancies between the analyst's comprehension of the analysand and the analysand's comprehension of the analyst can at this point lead to significant deepening of insight.

2. The analysand who feels himself successful in communicating his state of mind and experiences the ambiance of the analysis as that of a sustaining selfobject may then bring up aspects of a problem in a context of assuming or asserting some degree of responsibility. The analyst's sensitive perception of this often small but extremely meaningful shift to self-assertion can, by empathic mirroring, give a further sustaining boost to the analysand's experience of self-mastery.

3. The analysand who is now able to recognize and communicate his symptom, behavioral disturbance, pathological wish, etc., from a self-originating perspective will often in his associations provide evidence of an alternative or variant (often potentially more nor-

mal) disavowed self. The analyst's perception of this nascent alternative self-aspect gives focus to a struggle-in-depth (current or developmental).

4. The problem or disturbance then may be subject to a deeper, more causal interpretation guided by the nature of the material. If the analyst's understanding of the patient's associations warrants it, his interpretation will focus on the elucidation of an intrapsychic conflict. Alternatively, if in the analyst's view the material warrants it, the interpretation would be made with respect to a disturbance in the patient's relationship with a selfobject that has led to an experience of a defect in self-regulation. Each problem—the intrapsychic conflict and the disturbance in self-state—might be interpreted sequentially. As he listens empathically to the flow of the material, the analyst is guided in his timing and choice of interpretive subject matter by his understanding of the form that the difficulty takes in and out of the transference and by his reconstructions of antecedent forms and variants of conflicts or defects in self-regulation.

I now attempt to illustrate this sequence of interpretative work by the flow of Mr. N's associations and my perceptions and responses during a week in his fifth year of analysis. He began by describing a conversation he had had with his wife about ending analysis. How will he feel during his last hour? Would it be easier to taper off? After a silence he revealed a fantasy that I had become agitated and told him that he had refused to immerse himself in analysis for 5 years, and now he was worrying about leaving. He went on to talk about his desire to change his job and his memories of difficult times of transition in the past. Especially painful was a period in junior high when for the first time he had to take public showers. Everyone assumed that he was afraid to be nude in the shower room, but it really wasn't the nudity—it was taking the shower. He would go through it and try not to get wet. He did force himself to try to learn to swim. He was motivated by the horrible time his brother had experienced because of not being able to swim in high school. He was trying to prepare himself before that. I asked him to describe more about his feelings during his fantasy that I would criticize him for his failure to immerse himself. He was certain that I thought of him as only trying to avoid. I suggested that based on his disappointment with me whenever I failed to acknowledge his efforts and accomplishments, he may have feared I would not recognize that he also tried to master his fear as he had described with his successful effort to learn to swim. He agreed and stated that he knew that we had talked about his fear that if he immersed himself fully he would be hooked to me as he had been to his mother. But he didn't understand the shower and water. I encouraged his thinking about it. He said he could only think of disease, of his mother's warning against drinking from fountains. He would *never* touch a fountain!

Mr. N began the second hour by picking up directly on the material of the day before. This was unusual for him—an indication of personally felt investment in our shared effort. He said we had ended talking about disease from fountains. It would be just like him to take his mother's word without question. He mused about when this started. Ten or eleven? Probably earlier. Was it all the way back to Jay's illness? All he ever remembers is the scene of mother writing to Jay and asking Mr. N if he wanted her to write anything for him. I suggested that this memory may be treasured by him because it supports an illusion of calm at a time of fear. He wondered what he could have been afraid of. He was only 3 or 4. He only knew it was nephritis—a kidney disease. That's all. Well, there was the story about the doctor who did the wrong thing, and Jay almost died. I suggested that he may have become frightened of whatever in his little-boy mind he may have associated with Jay's illness. He answered, "Nothing I know of" in a tone of openness and appeal. I suggested, "Possibly something to do with a doctor who didn't know what he was doing and things to do with streams and flows and toilets." "Oh, oh, now that you say it, it does seem right. I feel it strikes a memory. Yes." After a silence, he said he thought about his mother complaining that his nephew wasn't yet toilet trained at 2. Her boys had been trained long before. He added it's ironic that something that started so well should then prove to be the source of so much trouble. He then described feeling confused. He wondered if he had gotten all mixed up about disease and toilets and water—feces, too? I responded that he may have gotten frightened about anything to do with the toilet and tried to avoid it as though it were connected with disease and danger. Excitedly he replied, "Knowing my mother, she would never have had the patience to explain it." I asked if he pictured her as reacting as he had fantasized me yesterday, getting agitated and saying you refuse to immerse yourself. "Yes, yes—that I'm stubborn—bad." I added,

"Then your concern about disease would have become lost in the struggle over your refusal to use the toilet, what your mother called your 'stubbornness.'" He acknowledged that is what he feels did happen, and he must have then felt lost. I proposed to him that as the issue got shifted to a battle over control, he would not have been able to easily get back to being the friendly, well-trained boy mother viewed him as and he always wishes to think of himself as. He responded, "That's very helpful. I see that, and it's helpful."

He began the third hour stating that yesterday's session had been very helpful, but he is dissatisfied with himself. It had to come from me. He feels that I had expected it to come from him, but he could not produce it. We reviewed his impression of "aggravation" in my voice, which he anticipated and heard when he had blocked and become unproductive. I asked him about my sense yesterday that he had felt open to my suggestions in a way that he frequently cannot let himself be. He then noted that for the first time he had opened his bill and really looked at it. He had feelings about my charging for a missed hour and directly questioned my judgment. I noted the closeness that he was allowing himself and wondered if previously touching and looking at my bill had been like touching and looking at the toilet—a source of very great danger. He exclaimed, "Of course—I couldn't even touch it—that's why even at home if I sat on the seat I held my buttocks from touching."

"I am back from a triumphant visit to the stadium," was his introduction to the fourth hour. He described being able to urinate in a stadium men's room for the first time in his life. He thought about the extreme embarrassment he had undergone in the past. He then associated to several areas of problems about privacy including having anyone know about his analysis. He remembered that he had felt appreciative of my suggestion that his mother had become confused by his stubbornness and hadn't understood why he was having trouble—what was the source of his fear? All she saw was that he had lost his training. I suggested that his being trained so early may have been largely by ritual rather than by being agreed on and worked out by speech, that when he lost the ritual he may have lost the easy flow into speech. He reflected for a moment and noted the similarity to his shifting from more fluid to more labored speech so often here if any tension mounts between us. I added that if speech became an accusation about his stubbornness, then the dialogue between himself and his mother would have been further derailed, forcing him back into ritual. He said like the ritual of having his bowel movements under the piano. He must have been trying to show her he was afraid, but he couldn't tell her. After a silence he said he'd been wondering why under the piano. I noted that he was raising an "analytic question" on his own. With unusual vigor he responded, "That's where mother and Jay would sit and play together. Maybe I had been saying: Shit on you, if you two play together and leave me out." Then, sadly, he reflected that he'd have been better off if he'd learned to play the piano, too. In his daydreams he is a violinist standing alone in a huge concert hall.[4]

It is consistent with the emphasis of the psychology of the self on selfobject transferences to recognize that this rather dramatic uncovering of the traumatic source of a childhood equivalent of a phobia that had become imbedded in Mr. N's character was not in itself curative. It was a foreground occurrence in the analysis that then permitted a systematic reexamination of the more basic transference and the intrapsychic conflicts that derived and persisted because of it. Some weeks later Mr. N stated his view of the effect on him of the developments in his childhood we had reconstructed: "It implanted in my mind a doubt that when something doesn't fit together nice and simply, I won't be able to do it at all, or I'll have a

---

[4]Mr. N suffered from a limitation in his use of metaphor and analogy that constituted a cognitive constriction in the ordinary use of symbolic process. This limitation can be conceptualized as a disturbance in the state of self, a crimping of self. His sensitivity to this impairment played a part in his reluctance to work "analytically" (symbolically) with transference material and with direct "associations" to elements of dreams or fantasies—in all of which the ability to draw an analogy is a prerequisite. This was also a source of one of the meanings of his appeal to me for help, that is, he wished me as an empathic selfobject to sense his cognitive constriction and the deleterious effect it had on his self-confidence. His wish was that I come to his aid to bridge his difficulty—to "uncramp" his mind, rather than ask him the ordinary analytic questions (what comes to your mind about this?). This type of question he felt exposed him to feeling inadequate without helping to identify the source of the problem. In time, as his limitation in appreciating and working with analogy and metaphor was recognized and his sense of failure understood, he became more adventurous in his attempts to "associate" symbolically, as the foregoing example of "why under the piano?" indicates.

Dr. Kohut, in referring to this aspect of Mr. N's problem, described it as a minor thought disorder and suggested that it represented a minor form of self-pathology probably originating in a disturbed selfobject relationship. Both Mr. N's parents appeared to be quite concrete and humorless in their thinking, and his own freedom to play with words may have been affected by the disturbed dialogue with his mother referred to in the material of this hour. It may be causal that his attempt at "playing" with metaphoric thought followed my interpretation of the disrupted dialogue.

terrible time with it." This disturbance in his sense of self-competence or efficacy became the central focus of the terminal phase of his analysis.[5]

Two fragments from his last week illustrate his state of mind at the termination: "I am thinking about this being our last week. Walking over I was looking at the neighborhood and realizing I won't be coming back on a regular basis. I felt sad and a little anxious. I'm leaving something important to me, but I have a good feeling about moving on to another phase of my life." I commented that looking forward gave him something to compensate for his sadness. He agreed and fell silent. I asked about his feelings, and he answered: "Tranquility. Peacefulness. Acceptance."

Later in the week we were analyzing a dream about war, fear, and snakes—elements that pointed to the danger of the eruption of his narcissistic rage into vengeance responses that destroy his capacity for efficacy and competence. I suggested he was concerned that without the analysis he might have trouble curbing the snake of his temper, the potential for engaging in holy wars. I added that the problem, as we had both come to see it, was: How could he experience the full range of his emotions, including anger, without fearing it would destroy the self he wished to be? He responded: "To be able to experience disappointment and anger, particularly with my mother, and not have it interfere with being the kind of person I want to be, is to accept my mother as she wants to be and not have it distract me from the approach I want to take. It means getting away from wanting it to be her who changes. It's to accept that we are different and not allow it to skew my approach to her and to my life. It is a continuing struggle, and it's very helpful to have the perspective I've gained."

---

[5]The sense of competence and efficacy pleasure develops as early as the first months of life as a behavioral pattern within the interactional matrix of infant and mother. It must be converted later into a series of operational choices in the period of separateness of self. Stechler and Kaplan (1980) describe this recurrent conflictual situation in the development of a normal little girl: "her behavior began increasingly to reflect a choice, i.e. when, in an empathic climate, she was presented with the necessity to choose between behavior that reflected the pursuit of the desire versus that which constituted an alliance with the parent, she chose the latter." The conflict surrounding these moment-to-moment choices constitutes, for many patients, a central dynamic around which the so-called positive and negative aspects of the transference turn.

SUMMARY

In conclusion, I wish to restate the six principles of psychoanalytic technique I have proposed:

1. The empathic vantage point for analytic observation is central.
2. Analysts form their constructions by having their perception shift between what the analysand is experiencing in the foreground and in the background. By foreground I mean the immediate content and meaning of the associations the patient is relating. By background I mean the more general status of the receptivity that the patient presumes he or she will receive from the analyst as a transference person, persons, or milieu.
3. Symptomatic alterations in the sense of self must be recognized. These may be restricted to depletion and enfeeblement or progress to states of fragmentation.
4. There is a need to follow patterns in each hour and in each sequence of hours that indicate subtle and gross fluctuations of the patients' way of sensing their state of self in relation to their way of sensing the analyst and the analytic milieu.
5. The analyst's perception is directed toward an appreciation of analysands' intentions as analysands would themselves perceive them.
6. There is a sequence for the interpretive effort of the analyst. Regarded overall, the aim of this sequence is to enable analysts to construct for themselves and for their analysands an "observation platform" on which both can stand and perceive the data of the analyst's empathy and the analysand's introspection.
   a. When analysts, through empathic perception, are able to construct a verbally communicable understanding of the patient's state of mind, they offer this initial bridging interpretation as a way to affirm and confirm the shared state of emotion-laden comprehension.
   b. Analysands who feel themselves successful in communicating their state of mind and experience the ambiance of the analysis as that of a sustaining selfobject may then bring up aspects of a problem in a context of assuming or asserting some degree of responsibility.

c. Analysands who are now able to recognize and communicate the symptom, behavioral disturbance, pathological wish, etc., from a self-originating perspective will often in their associations provide evidence of an alternative or variant (often potentially more normal) disavowed self. The analyst's perception of this nascent, alternative, self-aspect gives focus to a struggle-in-depth (current or developmental).

d. The problem or disturbance may then be subject to a deeper, more causal interpretation guided by the nature of the material. If analysts' understandings of the patients' associations warrant it, their interpretation will focus on the elucidation of an intrapsychic conflict. Alternatively, if in the analyst's view the material warrants it, the interpretation would be made with respect to a disturbance in the patient's relationship with a selfobject that has led to an experience of a defect in self-regulation. Each problem—the structured conflict and the disturbance in self-state—might be interpreted sequentially. As analysts listen empathically to the flow of material, they are guided in their timing and choice of associative subject matter by their understanding of the form the difficulty takes in and out of the transference and by their reconstructions of antecedent forms and variants of conflicts or defects of self-regulation.

REFERENCES

Kohut, H. (1977). *The Restoration of the Self.* New York: Int. Univ. Press.

Lichtenberg, J. (1979). Factors in the development of the sense of the object. *J. Amer. Psychoanal. Assn.* 27: 375–386.

———— (1981). The empathic mode of perception and alternative vantage points for psychoanalytic work. *Psychoanal. Inq.* 1: 329–356.

———— & Lichtenberg, C. (1972). Eugene O'Neill and falling in love. *Psychoanal. Q.* 41: 63–89.

Malin, A. (1982). Panel report: Construction and reconstruction: Clinical aspects. *J. Amer. Psychoanal. Assn.* 30: 213–234.

Ruskin, J. (1855). Letters on Landscape Painting.

Sander, L. (1980). Reporter: New knowledge about the infant from current research: Implications for psychoanalysis. *J. Amer. Psychoanal. Assn.* 28: 181–198.

Schwaber, E. (1979). On the 'self' within the matrix of analytic theory—Some clinical reflections and reconsiderations. *Int. J. Psychoanal.* 60: 467–479.

———— (1980a). Presentation at panel: Construction and reconstruction clinical aspects, *Amer. Psychoanal. Assn.* San Francisco, May 4, 1980.

———— (1980b). Self psychology and the concept of psychopathology: A case presentation. In *Advances in Self Psychology,* A. Goldberg, ed. New York: Int. Univ. Press.

———— (1981a). Empathy: A mode of analytic listening. *Psychoanal. Inq.* 1: 317–392.

———— (1981b). Narcissism, self psychology and the listening perspective. *Ann. Psychonal.* 9: 115–132.

Stechler, G., & Kaplan, S. (1980). The development of the self: A psychoanalytic perspective. *Psychoanal. Study Child* 35: 85–106.

15 Discussion of Paper by Dr. Lichtenberg

N. Treurniet, M.D.

In this discussion paper I try to elucidate Lichtenberg's six technical principles from my own viewpoint as a so-called "classical" analyst who is trying to integrate so-called "self psychology" within the matrix of existing psychoanalytic knowledge as it has been developed by Freud and by many creative analysts after his death. I appreciate the fact that Lichtenberg uses the expression "self psychological viewpoint" in the title of his presentation. The term viewpoint, rather than theory, creates an atmosphere of relativity that is further accentuated by his willingness to describe that viewpoint as he utilizes it. This atmosphere of relativity enhances the realization of our common aim: to help patients explore as much as possible their inner world to the fullest extent of their potentialities. Any obstacle to that aim must be recognized and overcome. Seen from the patient, these obstacles are both external and internal. They may consist of fantasied and/or real empathic failures, very often both. These real and fantasied empathic failures are a special and powerful source of resistance, but they are not the only source. Removing special resistances of fantasied and real empathic failures is a step by step process necessary to help patients overcome their basic resistance against relinquishing the fantasied wish fulfillment of their traumatized past existence; that is, their traumatized past states of self whether object-instinctual or narcissistic, libidinal or aggressive. In another paper Lichtenberg (1981) has called this the empathic process. Although this process is a necessary condition for the psychoanalytic process, it is not to be considered identical with it, nor it is an aim in itself. It is from this vantage point that self psychology deals with special resistances based on special disruptions of the working alliance. I now turn to the gist of Lichtenberg's paper.

Before treating the six principles of technique, first something should be said about the case. Mr. N was not broken. He was intact but constricted, inhibited, without ease or joy, living with a crippling dependence on his parents. I like Lichtenberg's choice. He sees the conflict in his patient, not in the theories. To place "selfobject disorders" versus "structural neuroses" is, I believe, a clinical invention based on polemic rather than scientific arguments. By his choice Lichtenberg did not join the one-sided, simplistic, and spurious polarity of defect and conflict. Mr. N represents more or less the usual average of the analytic patient population of our time. And by not contributing to the splitting tendencies that are always present between closely related groups with conflicting views, Lichtenberg again contributes to an atmosphere of relativity and ease, which is a precondition for the integrating tendencies that are present in Lichtenberg's presentation and to which I feel myself an exponent. But now the principles of technique.

The First Principle.   The first principle concerns the centrality of the empathic vantage point for analytic observation. I agree completely with Lichtenberg when he contends that "perceiving the analysand's state of mind, his immediate and general way of experiencing himself and others, his range of feelings and thoughts is . . . the critical task of analysis, but to do it requires the greatest discipline." But I strongly disagree with him when he equates the position of the imagined "outside" observer with that of the classical analyst.

This is exactly what Wallerstein (1980) meant when he identified the perspective that self psychology gives to classical theory as an imputed error from which self psychology then feels it rescues psychoanalysis. It is a clear example of an either/or dichotomy, in which a straw man has been set up to prove the superiority of the self psychological viewpoint, but the real opposition is that between bad technique—interpretations that exhort and blame—and appropriate technique—explanations without censure. Instead I would prefer to raise the level of discussion by pointing out that Lichtenberg at this stage of the analysis of Mr. N besides using empathic considerations also uses inferential statements. By conjecture he makes clear that Mr. N's resistance to introspection is an expression of the displaced protection against severe narcissistic traumatization as a child in the sphere of being seen while having drive-cathected bodily reactions as an expression of strong emotions while defecating under the piano. It is probably just as likely a conjecture that Mr. N can be expected to experience strong conflicts about separation-individuation and anality among many other conflicts. Of course all analysts use as a frame of reference for inference the entire body of knowledge they have acquired from their former empathic experiences, observations, the study of theory, and their incorporation of the literature of psychoanalysis. It is the inappropriate use of this knowledge in the form of inappropriate interpretations that is at stake. Inappropriate use is not the exclusive hallmark of classical analysis.

Lichtenberg calls attention to the need for discipline to maintain an empathic stance. This is especially true for the times when our patients test our ability to be dehumanized, to be depersonalized, to be used as an extension of the patient's self, in short, to be used only as a function. It is in this realm that Kohut's observations can be valued as significant contributions to our technique, although I have objections against some of his formulations on technical, not formal, grounds. I come back to this later in my presentation.

That Mr. N's resistance to introspection is of course a defensive maneuvre is beautifully illustrated by the sequence of material discharging into the flow of tears about the loss of his beloved dog. This sequence provided the basis for two significant entries into his mind: the importance of gentle persistence and the strength of his affectionate feelings. I would call your attention, however, to Lichtenberg's probably deliberate omission of a third and to my idea crucial entry into Mr. N's state of mind. Mr. N's disavowal of being distressed by drive-cathected thoughts, feelings, and memories like defecating under the piano, like cheating, stealing, and masturbating thinking of black girls, was lifted by the analyst's empathic persistence. This provided enough safety to express one of his probably most constricting conflicts which could be formulated somewhat like this: "Dogs can just as well be loved and mourned as human beings; that is, basically I experience myself sometimes as a sexual and aggressive animal because I was seen as such long ago by my parents. I want that animal to be respected and loved as I respected and loved my dog Connie."

It is not my intention to analyze Mr. N looking over Lichtenberg's shoulder. Technically, neither of the three entries should be interpreted in isolation, and much is dependent on the wording and the timing. I just want to call attention to a dimension that is in danger of being neglected by self psychology. Drive manifestations are not simply so-called disintegration products of a fragmented self. They are just the reverse. Drive-cathected states of past and present experience threaten the conscious self because of the often considerable shame and guilt feelings connected with the drive states. These states may have a fragmenting influence on the self-experience of the analysand if they are not empathically recognized as an aspect of the legitimate primitive self of the child that the patient once was. Given the right timing and wording it may be an empathic failure *not* to give that interpretation if the patient asks for it, so to speak, when he or she is ready. The drive-cathected wish should, of course, never be identified in isolation, as a pure wish and nothing more. It should always be embedded in a state of (always partial) wholeness: the literal revival of a memory of an experience in which a living self usually interacts with one or more real or fantasied objects, accompanied by significant affective experiences by which it has become split off from the development of the self or ego. This split is always the result of conflict. It represents for the patient an undesirable solution to his or her conflict and can often be replaced by a more desirable one.

The Second Principle. The task of analysts to form their constructions by letting their attention shift between foreground and background is to my idea the most encompassing indication of what we call analytic skill, and as such it has an immediate relevance for technique. Integration of foreground and background phenomena, however, does more. It creates the experience of depth, which in its connection with the category of time forms the basis for the conceptual development of our science.

In a very illuminating footnote Lichtenberg cites a child psychiatrist and a painter. The child psychiatrist, Professor Sander, illustrated the use of the concepts of background and foreground to explain the fitting together of mother and infant in the domain of time. The painter, John Ruskin, advocated the study of atmosphere, which defines and measures space. Theoretically, in thus connecting the basic categories of space and time, Lichtenberg is in excellent company. Freud was able to discover and create the analytic technique, with which a more or less two-dimensional, superficial surface phenomenon (i.e., the foreground social encounter between doctor and patient) gradually could be changed into a three-dimensional, developing process (i.e., the analytic process) in which the categories of time and space could coincide and synchronize. Every shift from foreground to background, every oscillation between surface and depth, a spatial phenomenon, thereby became in principle a possible opportunity to gather data about and reconstruct deeply buried events from the unique history of the object of study, a temporal phenomenon. In principle it is the same connection between time and space that is made by geology, or for that matter archeology, regardless of whether we visit the Grand Canyon or the remnants of the Minoan Civilization.

Of course, Freud did much more than discover this technique. Besides using it therapeutically, he employed the technique as a tool to create the until now most encompassing conceptual organization for explaining the development and functioning of the human mind.

One of the cornerstones of this conceptual organization is Freud's multidimensional way of thinking. He continually thought from more than one theoretical viewpoint at the same time or in succession without having made this always explicit. This sometimes makes it difficult to grasp the fundamental importance of his metapsychology, which, incidentally, was not a static phenomenon. Freud's theory formation can be described as an account of interaction that he time and again changed (Van der Leeuw, 1969). He conceptualized an interaction of different configurations, of different "parts," of different systems in the personality. In essence Freud's multidimensional way of thinking is characterized by a very felicitous integration of the forces present in all the dimensions we have at our disposal: the three of space and the one of time. One of these forces was constituted by our biological existence, and one of the crucial interactions has always been the interaction between biological force and cultural meaning, creating the viewpoints of drive conflict and conflict solution, the dynamic and the economic points of view.

I thoroughly agree with Van der Leeuw (1969) when he writes that the spatial representation, not the number, has Freud's preference. In this spatial representation the prevailing phenomena are characterized by motion and movement, by place and displacement and by division and partition of that spatial representation. And above all: these movements, displacements and divisions are powered and monitored by forces which, when attached to incompatible meanings give rise to the manifold vicissitudes of conflict and conflict solution so well known in our clinical and technical reality.

To be sure, the same spatial and temporal categories are discernible in Kohut's formulations of self-cohesion and self-continuity, but the qualities of cohesion and continuity are just as valid for the nonself-experience: the representation of the outside world. Moreover, in his earlier work, Kohut indeed enriched us with his illuminating descriptions of the defensive conflict solution of the vertical split. In his recent work, which constituted the birth of self psychology, he seems to have abandoned any reference to the conceptualization of conflict and conflict solution. The conceptualizations of conflict remain an indispensable factor in the understanding of the workings of the human mind.

Returning now to clinical and technical considerations, Lichtenberg's second (can we now call it multidimensional?) principle has important connections with many familiar clinical and technical psychoanalytic conceptualizations. Clinically, the foreground–background differentiation is intimately related to the concept of epigenesis, which by now is a very substantial part of our clinical psychoanalytic knowledge. To make a rather arbitrary listing, it appeared in the diagnosis of oral hysteria, in the differentiation of phallic-oedipal from phallic-narcissistic (Edgcumbe & Burgner, 1975), in the differentiation of mode and zone (Erikson, 1950), and in the concept of the anal penis in perversions (Chasseguet-Smirgel, 1974).

Technically, the foreground–background differentiation is central to our psychoanalytic work. It has been very clearly expressed in the work of that preeminent self psychologist avant la lettre, Donald Winnicott (1965). His conceptualizations of the holding environment and of the potential space as a re-creation of the early mother-child atmosphere in the analytic situation are very similar to Lichtenberg's description of "support systems that form and sustain self-cohesion and basic trust, optimism and a capacity for joy."

These qualities in the analyst and the ability to recognize them in the patient are a technical prerequisite for psychoanalytic work. The creation of a holding environment in the mother-child interaction forms the basis of the later ego functions of recognition, acknowledgment really, and memory. The disruptions of the holding environment unfortunately lead to the counterpart of these ego functions: disavowal and repression. This is the reason why every change for a schizophrenic patient is a loss instead of a gain and every new situation means a complete break; the break, or conflict, in the foreground also smashes the background. Only when the background organization is stable and predictable can the islands of the foreground experience be connected into a meaningful whole, ultimately leading to a more or less cohesive self-organization. And only when the background color and music of the analytic atmosphere are of a comparable (i.e., an essentially empathic) nature can the patient work with the analyst to fill this potential space gradually with all the foreground and background manifestations we see in the psychoanalytic process.

There is one problem, however, that I would like to accentuate. In order to offer the patient a predictable, empathic, and safe atmosphere, analysts must possess their own stable foreground and background organization. This is of course very much a function of the analyst's health, by which I mean that he or she should have incorporated a sound knowledge of analytic and extraanalytic reality. In other words, empathy and introspection are not enough.

An analyst's working mind operates by shifting between two more or less opposite poles: the subjective, empathic, introspectional pole versus the objective, observational, detached pole. The well-known conceptual constructs of the analyst's participating versus observing ego are an expression of this polarity. Elsewhere I (Treurniet, 1980) have expressed it as follows:

> The essence of the technical operations occurring in the psychoanalytic situation is a rhythmic interchanging and interacting alteration of two different functions of the analyst: the subjective stance, the (vicariously) introspective immersion in the patient, alternates with the objective stance, the more distant observation. This process is "transitional" in the sense that being in the one state we are never out of touch with the other. There is a rhythmical balance between observing and experiencing, between detachment and union [p. 372].

This observational pole, consisting of the analyst's knowledge and guarded by his ego function of reality testing, is just as indispensable for his technical skill as is the empathic-introspective vantage point. Therefore, I consider neither of these vantage points to be central in itself but only in combination with each other. Only then is it possible for an analyst to accompany the patient without getting lost. The patient should feel safe with him in order to use the potential space of the analysis to its fullest extent, that is, to let the foreground–background structure of his own representational world move as freely as possible, to let it become as upside-down and as inside-out in the topsy-turvy pattern of his own developing analytic process as he pleases. Analysts can only take care of that process and the patient if they are able to see if and when elements of the background–foreground world are in conflict: foreground against background or vice versa, oedipal versus pre-oedipal or the other way around, transference versus nontransference, and so on. Anything may be used as a defense against anything. Correct insight is only possible if one is able to view psychic phenomena as a result of meanings attached to forces, which (not always but often) are in conflict. Once in conflict, these forces create a demand for work and call for a conflict solution.

The theory that groups these meanings together as different systems with different functions but interacting in power relations is called metapsychology. The elements of this theory are not things or objects, conflicting or colluding as in the physical world. Rather, they are comparable to coordinates, meant to assist in orientation and without which one gets lost. The analyst, then, must have incorporated the knowledge warehoused in this theory, implicitly or explicitly, into his or her way of professional functioning. This is the background of my conviction that self psychology in the narrow sense is a gain to psychoanalysis, but self psychology in the broader sense is a grave and serious loss, especially from the viewpoint of technique. The metapsychology of the technique of self psychology in the broader sense is threatening to rob psychoanalysis of some of its most valuable technical conceptual tools, the dynamic and economic points of view.

Before I go on I would like to make the following point: The differentiation between the empathic-introspective and the objective-observational vantage points, between he inside and outside points of view as equally indispensable technical positions, should be clearly distinguished from the inappropriate use of either view-point in technique. Of course, the analyst can use the "outside view" as a countertransferential defense against a threatening commu-nication of the patient. But so can the empathic-introspectional van-tage point, the "inside view," be misused by the analyst to soothe the patient at a moment when his real need might be to come face to face with his own demands and rage. Here again one gets the im-pression that the self psychologist "rescues" a patient from the un-empathic classical analyst. This might be a sign of a one-sided "em-pathy-distrubution" in the analyst's judgment and assessment of the patient's past and parents.

As Wallerstein (1980) has pointed out, the discussion between self psychology and classical analysis is often conducted by self psy-chologists in terms of another discussion: that between good tech-nique and bad technique. Anyhow, it should be clear that I do not consider the first principle, the empathic vantage point as central. The second principle, the foreground–background principle, is vast-ly superordinate as a technical principle because it offers the best opportunity for a metapsychology of technique.

The Third Principle.   The recognition of symptomatic states of depletion, enfeeblement, or even fragmentation of the self is a very important approach to what I think is the most essential technical contribution of Kohut's work: the enlarged understanding of the meaning of interpretation, which paves the way for an interpreta-tion (of the meaning) of interpretation. By this I mean the under-standing, or rather acknowledgment and if necessary the interpre-tation, of the experiential influence of the unique and in essence unknowable nucleus of the analyst's personality on the unique and equally unknowable personality of the patient. This understanding cannot be differentiated strongly enough from what is generally understood by the universe of transference–countertransference manifestations. This understanding also implies the notion of a seeming paradox: real empathy, that is, empathy employed by someone who utilizes more sources of data gathering from reality than only empathy, implies the observation of its own limitations (Treurniet, 1980).

In his description of Mr. N's prolonged state of enfeeblement and depletion in the middle phase of his analysis, Lichtenberg touches on these most important issues. The first interpretation that served to lessen Mr. N's regressive distancing was a frank communication by Lichtenberg that he felt the patient perceived him as being out of touch with what he found helpful. In fact, this amounted to a quiet recognition by Lichtenberg that his capacities to understand his patient were clearly limited: in other words, a recognition of the limitations of the power of his empathy and at the same time a frank acknowledgment of the analyst's dependence on the patient as an independent center of experience and initiative in the cooperation of the analytic work, which is an acknowledgment of the patient's independent self. That this became so beneficial for the ensuing period of the analysis is borne out by the material that followed and the at least temporal resolution of Mr. N's related conflicts over separation from his parents. The key to this resolution was the awareness that Mr. N's successes were regarded by him more as the successes of his mother and his tutor than as his own. In this light he experienced every success in his analysis as a success of his analyst instead of the result of his growing and developing self. Insofar as this step to separation-individuation was for a variety of reasons too dangerous to make, the only possibility was to regress into a state in which he could disclaim the responsibility for his success and for his failure resulting in the reproach that his analyst did not push or revitalize him. The only possible solution to this conflict, the only way to make oneself felt, or literally one's self felt, then, consists of this maneuvre of mounting pressure on the analyst as a repetition of mounting pressures on the parents who did frequently collapse to this pressure. The paradoxical meaning, at least in this case, of the essentially defensive depletion is that there are situations in which one can exist only by making the other person feel that one is not there (for his, the other's aggrandizement). The crucial mutating experience for the patient I think has been the recognition by the analyst of the patient's separate existence as a person. This recognition of separateness cannot but enhance the patient's sense of dignity, to which he is fully entitled. In this case and at that phase of the analysis, the patient unconsciously experienced the interpreting analyst as his pushing mother, who utilized the patient as an extension of her own narcissistically enfeebled self-organization. For the patient to experience himself unconsciously as an extension of the analyst's self-organization is bound to have grave consequences for the working alliance at that moment. From then on, this background problem presents itself in the foreground until it is recognized, understood, handled, and interpreted by the analyst from a basic attitude that does not foster this unconscious fantasy of the patient.

Before discussing Lichtenberg's next principles, however, I cannot help drawing your attention to the fact that the clinical vignette used by him in illustrating his third principle clearly points to a conflict (over separation), not a deficit. Consequently, this vignette is no illustration of the value of self psychology in the broad sense. But neither are those used in his illustration of the other principles.

The Fourth Principle. The need to follow patterns in each hour and in each sequence of hours, which indicates subtle and gross fluctuations of the patient's way of sensing his state of self in relation to his way of sensing the analyst and the analytic milieu, is a most important technical qualification indeed. After one of his silences Mr. N stated he would like to ignore his fantasy.

Lichtenberg then called attention to his patient's wish to treat his own fantasy as a waste product, thereby implying that he had more respect for the products of Mr. N's mind than the patient had himself. The next clue to insight was the patient's description of his own feeling state as distant and "irritating," instead of irritated, thereby revealing again a significant aspect of his conflicts over separation-individuation; namely, his by now practically conscious connection that his analyst, like his mother, cannot tolerate his existence as an independent person who also needs distance. It is Lichtenberg's belief that only by a careful focus on this highly individualistic form of discontinuity can both analyst and patient obtain entry into the patient's state of mind.

Of course, I completely agree. Again, it is the respect for the patient's individualistic form that is the key experience of a truly analytic nonintrusive relationship which enhances the working alliance and willpower to work through this pre-oedipally determined conflict. The patient's "self-anesthesia" turned out to be a crippling solution of intense, probably oedipally as well as pre-oedipally determined, conflicts about emotional connectedness in general as a replica of the dangers of his connectedness to his mother and father in particular. For this, however, we do not need the theoretical contentions of self psychology: Again, the so-called deficit of the self-experience is clearly the result of conflict. Moreover, this technical maneuvre was a necessary but also preliminary step—a condition, an opening up. I am sure that after this opening up, the painful emotional connectedness with the parents has been relived, remembered, and worked through analytically. To leave it at the opening up, at the empathic understanding, would be to leave the patient in the lurch. I do not say that Lichtenberg did, but self psychology suggests—at least in theory—that it would be sufficient. Furthermore, this is clearly a vignette in which the resistance, the silence, and the fantasy had little to do with empathic failure but clearly can be seen as a manifestation of transference.

The Fifth Principle. According to Lichtenberg, "the analyst's perception is directed toward a focus in which impelling pressures are regarded as components of conscious and to-be-made conscious self-directed goals as the analysand would himself perceive his aims, ambitions, and ideals to be. By focusing on intentions as the analysand would himself perceive them, the analyst can recognize both contradictory intentions (conflict) and regulatory failures without an exclusive or narrow focus on competing drives or on externally identifiable manifestations of competing pressures between drives, defenses, and prohibitions." With this principle, as with the others, there is hardly a word with which a classical analyst could disagree. This principle is nothing less than a call for attention to the healthy part of the personality of the patient.

Understanding of the adaptive aspect of conflict solutions is of course a prerequisite for every analysis. Imposition of the analyst's own intentions, convictions, and solutions on the patient is wrong technique. This is true since the time of Freud, who repeatedly warned against it, and it has been raised to the status of a metapsychological viewpoint since Heinz Hartmann: the adaptive point of view. What, then, is the new quality, the contribution of self psychology, to this classical analytic principle? The very fact that a certain content of the ideal formation is the result of a conflict solution of course does not mean that the analyst loses sight of the importance of the function of this ideal for this patient. Mr. N's dutiful-son adaptation was, besides other things, a patently obvious reaction formation against murderous wishes. Interpretations of this constellation are naturally very insensitive and cause the depletion of any patient's self-esteem if they are made out of an empathic context with the phase and concrete material of the analytic process at that moment. That would be tantamount to wild analysis.

Any candidate who would do with a patient what Lichtenberg imputes here into classical analysis would cause the concern of his or her supervisors.

Before discussing the last principle, one other remark is in order. After Freddie's, the dog's, carefree romping in the yard had appeared into the analysis, Lichtenberg rightly suggested that Mr. N might have enjoyed similar romping but had become frightened. Mr. N could not, however, imagine himself ever doing that because his mother always made him wear shoes, a very sensible protection with snakes around. This piece of material is, as so many other pieces in this beautiful case illustration, a clear indication of Mr. N's conflict about becoming a freer, looser sort of person. Again, this is not a structural deficit, but an ego restriction as a result of conflict.

The Sixth Principle.   This principle deals with the sequence for the interpretive effort of the analyst in order to enable him to construct for himself and the analysand an "observation platform" on which both can stand and perceive the data of the analyst's empathy and the analysand's introspection. The aim of the first step is not the resolution of conflict; rather, it is the first way station, the first paving of the road that ultimately leads to the resolution of conflict. That the success of the patient in communicating his state of mind to the analyst, the success in making himself understood, creates an emotional climate, a preparation for "significant deepening of insight," in which the patient feels sustained is to my idea stating the obvious and means nothing less (and nothing more) than that the patient's feeling of safety should be guarded by the empathic tact of the analyst. This obviousness is obscured when it is translated into the terminology of a new theory, whose findings and real achievements, impressive as they are when seen in their real and limited, clinical and technical perspective, are based primarily on a better understanding of the conditions of the working alliance. The first two steps described by Lichtenberg are vital steps in securing the strengthening an atmosphere favorable as well as necessary for the development of an optimal working alliance, recognized as a vital element in technique by classical analysis a long time ago (e.g., the same steps and principles are described by Greenson, 1967). When and if this working alliance is sustained and secured, the third step is self-evident. The analysand only then feels safe enough to reveal intimate but vital information to recognize his symptoms, behavioral disturbances, pathological wish, and the like "from a self-originating perspective." It has much to do with a correct understanding and management of the affect of shame. This is no more and no less than the endeavor to create a climate in which the patient can progress to the next step—that he can feel for himself that, as Dr. Lichtenberg calls it, his "nascent alternative self-aspect gives focus to a struggle in depth, current or developmental." This is a somewhat complicated way to express these steps as preparations to let the patient experience himself to be in conflict with himself. Here again, the opposition is not that between a structural defect versus a disturbance in the relation with a so-called selfobject. Every pathological conflict situation, be it oedipal, pre-oedipal, adolescent, or latency, gives rise to a defective self-experience, or rather to a defective, considerably less than optimal, regulation of self-esteem. Defective experiences cannot be equated with structural defects as they have been conceptualized by classical analysis.

Although the technical sequence is beautifully carried out and described by Lichtenberg, he misses the point when he claims this to be the technique of self psychology versus classical analysis. As for the excellent and moving description of the working through of Mr. N's resistance against a working closeness and its defensive (not defective) replacement by the ritual, this is only another example of the structural consequences of an unmastered, unconscious conflict. The fact that a supposedly better and more empathic mother would have helped him to find another solution does not in any way support the theory that the conflict is caused by an unempathic mother or selfobject. The conflict is there, and the child needs help in overcoming it. In this case the relative absence of this help implanted in Mr. N's mind a doubt that "when something does not fit together nice and simply he won't be able to do it at all or he'll have a terrible time with it." Here the patient expresses better than the theory he is supposed to support that he was afraid to experience normal conflicts and did not get help in finding another solution. I think this is an essential element of parental as well as analytic help—the fact that the analyst as well as a parent sometimes functions as an extension of the patient's or child's self in that both are ready to take over a vital function of the patient or child if necessary. That vital function is the structuring of internal and external reality; it is here that problem solving and conflict solution are identical. That vital function is also the function of the so-called selfobject, or the selfobject aspect of the relationship, analytically defined as the basis of the working alliance (Lampl-de Groot, 1975). The fact that at the origins of self, at or before the psychological birth of the infant, the reality-structuring activity of the mother is identical with the drive-satisfying activity of the mother does not warrant the creation of a whole new psychology which tries to reduce all later developments of drive organization (and its conflicts and their vicissitudes) to deficits in the development of structure.

In reviewing Lichtenberg's contribution I was struck by his fine and refined description of his case as well as by the technical principles he employed. The way he utilized Kohut's technical and clinical findings showed how expertly he guided his patient into experiencing and working through his basic instinctual conflicts. Each of Lichtenberg's principles proved a valuable tool to pave the way to that goal. But I was also struck by the conceptual tour de force he had to employ in order to squeeze sound analytic knowledge into the crippled language of self psychology. The empathic vantage point had to prevail at all costs and when he clearly, and to my mind quite justly, used inferential knowledge implicitly and a so-called "structural defect" had to be proved, when there was only a question of an experience of self-deficiency as a defense against intensely feared wishes and needs.

Listening to self psychologists one invariably gets the impression that classical psychoanalysis has degenerated into an instrument to destroy the dignity and self-organization of our patients, the ambitions and ideals of people. To my mind, only a thorough reflection on the meaning of Kohut's method can furnish a possible answer to the question of why self psychology is so immersed in its own self-absorption that every connection with comparable and interesting work of so many other analysts in our professional world is so seriously severed. Or, to put it in other, more self-psychological words: Why is self psychology so patently unempathic with creations of its mental ancestors and siblings, if empathy is considered the major tool in the formation of psychoanalytic knowledge?

REFERENCES

Chasseguet-Smirgel, J. (1974). Perversion, idealization and sublimation. *Int. J. Psychoanal.* 55: 349–357.

Edgcumbe, R. & Burgner, M. (1975). The phallic-narcissistic phase: A differentiation between praeoedipal and oedipal aspects of phallic development. *Psychoanal. Study Child* 30: 161–180.

Erikson, E. H. (1950). *Childhood and Society*. New York: Norton.

Lampl-de Groot, J. (1975). Vicissitudes of Narcissism and problems of civilization. *Psychoanal. Study Child* 30: 663–682.

van der Leeuw, P. J. (1969). On Freud's theory formation. *Int. J. Psychoanal.* 50: 573–582.

Lichtenberg, J. (1981). Empathy and other vantage points for psychoanalytic work. *Psychoanal. Inq.* 1.

Treurniet, N. (1980). On the relation between the concepts of self and ego in Kohut's psychology of the self. *Int. J. Psychoanal.* 61: 325–333.

Wallerstein, R. (1980). Self-psychology and 'classical' psychoanalytic psychology: The nature of their relationship—A review and an overview. This volume.

Winnicott, D. W. (1965). *The Maturational Processes and the Facilitating Environment*. New York: Int. Univ. Press.

16 Discussion of Papers by Drs. Lichtenberg and Ornstein

Ernest S. Wolf, M.D.

A number of issues come into the foreground immediately when such complicated topics as are represented by Lichtenberg's and by Ornstein's papers are to be discussed. Both papers deal with aspects of the psychology of the self, and thus both are located at the frontiers of the scientific psychoanalytic enterprise.

In any living science there is always a forward edge where the whole system of the data, method, and theory of the field is in flux, and changed theory provides a new view of and gives new meaning to the previously accepted conceptualizations. In such cases the discussants have open one of several options among which to choose their approach. They can choose to stand with the older theory and challenge the presenter of novel ideas to demonstrate the usefulness of the proposed modifications or innovations. They can question the innovator about the soundness of the data, the applicability of the method, and the logic and coherence of the new theory. Distortions and innuendos not directed to substantive issues but to discredit the investigator *ad hominem* are not permissible in scientific discourse. However, in the heat of the controversies evoked by self psychology, such a rule is easily breached.

Alternatively, discussants can adopt a second option for their comments. They can accept the proposed innovation and by examining its impact on various problems, unresolved issues, and even on some apparently resolved ones, elaborate the consequences of the new theory for the whole scientific field in question. In my discussion here I take this second approach mainly. But before beginning I wish to make a few comments regarding the status and acceptance of the psychology of the self with psychoanalysis.

Science is a human activity in response to an unquenchable thirst for understanding and explanation, to know more and more with increasingly closer approximation to an unknowable truth. It is my belief that in science generally, not just in psychoanalysis, those theories survive that over a period of time prove themselves to be the most useful in furthering the growth of the scientific enterprise itself. Self psychology, it seems to me, has given the greatest impetus to the psychoanalytic scientific enterprise since ego psychology superseded id psychology. No one, at this point in the history of psychoanalysis, can foretell which psychoanalytic theories will survive and which will fall by the wayside. That will be decided in thousands of analysts' consultation rooms during millions of analytic hours over the coming decades. It will not be decided by the exposition of the most clearly defined and most precisely conceptualized theory, nor by the publication of the most instructive case histories of the highest fidelity. Indeed, these may illuminate important aspects of the psychoanalytic experience and thus point the analyst and the analysand into the most fruitful direction. But what will prevail in the scientific marketplace can only be explained *ex post facto,* not predicted with certainty.

I now turn to the papers by Lichtenberg and by A. Ornstein. However, my comments are not intended to challenge their presentations or to second-guess them (which is ever so easy when someone presents clinical material because one can always find additional or alternative interpretations), but to see how their insights might enrich our psychoanalytic knowledge. Lichtenberg's paper focuses on the details of the therapeutic process in psychoanalysis. Ornstein addresses herself to important theoretical and clinical issues raised by Kohut's reformulation of the Oedipus complex. Both papers are supported by clinical material, but as already mentioned, such clinical evidence should be viewed for its ability to highlight and evoke in the experienced psychoanalyst the familiar psychoanalytic situation. One should not attempt to use case reports as the equivalent of the actual clinical experience and try to prove or disprove something.

Lichtenberg presents an excellent paper on current topics in self psychology; in particular, he is concerned with technique. In harmony with traditional psychoanalytic thinking, he brings forth the clinical data upon which he then bases his theoretical elaboration. And in keeping with Kohut's injunction to eschew rigid definitions and final closures, Lichtenberg demonstrates how he applies six principles of technique to the psychoanalysis of a particular case. The result is an impressive elaboration of clinical and theoretical insights.

Lichtenberg's six principles of technique are in summary fashion: (1) to place empathy in the central vantage point; (2) to allow one's empathic perceptions to oscillate between foreground and background; (3) to pay attention to the state of the self, (e.g., depletion, enfeeblement, fragmentation, etc.); (4) to follow closely the fluctuations of the state of the self from session to session and within each session in the relation to analyst and to the analytic ambience; (5) to focus on the intentions of the self as perceived by the analysand; (6) to follow a certain sequence of steps in making interpretations in such a way as to allow the analysand increasing scope for expression of either a defect in self-regulation or of an intrapsychic conflict which can then be interpreted.

In my discussion I propose to relate Lichtenberg's six technical principles to the goal of analysis, that is, psychological health. P. Ornstein (1980) has published a detailed exposition of the concept of health as viewed from the standpoint of a psychoanalytic theory of the bipolar self. Kohut, furthermore, in an as yet unpublished manuscript, has succinctly defined health as that state when a reliable, continuous, and cohesive tension arc between the two poles of the self has become securely established in at least one sector of the personality.

But let me first very briefly review the six principles. Lichtenberg's first principle is the centrality of the empathic vantage point. This means that all the data used in psychoanalytic treatment are to be processed by the analyst in such a way as to reveal how the particular events from which the data originate are experienced by the analysand. That is, any event anywhere is experienced by the analysand in a specific manner, which depends on his or her total life history, or, to put the statement in still another form, the analysand's experience can only occur within a historically determined context that gives it meaning. For example, the analyst may hear the patient speak of his pleasure in planning a long trip to a favorite vacation spot, but at the same time, the analyst may become aware by introspection of a certain resonant uneasiness within himself. These sensory perceptions, whether perceived extrospectively (the tremulousness) or introspectively (the uneasiness), are data that inform the analyst in his attempt to sense himself into the inner experience of his analysand, and he interprets at this moment that the analysand is experiencing a degree of anxiety.[1] Not much can be said about the process of resonance that allows the analyst to relate his introspected uneasiness, a signal uneasiness, to the analysand's anxiety except that this capacity for *vicarious* introspection into the inner experience of others is trainable and, with experience, becomes increasingly reliable, similar to the trainability and increasing reliability of extrospective perceptions.

Armed with an introspective-empathic perception of the analysand's inner experience, the analyst can now view all the elements of the analysand's psychic life through the eyes of the analysand, so to speak. In his imagination the analyst can now station himself in the middle of the analysand's inner experience, the empathic vantage point, and construct hypotheses about how and why the analysand thinks and feels about his experience. To construct these hypotheses, the analyst processes the empathic introspective data together with extrospective data under the guidance of a theoretic framework (i.e., a psychoanalytic theory). More simply, the analyst tries to make sense out of the empathic observations by putting them together with extrospective observations within the framework of a theory.

---

[1]Both extrospective and introspective data are organized into perceptions along two different schemata in such a way that in the extrospective mode perceptions appear as if from the outside of the observed, whereas in the introspective mode perceptions appear as if experienced inside. Extro- and introspective percepts, therefore, are distinguished only by the different way the raw data are organized. The extrospective and introspective perceptions are then further processed, in psychoanalysis, by the consideration of psychoanalytic theory, history, and so forth to yield psychoanalytic interpretations. It is clear that data from both modes are needed to result in fully rounded encompassing interpretations. Extrospective data alone result in the construction of a lifeless, machinelike "mental apparatus"; introspective data alone result in imaginative, sometimes dreamlike, creations with an uncertain hold on reality. Scientific psychoanalysis combines both types of perceptions into the flesh and blood of real people in a real world.

Lichtenberg stresses the difficulty and the necessity of maintaining the empathic vantage point, and he points out that the greatest discipline is required. Discipline, derived from the Latin *discipulus,* meaning pupil (and the antithesis of *doctor,* which means teacher), does indeed describe what is required of analysts: to let themselves be instructed by the analysand's experience rather than by their own "superior" knowledge. This entails a very difficult, temporary negation of the analyst's intellectual self in the service of the analysis; a negation during which the analyst may experience himself uncomfortably as an extension of the analysand, as the analysand's selfobject. It is a discipline that requires the analyst's willing suspension of his belief in the reality of his own world and to accept, instead, for a time, the patient's world—a world that may strike the outside observer as an illusion—as the true operative reality. It corresponds to Freud's (1912) injunction: " [The analyst] should withhold all conscious influences from his capacity to attend, and give himself over completely to his 'unconscious memory' [p. 112]."

This leads me to Lichtenberg's second technical principle of recommending that analysts let their empathic perceptions oscillate between foreground and background. I believe Lichtenberg here tries to describe a background, overall ambience of a readiness to attempt a mutual understanding. We used to call this the therapeutic alliance, which means that the analysand for much of the time experiences the analyst as a sustaining selfobject presence. In contrast to this, Lichtenberg poses in the foreground the awareness of disturbances that arise in the self-selfobject relation between analyst and analysand, which can be delineated most clearly by comparison with the relative composure of the background ambience. It is the sustaining power of this background that allows foreground disturbances to occur without a total disruption of the analytic process.

Lichtenberg's third and fourth technical principles recommend focusing on the state of the self, its depletion or fragmentation, and following closely these fluctuations of the state of the self within each hour and from hour to hour. These fluctuations, sensed empathically, are profitably viewed as manifestations of selfobject responses that fail to sustain the formerly cohesive self-experience. The fluctuations in the state of the self become clues to the transference; for example, the depletions or fragmentations are the result of the unavailability of a needed, sustaining, mirroring, or idealizable selfobject.

However, the states of fragmentation or depletion are extremely painful and rightfully feared. Analysands may well act to prevent this fierce discomfort by all of the means at their disposal. Lichtenberg's patient, for example, through his silences tried to avoid saying something that might irritate the analyst and thereby destroy the equanimity of the minimally sustaining selfobject relationship that existed. Though he needed a deeper selfobject involvement to achieve a fully cohesive self, he preferred, for a long time, the self-anesthesia of a minimal relationship to protect himself against the potentially painful vicissitudes of a real connectedness. This constellation strikes me as akin to the schizoid personality's defensiveness. The careful, gentle, yet persistent analysis of such desperate defenses against the full development of a feared selfobject transference may take years before a full-fledged selfobject transference can become established and worked through. Perhaps many of the patients that now seem unanalyzable "borderlines" fall into this category.

Lichtenberg's fifth technical principle enjoins the analyst to pay special attention to the patient's intention, whether conscious or unconscious, as a way of detecting contradictory intentions (i.e., conflicts) without narrowing the focus exclusively on drives and defenses. In other words, by empathically grasping intentions from the "inside," so to speak, the analyst can recognize both self-esteem–enhancing and pleasure-driven goals. At any rate, Lichtenberg interpreted both goals and found out which interpretation was correct from a consideration of the patient's response.

Finally, Lichtenberg's sixth technical principle sets out a sequence of interpretive interventions. His use of the felicitous phrase "an observation platform" on which both analyst and analysand can stand to construct a verbally communicable understanding defines the condition that makes bridging interpretations possible so as to confirm shared states of emotion-laden comprehension: In short, the analysand knows he or she has been understood. This basic intervention creates the ambience that facilitates selfobject transference to be experienced and then explained. Moreover, I would add, it allows room for self-assertion, perhaps for the first time in the patient's life and thus may allow the patient to take some responsibility for himself, perhaps, also for the first time in his life.

I now attempt to relate Lichtenberg's technical principles to Kohut's definition of health and his theory of cure as viewed by the psychology of the self. In a forthcoming publication Kohut has further defined and outlined in greater detail than before his view of the curative process. He defines the goal of analysis as the establishment of an uninterrupted tension arc from basic ambition via basic talents toward basic ideals. For the process of cure, Kohut outlines a three-step movement of: (1) analysis of defenses against the transference; (2) unfolding of the transference; (3) opening of a path of empathy between the self and the selfobject and thus establishing and widening a state of empathic resonance.

Specifically, the repressed or disavowed archaic narcissistic relationship that had continued to link the defective archaic self to its archaic selfobject (e.g., archaic mergers and archaic twinships) during a successful analysis comes to be replaced by a qualitatively different relationship to mature selfobjects, namely, by an empathic resonance that emanates from the selfobjects of the social surround of adult life. This change comes about through transmuting internalizations that allow the increasingly healthy self to identify and to seek out in the most human aspects of the present-day reality the appropriately available resonant selfobjects.

Clearly, it follows from these definitions that it is the structural strengthening of the self—whether it is conceptualized as increased cohesion of the constituents, as increased firmness of the self-boundary, or as an increasingly continuous and uninterrupted tension arc between the self's poles—that allows it to discard no longer needed defenses of the self in favor of more open responsiveness. In other words, it allows the strengthened self to replace archaic merger modes of selfobject relationships with maturely resonant selfobject ties, the empathic resonance. Kohut suggests that this change comes about by a combination of two routes: (1) transmuting internalization builds structures; (2) the sustained echo of empathic resonance that pervades the analytic relationship most of the time encourages the analysand to search for available resonant relationships also in the surrounding world.

Lichtenberg's six technical principles can be said to create conditions for such a curative process to become established. For example, the centrality of the empathic vantage point is not only a necessary step in analytic data collection, but it also demonstrates to the analysand that an empathic stance is possible, which for many analysands comes as a totally unexpected surprise. In addition, a sustained and stable empathic stance, by holding out the hope that the traumatically faulty responses of the archaic infantile selfobject might not be repeated again, encourages the mobilization of the repressed and disavowed selfobject needs, albeit at first under cover of defenses, and finally creates the ambience in which even these defenses can be discarded.

Most of the other technical principles, such as focusing on the state of the self, following its fluctuations from session to session, relating it to intercurrent stimuli and to the self's intentions, are all designed to diagnose correctly the inevitable disruptions of the transference and, with the aid of these diagnoses, when expressed through correct and tactful interpretations, to restore the transferences to their previous harmonious state.

I would like to add some theoretical elaborations. On a previous occasion I have described the psychoanalytic configuration as having a bipolar structure, analogous to the structure of the self, with the analyst at one pole and the analysand at the other. Again, in the analytic situation one can also observe a tension that emerges from the *convergent* attachment of analyst and analysand as a consequence of their mutual analytic endeavor while at the same time the individual self of each participant strive for self-realization in *divergent* directions. This analytic configuration has a beginning, a middle, and an end. Its course cannot be predicted, and it seems to have a life of its own. Only in retrospect can it be seen that, in the main, the course of the analysis was determined by the participating constituents, the analyst and the analysand (Wolf, 1979).

Translated into more experiential language, one aspect of being analyzed can be described as the growing awareness that one is not totally free, but part of a larger process that inexorably draws one toward some goal of its own. Both analyst and analysand are subordinate systems within a larger system, the analytic configuration. In the initial, defensive phase of analysis, it is the analyst's task by appropriate interpretation to demonstrate the fear of, but also the rewards for, being part of such an analytic system. But perhaps even more decisively than interpretation, it is the participation of the analyst in such a larger configuration that comes to be experienced by analysands as not only benign but liberating of their own expressiveness. The boundaries of the analysand's self, as he or she follows the basic rule, begin to fade and the self expands to include the whole analytic configuration. We observe this in the phenomena attending the state of a harmonious selfobject transference. For not only has the analyst become a selfobject for the analysand, but this is now true also for the whole analytic configuration with which the analysand has become merged.

The analytic configuration is a self-selfobject unit, which in some ways never dissolves again. Within this analytic configuration there develops a capacity for resonant communication as the boundaries of the participating analyst and analysand are temporarily suspended by a merger into the larger selfobject unit of the analytic configuration. Even after the so-called termination of the analysis, there remains the capacity for resonant communication, which will now be available when entering into the self-selfobject configurations of daily life. This readiness for empathic resonance, not only with the analyst-as-selfobject but with any available selfobject of the surround, is the measure of the cure in psychoanalysis. Let us now turn to A. Ornstein's paper on the oedipal selfobject transference.

Ornstein tackles the complicated relationship between infantile sexuality and the development of the self. As background to Ornstein's considerations it is useful to state briefly Kohut's reformulation of the oedipal problem. Kohut differentiates between an oedipal *stage* (referring to the normal state of experiences at that age) and the Oedipus *complex* (referring to the pathological distortion of the normal stage). The normal oedipal stage encompasses the conflict engendered by the affectionateness and by the assertiveness of the oedipal-age child and the pursuit of his age-appropriate wishful fantasies for exclusive and tender attachment to the heterogenital and the homogenital parent. Both parents are the carriers of needed selfobject functions (i.e., the mirroring functions and the idealizing functions). When the parent fails in these selfobject functions, the child's self suffers the disintegrating experiences that may and do result in the distortion of the normal conflicts that occur during the oedipal phase into the pathological conflicts that have been called the Oedipus complex. It is the sequelae, not of the normal conflicts of the oedipal phase, but of their distortion into the pathological conflicts of the Oedipus complex that results in the neurotic drives, neurotic defenses, neurotic symptoms—the classical neuroses that psychoanalysis has investigated so well during the first century of its scientific development.

Ornstein, in her case report, makes brief reference to such a typical neurotic constellation, namely, a minor sexual inhibition. The mother's response to the patient's normal oedipal sensuality was an unempathic counterseductiveness that heightened the youngster's erotism into a dangerous overexcitement, which tended to disintegrate his still vulnerable self and against which inhibitory neurotic defenses had to be brought into play. There is no difficulty in integrating self psychology with classical analytic views here if we are willing to accept the clinical evidence pointing to sexual overstimulation by the selfobject milieu as the primary pathogenetic agent instead of postulating an inborn excessive libidinal drive.

It is well to keep in mind here that the vulnerability of the self was not only due to the youngster's tender age but also, and probably primarily, because the father demanded that the patient comfort his mother by crawling into bed with her when he was already of school age and in his early teens. Empathically, we can easily imagine the mental state of the child: Overstimulated sexually, he feels misused and misunderstood by both parents in their disregard for his own needs. Translated into the language of self psychology, he is likely to have experienced this disregard as a deficient response to his need for a mirroring selfobject function performed by his mother.

Furthermore, the case history demonstrates a traumatic disillusionment in the idealized parental selfobject function carried by his father. The father was experienced as helpless and unable to protect the youngster so that the father's image became incompatible with the youngster's need for an idealizable image. Such a lack of age-appropriate selfobject responses weakened the child's self and thus contributed to its disintegration. As a consequence the normal affectionateness and sensuality are no longer an integral part of a cohesive self but become distorted into pathological sexuality: the Oedipus complex.

But Ornstein goes further in her conceptualization. She proposes that in her case, the child's frustrated need for admiration from the idealized father became intensified by the disintegration products (i.e., the pathological sexuality) into a wish for sexual closeness to the homogenital parent (i.e., a homosexual wish). Her clinical observations seem to support Anna Ornstein's formulation. Thus, Ornstein shows us that the so-called negative Oedipus complex is a consequence of self-disintegration also and not a part of the normally occurring oedipal phase.

Ornstein also demonstrates the technical point that the revived needs for oedipal selfobject responses from the analyst may be successfully responded to by an analyst of either gender. Thus, her patient's demands for an idealizable male analyst turned out to be an expression of the need for empathic understanding and interpretation of the wish for a strong, nondisappointing, idealizable male selfobject. In meeting the need for empathic understanding and interpretation, the analyst provided the basic response needed for the selfobject transference regardless of her gender.

With the Oedipus complex thus reconceptualized as a pathological miscarriage due to failures of the selfobject milieu of the oedipal phase, one may now question what role, if any, the normal oedipal phase plays in the consolidation of a cohesive self. It is clear that the parent who is empathically in tune with his child's needs will neither respond with a traumatic rebuff nor with an attempt at gratification that would turn the child's sensuality into an aroused sexuality. Optimally, there would be some frustration carried out with an empathically perceived grasp of the child's state of need for selfobject responsiveness, but not for physical gratification. Such optimal frustration results in a strengthened self because the mild discomfort attending the frustration in the context of an empathically responsive selfobject ambience allows the self a maximal opportunity to use its own self-soothing resources to the fullest: The self turns to other satisfactions, particularly the joyful exercise of newly acquired skills. The attuned parent, therefore, provides the milieu that draws the oedipal-phase child onward into latency and beyond.

Finally, Ornstein calls attention to some issues about the formation of psychic structures that help to clarify this confusing aspect of psychoanalytic theory. Ornstein contrasts two means by which aspects of a selfobject can become part of the self. Transmuting internalizations taking place in small doses eventuate in psychological structures that develop in relation to phase-appropriate selfobject responses. The appropriate selfobject responses facilitate the transformation of archaic narcissistic structures into structures that are in harmony with the particular child's needs and specifically fit his unique skills and talents. In contrast, gross identifications represent a particular attempt at internalization in which relatively massive psychological characteristics of another person are "taken in" and become, generally for defensive reasons, a temporary or more lasting compensatory part of the self.

I find Ornstein's differentiation here quite plausible and supported by her clinical evidence. In her portrayal of transmuting internalizations she demonstrates how we can describe a process in experience-near terms and avoid terminology and metaphors that basically refer to a mechanistic model of a mental apparatus with quantities of mass (object identifications) cathected by energy which are moved in and out (e.g., introjected and projected). Conceptualizing on the basis of the metaphor of the self and its selfobjects as it began to emerge in Kohut's *The Restoration of the Self,* Ornstein demonstrates that through the minute accretions of transmuting internalization, genuine ambitions and ideals are built up. Alternatively, gross identifications in which a person, let us say a child, attempts to become more like another person (e.g., a parent) proceeds by way of disavowing those aspects of the self that seem discordant with an idealized selfobject. Far from taking anything in, I believe such "identifications" are achieved by sacrificing aspects that genuinely are self, and the self, therefore, becomes impoverished. It is understandable why gross identifications often strike us as pathological.

Self psychology must still wrestle with the need to reconceptualize the process of transmuting internalization to free it of its roots in a mass and energy model. Kohut has led the way in this reformulation by introducing the concept of empathic resonance. The analysand's seeking of archaic mergers is replaced by empathic resonating as the end point of the therapeutic process. This change to empathic resonance leads to psychological change. How can we understand this and still stay logically consistent within our self-selfobject model? Does an increased capacity for empathic resonance require the acquisition of new psychic structures? Or does it require the loosening of all-too-rigid boundaries, the lifting of barriers within the self that interfere with free communication within the self-selfobject system? I tend toward the latter view, and I belive by his use of the word "resonance" Kohut was tending toward the use of a systems metaphor, in that resonance is a total system response, a reverberation of a whole configuration that is impeded by trying to narrow down on any of its parts.

The choice of the most suitable metaphor to express psychological knowledge is not a task for a brief discussion, but for years of strenuous thought. It is spurred by the clear presentation of clinical data derived from the self psychological viewpoint exemplified by both Lichtenberg and Ornstein. Probably, our choices of metaphors must be tentative at any rate, for new data and new theories bring new problems and new opportunities. Freud once recommended that we change our metaphors frequently to avoid their becoming stale and reified. Let us have the courage to make the necessary changes.

REFERENCES

Freud, S. (1912). Recommendations to physicians practising psychoanalysis. *S.E.* 12: 112.

Ornstein, P. (1980). Self psychology and the concept of health. In *Advances in Self Psychology*, A. Goldberg, ed. New York: Int. Univ. Press.

Wolf, E. S. (1979). Transferences and countertransferences in the analysis of disorders of the self. *Contemp. Psychoanal.* 15: 577–594.

IV SELF PSYCHOLOGY AND PSYCHOTHERAPY: THEORETICAL AND CLINICAL CONSIDERATIONS

17 Self-Psychology: Relevance to Psychotherapy

Samuel Kaplan, M.D.

Critics and proponents of self psychology often achieve a consensus in their acknowledgment of the usefulness of Kohut's contributions to their clinical work. In his masterly introduction to Kohut's writings P. Ornstein (1978) emphasized that Kohut's lectures, papers, and books reflect the constant interplay of clinical and theoretical elements. Thus, according to Ornstein, when Kohut explicates psychoanalytic theory, he underscores the relationship between theory and method so that "the reader . . . aided in recognizing how a particular concept arose and what it was to explain [p. 39]."

Kohut's seminal paper, "Introspection, Empathy, and Psychoanalysis" (1959), heralded the basic methodology that permitted him to refocus on the analytic data provided by his patients so as to discover and elucidate the mirror and idealizing transferences. His subsequent writings are replete with clinical illustrations that spell out his evolving analytic approach to selfobject transferences and his concept of transmuting internalization as both a developmental process and a crucial aspect of the therapeutic enterprise.

Kohut's earlier discoveries flowed from his treatment of narcissistic disorders. He differentiated this group of patients from the wider and more encompassing diagnostic entity of "borderline" conditions and demonstrated that patients classified under this narrower nosologic entity could be successfully analyzed. Basch (1981) pointed out that the nature of the transference does change in narcissistic disorders, but he states:

> . . . its management does not. There is no role playing on the part of the analyst in a misguided attempt to provide the patient with a meaningful experience over and above the analytic one. . . . [The analyst] no longer finds himself impelled to actively interfere with the development of the mirroring or the idealizing transference . . . (I)n the mirror transference as in the idealizing transference, Kohut advocates that we do no more and no less than we do with psychoneurotic patients. That is, foster the patient's associations, avoid premature closure, depend on the unconscious to provide the material, interpret it appropriately and engage the patient in the working through process till insight is demonstrably achieved [p. 342].

As analysts became increasingly familiar with Kohut's writings, they expressed their enthusiasm for the help they obtained in their clinical work with narcissistic disorders as well as with a variety of diagnostic categories.

Over time, concepts and techniques developed in the crucible of clinical psychoanalysis began to be applied to dynamic psychotherapy. The papers presented here can be viewed as a beginning exploration of what the authors hope will be an expanding arena for the fruitful application of self psychology to the theory and practice of dynamic psychotherapy. As we build on the concepts elaborated by the authors and discussants, we may be able to discover how useful a psychotherapy based on self psychology can be, and how specific and focused an approach can be delineated.

The paper by Basch offers an opportunity to explore the place of self psychology in psychotherapy from a historical perspective. As suggested by the title, Basch briefly discusses the place of theory in scientific enterprises, notes that we do not yet have a theory of psychotherapy, and then seeks to demonstrate that self psychology "paves the way for the formulation of such a theory." He draws our attention to the constant interdigitation of clinical practice and theory in Kohut's writings. Thus, Kohut's experiences with patients with narcissistic disorders led to his early reformulation of limited components of psychoanalytic theory. These theoretical modifications, then applied to the clinical situation, forced him to further, more extensive reformulations of theory. This still ongoing process provides us with a series of concepts that can be applied to dynamic

psychotherapy. Basch focuses our attention on central conceptualizations of self psychology as they now become the basis for a theory
of psychotherapy. Thus, he highlights the role of "interpretation
regarding the disavowed emotional aspect of selfobject relationships
as these are manifest in the transference" and suggests that these
can be effectively dealt with in psychotherapy.

We are offered a pungent, articulate response to this paper by
Michels. He takes issue with Basch's understanding of the history
and evolution of traditional psychoanalytic theory. He then reviews
the clinical data offered by Basch and offers an alternative way of
conceptualizing the experience detailed by the author as he found
his own way to understanding and helping his patient. It is Michel's
contention that the essential shift in Basch's approach to his patients in psychotherapy was not primarily the result of a change in
the theory he employed. Rather, he views the critical transformation as the outcome of the author's "new relationship to theory."
Michels spells out his perception of this shift in some detail and
concludes that "our therapeutic work requires creative imagination,
and we welcome new theories that assist that imagination."

London's paper seeks to spell out explicitly the nature of the
transferences in a patient ordinarily diagnosed as borderline. The
paper presents an unusually self-revealing report on the therapeutic interaction between therapist and patient. London makes it
quite clear in his discussion that his intent is to initiate a serious
study on the place of confrontation in self psychology. His own vantage point is clearly articulated in his statement that "efforts to
gratify [a patient's] demands by turning a professional therapeutic
relationship into a personal friendship may bring short-term relief
to the patient at the risk not only of therapeutic failure but of untoward regressions and serious complications of iatrogenically induced dependence." He seeks to clarify his conceptualization of confrontation by distinguishing among "an interpretation, the communication of empathic understanding, and a confrontive response."
He draws attention to those situations in which the therapist, experienced as confrontive, serves to sustain the patient's self.

It might be a rewarding experience for the reader to study Bach's
discussion and then to reread London's paper. In this remarkably
lucid exploration of clinical data offered by London, Bach presents
an original approach and helps us understand the patient's inner
experience. Flowing from this alternative perspective, Bach reex-

amines and reformulates the specific technical issues raised by London. The logic of Bach's understanding of the patient, as revealed in his study of the emerging selfobject transferences, leads him to reevaluate the therapeutic process. In this clinical context he then expresses serious doubts about London's new hypothesis of the "confrontive selfobject transference." Furthermore, he questions the validity of placing this notion on the same conceptual level as the mirroring or idealizing transferences.

These papers and discussions sharpen our focus on the relationship between theory and practice. Clearly, we do rely on theory insofar as it provides us with a map and helps us make order out of a patient's verbal and nonverbal communications. However, we do recognize the danger of superimposing any new or old theory on the clinical data. The result may be an illusory aura of certainty, if we have thereby only succeeded in creating a psuedo-orderliness. The authors and discussants have provided us with significant and challenging concepts to help us as we struggle to develop a useful theory of psychotherapy. Such a theory could indeed serve us well in our psychotherapeutic endeavors. In his closing comment Dr. Smith will further elaborate on these papers.

REFERENCES

Basch, M. (1981). Self object disorders and psychoanalytic theory: A historical perspective. *J. Amer. Psychoanal. Assn.* 29: 337–351.

Kohut, H. (1959). Introspection, empathy, and psychoanalysis. *J. Amer. Psychoanal. Assn.* VII: 459–483.

Ornstein, P. (1978). *The Search for the Self,* Vol. 1. New York: Int. Univ. Press.

18 The Significance of Self Psychology for a Theory of Psychotherapy

Michael Franz Basch, M.D.

A scientific theory is simply a formal description of a pattern or patterns of expectation that we bring to a particular situation. When we do not know what to expect, we cannot become organized, and if we cannot become organized, we tend to become anxious. If that state of affairs lasts for any length of time, we cease to function effectively. So another way of looking at theory is to view it as a device for preventing, controlling, or resolving anxiety by creating order.

Strange as it sounds at first blush, theory comes before facts. We are taught to believe that the scientific method requires that we gather data and then formulate a theory. But it is obvious that this sequence cannot be true. Sensory input that finds no established ordering framework is just noise, not information; that is, it is not and cannot be organized. Recall the first time you looked into a microscope or heard a foreign language spoken. What you saw or heard had no meaning. You have to teach people what to expect; then they can make sense out of what they experience, or rather, they can experience once you teach them what to expect. Therefore, the pattern of expectation—the unspoken theory—must precede observation. Observations, in turn, can change theory by altering or refining expectations; the process can then go back and forth depending on the need and the creative capacity of the individual in question.

I maintain that we have not had a truly functional theory of psychotherapy, a situation that has hampered the practice, teaching, and development of that art. Furthermore I believe, and endeavor to demonstrate in this paper, that one of the contributions of self psychology is that it paves the way for the formulation of such a theory.

Knowing what one wants to say is one thing; actually putting it down on paper is another. I had some difficulty in choosing a format for presentation to a large and varied readership. Much as I might want to do so, I cannot possibly anticipate what particular concerns each reader might bring to this discussion of the significance of self psychology for psychotherapy. I take an ontogenetic approach, using my experience as a student, practitioner, and teacher to illustrate what I consider to be the signal contributions made by Kohut's work to the field of psychotherapy. I trust that by doing so I engage your interest sufficiently to use my idiosyncratic narrative as an aid to rethinking the larger and more abstract issues.

Let me begin by outlining the history and nature of the problem posed by the relationship of psychotherapy and psychoanalysis as I understand it. Freud demonstrated through psychoanalysis that neurotic disturbances represented arrests or aberrations of sexual development eventuating in an oedipal conflict that could potentially be undone through the promotion of insight into the unconscious reasons for the patient's difficulties. This discovery raised hopes that the psychoanalytic method could be modified so that the treatment would be both less demanding and have wider applicability while still achieving a cure based on understanding the meaning and origins of the patient's problems. So began what today we call psychoanalytically oriented, dynamic, or insight psychotherapy.

In the process of transforming psychoanalysis into psychotherapy, many significant modifications were made in Freud's approach. The patients generally sat up rather than lying on the couch; they were seen once or twice a week rather than on an analytic schedule; and the therapist was not necessarily an analyst and might not have had any personal psychoanalytic treatment. But what did not change was the theoretical position that the therapist took vis-à-vis the patient; that is, all nonpsychotic patients were treated as if they had the relatively mature character structure and the capacity for object love that is the hallmark of the psychoneurotic patient and the *sine qua non* for the classic transference neurosis. The Oedipus conflict discovered by Freud as central for psychoneurotic pathology became the focus for development generally. The resolution of the Oedipus conflict, which made neurotic symptomatology unnecessary and let the erstwhile neurotic person integrate sexuality with the rest of his life, now became thought of as the gateway to maturity for everyone. The vicissitudes of infantile sexuality became the index of development. Maturation consisted of a progression from oral to anal to phallic sexuality, culminating in the Oedipus conflict, whose resolution paved the way for genital primacy and adulthood (Basch, 1983).

A patient's pathology was assessed in terms of the level of infantile sexuality at which he had been arrested. It was expected that if he could be helped to free associate, he could be shown his problematic relationships with parents, siblings, and other important figures that had led to his conflict as well as the resulting misdirected attempts at discharging sexual and aggressive instinctual energy. It was believed that such interpretation would, like a key in the lock, open the door to insight, maturation, and the resolution of whatever symptoms had brought the patient to therapy in the first place. But the results were not always what had been expected. A large number of patients did not respond to this approach and either left treatment or became involved in an interminable therapeutic relationship that seemed to lead nowhere.

Psychotherapists were divided in their attempt to improve the situation. Roughly speaking, two groups were formed. One group rejected the constraints put on therapy by the single-minded goal of investigating and rechanneling the patient's infantile sexual and aggressive development. These therapists chose, instead, to take the patient's presenting complaint at face value and tackle it directly. Behaviorism and all its offshoots—including cognitive and learning therapies, biofeedback, hypnotic and other forms of direct suggestion, abreactive, cathartic, affect-directed therapies, client-centered therapy, family therapy, and other therapies geared to improving interpersonal relationships—emerged. Sometimes it almost seems as if any given complaint will sooner or later bring forth a therapy that claims to address that particular difficulty and then generates a theory that sees in that problem the embodiment of humanity and the human past and present. Paradoxically, although all these so-called schools of therapy are united in only one respect (viz., their vociferous rejection of psychoanalysis), they have in fact repeated its history when they undermine often valuable and validatable insights by claiming too much for them.

Undaunted when confronted by the failure of modified psychoanalysis to deliver the hoped-for benefits, the second group of therapists responded by becoming more doctrinaire. Because the theoretical position of psychoanalysis was considered to be immutable and beyond discussion (though Freud had never taken such a rigid stance, changing his theoretical formulations often enough while he was still alive), the blame for therapeutic failure had to be assigned to the patient and/or to the therapist. The terms "weak ego" and "borderline" were employed as euphemisms for patients who did not lend themselves to an associative approach and/or did not respond with improvement to attempts to reconstruct their childhood in the light of their complaints. By attaching the appropriate diagnostic formula, large numbers of patients were designated as being beyond therapeutic help. But the therapists, too, came in for their share of the blame. Not so long ago, students were regularly subjected to the equivalent of an examination of conscience by teachers and supervisors, and any deviation in their thinking from the accepted instinct theory of development was an indication that the student needed an analysis or more analysis.

I clearly remember how I and my fellow residents sat frightened and passive with our patients. We were passive because we felt we had to limit ourselves to encouraging patients to say what they were thinking and then wait for them to give us the opportunity to connect the present problem to earlier experiences in their family relationship. We were frightened because we firmly believed that everything we might say or do had an immediate and significant sexual or aggressive implication for the patient. We really thought that to say or do anything other than interpret the genesis of the patient's problems would destroy our therapeutic, neutral stance, establishing an equivalence in the patient's unconscious between us and those earlier seductive and/or punitive figures who were responsible, we believed, for his or her problems.

Many in this group of therapists who remained committed to the idea of cure through insight shared a secret conviction that psychotherapy was at best makeshift and that psychoanalysis was the only treatment worthy of the name. They were further united by a disdain for all other attempts to investigate the human condition, including experimental, learning, cognitive, and other aspects of academic psychology, as well as all other forms of therapy. Because all these forms of treatment were obviously no more than a resistance to psychoanalysis, their protagonists were to be pitied, not studied. The result of this kind of training was that we learned both a theory and a method that were not applicable to our patient population and at the end of our apprenticeship were left ill equipped to perform the job that we were now certified as being able to do. We had, in other words, been taught to do a form of pseudo-psychoanalysis, a practice that, to my knowledge, is still not uncommon today.

Let me illustrate this with a clinical vignette. A graduate student, whom I call Martin Young, came to see me shortly after I had entered private practice and before I had obtained any analytic training. Mr. Young was feeling hopeless and depressed, because he could not seem to complete his thesis. A diagnostic interview showed that the patient seemed to have the requisite intelligence to master his work and that his undergraduate record had been good. Because he was entering his father's field, I assumed that his failure represented a punishment for daring to compete with his father and that to succeed in his work would represent a forbidden, symbolic, oedipal victory. In exploring the patient's family situation with him over a period of time, I found that he saw his childhood relationship to his father as one marred by the loneliness and longing experienced during the father's frequent absences on business trips, which sometimes lasted for months. Anger, competition, and rivalry did not seem to be in evidence. I assumed, however, that the lack of negative feelings toward his father represented a defensive maneuver, and I suggested this to the patient. The patient eventually recalled the tension and the fears he experienced when his father would take his mother along on shorter trips for a week or two at a time, leaving him and his 3-year older sister in the care of a housekeeper. On one such occasion, when he was 5 or 6 years old, his sister enticed him into playing the "doctor game" with her, and they exposed their genitals to one another. She then threatened him with all kinds of punishment if he dared tell anyone what they had done. The patient remembered that after his parents came back he was, or so it seemed at least to him in retrospect, frightened for months that he would somehow betray the secret or that his parents would detect it. He recalled having difficulty sleeping at that time because he feared that he might talk when asleep and reveal all. I interpreted this as a displacement from his incestuous desire for his absent mother, a desire and excitement stirred up by the exposure to his sister's genitals. As far as I was concerned, this was the real secret that he was afraid to give away while asleep. Perhaps, I hypothesized, his learning difficulty had to do with having learned too much too early; forbidden things that only fathers and not little boys should know and so on. The patient was an obliging sort, eager to please, and was quick to accept what I had to say as plausible, and he usually managed to associate to material that could be seen as confirmatory. However, in spite of the so-called "insight" he gained over the months we worked together, there was no particular improvement in his ability to do his work or in the depressed feelings from which he suffered as a consequence.

I am sure that many of you are by now amazed by my naivete, first because I apparently thought I could revive and resolve an oedipal conflict in once- or twice-a-week psychotherapy; second because I was trying to do this work without having had at that time any psychoanalytic training; and third because I was trying to obtain results by using the patient's version of his history as a basis for interpretation instead of limiting my interventions to whatever might be revealed through his transference to me. But do not judge me too harshly yet. Then as now, at least in the training programs that I am acquainted with, Freud's schema of psychosexuality, that is, the oral, anal, and phallic phases of development, the centrality of the Oedipus complex, and the dynamics and genetics of defense against instinctual drives, were often the beginning and the end of what we learned about human maturation. How was I to know that experienced, reasonably talented psychotherapists did not pay any attention to these formulation when they actually did their work and that they only then wrote up their cases in the literature as if they had been guided all along by these theoretical considerations? Of course, I saw an oedipal conflict, or a retreat from an oedipal conflict, behind every symptom the patient brought to me. But theory is a two-edged sword. Once one accepts a particular theory, that framework colors what one perceives. Precisely because it spares one the anxiety of not knowing, it is difficult to disregard or call one's theory into question when one ought to do so. Instead, the tendency is to disavow or alter the significance of discrepancies and, by doing so, give the illusion of a fit between theory and observation. For instance, I was aware that this patient did not demonstrate rebelliousness and competition in the therapeutic relationship, but I assumed that he was simply defending himself against these impulses. I looked all the harder for the evidence that I knew must be there and blamed myself and my lack of experience for my inability to detect it.

Still, you will say, when I saw that what I was trying to do was not working I should have had the sense to try a different approach. Brave words, but we were strictly enjoined from doing anything other than interpreting the dynamics of psychosexuality and the family romance, even though we were taught at the same time that the transference was a dangerous business outside of analysis and that we had to be very careful to quickly dissipate and generalize any emotional overtures that the patient made toward us. We were warned that anything other than interpretation was to act out with the patient. To show an interest in what patients were saying was to be seductive; to help, advise, or guide patients in their associations was to be manipulative; to presume to help them deal with activities outside the session was to have succumbed to the heresy of behaviorism. You were not even supposed to *question* patients if you were puzzled by something they said for fear of contaminating the spontaneity of free associations.

Eventually Mr. Young and I ran out of things to say to each other, and long silences ensued during which I would encourage him to say what he was thinking, and he would tell me that he was not thinking of anything. But one day he admitted that he was thinking of something, namely, some reading he had been trying to do for his thesis. It was mundane stuff that had nothing to do with therapy. Perhaps it was prescience on my part, or more likely desperation, but in any case, I reminded him that he was obliged to tell me whatever was on his mind and, if it was about his thesis, so be it. He obliged with a résumé of what he had read that day. I of course expected that this superficial material was resistance to more significant content that would spontaneously emerge, directly or indirectly, as he kept on talking. But nothing of the sort happened. Instead, the patient took the opportunity in this and in subsequent sessions to discuss his work and his reading with me. Against my better judgment I found myself increasingly interested in what he was saying and drawn into what I considered to be his defensive behavior by discussing this material with him. It was certainly more stimulating than sitting around and saying, "What occurs to you?" and fighting off sleepiness and boredom, but I was not comfortable with his turn of events, feeling I had been seduced by the patient into "acting out" his wish to have me as a friend and mentor rather than as a therapist. Where was my impartiality, my objective stance, my therapeutic neutrality? I considered myself more or less lost to dynamic psychotherapy and, certainly, to the analytic career that I eventually hoped to undertake. It was years before I read Freud's statement regarding the management of countertransference to the effect that one should not give a patient too little just because one loves him too much. So I suffered, feeling very much alone in my fall from therapeutic grace. Mr. Young, however, did not share my sense of failure but felt rather excited and pleased that I could care about him as a person and take an interest in his daily life.

As we talked more about his work, it became clear to me that the patient's fear of being found wanting was the immediate reason for his inability to complete any portion of his thesis. He was by no means lazy. He had voluminous notes, if anything a surfeit of material, but whatever he tried to do with it seemed to him not good enough, and he was convinced that the members of his department would share that feeling. I thought that behind this reluctance to submit his work to his professors or to present it in seminars was a fear of his competitiveness and the patricidal impulses that the competitiveness represented. I had heard about times when phobics have to be put into the situation that they dread most so as to mobilize their anxiety and stimulate their associations. I took a chance and asked Mr. Young to bring me the portion of the work that he was talking about that day so that I might better understand the details he was bringing up. Although he was at first fearful that I might be critical in the pejorative sense of the word, it was also clear that Mr. Young was pleased by this additional show of interest on my part. Our subsequent discussions of his writing led him to bring in other portions of his thesis that he had worked on and then put aside. My ability to understand quite clearly what he was trying to say in his papers and my obviously positive attitude about them gave him the courage and the confidence to let others at the university judge his productions. He met with a generally favorable response. He began to do better in his work and proudly brought me the news of his progress. I kept looking in vain for oedipal rivalry, possible fantasies about outdoing me or in some way hurting me through his achievements. As his confidence in himself improved he spontaneously talked more about his father, but always in terms of his past longing and with the recognition that what he missed then was the kind of relationship that he and I now had.

As the patient was increasingly able to permit himself to succeed in his classroom work, he spoke in more detail about other areas of his past and present life. For our purposes it is not necessary to detail those sessions. In terms of his present-day life I found that apart from his work difficulties he was doing well. His relationship with peers of both sexes was good, his capacity for heterosexual fulfillment was unimpaired, and he had a number of nonwork-related hobbies and activities he enjoyed. As our treatment progressed Mr. Young became pleased with himself and eventually suggested that because he was getting good grades once more, perhaps his therapy could be terminated. I agreed, but I had some reservations. Mr. Young was grateful to me and credited me with his improvement, but I felt I had failed to do a proper job and had at best given the patient superficial "support" rather than insight.

It took some years and repeated experiences of the sort just described to make it clear to me that the patient's priorities are not necessarily or only evasions of some hidden truth, but can also be indicative of something that needs to be dealt with as such. As I became more expert at my job with the help of my patients, I found myself becoming increasingly interested in hearing about what patients *did* yesterday rather than in what was *done* to them years ago. Also, having heard about their problems, I insisted that they also tell me about those aspects of their lives that were not problematic: what gave them joy, as well as what made them sad; where they succeeded, as well as where they failed; whom they had helped, as well as whom they had hurt. I did not direct patients to their past or to their family history because I found that the historical, genetic material emerged as a matter of course as the patient made himself, and not just his problem, understood. Penis envy, sibling rivalry, castration fear, the primal scene, and all the other things I had learned and was learning more about (for I had in the meantime managed to get myself accepted for analytic training) seemed to play no great part in my psychotherapeutic experience. If such matters did surface in the dreams or associations of my psychotherapy patients, they were not pivotal. What came up over and over again were the hidden wishes for love and understanding, the shame, often masquerading as anger or bravado, that was frequently associated with such desires, and the concomitant inability to voice and thereby become conscious of what it was that was really troubling them. Much of my work seemed to be with people who had remained childlike, immature in some significant respect, and who almost seemed to be marking time, waiting for someone to help them understand *what* it was they missed; the "why" then took care of itself. As soon as I was able to draw on my memories and emotions as the patient stimulated them with associations and once I stopped worrying about what this or that association *should* mean in terms of infantile sexuality, I seemed to find the words that both communicated understanding to the patient and enabled him, in turn, to progress and achieve the necessary insight that let him not only see what was wrong but do something about it and then part from me.

Over the years as my colleagues and I became more open with one another, I learned that we had all made modifications in technique that let each of us, in his or her own way, deal with and work comfortably with our patients. We all tended to look at the totality of our patients' development, tried to see as clearly as we could what it was that they were doing to defeat themselves, and then helped them to look at that issue as best we could. Insight and understanding were promoted, but it was related to failures of communication and learning, to self-defeating problem-solving techniques, and above all, to the inability to know and deal with emotions in an appropriate manner. The task of the psychotherapist, it seemed to us, was much more related to the ancient adage "know thyself" than to "know thy oedipal conflicts." Surprisingly, however, the realities of the consulting room seemed to be forgotten in the classroom. In psychotherapy training programs, even more so than in psychoanalytic institutes, what is taught in lectures and written in textbooks has very little in common with what actually transpires in the therapeutic situation. As I have mentioned, once in practice psychotherapists learn to listen to patients and, though encumbered by what they think they have learned about psychopathology, make those necessary compromises in technique that eventually allow them to become effective practitioners. However, when former students in turn become teachers, diffident about what they feel are deviations from accepted teachings and lacking a theoretical framework that would let them deal systematically with their experiences, they often as not promote in the classroom the very approach

they have learned to shun in their consulting room. I know colleagues who are excellent therapists and who would never force one
of their patients onto that Procrustean bed, but nevertheless, they
teach the psychoanalytic theory of neurosis as the paradigm for
psychotherapy to their students. Apparently, in the absence of a
valid explanation, an inapplicable one is preferred to none at all,
illustrating the fact that the brain needs theories to serve as an
integrating matrix, that is, as a pattern of perceptual expectations
through which it can organize, evaluate, and respond to stimuli
(Basch, 1975b, 1976b).

What dynamic psychotherapy has inherited from psychoanalysis
is an unfortunate confusion between methodology and theory or
between a specific psychoanalytic theory and a potentially larger,
more encompassing general theory. When Freud decreed that the
neuroses taught us what we needed to know about normal development, he created a framework that was too narrow to account for
either the many facets of development that can be inferred from
direct observation of infants and children or for those opened up to
inspection by the transferences formed in their treatment by those
patients who are suffering from functional disturbances other than
the neuroses.

The disappointment with psychoanalytic psychotherapy, to which
I alluded previously, is attributable to Freud's misunderstanding
about the nature of this discovery. As I have documented elsewhere,
Freud's desire to establish a general psychology led him to see the
results of the psychoanalytic method as corroborating a theory of
mental development and functioning that he had postulated in all
its details prior to discovering psychoanalysis and whose premises
we now know to have been in error (Basch, 1975a, 1975b, 1983,
1981a, 1981b). In the process he failed to see that his method was
both narrower and deeper than he supposed. Psychoanalysis, the
investigation of the meaning of human behavior—including, of
course, thought, whose effects are intracerebral—in and of itself can
never generate a total psychology. With the tools of psychoanalysis,
introspection, and empathy, we see the effects of various developmental processes on thought and behavior, but the origin, nature,
evolution, and maturation of those developmental processes are the
purview of psychological research using different tools.

Only a theory that includes the findings of both analytic and
observational psychology and then integrates them with the appropriate neural sciences can be a general psychology of the sort Freud

envisioned. Although more limited in some respects than he had supposed, the psychoanalytic method and what can be learned from the transference has greater possibilities than Freud suspected. It is here that the work of Heinz Kohut finds its place.

I recall very well the impact Kohut's (1978) early papers had on our practice of psychoanalysis. Then as now, patients with narcissistic personality or behavior disorders formed the bulk of an analyst's practice, and literally overnight, analyses that had been stymied in spite of the best efforts of analyst and analysand became productive, once it was understood that what had been assumed to be resistance to transference was transference material in its own right and had to be dealt with accordingly (Basch, 1981b). So we might say that Kohut's discoveries first brought about a technical or methodological change in the practice of psychoanalysis, although their implications for psychoanalytic theory were not appreciated for some time. In psychotherapy it was the other way around. It was as if a theoretical floor had been slipped under the idiosyncratic technical innovations and methodological modifications that made psychotherapy a viable treatment in the hands of the experienced practitioner. As an analyst coming upon Kohut's work I had an "Aha!" experience. As a psychotherapist my reaction was: "Oh, so that's the meaning of what I have been doing." As a result of the advances made by self psychology, it should no longer be necessary for future generations of psychotherapists to have to repeat the frustrating and wasteful learning pattern that I described earlier.

As we know from his "The Two Analyses of Mr. Z" (1979), Kohut initially approached his patients with the traditional understanding of development based on the analysis of the neuroses. Demands other than those reflecting the sexual and hostile strivings of the oedipal period were interpreted as evasions of those feelings, so-called resistances to the oedipal transference. In the second analysis of Mr. Z, Kohut shows how the experiences reported by him in *The Analysis of the Self* (1971) had modified his approach. His method of conducting an analysis had not changed; it remained based on the fundamental premises laid down by Freud, namely, that cure was effected through promoting the patient's understanding of his pathology. This understanding was made possible by the interpretation and working through of the patient's transference to the analyst. What had changed was Kohut's grasp of the scope of the transference. Similar to Freud's experience, an insistent patient

(Miss F, *Analysis of the Self,* p. 283 ff.) had led Kohut to reconsider certain presuppositions he had brought to her treatment. This experience helped him recognize that a patient's immature demands and behavior are not necessarily *resistances* to instinctual transferences but may in themselves be evidence of transferences of another sort. He found that what is being reenacted through them is a patient's earlier frustrated attempt to develop a reasonable and functioning self; that is, to acquire those abilities that will let him maintain a viable self-esteem and a sense of self that will stand him in good stead in good times and bad, when alone and with others, when successful and when disappointed. Such maturation requires an atmosphere in which a patient can learn to develop, mobilize, identify, and work on fulfilling age-appropriate ambitions, gaining in this way a sense of mastery over his fate. In addition, he can have the opportunity to relate to models that will serve as ideals permitting him the experience of a nondestructive union with admired others. Such experiences have their prototype in the earliest union of the infant with his parents. Optimally, they prepare the way for the capacity to ally oneself with and draw strength from relationships and institutions that transcend the self without destroying it. Between them, ambitions and ideals form the psychological balance that Kohut has called the bipolar self. It is in the service of ambitions and ideals, between the two metaphorical poles of the self, that the capacities to perceive, to learn, to feel, to reason, and to create come together in what we call character.

Although only sketchily outlined here, Kohut has provided us with a framework for understanding the motivation for behavior that is comprehensive, open-ended, and does not contradict the findings of other related scientific studies of development.

I have been especially impressed with, and have written elsewhere about, the differences between the traditional psychoanalytic outlook based on an extrapolation from psychoneurotic pathology (which pictures the infant as a reflex organism, essentially asocial, seeking only freedom from stimuli, satiation, and sleep, and for whom maturation is, when all is said and done, a progressive deprivation of instinctual gratification and a distortion of his natural animal-like state), and the evidence demonstrating that even the newborn gives every indication of being very much a social, *human* being. As such he is stimulus hungry, eager to and capable of communicating with and learning from those around him, and furthermore, one whose instinctual needs, given the opportunity to do so in an age-appropriate manner, are fulfilled by, rather than opposed to, socialization (Basch, 1976a, 1977). The concept of development as an ongoing process of communication that, from the beginning of life to its end, depends on the ability and opportunity of an individual to make what he does and what happens to him part of the meaningful continuity that Kohut calls "self" is not only a very useful framework for understanding our patients but is also in keeping with findings of other branches of psychology.

Instead of teaching our students a theory of development that they will have to discard as meaningless for their work, self psychology enables us for the first time to synthesize a theory of development in which a psychoanalytic theory of motivation can be united with what has been learned by other branches of psychology about the development of perception, emotions, and thought. Using such a theory of development we can teach even beginners to relax, become aware of their reactions to the patient's behavior in the therapeutic situation, and use their inner response to guide them in their search for appropriate therapeutic intervention. In other words, self psychology permits the therapist's empathy to be used systematically in helping the patient. For years we have been encouraging our patients to introspect—to say what occurs to them, to report whatever is on their mind, and so on—not realizing that the therapist's freedom to be empathic is a prerequisite for patients' feeling safe enough to permit themselves to do so. The bipolar self and its attendant redefinition and expansion of the concept of transference are like a safety net beneath the therapist that gives him the freedom to experience the patient and his reactions to the patient without fear of falling too far if he loses his footing.

The concept of the selfobject completed the transformation of Kohut's theory from a schema directed to the treatment of a particular group of patients, the narcissistic personality disorders, to a hypothesis that had universal application. Psychotherapy, as I have elsewhere documented at greater length (Basch, 1980), cannot hope to deal satisfactorily with oedipal content because repressed infantile sexual conflicts need to be worked through in an ongoing analytic transference. So for practical purposes, we have had no theory of technique that has been useful to the psychotherapist. However, interpretation regarding the disavowed emotional aspect of selfobject relationships as these are manifest in the transference can be dealt with effectively in psychotherapy (Basch, 1980).

For example, had I been able to approach Mr. Young's case with a knowledge of self psychology, I would not have jumped to the conclusion that his difficulties of necessity had to be based on oedipal rivalry. Instead of coming to premature closure I would have had the theoretical support enabling me to listen empathically to his expressions of loneliness and need for his father, explored this idea further with him, and then waited to see if and how that supposed need would have played itself out in the transference relationship with me. I think it cannot be stressed enough that self psychology does not tell us what to find, but rather where to look and how to listen. It is a misunderstanding, whose source is not to be found in any of Kohut's writings, that self psychology eliminates or downplays the significance of psychosexuality or the potential oedipal conflict that can develop as a result of selfobject failure in the area of drive discharge and development. Self psychology is inclusive, not exclusive; it rules in, not out. It is entirely possible, and has happened to me in cases whose presenting symptomatology was similar to Mr. Young's, that the transference that developed indicated that patient's work or learning inhibitions were rooted in oedipal difficulties. If I am convinced that repressed infantile sexual wishes will have to be mobilized in the transference before the patient can be helped, I definitely recommend that a psychoanalysis be instituted because psychotherapy will, at best, have limited success. If, however, as was the case with Mr. Young, emotional deprivation rather than instinctual aberration is responsible for the patient's difficulties, it is now possible to interpret the resulting transference along those lines.

Psychotherapy often requires us to enter the lives of our patients much more actively than does psychoanalysis. Now it is possible to accompany that activity with interpretations of the selfobject needs the patient is demonstrating. This approach enhances our efficacy and permits the promotion of the sort of insight that was only possible previously in the analysis of psychoneurotic patients. I do not think I would have *done* anything much differently with Mr. Young than what I eventually did. What I now do much more effectively is to interpret to such patients the transference significance of what it is we are doing together.

In summary, then, we could say that Kohut's work finally makes the method of psychoanalysis applicable to the various psychotherapies. By expanding and explaining the concept of transference Kohut has laid the basis for a comprehensive theory of psychotherapy that will not only help those of us who have experience to engage in what we do better than we could before, but will let us teach our students a truly useful series of hypotheses about the origin, nature, and management of psychological tension. Concepts that can be used to good advantage from the very beginning of their clinical work.

REFERENCES

Basch, M. F. (1975a). Consciousness and Freud's "Project." *Ann. Psychoanal.* 3: 3–19.

———— (1975b). Toward a theory that encompasses depression: A revision of existing causal hypotheses in psychoanalysis. In *Depression and Human Existence*, E. J. Anthony & T. Benedek, eds. Boston: Little,Brown, pp. 485–534.

———— (1976a). The concept of affect: A re-examination. *J. Amer. Psychoanal. Assn.* 24: 759–777.

———— (1976b). Psychoanalysis and communication science. *Ann. Psychoanal.* 4: 385–421.

———— (1977). Developmental psychology and explanatory theory in psychoanalysis. *Ann. Psychoanal.* 5: 229–263.

———— (1980). *Doing Psychotherapy*. New York: Basic Books.

———— (1981a). Psychoanalytic interpretation and cognitive transformation. *Int. J. Psychoanal.* 62: 151–175.

———— (1981b). Selfobject disorders and psychoanalytic theory: A historical perspective. *J. Amer. Psychoanal. Assn.* 29: 337–351.

———— (1983). An operational definition of "self." In *Developmental Approaches to the Self*, Benjamin Lee, ed. New York: Plenum Press, pp. 7–58.

Kohut, H. (1971). *The Analysis of the Self*. New York: Int. Univ. Press.

———— (1978). *The Search for the Self: Selected Writings (1950–1978)*, P. H. Ornstein, ed. New York: Int. Univ. Press.

———— (1979). The two analyses of Mr. Z. *Int. J. Psychoanal.* 60: 3–27.

19

Discussion of Paper by Dr. Basch

Robert Michels, M.D.

Dr. Basch's presentation is lucid, lively, and marked by the cognitive clarity that is familiar in his writing. These are all characteristics that endear him to readers and audiences, but they can make difficulties for a discussant, for what is one to say? However, he has been generous to me in this paper because, in some fundamental respects, I believe we disagree.

He begins with a discussion of the nature of scientific theory, a subject about which his earlier contributions are among the most important in the psychoanalytic literature. He proceeds to discuss psychoanalytic theory and its relationship to psychotherapy, the subject of his recent monograph that is rapidly becoming a classic textbook of psychoanalytic psychotherapy. He then offers an instructive case example about himself as a young therapist, describing his early difficulties and the technical innovations that he developed and that rescued him and his patient, innovations that he experienced as opposed to the theory he then believed to be true. Finally, he discusses the impact of self psychology on the learning and practice of psychotherapy and expresses his conviction that, unlike traditional psychoanalytic theory, it would have facilitated his maturation into a skillful psychotherapist and that it offers a vastly preferable theoretical base for psychoanalytic psychotherapy. I begin my discussion with his second issue, traditional psychoanalytic theory and its relation to psychotherapy. I then comment on the two psychotherapies "by Dr. B" and the contrast between traditional psychoanalytic theory and self psychology as frameworks for psychotherapy. Finally, I end where Dr. Basch starts, with the nature of the theory and its relevance for psychoanalysis and psychotherapy.

Dr. Basch tells us that his understanding of psychoanalytic theory was that "A patient's pathology was assessed in terms of the level of infantile sexuality at which he had been arrested . . ." and that therapy had a "single-minded goal of investigating and rechanneling the patient's infantile sexual and aggressive development." He was "strictly enjoined from doing anything other than interpreting the dynamics of psychosexuality and the family romance . . ." He now believes that "Freud decreed that the neuroses taught us what we needed to know about normal development . . ." and that "the traditional psychoanalytic outlook . . . pictures the infant as a reflex organism, essentially asocial, seeking only freedom from stimuli, satiation, and sleep, and for whom maturation is . . . a progressive deprivation of instinctual gratification and a distortion of his natural animal-like state . . ." Whose traditional psychoanalysis and psychoanalytic theory of development is this? A. Freud, H. Hartmann, R. Spitz, E. Jacobson, M. Mahler? I do not believe they would recognize it!

Dr. Basch knows a great deal about the evolution of psychoanalytic theory, and unless he is a great deal older than he looks, he certainly knows that the various fragments of once held views contained in these passages no longer represented psychoanalytic theory many years before his training. He has chosen to caricature traditional psychoanalytic theory and along with this to ignore the various fragments of suggestions for psychoanalytic psychotherapy that had already been formulated by Bibring, Gill, and others well before Dr. Basch's training. Why has he done so? Were his teachers that bad, or perhaps, is he trying rhetorically to emphasize an important point about the role of theory in the clinical situation? I return to this issue later.

Let us now turn to young Dr. Basch as psychotherapist. His method of approach is described clearly. For example, "*Since* he was entering his father's field, I *assumed* that his failure represented a punishment . . ." And again, "I *assumed* . . . that the lack of negative feelings . . . represented a defensive maneuver . . ." Or consider his interpretation of a sleep disturbance as a displaced incestuous

desire, apparently without supporting evidence. Dr. Basch is searching for data that fit his theory, as a good scientist should. However, I
believe that Freud's and our traditional instructions for psychoanalysts are not that they function like scientists working in the
laboratory. We hear none of the free floating, evenly hovering attention, of the relaxed access to his own inner life, of the mental state
Freud and traditional psychoanalysts have always associated with
the therapist's role. This is hardly surprising. Dr. Basch was a
young student, and he is making one of the most characteristic
errors of young student therapists: trying to prove the theory and
please his instructor rather than listening to his patient with the
theory as an aid to understanding what he hears. Dr. Basch is testing psychoanalytic theory, not treating patients, and it should not
surprise most of us that it fails that test.

However, Dr. Basch rescues himself. Although he describes himself as frightened and passive, he does have the courage to come out
from behind his theory and meet his patient face to face, and once he
does so good things happen. He learns about his patient's life and
problems in life, and his patient gets better. But I am troubled by
the other things that Dr. Basch claims to have learned from this and
similar experiences. He states: "Penis envy, sibling rivalry, castration fear, the primal scene, . . . seemed to play no great part in my
psychotherapeutic experience." My own impression is that each of
these concepts has been a valuable tool for organizing my impres-
sions and understandings of the lives of the people I meet in psychotherapy. I do not think Dr. Basch believes that infantile sexuality is
only relevant for the analyzable, but this passage almost suggests
that he does. The same issue reappears when he states: "If I am
convinced that repressed infantile sexual wishes will have to be
mobilized in the transference before the patient can be helped, I
definitely recommend that a psychoanalysis be instituted since psychotherapy will, at best, have a very limited success." This would
seem to indicate that classical neurotic patients can be treated by
psychoanalysis but are not amenable to psychotherapy, whereas
patients with narcissistic disorders can be treated by either psychoanalysis or psychotherapy. To say the least, this is a surprising
view!

Dr. Basch sees self psychology as a remedy for many of the evils of
the psychoanalytic theory he tried to apply as a psychotherapist. I
think that we would all agree; in fact, almost any broad view of man

would be superior to the partial and inhuman model he felt he should be using. (Indeed, it is somewhat bewildering to me that, with the view of psychoanalysis that was presented to him early in his training, he persisted in his desire to become a psychoanalyst. However, his shift to a better, although forbidden, mode of treatment with his patient and his persistence in his studies only demonstrate what wise educators have long known about the weakness of their impact on their students.) Dr. Basch found the terms and categories of self psychology far more helpful in organizing his experiences with his psychotherapy patients. Ambitions, ideals, the central role of communication in development, and the self aided him far more than drives, defenses, conflicts, and compromises. I think that many would take issue with his assertion that "self psychology enables us *for the first time* to synthesize a theory of development in which a psychoanalytic theory of motivation can be united with what has been learned by other branches of psychology about the development of perception, emotions, and thought." He would seem to be dismissing several decades of developmental ego psychology without explaining why.

However, although questions of priority or uniqueness of a theory may be important for historians or sociologists of science, or for the narcissism of scientists, they are not really important for the science itself. Whether it is the first or only psychoanalytic theory to do so, Dr. Basch makes clear the vital thing that self psychology allows him to do as a psychotherapist: "Using such a theory . . . we can teach even beginners to relax, become aware of their reactions . . . and use their inner response. . . . [The theory] . . . gives . . . [the therapist] the freedom to experience the patient and his reactions to the patient without fear of falling too far if he loses his footing." It has been a long way around, but I believe that we have rediscovered Freud's attitude of evenly hovering, relaxed, unfocused listening, and as far as I am concerned the goal is so essential to psychotherapy that we should not complain about how circuitous the journey may have been.

This brings me to my last, and Dr. Basch's first, point: the nature of theory and its relevance for psychoanalysis and psychotherapy. Dr. Basch opens his paper by telling us that a scientific theory is simply a formal description of a pattern or patterns of expectation that we bring to a particular situation. That is true, but of course it is also true of many other things that are not scientific theories.

Astrology, religious systems, and superstitions also involve patterns of expectation, and so does Greek tragedy, Western music, or the Elizabethan sonnet. Self psychology, like libido theory and many other systems of psychoanalytic thought and interpretation, involves patterns of expectation, but that does not make it a scientific theory.

Scientists use scientific theories to guide their observations and experiments, and very occasionally, they employ the results of these observations to modify their theories. When they are creating new theories (the extraordinary science of Kuhn), they dream, float, imagine, relax, regress in the service of the ego, and in general draw on deeper levels of their mental capacity. When they are using theories that already exist (the ordinary science of Kuhn), they work, think, attend, focus, calculate, and solve problems. The psychoanalytic geniuses who create new theories, the Freuds, and Kohuts, and others, work much as do Kuhn's extraordinary scientists. However, the psychoanalytic clinician employing an existing theory is not at all like the ordinary scientist, and this difference is at the heart of the role of theory in psychoanalytic practice, as well as the heart of Dr. Basch's early difficulties in psychotherapy. The question is not so much what theory is used, but how it is used. I believe that Dr. Basch's critical transformation was not to a new theory, but to a new relationship to theory. If I might borrow the spatial metaphors that are now unemployed, the question is where the theory is located. Dr. Basch started out with a crowded office; the theory between himself and the patient interfered with their relationship. Psychotherapy should be conducted with as little as possible between patient and therapist. The theory is not absent, but it is inside the therapist (or perhaps behind his shoulder whispering in his ear). It is not something that he tests to see whether it is true or false, but rather something that suggests meanings, enriches the possible range of associations, and enhances understanding. Theories that are scientifically almost absurd can be clinically rich; libido theory is an example. Other theories that are scientifically elegant can be clinically empty; general systems theory has yet to rise above this description. The clinician uses theory not as a hypothesis for testing, but as a source of enrichment to the meanings that he brings to the patient's experience, a way of drawing on the collective experience of psychoanalysis since Freud in addition to his own, and in addition to his knowledge of art, culture, history, the humanities, and theories of child development. All of these are potential sources of interpretations, and as clinicians we have little concern with their inconsistencies or logical flaws. The task is not one of validating hypotheses or constructing an overarching unified field theory; rather it is enriching the network of meanings that we use to understand our patients' lives. A scientific theory is valued if it suggests experiments that could disprove it. A psychoanalytic theory is valued if it suggests interpretations that further an analysis.

A theory is a kind of mental structure, and we know that there are many ways to look at mental structures. They have origins and developmental causes, they have adaptive functions, they organize and simplify external reality, and they relate it to the preexisting inner world. Scientific theories can exist and be studied "out there," but a psychoanalytic theory is of no value to the clinician until it is well internalized and part of his analytic self. Indeed, for beginners, theories are often transitional objects. They keep the young therapist from getting too lonely and offer him something to suck on and pacify himself with on a long winter night. A theory operates like a language, organizing the categories of perception and action, often without our awareness. In this regard a new theory can be like a second language, allowing us to know and do new things and also making us more aware of our old theory, our first language, and how it shaped our experience. An educated person knows that his or her language is not the only possible one and is less likely to believe that its rules and tenses are the way the world really is, rather than the way he or she has learned to perceive it. Dr. Basch as a young therapist learned one language; he then found it inadequate and now has discovered a second one that he prefers. However, all languages have limitations, and any one can constrict the awareness of its user. One moral to take from Dr. Basch's tale may not be the advantage of his second language over his first, but rather the advantage in knowing two languages rather than one and therefore recognizing that any language is only one of several that are possible. It helps keep language or, to break the metaphor, theory in its place, somewhere other than between patient and therapist.

If theory is like a psychic structure, one of the questions raised by Dr. Basch's paper is whether traditional psychoanalytic theory represents a case of arrested development, requiring a transmuting internalization, or alternatively, whether there is an intersystemic conflict between structural theory and self psychology. I do not know the answer to these questions, but I do believe that even if the development has been arrested, there is potential cohesion rather than fragmentation, and the conflicts I detect do not seem to be pathologic. Our therapeutic work requires creative imagination, and we welcome new theories that assist that imagination. Dr. Basch has demonstrated that self psychology can do just that.

20

Confrontation and Selfobject Transference: A Case Study

Nathaniel J. London, M.D.

INTRODUCTION: DEFINITIONAL CONSIDERATIONS

The place of confrontation in self psychology has yet to be clarified. Still, the concepts of self psychology are particularly suited to advance our understanding of confrontation. The confrontations to which I refer in this paper generally serve to promote a patient's cohesive self and are fully empathic. Unempathic confrontations are only touched upon in terms of misuses of confrontation. Whether one uses Kohut's (1978) definition of empathy—"the recognition of the self in the other [p. 705]"—or any other definition, empathy is a way of organizing observations; it is not a technique. Because one's empathy may be employed in any clinical technique, the use of empathy in interpretation, in the communication of empathic understanding, and in a confrontive response merit comparison.

In an *interpretation* the therapist provides meaning and significance to the patient's experience within the context of their interaction. The interpreting therapist, optimally together with the patient, considers the patient and their mutual work from an objective viewpoint. In the *communication of empathic understanding* the viewpoint is different. The therapist adds meaning to the patient's experience and their interaction from the subjective viewpoint of the patient. In a *confrontive response* the therapist interacts with

247

the patient from his own subjective viewpoint—to some degree he commits his person and personality to the clinical interaction.

The subject of confrontation is particularly pertinent to borderline patients. In setting limits or opposing a patient's peremptory demands, it may be hard to maintain optimal empathy. Such confrontations are not misuses of confrontation and may prove better examples of correct empathy than placating the patient. But the focus of this paper lies elsewhere, specifically, on those situations in which the therapist, because he is experienced as confrontive, serves to sustain the patient's self. This may be observed at times even with misuses of confrontation, such as the use of confrontation as an end in itself (Zinberg, 1973) or "confronting a patient with reality" without regard for how or why the patient may hold to a different integration of reality. In such situations the confronting therapist may be experienced by the patient as part of his self in ways readily explained by the theory of selfobject transferences. In the case to be presented, however, the confronting psychotherapist was not experienced as part of the self but as an independent center of initiative. This raises an interesting question for self psychology: Must the selfobject that promotes a cohesive self necessarily be experienced as part of the self?

DIAGNOSTIC CONSIDERATIONS
CONCERNING BORDERLINE STATES

The contributions of Kohut (1971, 1977) and Adler (1979) both consider the distinction between borderline personality disorder and narcissistic personality disorder dependent to a considerable degree on the developing clinical situation. Within certain limits the same patient may appear borderline in one clinical situation and narcissistic in another. Kohut defined a narcissistic personality disorder as one in which selfobject transferences develop that allow tolerance for regression and the activation and interpretation of archaic selfobject transferences. He considered such clinical development evidence for a cohesive self and cohesive idealized archaic objects. As for the borderline patient the central area of regression involves experiencing a fragmented body-mind-self and selfobject, which cannot be psychologically elaborated. According to Kohut (1977), where there is evidence for such regressive developments, the patient is "in principle not analyzable [p. 192]."

Although the differences between Kohut and Adler may be more apparent than real, Adler's vantage point leads to a different focus, which appears more optimistic with regard to borderline states. He maintained that a borderline patient may gradually develop selfobject transferences as holding introjects become assimilated, so that he may be treated similarly to a narcissistic personality disorder. Adler viewed the main therapeutic task as fostering a situation in which selfobject transferences can emerge and pathological aspects can be interpreted. Though keeping as an open question Adler's therapeutic optimism with regard to the potential analyzability of borderline patients, the focus of this paper is close to Adler's, that is, on the nature of the transference where stabilizing selfobject transferences have not formed.

CASE PRESENTATION[1]

Review of a record of psychotherapy during an arbitrarily selected 2-month period indicated decisive, favorable changes in the clinical process, in the nature of the clinical interaction, and in the patient's level of integration. The patient established a more stable selfobject transference in the context of an interaction with a particular quality: He experienced me as confrontive in a particular way. The favorable changes appeared to result from a partial resolution of this patient's demands for confrontation.

It is not the purpose of this report to advocate the use of confrontation as a deliberate technique in psychotherapy. In fact, caution is emphasized with respect to "being confrontive" in various ways that such technical advice is commonly understood. The focus is rather on the nature of the clinical interaction in the context of a spontaneously unfolding process. I would question whether anyone could have made contact with this patient at this point in treatment without at least being *experienced* by the patient as confrontive and

---

[1]The following case has been disguised so that the patient would be recognizable only to himself. Accuracy has been sacrificed for the purposes of disguise, for conciseness, and to emphasize the theoretical issues. However, care has been taken to convey the events of the clinical process accurately without regard for any theoretical formulation. Should the patient, perchance, gain access to this report, he should understand that it is not a full portrayal of my understanding of him. He does understand that I regularly consult with my colleagues about my work, while maintaining confidentiality. This presentation is part of such consultation.

without being actually confrontive to some degree. This report is concerned not only with establishing a stable selfobject transference in such a situation but, more significantly, with resolving such a selfobject transference in a way that furthers the treatment.

Carl Y, age 24, had a long and dramatic psychiatric history and an even longer and committed ambition to be a creative writer. His short-lived marriage appeared as a pathetic reenactment of his involvement with a disturbed younger sister. His past history and mental status examination was consistent with many of the criteria for borderline personality disorder described by Perry and Klerman (1980). He was highly volatile and emotional. Although generally appearing submissive and forlorn, he was capable of intense, angry outbursts to the point of assaultive gestures toward persons and property (he was never actually damaging in his behavior, although he had been so misinterpreted). Suicidal ruminations had been frequent. There had been a number of hospitalizations. He always reacted strongly to any separation. He was prone to paranoid states with specific preoccupations with being poisoned. These states could be so transient as to be only momentary. Quite separate from these paranoid reactions, he also maintained a paranoid attitude in attributing the sources of his psychological difficulties to the manner in which his parents reared him. That there was more than a kernel of truth to this paranoid attitude is an understatement, but his paranoid attitude made it hard to bring his unhappy childhood experiences into focus in the treatment. No evidence of schizophrenia was evident in the history he provided or in my observations of him.

Carl always made good contact with others and was capable of strong involvements to the point of overinvolvement. He was psychologically minded and perceptive. His intimate relationships were prone to intense idealizations and disillusionments, but he was otherwise astute and sensitive in his assessments of others. Similarly, within the sector of his emotional disturbance, there was a pathological self-centeredness and sense of entitlement of which he was deeply ashamed. He had solid values and a concerned and generous spirit toward others. Frequently, others took unfair advantage of him.

Carl's intensity was his most striking quality; it was an intensity that remained constant whether he was depressed or elated. It could be exhausting both for himself and for others. More often than not, his treatment sessions involved use of his acute intelligence and gifted command of language to produce a torrent of words. He and I recognized early in our work together that his remarkable capacity for insight would be a problem. These insights could be viewed as intellectualizations, but they also represented an impressive exercise of his intelligence. His discoveries about himself were consistently precise and well documented. The problem was that they were generated in such profusion that, as in keeping with Gresham's law, the excess of insights tended to drive out or depreciate the few insights that might have had a decisive impact on his life. The content of each hour was very detailed and full of connections; yet it was impossible for me to recall, in full, the details of any single session. I have frequently been unable to keep up with Carl's rapid associations, but I have never for a moment found him boring or obscure.

It is hard to say to what degree Carl had a cohesive self. He certainly had a firm sense of identity—a coherent integration of goals, values, and ambitions. There was no evidence for a disturbance in evocative memory as noted by Adler with respect to severe borderline states. There were major amnestic areas. He could not recall any experience with his father before adolescence, whereas other preadolescent memories were vivid. He showed evidence of fragmentation when misunderstood—with hypochondriacal symptoms, psychosomatic symptoms, and paranoid experiences. He did require that I understand him accurately, but I am not sure how much he required my recognition in order to maintain a cohesive self. Evidence for the emergence of derivatives of an archaic grandiose self are presented later on. Although Carl appeared initially as a borderline personality disorder, other diagnostic possibilities remained to be ruled out. Severe mixed psychoneurosis (hysterical and obsessional), narcissistic personality disorder, and bipolar affective disorder (manic-depressive) were all possibilities.

Carl sought psychoanalytic treatment with me following a dramatic disruption of a long-term treatment in psychotherapy. He was overwhelmingly depressed and despairing of his future, with suicidal ruminations. He was working independently at his creative writing but had no gainful employment. Paranoid elements were prominent, most immediately with respect to an eccentric and intrusive landlady. Emotional displays and tantrums were frequent. With respect to all the emotionality and depression, Carl informed me that he was scarcely in touch with these feelings. He was more pervasively aware of a bewildering and frightening sense of emptiness. I did sense a workable treatment situation and a patient with high motivation. I was concerned at this point about his potential for psychotic disorganization and had no reason to know that he could tolerate the regressive pull of a psychoanalytic situation. He was disappointed when I told him that I was unwilling to consider psychoanalysis at this time, but we could reconsider the matter when he had developed a more stable life situation. We began psychotherapy on a twice-weekly basis.

The opening pages of the psychotherapy were not easy for either of us. He responded well to my firmness in setting limits so long as I was fair and my reasons were made understandable. His feelings about his previous treatment were in the foreground and required a good deal of tact and understanding on my part to clarify the issues. It was hard for him to understand my approach to him, particularly with respect to issues of neutrality and abstinence. On the other hand, my neutrality, objectivity, and firmness also served as a relief and comfort to him. His sense of humor meshed well with mine in a way that proved very helpful. In general, I appealed to the mature and reflective aspects of his personality. The professional nature of our relationship and my professional integrity were consistently and explicitly recognized by Carl. In fact, these factors, along with what he saw as my competence, were valued and came to sustain him at difficult times.

There were confrontations that proved significant. Early in the treatment I asked him to change an appointment to suit the needs of another patient. Carl flew into an awesome rage. The origins of his anger and distrust of me were made very clear: This was another example of repeated instances in which people took advantage of him and put the needs of others ahead of his own. I had a few days to consider the matter and concluded not only that the appointment change was necessary but that I could not tolerate accommodating the nature of my practice to his needs. His fury remained unabated. Neither interpretation of my empathic failure, an appeal to reason, nor just riding out the emotional storm seemed likely to settle the matter and allow for a manageable treatment situation. I finally told him with constraint, but with a feeling of genuine anger and in frankly vulgar terms, something to the following effect: I understood that he was afraid that I would take advantage of him, that I understood why that was such an important issue for him, but that he had to understand that I could not allow him to exploit me either. He immediately calmed down and proceeded to explore the issues relative to this confrontation in a fruitful way, including some significant connections to the past. I have since thought a great deal about the significance of this confrontation. I had been genuinely provoked and was in a state of temporary regression as I responded as best I could to what I felt was an assault on my essential freedom of action. I submit this confrontation as an example of meeting the borderline patient at his or her level of regression and on a level of action. I do not think it would have proved effective if it had been contrived or if I customarily felt free to respond in such a manner.

After a time the emotional storms subsided, and there were indications of an idealizing transference. The torrent of words slowed to merely a rush. I was able to tune in and respond not only to the misunderstandings and mistreatments he had repeatedly received from his parents and others but to his considerable assets and capabilities. He readily participated in my efforts to understand my empathic failures as they occurred. All this was a new experience for him, and he thrived on it. He did complain from time to time that my attention to his assets somehow interfered with gaining access to a dark side of himself. He wanted to bring that out and particularly to connect his problems with his difficulties in childhood. He was concerned that I only wanted to reinforce his strengths and cover up the problems. He would then think about an analysis with both wishes and fears. There was a persistent fantasy that he would have to become psychotic in order to resolve his problems and his fear that I would reject him when that occurred.

A selfobject transference with elements of mirroring and idealizing was now providing some measure of stability. The evidence for this was quite clear but is not fully documented here in the interest of conciseness. Yet, Carl's vulnerable self was still functioning on an archaic level close to primary process organization, as evidenced by an incident in the tenth month of treatment. He complained of feeling unexpectedly depressed and somewhat crazy. Paranoid concerns suddenly returned. He now had a job with a publishing firm and recently went to dinner with his parents. He wore a new coat and tie for which his mother complimented him. Ordinarily, he dresses in a manner he describes as weird and eccentric. On reflection, he considered the coat he wore to the dinner not exactly his style. It was more befitting his mother's taste; too *conservative* and not very masculine. The next day, he enthusiastically entered into a political debate with a female co-worker. He had entirely contradictory opinions about the point in question, but he joined the adversary spirit of the discussion and aggressively argued one side in opposition to the young woman. She then accused him of using a *conservative* argument, an accusation that rekindled his feelings about the conservative coat. As he told me this, we could now both recognize that this experience set in motion a state of fragmentation. His depression and paranoid feelings followed this confrontation with disparate aspects of himself and his conflicted identifications.

During this phase Carl would talk throughout the hour and would be distressed if I interrupted. Yet, he always asked for my personal reaction to what he was telling me. My responses were never quite enough. That is to say, he appreciated my empathic understanding but yearned for something more in terms of my personal responses. He frequently complained that he didn't know anything about me.

Toward the end of a year of psychotherapy, the indications of a grandiose self began to emerge. The initial references were to his body-self. In one hilarious hour he began to boast of his physical prowess. He insistently and persistently challenged me to arm wrestle with him to demonstrate his superior strength. I have always taken pride in my intuitive grasp of the difference between responsiveness and gratifications that go beyond analytic abstinence. Arm wrestling with a patient immediately appeared to me as an inappropriate gratification. Yet, my respect for the sensitivity of his emerging grandiose body-self led me in the end to accept his challenge. He won, but I believe he felt content that I gave him a fair fight. In retrospect, I realize that the contest was the very model of confrontation on a regressive level of action, which is a main concern of this paper. The fact that this was the only occasion when Carl sought physical contact with me is further evidence for the reactivation of an archaic grandiose body-self. More significantly, and with intense feelings of embarrassment, he next began to reveal ideas that he had a brilliant mind and a great potential for creative achievement. It may even be true that this gifted young man indeed has such potentials. The important point is that such a view of himself was experienced by Carl as grandiosity. At this time teachers and friends also began to respond to his potential. This led to an invitation to study for a semester in a creative writing program at a state university in a distant part of the country. Carl was eager to go, and I did not stand in his way. At this point I recognized his considerable improvement, but I also had good reasons to conclude that there had so far been no significant structural change.

After several months Carl wrote a glowing account of his success in this program along with generous praise for me and our work together. Two weeks later he returned in an agitated overactive state, unable to sleep. He had become intensely involved with a woman teacher and dropped out of the program, ostensibly to avoid disrupting the teacher's marriage. He talked incessantly and informed me that he was a genius. I thought he was in the midst of a manic episode. There was not really a flight of ideas, but he was somewhat tangential. He would stick to the subject in his usual intelligent and creative way, the subject being a description and formulation of his life history and current psychological crisis. But the torrent of words was endless and seemed to lead nowhere. He insisted that he wanted to tell me of his recent experiences, but few details emerged. A trial of lithium seemed indicated. I explained my reasoning to Carl and recommended consultation with a clinical psychopharmacologist. The effect on Carl was of a truly massive empathic failure. Even thinking of him in diagnostic terms was an assault on my viewing him as a whole person. He stormed out of the office vowing never to return, and it was touch and go for a while whether he would continue. He never saw the consultant, and the manic episode subsided in about 2 weeks. We continued to meet, although to his dismay my schedule would permit sessions only once a week.

I responded to this crisis not with further confrontation but with a detailed exploration of the meaning of his reaction. That is to say, I never backed down on my recommendation for a psychopharmacologic consultation, but clarification and interpretation of his reaction to my recommendation, including the connections to the past, occupied much of our work for the next 8 months. Over this period he complained regularly of feeling depressed and at the same time kept informing me of steady progress in his life. Most significantly, the complaints of emptiness disappeared. He now had feelings even though he didn't like them. Whenever he was praised at work for his achievements, he tended to react with some form of depression or fragmentation. It seemed to me, as I interpreted him in various ways, that his grandiosity now had to be concealed, and anything that would breathe life into it was experienced as an assault.

I began to keep process notes of our sessions when Carl returned from a planned vacation. He started off with a serious complaint. Despite my competence and his trust in me, I wasn't doing him any good. He was much better, but he did it all by himself—some of it out of spite, as if to show me. He knew he needed more treatment, but I don't help him; I don't say anything; I don't help him to talk about his past; I don't help him get out the crazy stuff within him; he should quit, and if he stays, it will only be for me to help him to leave me. He can't leave now because of his fear that he'll crack up if he stops seeing a shrink. His complaints became more and more uncontrolled in what I experienced as a merciless verbal attack on me. But Carl insisted that he had no desire to attack me. Rather, he was doing what he could to get me to respond—to confront him—to help him open up. Over the next 2 months, Carl was considerate and thoughtful but unrelenting in his efforts to get me to be more confrontive. I let him know that I heard him.

Initially, I also told Carl that his sense of a dark side of himself, which he wanted me to bring out, could be an illusion. His immediate reaction was an acute sense that I was laughing at him. The atmosphere deteriorated, and he left angrily, telling me that he didn't want to come back. Carl could hardly have understood what I meant in telling him that his "dark side" might be an illusion. We spent the next 2 months exploring the subject. But it was my first attempt to raise a serious question that had been on my mind for some time. I wanted to know if the dark side represented his psychotic potential—what Kohut (1977) described as a central area of regression, which cannot be psychologically elaborated—or if there were indeed well-formed ideas and fantasies that I had somehow not helped him to elaborate. His initial response was a paranoid feeling that I mocked him, and it was only the beginning.

Carl thought about what I said regarding illusion and made some sense of it even though still far from what I had in mind. He explained that his friends had no trouble seeing the dark side of him. But if he talked to me about his miserable childhood, I would just say, "I've heard that before." There was some basis for his complaint insofar as I repeatedly challenged his conviction that he was permanently damaged by his childhood experiences. Carl said that he would prefer that I ask him why these childhood events still troubled him so much. I fully agreed and rephrased his question to why these events continued to "haunt" him so. Carl went on to document considerable improvement in his life. He stressed that his mistreatment by his parents as well as other important figures gave him good reason to be suspicious of me. In his outburst at me during the last session, he wanted to challenge me to be more confrontive, and it worked. What I said about "illusion" or being "haunted" gave him something to think about. During this session, Carl was more subdued, reflective, and capable of self-observation than I had ever seen him. Subsequent interviews took on a coherence and continuity at a higher level than before. A decisive and favorable turning point in the treatment had occurred. It so happened that I informed him during this interview that we could resume sessions twice a week. Perhaps the improvement derived from the increased frequency in meeting.

On reviewing the record, however, the decisive factor appears to involve the issues around confrontation. As Carl experienced this development, he had finally succeeded, in his own confrontive way, in getting me to become more confrontive and responsive—to be freer in expressing my personal reactions to him in a way he found integrative. To my best opinion, I do not believe that I actually became more or less confrontive or responsive. The so-called confrontations at the beginning of this phase were simply emotionally charged words like "illusion" or "haunted," to which he responded as if I were more confrontive. What was decisive, to my view, was not any confrontation per se. Rather, it was that I heard his complaint and accepted his demand for confrontation as his contribution to the treatment and as something worthy of consideration. Looking back, it seems that I had never rejected these demands, and I had frequently been confrontive. Yet, in a subtle way I had treated his demands for confrontation as an obstacle to be overcome without actively engaging him in the meaning of these demands. It was particularly important that I fully understood that his attack on me was not malicious or manipulative, as he had so often been accused of in the past, but that his attack was in the interest of furthering our work. As if to confirm the point, Carl then told me that his father had just accused him of deliberately neglecting a business matter, although his motives had actually been constructive. Carl next reported that his best friend was drinking too much, and he started a well-organized campaign to confront his friend about the drinking problem. This is the best evidence I have that introjective processes were at work—that he was becoming confrontive in the way he wanted me to confront him.

A supervisor at work, one whom he respected for his competence but not as a person, dramatically confronted Carl with a harsh criticism. He then told Carl that he wanted to shock him in order to help him bring out his "real" feelings. Carl told me with some pride that he cried "real tears." For my part, Carl's so-called real tears seemed a compliance with his supervisor in keeping with his yearning for a dramatic confrontation. I was reminded, I told him, of a colleague who was accustomed, at a particular point in a developing treatment situation, to call his patient by his first name. Invariably, the tears would flow, and the patient would become hooked into the treatment. I added that I did not respect that kind of manipulation, and Carl was obviously moved by what I had said. I believe that what I told Carl was the most important confrontation of all: to confront him with the misuses of confrontation. It was precisely then that Carl, for the first time, began to tell me in detail of his involvement with his teacher at the state university. In summary, he admired her tremendously, they were exquisitely attuned in interests and values, and she idealized him. For the first time, he truly felt in love as well as merged with her. Despite his respect for her teaching, he began to feel that she wanted to control him in his work and that was becoming intolerable. There was also a grandiose quality to her aspirations which worried him. He also feared disrupting her marriage, and he fled the course.

As he again demanded my personal reaction, I commented that there seemed to be some problems in the way he loved. Carl was indignant: "No one has the right to presume how another person should love!" I said that perhaps I should not have used the word "problem." Carl boldly rejected my apology: He wanted me to say what I thought even if it angered him. We reviewed the whole matter of his intolerance to being seen as having a problem—to being viewed in diagnostic terms. He was devastated when I recommended lithium because it reminded him of all his mother's criticisms when he was 9 years old: that he was flying high and headed for a fall; that he was too tense; that he was manipulative, malicious, and selfish. The pediatrician placed him on a sedative. He reacted with fears of going crazy. I considered, although I dared not tell Carl at this point, that he may well have had a manic mood swing at that time. Carl had told me at the outset of treatment about his mother's eccentric and punitive responses to his turmoil at age 9. He now told me of his subjective experiences. He had explicit sexual preoccupations centered around frantic masturbation. He developed massive obsessive-compulsive symptoms including rituals, prayers, doubting, and preoccupations over touching. One specific masturbatory fantasy was that he was the director of an institution for people with sexual problems, and he treated them by caring for them like infants. The physical care was sexually exciting.

After several sessions devoted to telling me about this childhood disturbance, Carl then revealed, with great embarrassment, another feature of his experience at the state university. There was a moment when it felt to him that his past, present, and future all came together. He had a sense of greatness that he knew he possessed ever since childhood. In this quality of greatness he emphasized his capacity for the documentation of emotional experience. This sense of greatness is partly a burden because it alientates him from others. Carl also emphasized that he does not experience this greatness as part of his self—it is something within him, but not part of him. About this time, he told me something related by his mother, which he cannot remember. In his childhood he and his father regularly played chess and other intellectual games. At the point that he would succeed and excel at the game, his father would become angry and pick on him. Whether or not his mother's account is accurate, it is consistent with a theme that Carl's talents and abilities were stimulated only to be depreciated at the point of success. There is evidence that this theme has been prominent in the transference, but I have not yet been able to confirm the point with Carl.

To review this phase of the psychotherapy, Carl made strenuous efforts to get me to become more confrontive. A transference situation developed in which he experienced me as confrontive and as personally involved and committed in a way that promoted a more cohesive self. But I had my own demands for Carl. I wanted to know whether the dark side of him represented an inner life connected with a cohesive self or whether it was an illusion—a dark side that was only his vulnerability to psychotic fragmentation. It was precisely when I conveyed to Carl not only my sincerity but also my rejection of confrontation to exploit rather than to understand him that he began to let me in on the dark side. Specifically, he presented detailed accounts of his involvement with his teacher, as the embodiment of an idealized archaic object, and of the emergence of a grandiose self. He also revealed many vivid details of his emotional disturbance at age 9, which one may presume to be connected to the emotional turmoil at the state university. The entire level of his interaction with me showed improvement. He deliberately tried to slow himself down, to become more reflective and more aware of his inner experience. There was another disturbed period with depressed and suicidal feelings. At this time, he had a fantasy that he would die of an illness, that I would come to his funeral, and he wondered how I would react. In place of his earlier recurrent feelings that he did not know me and could not tell if I had any personal reaction to him, he was now able to entertain fantasies about my personal reaction to him at his funeral.

During this time, Carl not only continued to ask me to become more confrontive, but he was openly critical of any interpretation of empathic failures. Whenever I tried to explore regressive shifts in relation to his interaction with me, he felt that I was trying to push him into a more intense involvement. He felt patronized by such efforts. The very measures that had proved successful during the earlier periods of mirror or idealizing transferences were now unacceptable. The only empathic failure we could fruitfully explore was my failure to accept and value his demand for confrontation. Carl also spontaneously brought into our discussion an obvious oedipal theme in his life—his repeated preoccupation with losing the girl he loved to a less worthy male rival. It was striking that any effort of mine to respond to this issue led to fragmented behaviors; he felt pressured by me and became argumentative and guarded.

The culmination of our discussion about whether his dark side was an illusion came when I told him that he had answered my question and that I was now convinced that he did have an inner life that warranted our attention. He was thrilled but also dumbfounded that it had taken me so long to figure this out. His view of himself was of someone given excessively to fantasy. He turned the discussion to his need for me to view his distress, now as in the past, as provoked by others and external events—what I described earlier as a paranoid attitude. He insisted that the abuse he had received was real and not fantasy. I said something to the effect that fantasies are always connected with what is real and have their own reality. This statement had a profound effect on Carl, and his understanding may be summarized as follows: His mother, as well as others, constantly accused him of misperceiving or distorting reality. Though he knew this was not so, he also came to doubt his own perceptions of reality. Accordingly, he deliberately struggled to push his fantasies aside, concentrate on accurately perceiving reality, and get me to confirm that his perceptions were accurate—that he had been misunderstood and victimized. This formulation provided by Carl leads to a conclusion that his demand for confrontation as well as his paranoid stance was partly defensive. He sought my personal reactions to guarantee that he was realistic and concealed his fantasies for fear that I, too, would attack him for distorting reality, for being crazy.

Carl's formulation of a defensive aspect to his need for confrontation is an important part of the treatment work at this point, but it is only a minor aspect of his need for confrontation as he has since come to understand it. Further consideration of Carl's need for confrontation are presented in the discussion that follows. His defensive need for confrontation may explain his paranoid stance with regard to his parents. It does not explain the quite different transient paranoid reactions in response to empathic failures, reactions which did appear as manifestations of fragmentation. There is reason to consider that a patient may have a cohesive archaic grandiose self and also have fragmented body-mind-self and selfobject experiences that cannot be psychologically elaborated. Carl initially appeared as a classical borderline personality disorder, but he now appears as a narcissistic personality disorder. A definite diagnosis is still deferred. Bipolar affective disorder remains a possibility. Even more evidence of psychoneurotic features has emerged. A diagnostic assessment of Carl is difficult, to say the least.

There is evidence that Carl's level of interaction with me shifted to one that was more integrated and less paranoid. To illustrate the point, consider Carl's depressed and paranoid reaction when his coworker accused him of being conservative, because it reminded him of his "conservative" coat. His vulnerability to a single word was on a primary process level. The same theme reemerged at this point in the treatment at a higher level of integration. Carl began a session by informing me that he had bought an expensive topcoat at a bargain price. The rest of the session was devoted to a recent anguishing argument with his mother, one which he felt he handled better than in the past. There was mention of his mother's frustrated longing for Carl to take his place in the community as a member of his father's club. As Carl got up to leave, he put on his new coat. I smiled as I looked at him. He asked why I smiled. I told him that I was hesitant to tell him, but he insisted that I go ahead. I said that the coat had just the preppy look for his father's club. He acted upset in a teasing way and asked me if it could be anything else. I replied that it could be a good-looking coat quite apart from his father's club. "Couldn't it be a bum's coat?" Carl asked. I replied, "No way!" Carl gave me the finger and jauntily walked out the door.

DISCUSSION

Borderline patients often thrive on an attitude of firmness and bluntness (Cameron, 1961). An early development in the direction of a selfobject transference occurs when the patient relies on the therapist's organization of the patient's self to maintain a measure of cohesiveness. In myriad verbal and nonverbal ways, a therapist reflects back to the patient his psychological image of the patient. Fragmentation experiences follow when the therapist overestimates or underestimates the patient; cohesion is promoted when he is on the mark. Although it is often of crucial importance to contact the patient at his mature level of functioning, it is equally crucial to be able at certain times to contact the patient at his level of regression. Such contact is often established at a level of action quite different from any conventional psychoanalytic interpretive stance. Furthermore, borderline patients characteristically activate regressive responses in the therapist, which may be fruitfully utilized in the treatment (Kernberg, 1972). It should be noted that these well-known clinical observations with respect to regression and action in borderline patients have been used to justify what I would consider wild activity by the therapist. The responsiveness on a regressive level or on a level of action to which I refer is far from wild but is rather experienced by patient and therapist as well as attuned.

Borderline patients frequently demand "make me feel real" or demand that the therapist "be more real." Such patients are frequently viewed as seeking personal intimacy or a cure through love as resistance to the therapeutic task. Another common understanding or, rather, misunderstanding is that the "empty" patient requires mothering responses in order to make up for something not provided in childhood—another version of the cure through love that may be justified by one or another theory of developmental deficits. However one may understand these damands to "make me feel real," efforts to gratify such demands by turning a professional therapeutic relationship into a personal friendship may bring short-term relief to the patient at the risk not only of therapeutic failure but of untoward regressions and serious complications of iatrogenically induced dependence. A full discussion of the subject is beyond the scope of this paper. Suffice it to say that the crucial factors may lie more in the grandiose fantasies of the therapist than in any understanding of the patient. As for the patient, though we have many theories to explain the feelings of emptiness and the wish for the therapist to "be more real," the subject deserves to remain an open research question. It is certainly appropriate to consider that such demands reflect primitive transference needs similar to Carl's demands for confrontation.

The patients who characteristically offer such complaints often thrive on a treatment involving a high degree of confrontation. Consider the plight of an analyst who struggles vainly to use sophisticated skills and knowledge to establish a workable treatment situation, only to lose the patient to a naive therapist who forms a "holding environment" based on the most simplistic and banal confrontive techniques derived from one or another of the new modalities. Such naive treatments achieve only very limited goals at best, but patients often choose them. Furthermore, confrontations can be terribly abused and serve as the very antithesis of a psychoanalytic orientation. "Confrontation with reality" is frequently misused to demand social conformity at the expense of any chance of empathic contact or understanding of a patient. Other confrontations become an excuse for wild analysis or for subjugating and humiliating the patient according to one set of beliefs or another. Zinberg (1973) has discussed the problems of confrontation when it is used as an end in itself rather than a means to an end. All this notwithstanding, there is a place for confrontation in psychoanalytic psychotherapy. Buie and Adler (1973a, 1973b) have thoroughly discussed the uses and misuses of confrontation in the psychotherapy of borderline patients. In the interest of conciseness, their contribution are not reviewed here. Rather, I consider the contributions of self psychology with respect to the meaning of confrontation.

Selfobject transferences, such as a *mirror* or *idealizing* transference, serve to sustain a cohesive self (Kohut & Wolf, 1978). Carl showed evidences of such transferences in the course of his treatment. In the phase of his treatment under study, however, Carl achieved a more cohesive self in the context of an interaction in which he experienced me as *confrontive*. I emphasize Carl's experience, because whether or not I was actually confrontive is a pertinent but separate issue. A formulation of a *confrontive selfobject transference* might be appropriate. Such a formulation would be similar to Wolf's (1980) description of an ally-antagonist maternal selfobject, where the mother is free to confirm the child as an ally and simultaneously oppose his healthy aggression.

Confrontation, a term that can be applied to diverse clinical situations, is more evocative than precise. Something, someone, or some idea is faced, set in opposition, or compared. There are forms of confrontation quite different from the clinical interactions described here. Perhaps some more exact designation could be found that would capture the particular quality of personal responsiveness so central to Carl's demands for confrontation. Nevertheless, I believe that Carl's demands for confrontation correspond generally to what is understood as confrontive in the mental health field today and may prove useful not only to clarify the optimal uses of confrontation but to understand the misuses of confrontation better. Patient's demands, such as for a cure through love, for relief of emptiness, or for dramatic confrontations, may have a great deal in common. Such demands may be developed, inhibited, or exploited depending on the responses of the therapist.

Carl's treatment remains incomplete, and it may turn out that his need for confrontation involves very specific issues that have not yet emerged. As for the quality of the confrontive interaction he sought, he experienced me as an independent center of initiative. By contrast, the patient in a mirror transference cannot tolerate the therapist as a center of initiative. In an idealizing transference the therapist's independent cohesive self may be esteemed but is not confronted. For example, a therapist may be idealized for his confrontive qualities regardless of whether any meaningful confrontation takes place. Such was the case with Carl's idealization of his supervisor who "made" him cry real tears. Further qualities of the therapist that proved integrative for Carl had to do with personal commitment, with a center of will, or with what Erik Erikson called "the meaning of meaning it."

Confrontations are necessary and inevitable in all forms of psychotherapy. However, the focus of this paper is on those clinical situations where the therapist, because he is experienced as confrontive, serves to sustain the patient's self. Considerations of neutrality, abstinence, and psychological distance, not to mention respect for the patient, place serious and significant constraints on the use of confrontation. I would even reject the idea that one *ought to be* confrontive with borderline patients. Rather than such a priori determination, confrontation would seem appropriate when a borderline patient behaves in a way that such a response would be genuine and in keeping with the treatment process. Confrontation should be consistent with the therapist's empathy and constantly tested in terms of the patient's response.

Carl's demands for confrontation, as they evolved and were partly resolved, can stimulate any number of hypotheses. Where confrontation implies a sense of clashing or opposition, Hartmann's (1953) suggestion as to the role of aggression in structure formation seems pertinent. Yet, it is not clear whether the decisive factor for Carl's progress was my aggressive firmness, my openness, or some other factor. In Cameron's clinical report (1961) the patient incorporated his qualities of firmness, in the context of an idealizing and merging transference, to deal with a tyrannical maternal introject. Carl has shown some evidence for such processes. Yet, his demands for confrontation mainly appear as a striving for integration in opposition to the therapist's self, experienced by him as independent and empathic, rather than as a merging transference.

While deferring any definitive conclusions about Carl's demands for confrontation, certain issues have clearly emerged from the treatment so far. I have already mentioned a defensive aspect—that Carl sought my responses rather than reveal his own inner experiences because of his fear of my reaction. Although this defensive motive is the least important in explaining his "confrontive transference," its clarification within the treatment process was an important part of the work. At a later point in the treatment, Carl thoughtfully explained that he wanted me to be confrontive because he needed me to be a "firm center." I understood this to mean that he needed to know that I had a cohesive self and, more specifically, that I was not vulnerable to merging with him when he began to reveal more regressive levels of his experience. The most significant consideration of all was Carl's repeated emphasis that my confrontations would help him to elaborate the dark side of himself. His inner life was extremely rich and detailed, but it was also chaotic, confused, and fragmented. Two colleagues have suggested helpful metaphors to bring out this significance of his need for confrontation. Meyer S. Gunther referred to my confrontive presence as a "template" against which Carl could organize his chaotic experiences. Wolf (1980b) referred to self-boundaries and even to a metaphorical "skin" of the self, which could be consolidated and strengthened in the context of a confrontive contact.

Since writing up this presentation, Carl's demands for confrontation have subsided, and he has shown an objective interest in understanding what he now considers excessive needs for confrontation or personal responsiveness. Although the developmental roots of these needs are still not clear, one factor among many seems worth mentioning. His overly concerned parents were constantly *talking* about him, either criticizing or sometimes approving, with excessive references to him in the third person. Carl experienced himself as denied that direct sense of how his mother and father experienced him, which is the essence of personal responsiveness. His longstanding provocativeness, particularly as it became concentrated in the transference in his demands for confrontation, appear as his attempts to wrest such responsiveness from an unyielding environment.

CONCLUSION

Study of the record of treatment of Carl Y over a 2-month period indicated the organization of a more cohesive self as he came to experience his therapist as more confrontive. Carl's complex needs for confrontation have been described, although only a few of the possible meanings of these needs have been enumerated. I have emphasized a need to experience me as an independent center of initiative and as an ally–antagonist, as well as the role of aggression in structure formation. The "clarification, interpretative work and empathic support" (Adler, 1979) required to develop and ultimately resolve such a transference have been described. In other words, although the meaning of this patient's needs for confrontation is important, it is even more important to understand the means to engage him in the treatment process. Whether or not a therapist is confrontive in a given situation is a matter of clinical judgment, which lies beyond the limits of this discussion. This case study serves to illustrate the importance of accepting the patient's demands for confrontation as an integral part of the treatment and does not necessarily require that the demand be gratified. It is suggested that the patients who demand a cure through love, relief of emptiness, or dramatic confrontations may have similar needs expressed in these diverse ways. The precise transference needs or demands of patients who seek confrontation require further clarification and may vary from one situation or patient to another. With respect to the theory of self psychology, the role of the selfobject in promoting a cohesive self in the clinical situation has been emphasized. An implicit question has been raised, however, as to whether the selfobject must necessarily be experienced as part of the self. Such experiences involve complex matters of psychological distance and may be hard to assess. The crucial issue may be that the selfobject serves functions necessary for a cohesive self.

REFERENCES

Adler, G. (1979). *Transference, Real Relationship and Alliance.* Paper presented at the fall meeting of the American Psychoanalytic Association.
Buie, D. H. & Adler, G. (1973a). The misuses of confrontation in the psychotherapy of borderline cases. In *Confrontation in Psychotherapy,* G. Adler & P. G. Myerson, eds. New York: Science House, pp. 147–162.
———— (1973b). The uses of confrontation in the psychotherapy of borderline cases. In *Confrontation in Psychotherapy,* G. Adler & P. G. Myerson, eds. New York: Science House, pp. 123–146.
Cameron, N. (1961). Introjection, reprojection, and hallucination in the interaction between schizophrenic patient and therapist. *Int. J. Psychoanal.* 42: 86–96.
Hartmann, H. (1953). Contribution to the metapsychology of schizophrenia. *Psychoanal. Study Child* 8: 177–188.
Kernberg, O. *Object Relations Theory and Clinical Psychoanalysis.* New York: Jason Aronson.
Kohut, H. (1971). *The Analysis of the Self.* New York: Int. Univ. Press.
———— (1977). *The Restoration of the Self.* New York: Int. Univ. Press.
———— (1978). *The Search for the Self.* New York: Int. Univ. Press.
———— & Wolf, E. (1978). The disorders of the self and their treatment: An outline. *Int. J. Psychoanal.* 59: 413–426.
Perry, J. C. & Klerman, G. L. (1980). Clinical features of the borderline personality disorder. *Am. J. Psychiat.* 137: 165–173.
Wolf, E. (1980). On the developmental line of selfobject relations. In *Advances in Self Psychology,* A. Goldberg, ed. New York: Int. Univ. Press, pp. 117–130.
Zinberg, N. (1973). The technique of confrontation and social class differences. In *Confrontation in Psychotherapy,* G. Adler & P. G. Myerson, eds. New York: Science House, pp. 271–302.

21 Discussion of Paper by Dr. London

Sheldon Bach, Ph.D.

While listening to the paper by Dr. Basch, I was reminded of a poem by Jacques Prévert which tells of an academic painter vainly trying to paint a still life of an apple. The painter is obviously perceiving the apple through the prism of centuries of tradition in still-life painting. So he paints, rubs out, repaints, but all in vain—he seems never quite able to catch the apple in its essential self, its veritable appleness. At that moment Picasso wanders by, sizes up the scene in a moment, walks over, picks up the apple, and takes a bite out of it. And the apple says: Thank you, Picasso!

In this sense I thank Dr. Basch for reminding us that sometimes accepted ideas tend to obscure rather than to clarify reality and that from time to time we must take a fresh look; we must bite the apple ourselves and have faith in our own gustatory experience. However, I should qualify this by noting that Freud himself, that most complex of geniuses, often maintained that both his theory and technique were largely provisional and indeed remarked in 1916: "The narcissistic neuroses can scarcely be attacked with the technique that has served us with the transference neuroses. . . . Our technical methods must accordingly be replaced by others; and we do not know yet whether we shall succeed in finding a substitute [p. 423]."

Today there are many who feel that we have indeed succeeded in finding a substitute, or rather a series of complementary approaches that enable us to deal with heretofore scarcely treatable disorders in

269

a way that no longer depends largely on the talent or intuition of one particularly gifted therapist but which can be taught as a descriptive explanation. Whether indeed self psychology forms a more general theory of which classical psychoanalysis is only a special case, whether it is a complementary theory, or whether it is something else entirely is a hotly debated issue, which I do not even propose to engage in. Personally, I cannot help but think that the difficulty of integrating a growth theory with a conflict theory has something to do with that uniquely human ambiguity, namely, the difficulty of integrating a subjective sense of *who* one is with an objective sense of *what* one is—two perspectives that are never quite concordant. Therefore, I tend to favor an approach that allows for a multiplicity of perspectives on the same phenomenon. But be that as it may, I have little doubt that self psychology has opened clinical vistas that we have only begun to appreciate, explore, and verify.

Let me turn now to Dr. London's case, which raises so many interesting questions. We must be especially grateful to him because he has told it like it is, without trying to tidy up the parameters, a move which might have made him impervious to criticism but would certainly have deprived us of the liveliness characteristic of this particular treatment. I must admit that when I first read a draft of the case I was overcome with a sense of confusion and puzzlement. It was certainly not a classical neurosis, nor apparently even a narcissistic personality disorder. What was one to make of it? How was one to get to the heart of the matter? Trying to clear my mind of all preconceptions, I studied it in the hope that some answer might yet emerge from the dark side of my own self.

What eventually did come to me was the rather obvious thought that both the patient, Carl, and the analyst were trying very hard to discuss his fears and anxieties about engaging once again in some kind of selfobject transference, particularly his fears of a merging transference. A major theme appeared to be the patient's subjective sense of aliveness and deadness, of fullness and emptiness, a fullness that, as in his torrent of words, might lead to overexcitement and insanity or a bewildering and frightening emptiness, which might lead to depression, apathy, and death of the self. In this sense, Carl's tremendous hunger for confrontation might be viewed as a demand that the therapist allow himself to be used as a vehicle for the elaboration of the patient's excitement within a context of control. Let me try to document this initial perception.

We know from the history that Carl came for analysis following the dramatic disruption of a long-term psychotherapy. Depression, emotional displays, and tantrums were prominent, but he maintained that he was scarcely in touch with these feelings. He was more pervasively aware of a bewildering and frightening sense of emptiness. This bewilderment and emptiness impressed me, because it so clearly paralleled my own countertransference reactions on first reading the case. This split between Carl's mental emotionality, which looks like displays and tantrums when seen objectively, and his subjective experience of deadness can be seen as a disconnection from his archaic body ego, as a kind of false-self superstructure, and as a powerful defense against his fear and desire for regression to a selfobject transference.

The analyst too was concerned at this point about the patient's potential for psychotic disorganization and was unwilling to consider analysis, a decision to which Carl reacted with great disappointment. Thus, in the opening gambit, the patient had asked for psychoanalysis and had been told that he may be so full of crazy excitement that either he or the analyst would not be able to tolerate it.

In the first confrontation, about changing his appointment, Carl is of course reassured to learn that the analyst can set limits to a patient's rage and that they both can survive it. But he then became concerned that the analyst was trying to cover up his madness, which the patient needed to express. Dr. London says that "there was a persistent fantasy that he would have to become psychotic in order to resolve his problems," a fantasy which may well have been shared, with the patient representing the wish and the analyst its prohibition. And indeed, the fantasy did become reality; a sort of compromise formation is arranged in which Carl went elsewhere to become crazy. But I am running ahead of the story—let me backtrack a few months to the strange episode of the "conservative" argument and the "conservative" dress.

First off, it seems to me that Carl's very identity was intimately related to his being oppositional and confrontive. This was how he protected himself from fears of merging, grandiosity, and regressing in the transference. We may note that in the political debate with a colleague he had entirely contradictory opinions, but aggressively argued in opposition to the young woman. One might say that, to some extent, negation *was* his identity. Thus, in a world where other people are ostensibly sane, his uniqueness consisted partly in his being mad. Ordinarily, we know he dressed in a manner that *he* described as weird and eccentric; that is, in a manner that openly displayed his madness. When his mother complimented him on his conservative dress, he experienced this exactly as if his analyst were trying to cover up his madness. He felt that his weirdness was an authentic and genuine part of his identity; both a defense against merger and an aspect of his archaic grandiose self that he was fearful of expressing. Identifying with the prohibiting aspects of mother and analyst, he momentarily lost contact with the wish to display himself, however crazy he might look. Depression and paranoia followed upon this failure of nerve.

But the process of the development and emergence of this grandiose and oppositional part of his self would not be stopped. A month or 2 later he was boasting of his physical prowess and urged the analyst to arm wrestle with him in order to demonstrate his superior strength. Once again the analyst was placed in the position of containing the patient's grandiosity and, in fact, physically contested with him. Let me bypass for the moment a consideration of whether this was the best possible technical response in order to trace the continuing evolution of the grandiosity. Shortly thereafter Carl revealed, with extreme embarrassment, that he had a brilliant mind and a great potential for creative achievement. He experienced this as shamefully grandiose, and it was at this point that things got a bit out of hand and the mirroring transference, if one may call it that, failed. Unable to deal with his own shame, fears of grandiosity, and longing for merger, Carl was compelled to seek another arena by going off to the state university to act out his fantasy that he must become psychotic in order to resolve his problems. Here we might pause to speculate on the significance of this disruption in the treatment.

If we examine Carl's account of the manic episode that culminated his involvement with his teacher, an episode that seems clearly a displacement from the transference, obvious parallels come to mind. The patient admired the teacher tremendously, he and she were exquisitely attuned in interests and values, and she idealized him. For the first time the patient felt truly in love as well as merged with her. Despite his respect for her teaching, he began to feel that she wanted to control him in his work, and that became intolerable. There was also a grandiose quality to her aspirations that worried him. He also feared disrupting her marriage, and he fled the course.

Substituting therapist for teacher, we may well wonder if the patient wasn't talking about primitive fears of merging and differentiating, of loneliness and rage, of fears of destroying the selfobject or of being destroyed by it. Perhaps this fear and rage had not been adequately addressed on their primitive experiential level; perhaps what looked like an idealizing or mirror transference was *both* a re-creation of an earlier traumatized state and *also,* at least in part, a defense against further exploration of these issues. In other words, the analyzable transferences that Kohut describes already imply a considerable developmental achievement of self-cohesiveness, whereas this patient's problems to some extent still lie in the earlier stages of self-pacification and especially self-unification.

But notice—regardless of our speculations about what might have been—the patient actually returned, and the therapeutic process continued. To those of us who are continually making mistakes, a group in which I must unfortunately include myself, this fact alone should be very reassuring. And indeed, the patient and therapist were reunited only to repeat once more the very difficulty from which I believe he had fled. He returned in an ambivalent manic state, enraged at his sense of defectiveness and humiliated that he *must* come back, wanting acceptance and containment, but being frightened of it and furious at the same time. The therapist was also frightened, just precisely as I *know* I would have been, and offered him lithium instead. But the episode subsided on its own, and most significantly, the complaints of emptiness now disappeared. The eruption from the depths seemed to have served its purpose; both participants survived, and Carl was now able to *have* feelings even though he may not have liked them. But he was still frightened of them, and Dr. London now consistently interpreted his reactive depression or fragmentation whenever the patient feared that his grandiosity would be triggered without sufficient self-structure or transference to support it. Here I feel that an opportunity may have been missed to deal, at least retrospectively, with the patient's anger, humiliation, and fear of closeness in the transference. After all, why did Carl need to leave treatment in order to begin to experience real feelings for the first time?

And in fact he returned from a planned vacation with complaints that the therapist *still* wasn't helping him bring out the madness from within him, what he called his "dark side." The analyst, who was concerned that the patient's "dark side" may have been very dark indeed, asked him if it might be an illusion. I believe that this "dark side" contains, among other things, the patient's oppositional identity, the negation that he needed to feel real; and telling him that *it* might not exist was the same as suggesting that *he* might not exist, or that the analyst was unprepared to deal with it. On the other hand, acknowledgment that the patient was haunted or conflicted became once more a recognition that he was fully accepted and really there.

At about this point in treatment, with the manic episode well behind, sessions were resumed on a twice weekly basis. Both patient and analyst were now feeling more comfortable with each other; they had weathered the crisis and were less anxious about each other's "dark side." Perhaps the patient interpreted more frequent sessions as a statement that he had less reason to fear his madness. At any rate, he now began to reintegrate the control that he had heretofore projected on the analyst. He seemed no longer afraid to talk about his crazy experiences; he recounted the manic episode at the state university and also a related episode at age 9 when his mother had him medicated to control a manic "high."

This turmoil at age 9 seemed an especially apt demonstration of how inadequate environmental response may lead to ever more frantic demands, self-stimulating masturbation, obsessive-compulsive symptomatology, and ultimately, to fragmentation. The masturbatory fantasy of directing an institution for people with sexual problems whom he cared for like infants is on one level a reversal and fragmentation of his own wish to be seen and cared for as a whole, self-contained, live person. He had been forced to become his mother in his head: nurturing, life-giving, and yet directive and containing. Another way of saying this is that the fantasy tried to compensate for inadequacies of early mothering that led Carl to a kind of precocious development, in which an excited "mental emotionality" was split off from the body-ego, so that he could demonstrate tantrums, emotional displays, and depressions, but nevertheless *feel* empty and dead inside. Obviously, to speak of faulty environmental responses in this and earlier interactions is shorthand for a very complex state of affairs in which the patient's own psychological contributions and native endowment may be too easily overlooked. From the data at hand, we are simply unable to say whether anyone could have provided adequate mothering for this particular infant.

And yet as clinicians we must be impressed with the awesome power of the transference in its persistent demands, however distorted, to obtain what the patient felt he needed in order to become whole again. Failing with his mother, he had transformed her demands to the father's intellectual sphere and had failed again. Failing in a prolonged therapy, he had come to Dr. London, and through the vicissitudes of a difficult treatment, he practically obliged Dr. London to repeat the traumatic situations with him and, ultimately, to become just the sort of a therapist he felt he needed. To do this, of course, he needed a therapist who was devoted but tenacious and yet open-minded and willing to learn from his patient and his mistakes. Fortunately, he found such a person in Dr. London, and it would seem that the ultimate prognosis for this interaction is a good one.

In conclusion let me just briefly touch on some of the questions Dr. London raises, especially the ones on which we may not see eye to eye. To confront the issue directly, I have some difficulty with the concept of confrontive selfobject transference. Try as I may, I cannot see this on the same conceptual level as the mirroring or idealizing transferences, if only because in confrontation the therapist is not experienced as part of the phenomenal self-system. More importantly, mirroring and idealizing selfobject transferences are developmental concepts, which have to do with arrests in growth subsequent to the development of a more or less cohesive self. If one is to make developmental analogies with a confrontive transference, they would seem to lie in an earlier period and relate more to differentiation, self-definition, and self-unification rather than to problems of optimal disillusionment. In this sense the concept of a "template" against which the patient could organize his experience, or a self-boundary that is stimulated and strengthened by confrontation, or even an identity that exists only in opposition to the object all refer to a period before the consolidation of a cohesive self.

But the need for confrontation in this patient is probably very complex and exists on many levels simultaneously. The first level was clearly defensive and involved his fear that he had misperceived reality as his mother so often accused him of doing, and that his therapist would not tell him the truth about this. Thus, his very attempts to engage a workable selfobject transference foundered on the fear that his therapist might not be a reliable object and especially on the fear that the therapeutic balance between closeness and distance was not reliable enough to sustain him. From another viewpoint, this can be seen as a fight against merging or a struggle to negate a developing attachment.

On another related level one might see the patient's confrontive needs as a demand that the therapist have a presence, that he be really there, really alive, self-sufficient, indestructible, and not totally susceptible to his fantasies of omnipotent control. In this sense the therapist's presence as a real person in the real world is a *sine qua non* for the engagement of *any* transference paradigm, particularly with the more disturbed patients who worry that their own existence is only a fantasy or a negative construction. Certain borderline patients need to kill the therapist in fantasy in order that he may survive in reality and become usable by them. It seems to me that Carl's demands for confrontation were aimed at establishing the therapist's *presence* or "thereness," and this implies that one or both of his parents may have failed him in this respect.

I have tried in addition to point to a prominent defensive and developmental aspect, namely, his need to know that Dr. London could sustain and contain him in the selfobject transferences. Once satisfied with this, the patient could lend himself to the transference, and indeed, his demands for confrontation have subsided and are now being retrospectively analyzed.

Finally, I feel obliged to say a word about the great arm-wrestling scene. In principle, I am not opposed to reasonable parameters when working with certain patients. But they are to be used reluctantly when they keep us from understanding what is really going on; indeed, they may help to suppress the very feelings the patient is trying to voice. For example, is the hilarious boasting about his physical prowess a manic attempt to deny feelings of weakness, depression, and emptiness? Is it an attempt at separating to counter his fears of merging? Or is it a test to see whether they can engage without destroying one another? Is he producing a physical confrontation because only through opposition can he feel alive? Above all, I wonder if Carl was wrestling with his therapist in order to touch him and be touched by him, precisely because he felt *out of touch* with the therapist and with himself. Like Jacob wrestling with the angel, the patient wanted to know the therapist's name and be blessed. These are all issues I would have tried to pose to the patient in one way or another instead of participating in a kind of collusive reality-testing, which avoids the underlying fantasies. But of course, I was not in the heat of the battle, and Dr. London was.

One aspect of this incident may have been an attempt to heal the split between Carl's mental emotionality and displays and his archaic body-ego, which experienced only emptiness. It was *after* this episode that he fled to the state university and engaged in a relationship with his teacher, and it was only after his return that he could begin to experience real feelings even though he didn't like them. This marked a significant turn and was the basis for the establishment of a workable transference.

I do not know whether it was necessary for this resolution to occur via the third person intermediary of the teacher's body, or whether it could have happened through some empathic interpretation of his need to be touched, cared for, and held as in his masturbation fantasies. In any case, it would be interesting in retrospect to know just what had been on his mind and even to see if he now feels that it could have been handled differently.

In discussing parameters with patients years after the event, I have often been surprised and enlightened to discover just what it had been that they needed from me at a particular time. If the dialogue with Carl continues, as I have every hope that it will, we may yet learn something more from that always inexhaustible source of psychoanalytic knowledge, namely, our patients.

REFERENCES

Freud, S. (1916–1917). Introductory Lectures on Psycho-Analysis (Part III). *S.E.* 16.

22 Closing Comment

Sydney Smith, Ph.D.

The two major papers in this section together with the two discussions have attempted to come to grips with specific and important issues in dealing with a treatment approach that emphasizes issues of the self. In making this effort, these papers grapple with issues we have encountered for years in applying psychoanalytic technique and theory to psychotherapy, but now an attempt is made to look at these problems through a different lens. In part because of the vantage point offered by self psychology, the old issues appear anew as lively and fresh, but they also are lively because we are ever embarking on the perils of relating to our humanly complex patients with the instrument of our own personalities. Without belaboring the discussions, perhaps we could breach one or two final points not made by either Bach or Michels.

London's paper raises the question of how useful action is as opposed to interpretation in the therapeutic setting. Action is usually avoided because it leads to gratification that we generally think of as impeding rather than helping progress in treatment, and there can be no doubt that London's patient was gratified by her physical duel with him. But questions remain: If actions are undertaken, what then happens to the patient's and the therapist's pleasure in the action and the attendant drama, and in what ways are these behaviors reflected in the structuring of the transference roles?

Basch's paper again brings up the argument between conflict theory and defect theory, a controversy that presently sees many psychoanalysts on one side and self psychology on the other. Whatever side of this argument the reader supports, the papers presented in this section indicate that a reconsideration of this issue may be in order and that the approach to patients cannot be through metapsychology alone. Authors on all sides agree that clinical acumen and sensitivity are required.

The major significance of these papers is the attempt they make for the first time to apply the concepts of self psychology to the general problems of psychotherapy. In this effort the papers have made a valuable beginning, and the two discussants have offered exactly the kind of constructive response that gives the task a forward thrust. This task would appear to be one of determining through successive studies the formal aspects, strengths, and limitations of a psychotherapy based on self psychology. Undoubtedly these papers will be regarded as pioneering stimuli to the promising developments that will follow.

V SELF PSYCHOLOGY: IMPLICATIONS FOR PSYCHOANALYTIC THEORY

23 Prologue

Melvin Bornstein, M.D.

New concepts in psychoanalysis may be stimulated by clinical observations, but a major test of their originality, value, and power takes place within the theoretical realm. Some new insights are easily assimilated into existing theory; others require alterations in the significance assigned to known factors. Some insights are regarded by their proponents as so unique in perspective and so divergent in approach that a new theory is required. Self psychology clearly started out to be an addition to existing psychoanalytic theory. Later, many of its proponents and adversaries stated that its precepts constituted a sizable alteration in existing theory but that a complementary accommodation could be made. More recent proposals have been regarded by some as constituting a new general theory or at least an alternative theory to both ego psychology and object relations theory.

This section contains four theoretical papers. The papers by Stolorow and Goldberg deal with specific theoretical issues that have been generated by self psychology. The contributions of Wallerstein and P. Ornstein constitute far-ranging attempts to place in focus the scope of the contribution of self psychology in relation to psychoanalytic theory in general. Each of the four papers takes up a number of specific isses, many new and many controversial. Along with an exploration of the specific issues, the reader may wish to consider the broad theoretical question: Can or should self psychology be integrated within existing theory, or is self psychology now or on its way to becoming a separate theoretical entity?

In the first paper in this section Stolorow takes his stand with those who would replace traditional metapsychology. He then compares the phenomena-near theory of self psychology with his own theory and those of Klein, Schafer, and Atwood. Stolorow states that the issue of whether the self is a supraordinate concept is a problem of metapsychology and therefore it can be dismissed. Stolorow holds that the crucial problem becomes a set of empirical questions concerning the degree to which a firmly demarcated self-structure predominates in the organization of a person's subjective state. From this viewpoint self psychology is concerned with the development of the structuralization of self-experience. Stolorow believes his approach permits a complementarity between a psychology of conflict-ridden but firmly consolidated psychic structures and a psychology of missing or precarious psychological structures.

Employing an experience-near structural viewpoint, Stolorow examines the concept of transmuting internalization during a successful analysis. He describes two developmental processes that comprise transmuting internalization: (1) the patient's acquisition of functions involved in the maintenance of self-cohesion, self-continuity, and self-esteem; (2) the structuralization of self-experience whereby the analyst's empathic understanding facilitates the reactivation of stalled developmental processes and the reorganization of the subjective field, building up an increasingly differentiated self-structure.

In the second paper in this section Goldberg mounts a direct challenge to existing psychoanalytic theories. Unlike Stolorow, who aims for a working complementarity retaining structural concepts by modifications, Goldberg attacks a bastion concept of the structural hypothesis. According to Goldberg internalization, as it is treated in classical psychoanalytic theory, by its preoccupation with the dichotomy between inside and outside, places undue emphasis on discrete boundaries between people. He suggests that an analysis of the phenomena subsumed under internalization refers to the inner experience of *ownership, privacy,* and *representability.* Goldberg believes that an advantage of his alternative theoretical model for internalization is that it shifts the emphasis to sharing and to the bridging of separateness by a communicative link. In studying Goldberg's presentation the reader can reconsider the many clinical entities subsumed under internalization and determine how well these are accounted for by ownership, privacy, and representability. Does the reader agree that this self-psychological model offers greater flexibility and freedom in conceptualizing experiential relationships than a model based on complex transformations from "outside" to "inside?"

In a carefully thought out evaluative commentary Wallerstein describes two aspects of self psychology: a clinical theory that he values highly and a general theory about which he has serious questions. Wallerstein believes that in its delineation of narcissistic phenomena as discerned in the specific narcissistic mirroring and idealizing transferences and their counterpart, the specific countertransferences, self psychology makes its most precise contribution to psychoanalysis. In contrast to his appreciation of the clinical theory, Wallerstein is critical of aspects of the general theory of self psychology. He describes many complex issues that reflect areas of serious controversy between the theories of self psychology and those of classical psychoanalysis. He gives particular emphasis to what he regards as a false dichotomy between a deficit and a conflict model. He accuses self psychology of equating conflict with pathology rather than acknowledging that conflict is a fundamental aspect of the human condition. To buttress his argument Wallerstein proposes a broadened definition in which conflict is regarded as tension between contradictory wishes of all sorts—a definition he believes self psychology could accept without weakening its position. In addition, Wallerstein is critical of what he considers to be self psychology's one-sided emphasis on empathy. Too much reliance on empathy in analysis can lead to knowledge that is incomplete or incorrect, and he adds, it places undue responsibility for therapeutic difficulty on the therapist's being unempathic. Moreover, a one-sided emphasis on empathy encourages an overevaluation of external events. Overall, Wallerstein objects to the trend of self psychology to redefine psychoanalysis narrowly in terms of an empathic introspective awareness within the selfobject context, a view he believes is a theoretical reductionistic oversimplification.

Wallerstein advises psychoanalysis to maintain one classical theory so that the phenomena of complex mental states that it studies can be embodied within its one (Freudian) paradigm and thus retain a perspective of overdetermination and of multiple (metapsychological) points of view. He repeatedly emphasizes that the optional metaphors for psychoanalysis lie within the unifying language and thought conventions of "both/and," rather than the splitting and dichotomizing thrusts of "either/or."

P. Ornstein's discussion ranges over the ground covered by Stolorow, Goldberg, and Wallerstein and provides a basic statement of the assertions of self psychology. The essence of Ornstein's argument is that self psychology constitutes a clinical and theoretical point of view so radically different that it is a separate competing basic hypothesis. Thus, Goldberg's effort to replace the concept of internalization employed by all other psychoanalytic theories with concepts of ownership, privacy, and representability is in line with the attempt of self psychology to use experience-near metaphors. But Ornstein rejects the attempts of Stolorow and Wallerstein to treat self psychology as complementary to, or able to be included within, a modified structural theory. Because the issue of conflict versus deficit is the main sticking point, Ornstein devotes his major effort to establishing the superiority of self psychology's concept of deficits to explain transference phenomena. The reader must follow Ornstein through a series of intricate arguments by which he attempts to demonstrate that the clinical data now understood as the result of primary conflict can be better accounted for by an understanding of structural deficits that develop from traumatic disruption of the empathic bond between self and selfobject.

24

Self Psychology—A Structural Psychology

Robert D. Stolorow, Ph.D.

Just as the self has been characterized as bipolar in its structure and development (Kohut, 1977), self psychology too has been bipolar in its evolution. Its first nodal point, *The Analysis of the Self* (Kohut, 1971), was a monumental clinical contribution, extending psychoanalytic understanding and treatment to those disturbances in self-experience that we call "narcissistic." Explicated in this book were such essential clinical discoveries and theoretical ideas as the "narcissistic transferences," the concept of a "selfobject," the concept of "transmuting internalization," and the proposition that narcissism and object love have conceptually separate lines of development. In the first phase in the evolution of self psychology, these contributions were, quite understandably, still grafted to the Procrustean bed of Freudian metapsychology and were voiced in the language of traditional "mental apparatus" psychology and "drive-discharge" theory. In contrast, in self psychology's second nodal point, *The Restoration of the Self* (Kohut, 1977), these seminal clinical discoveries and conceptualizations were freed from the strictures of classical metapsychology and boldly reformulated within a new theoretical framework placing the experience of self at the center of psychoanalytic inquiry. This framework, I believe, constitutes no less than a new scientific paradigm for psychoanalysis. I would characterize it as a *developmental phenomenology of the self,* because it is principally concerned with the ontogenesis and structuralization of self-experience, its conscious and unconscious constituents, and their normal and pathological developmental vicissitudes. This new paradigm, involving a conceptual shift from the motivational primacy of instinctual drives to the motivational primacy of self-experience, enables us to comprehend a wide variety of pathological states and psychological products from the standpoint of a person struggling to maintain a sense of self-cohesion in the face of threats of self-disintegration, rather than from the standpoint of a mental apparatus processing drive energies and dealing with instinctual conflicts. Infantile "drive" experiences are no longer to be regarded as primary instinctual givens, but as "disintegration products" that occur when a precarious self-structure has not been properly supported. "Fixations" at various pleasure aims associated with the erotogenic zones, for example, are seen as stemming from efforts to counteract feelings of inner deadness, self-fragmentation, and self-loss. Similarly, destructive rage is viewed not as the manifestation of an elemental instinctual viciousness, but as a secondary reaction to the traumatic empathy failures of caregivers that have menaced the cohesion of a vulnerable self-structure.

In this paper I attempt to clarify further the distinctive features of self psychology as a scientific paradigm by exploring its relationship to some other innovative ideas that have recently fermented within the field of Freudian psychoanalysis. In this way I hope to highlight Heinz Kohut's unique contribution to psychoanalytic thought.

Among recent critiques of Freudian theory, some of the most constructive have been those that rest upon George Klein's (1976) clarifying distinction between the metapsychology and the clinical theory of psychoanalysis. Metapsychology and clinical theory, Klein held, derive from two completely different universes of discourse. Metapsychology deals with the material substrate of subjective experience and is thus couched in the natural science framework of impersonal mechanisms, discharge apparatuses, and drive energies, which are presumed to "exist" as entities or events in the realm of objective reality. In contrast, clinical theory, which derives from the psychoanalytic situation and guides psychoanalytic practice, deals with intentionality and the personal meaning of subjective experiences seen from the perspective of the individual's unique life history. Clinical theory asks "why" questions and seeks answers in terms of personal reasons, purposes, and individual meanings. Metapsychology asks "how" questions and seeks answers in terms of impersonal mechanisms and causes. Klein wished to disentangle metapsychological and clinical concepts and to retain only the latter as the legitimate content of psychoanalytic theory. For him, clinical psychoanalytic constructs constituted a self-sufficient psychological theory uniquely suited for guiding the investigation of the data of the psychoanalytic situation.

It is my contention that self psychology, in its mature form as a new scientific paradigm, is essentially a clinical psychoanalytic theory in Klein's sense. This, I believe, is one of its principal virtues. The central theoretical constructs of self psychology were derived directly from the psychoanalytic situation—specifically, from sustained, empathic-introspective immersions into patients' subjective worlds as reflected in the microcosm of the transference (Ornstein, 1978). Correspondingly, self psychology's central constructs pertain to the realm of the experience-near and therefore embody a personalistic, rather than a mechanistic, perspective. These two features of clinical theory—experience-nearness and derivation from the clinical situation—are nowhere better exemplified than in the concept of a selfobject, the foundational construct upon which the theoretical framework of self psychology rests. This concept of an object experienced as incompletely distinguished from the self and serving to maintain the sense of self finally lifts the shadow that fell upon Freud's (1914/1957) theory of object choice when he tried to formulate the personal, narcissistic *meaning* of attachments in terms of the impersonal workings of an energy-discharge apparatus. More importantly, the concept of a selfobject radically alters our understanding of the meaning of patients' experiences in the analytic situation. As Evelyne Schwaber (1979) has aptly observed, our listening perspective is refined and broadened to encompass the "perceptual validity" of a patient's use of the analytic bond as an essential aspect of his own self-experience. Our interpretive focus is shifted from what patients might wish to ward off to what they need to restore and maintain (Stolorow & Lachmann, 1980)—to the idealizing and mirroring ties, thwarted during the formative years, which they now come to rely on for their sense of self-cohesion, self-continuity, and self-esteem.

To sum up so far, self psychology can be shown to meet the essential criteria for a clinical psychoanalytic theory. Its fundamental constructs are derivative of and uniquely appropriate to the meanings that can be apprehended in the psychoanalytic situation through empathy and introspection. In this respect self psychology promises to make psychoanalytic theory more scientific—that is, more closely grounded in psychoanalytic data. Such rootedness in psychoanalytic data contrasts sharply with those classical metapsychological constructs that are remnants of 19th-century physiology and are essentially unrelated to the psychoanalytic situation.

One of the most comprehensive efforts at constructing a clinical theory for psychoanalysis has been offered by Roy Schafer (1976). In his valuable critique of metapsychology he demonstrates that its structural-energic concepts represent unlabeled spatial metaphors, concretistic reifications that treat nonsubstantial subjective experiences and fantasies as though they were thinglike entities. He proposes to dispense entirely with these reified constructs and to replace them with a theoretical framework called "action language." This language brings to focus the person-as-agent—that is, the person as a performer of actions who consciously and unconsciously authors his own life. Within this language the subject matter of psychoanalytic conceptualization becomes action itself, especially disclaimed actions, as well as the individual's conscious and unconscious personal reasons for his actions.

Although there are certain broad similarities between action language and self psychology (they are both personalistic and holistic theories rather than mechanistic and atomistic ones), a careful scrutiny of the two frameworks reveals that they address fundamentally different empirical domains. Action language *presupposes* that the sense of self-as-agent—the experience of the self as a demarcated and abiding center of initiative—has been firmly consolidated. In contrast, self psychology is concerned with understanding just those subjective states in which the sense of self-as-agent has remained undeveloped or atrophied as a result of developmental interferences and arrests. Psychological configurations that are remnants of developmental voids or traumatically aborted developmental thrusts cannot be fruitfully conceptualized as purposefully performed actions. Thus, action language may be well suited for conceptualizing instances of intrapsychic conflict in which the attainment of a cohesive self-structure can be presupposed, but it cannot cover the clinical domain that has been the central concern of self psychology—the domain of missing, vulnerable, fragmentation-prone psychic structure.

In an earlier paper (Stolorow, 1978) drawing on work in collaboration with George Atwood (Stolorow & Atwood, 1979), I proposed that psychoanalysis as a clinical theory is best viewed as a structural psychology concerned with the nature, developmental vicissitudes, multiple functions, and therapeutic transformation of the psychological structures that organize a person's subjective experiences in general and shape the patient's (and analyst's) experiences of the analytic relationship in particular. In characterizing psychoanalysis as a structural psychology, I conceived of psychological structures not as contents or components of a mental apparatus, but rather as systems of ordering or organizing principles (Piaget, 1970)—cognitive-affective schemata (Klein, 1976) through which a person's experiences assume their characteristic patterns and meanings. This concept of psychic structure provides an experience-near framework for understanding the claim that classical conflict psychology aims for the realignment of existing pathological structures, whereas self psychology is concerned with promoting the development of structure that is missing or deficient.

In this context, how should we conceptualize the self? In referring to the self Kohut (1977) has tended to intermingle two meanings that I believe should be more sharply distinguished. Specifically, I suggest that we invoke the concept of *the person* when referring to an *agent* who initiates actions (Schafer's terrain) and reserve the term *self* for referring to the *structure* of self-experience. I make this terminological choice because I believe that Kohut's most important clinical discoveries and theoretical ideas pertain principally to the self as a psychological structure through which self-experience acquires cohesion and continuity, and by virtue of which self-experience assumes its characteristic form and enduring organization. His central contributions to our understanding of psychopathology and treatment concern those states in which the psychological structure that organizes the experience of self is missing or defective and in which archaic ties to selfobjects are required to restore and sustain a subjective sense of self-cohesion, self-continuity, and self-esteem.

In what sense, then, can we characterize the self as supraordinate? Should we picture it as supraordinate to a mental apparatus as Kohut (1977) has suggested? I would argue instead that the new concept of the self and the old concept of an energy-disposal apparatus exist on entirely different theoretical planes deriving from entirely different universes of discourse. From the perspective of psychoanalysis as a structural psychology, the metapsychological problem of the supraordinance of the self becomes transformed into a set of clinically crucial *empirical* questions concerning the degree to which a firmly demarcated self-structure predominates in the organization of a person's subjective field.

Similar considerations lead me to propose a revision of Kohut's (1977) conception of the complementarity between self psychology and mental apparatus psychology. I do not believe that a framework emphasizing the structuralization of self-experience and a framework emphasizing the processing of drive energies could every truly complement one another in guiding clinical psychoanalytic work. Following Klein (1976) and Schafer (1976) I would dispense with the mental apparatus concept altogether and envision the essential complementarity as one between a psychology of conflict-ridden but firmly consolidated psychic structures and a psychology of missing, precarious, and disintegration-prone psychic structures. A singularly important clinical implication of this revised concept of complementarity is that in *every* psychoanalytic treatment the analyst should continually assess whether at any particular juncture he is being experienced predominantly as a separate and whole object assimilated to conflict-ridden psychological structures firmly consolidated in the patient's past or as an archaic selfobject in a prestructural tie that substitutes for the patient's missing or precarious psychological structure. The results of this ongoing assessment will directly determine the therapist's perspective for analytic listening, his framing of precise analytic interpretations, and his conceptualization of the course of the analysis and its therapeutic action (Stolorow & Lachmann, 1980).

To exemplify further my characterization of self psychology as a structural psychology concerned specifically with the development and structuralization of self-experience, I turn now to an examination of the concept of transmuting internalization, the structure-building process set in motion during the working-through phase of the analysis of narcissistic disturbances.[1] In *The Analysis of the Self,* the process of transmuting internalization was formulated within the assumptions of mental apparatus psychology and the

---

[1]The discussion of transmuting internalization was taken from a broader exploration of the psychoanalytic concepts of the inner and the outer worlds appearing in Atwood and Stolorow (1980).

drive-discharge model: Repeated empathic interpretations of the patient's experiences of optimal frustration by the narcissistically invested selfobject result in a process of fractionalized withdrawal of narcissistic cathexes from the object and a concomitant redeployment of these cathexes in the gradual formation of particles of psychic structure, which now exercise the functions that heretofore had been performed by the object. I emphasized earlier that in *The Restoration of the Self* Kohut for the most part dispensed with these metapsychological constructions and framed his formulations in terms of a developmental phenomenology of the self. However, the implications of this theoretical shift for reconceptualizing the process of transmuting internalization have not yet been worked out in detail.

From the standpoint of a developmental phenomenology of the self, it can be shown that embedded in the concept of transmuting internalization are two closely interacting but conceptually distinguishable developmental processes. The first of these, emphasized by Marian Tolpin (1971), concerns the person's *acquisition of certain functional capacities* (e.g., soothing, comforting, and mirroring) involved in the maintenance of self-cohesion, self-continuity, and self-esteem—capacities which the patient (or child) had formerly relied upon the selfobject to provide. In referring to the person's acquisition of these capacities as "internalizations," Kohut adopted Hartmann's (1939) conception of internalization as a process through which autonomous self-regulation replaces regulation by the environment. Schafer (1976) has argued persuasively that to call this process internalization introduces misleading physicalistic and spatial reifications and that the development of a person's self-regulatory capacities may be more adequately conceptualized in nonspatial terms. I would hasten to add, however, that the patient may *experience* this developmental process as a relocalization of the selfobject's functions in *phenomenological space,* whereby they become assimilated into the self-structure (Lichtenberg, 1978). Here the term internalization may be properly applied.

Closely intertwined with the acquisition of self-regulatory capacities is the second developmental process embedded in the concept of transmuting internalization: the *structuralization of self-experience.* This process, in turn, can be broken down further into two components. In the first of these the analyst's nonintrusive neutrality and consistently accepting and empathic understanding of the patient's archaic states and needs come to be experienced by the patient as a *facilitating medium* reinstating the developmental processes of self-articulation and self-demarcation that had been traumatically aborted and arrested during the patient's formative years (Stolorow & Lachmann, 1980). Thus, certain articulations and structuralizations of self-experience are directly promoted in the medium of the analyst's empathy, a process which need not include internalization per se. The second component of self-structuralization involves internalization proper: those enduring reorganizations of the subjective field in which experienced qualities of the mirroring or idealized selfobject are translocated and assimilated into the patient's increasingly differentiated self-structure. To describe the myriad internalizations that contribute to the structuralization of the nuclear self is far beyond the scope of this paper. Hence, I restrict myself to a brief description of the internalizations of the analyst's empathic qualities which can occur during the working-through phase. I essentially describe certain developmental transformations of the experience of feeling understood, without addressing in any detail what it is the analyst understands at any particular juncture in treatment.

Such internalizations may be seen as proceeding through a number of steps. Repeated experiences of being understood by the analyst and the evolving perception of the analyst as a progressively more differentiated, empathically inquiring object enable the patient to form a complementary perception of himself as a person who has been and can be empathically understood. Here we see self-articulation in the medium of the analyst's empathy, but not yet internalization. Further structuralization through internalization proper is promoted by the repeated analysis of the patient's manageable, nontraumatic experiences of the absence of the analyst's empathy, which may result either from empathic failures or separations. At first the patient may fill the void by becoming able to invoke an image of the analyst's empathic responsiveness during the period of its experienced absence, thus restoring the lost feeling of being understood. During this phase, a patient undergoing a separation from the analyst may describe a feeling that the analyst is somehow "available" and "there," even though not physically present and not distinctly localized in subjective space. In such instances the analyst crystallizes in the patient's awareness as a transitional empathic presence. Gradually, as Kohut (1971) has described, the patient comes to experience a "shift . . . from the total human context of the

personality of the object to certain of its specific functions [p. 50]."
As Lichtenberg (1978) notes, he becomes able, without needing the
concrete images of the analyst, to minister the lost empathic re-
source but as an integral part of the fabric of himself." Hence, with
the patient's acquisition of the capacity for empathic self-observation and a corresponding perception of himself as a person who can
vation and a corresponding perception of himself as a person who can
empathically understand himself, the internalization of the analyst's
empathic qualities becomes fully integrated into the subjective self.
The quality of empathic understanding, formerly felt to be the property of a selfobject, has now become an enduring feature of the
patient's self-experience, contributing vitally to its structuralization.

To summarize, a consistently phenomenological perspective
makes it possible to clarify the concept of transmuting internalization and to demonstrate that it combines a number of complex,
interacting developmental processes: the acquisition of self-regulatory capacities, the facilitation of self-articulation, and internalization proper. Furthermore, a strict focus on the patient's subjective
field shifts the accent from the notion of "optimal frustration" (a
somewhat experience-distant concept originating in drive-discharge
theory) to the crucial role in the structuralization of self-experience
of *optimal empathy* (a more experience-near concept that is more
compatible with the new paradigm of self psychology).

In exemplifying my understanding of self psychology, it is no
accident that I chose to focus on one of its central developmental
constructs. From the vantage point of self psychology as a structural
psychology, Kohut's proposal that narcissism follows its own separate line of development can now be seen as inviting the construction of a detailed developmental psychology of the self-structure,
fleshing out his broad descriptions of the child's early ties to mirroring and idealized selfobjects. Such a developmental psychology
might begin to spell out the complex interplay between the ontogenesis and structuralization of self-experience, the vicissitudes of
object relations, cognitive and affective maturation, and psychosexual development (Stolorow & Lachmann, 1980). As seen in Kohut's
reformulation of drive experiences, the addition of the self-psychological perspective can radically alter and expand our understanding of these other developmental progressions. A comprehensive
developmental phenomenology of the self can provide the basis for a
revised, more embracing, developmentally based system of psychopathology, the foundations of which have already been set (Gold-

berg, 1975; Kohut & Wolf, 1978; Stolorow & Lachmann, 1980). It can also provide a framework for an increasingly refined understanding of the vicissitudes of transference and countertransference in the psychoanalytic situation, viewed in terms of the intersubjective interplay between the differently organized self-structures of patient and analyst (Stolorow, Atwood & Lachmann, 1981). Most important of all to our analytic work with patients, the theoretical framework of self psychology has extended the limits of our capacity for empathic understanding and hence of our therapeutic effectiveness to hitherto inaccessible regions of human subjectivity.

REFERENCES

Atwood, G. & Stolorow, R. (1980). Psychoanalytic concepts and the representational world. *Psychoanal. Contemp. Thought* 3: 267–290.
Freud, S. (1914). On narcissism: An introduction. *S.E.* 14: 69–102.
Goldberg, A. (1975). A fresh look at perverse behavior. *Int. J. Psychoanal.* 56: 335–342.
Hartmann, H. (1939). *Ego Psychology and the Problem of Adaptation.* New York: Int. Univ. Press, 1958.
Klein, G. (1976). *Psychoanalytic Theory: An Exploration of Essentials.* New York: Int. Univ. Press.
Kohut, H. (1971). *The Analysis of the Self.* New York: Int. Univ. Press.
_____ (1977). *The Restoration of the Self.* New York: Int. Univ. Press.
_____ & Wolf, E. (1978). The disorders of the self and their treatment: An outline. *Int. J. Psychoanal.* 59: 413–425.
Lichtenberg, J. (1978). *Transmuting Internalization and Developmental Change.* Paper presented at the Chicago Conference on the Psychology of the Self, October.
Ornstein, P. (1978). Introduction: The evolution of Heinz Kohut's psychoanalytic psychology of the self. In *The Search for the Self.* New York: Int. Univ. Press, pp. 1–106.
Piaget, J. (1970). *Structuralism.* New York: Basic Books.
Schafer, R. (1976). *A New Language for Psychoanalysis.* New Haven, Conn.: Yale University Press.
Schwaber, E. (1979). On the "self" within the matrix of analytic theory—Some clinical reflections and reconsiderations. *Int. J. Psychoanal.* 60: 467–479.
Stolorow, R. (1978). The concept of psychic structure: Its metapsychological and clinical psychoanalytic meanings. *Int. Rev. Psychoanal.* 5: 313–320.
_____ & Atwood, G. (1979). *Faces in a Cloud: Subjectivity in Personality Theory.* New York: Jason Aronson.
_____ _____ & Lachmann, F. (1981). Transference and countertransference in the analysis of developmental arrests. *Bull. Menning. Clinic* 45: 20–28.
_____ & Lachmann, F. (1980). *Psychoanalysis of Developmental Arrests: Theory and Treatment.* New York: Int. Univ. Press.
Tolpin, M. (1971). On the beginnings of a cohesive self: An application of the concept of transmuting internalization to the study of the transitional object and signal anxiety. *Psychoanal. Study Child* 26: 316–354.

25

Self Psychology and Alternative Perspectives on Internalization

Arnold Goldberg, M.D.

Psychoanalysis seems poised in its theoretical stance between two worlds. The first is that of our classical theory—one that is based on the principles of all natural science, one that is familiar, has served us well, and yet one that is periodically attacked for its mechanical and outdated models. The other position is less clear. It ranges from simple efforts to rid us of psychic energy and similar concepts to those elaborate and detailed endeavors that urge analysis to abandon all scientific pretense and/or to establish itself as a discipline similar to history or even art. This latter stance is, more often than not, felt to be of passing interest to analytic scholars but rarely seems to be of much clinical importance. Somewhere in between is a position of examining new, but still essentially scientific, alternative theoretical positions. Self psychology may offer us such an opportunity. Of course, only when clinical necessity demands a modification of theory should a tried and tested way of looking at things be reexamined and should alternative theoretical outlooks be entertained. In the evolution of any new theory, we see a time during which parallel use of the old theory usually precedes replacement. Theories are not fighting it out for the truth, but rather are vying over maximum usefulness. Only the exercise of a theory allows one to make reasonable choices, and only a flexible approach allows one to be objective.

The original presentations of narcissistic disorders by Kohut were cast in classical theories and, for the most part, found a home there. Any criticisms of the theory were telling both before and after self psychology came upon the scene, but no more than before. The struggle over the problematic role and definitions of the self remained as critical when Hartmann (1953) first tried to explain its metapsychological position as when Kohut (1971) elaborated its clinically relevant problems. I think the point at which classical theory simply could go no farther (with all of its shortcomings still in mind) was with the clinical fact of enduring and maturing selfobjects, which are persons who are felt as part of one's own self and whose role as such does not disappear as development proceeds. This bit of clinical data states that people maintain lasting selfobject relationships throughout life as part and parcel of normal growth and development. It seems to be the case that such a position cannot be well pictured, or realized, or even discussed with our present concepts of internalization, which posit that continuing growth and structuralization lead to adult positions of independence and autonomy (Mahler, 1968). Let us, for the moment, resist the temptation to tamper with and modify our classical theory further and test whether alternative theoretical models might help to extend our vision of clinical material and thus ultimately lead to a more major restructuring of psychoanalytic theory.

The evolution of thinking about the activities of scientists has moved from the absolute positions of rules for obtaining similarly absolute truths to those of a dialectic leading to the assumption of relative truths that reign for a variable period of time (Toulmin, 1979). Though it may be disquieting to some that each and every scientific arena is subject to inevitable growth and change, it is equally relieving to others that we can enjoy a flexible approach to the consideration, as well as the eliciting, of scientific data.

One of the supposed revolutions in the philosophy of science has been the position that all of our theories stem from and depend on some form of sentence/picture model, which is used to derive rules or laws to explain and cover the so-called empirical data (Harre, 1976) that is gathered by the use of such a theory or model. When and if we come across a poor fit between model and data, we have a choice of ignoring the data (after a period of trying to confirm their validity) or modifying our model. In psychoanalysis our models run close to what others call metaphors. Some even say that we should change metaphors periodically to keep our ideas fresh and vigorous, because a tendency among most investigators is to defend a model with a vigor amounting to a defense of a person's reality. The following work on internalization is a reconsideration of the effectiveness of one of the metaphors most congenial to psychoanalysis.

It seems so obvious that an individual has internal thoughts, feelings, and ideas that it may seem more comical than heretical to consider its denial.* "Inside" and "outside" permeate our language, perceptions, and thoughts to such a degree that, nowadays, normal development posits it as a necessary achievement to clarify and establish this boundary, and psychological pathology often corresponds to a failure in this delineation. The rule has become: What is external must become internal. The agreed definition (Schafer, 1968) for this sequence is: "Internalization refers to all those processes by which the subject transforms real or imagined regulatory interactions with his environment, and real or imagined characteristics of his environment, into inner regulations and characteristics [p. 9]." The most complete and thorough review of the topic appears in the now disavowed (by the author) book of Roy Schafer (1968), wherein he accepts and reviews the positions of the subject as agent, object, and place and equates inner with each and all of these points of view (i.e., the inner agent, the inner object, and the inner place). The crux of the problem concerns the word "inner." This directs our attention to those considerations of the conception of minds as being places or as occupying space.

To take the last of the triad (i.e., place) first, we can agree that we tend to think of ourselves as a contained and separate entity or body with a clear and recognizable difference from others. Even the most concentrated emphasis on the idea of using others as part of ourselves always runs up against the sharp picture of our distinctive physical or even psychological uniqueness. What is mine always seems to fall inside a frame of sorts. This enhances the feeling of being self-contained and leads to the consideration of others as falling necessarily outside that frame. Freud (1915) first posited the difference between inside and outside as based on stimuli: Those

---

*Note: For a philosophical approach to the problem see Hilary Putnam *Reason, Truth & History,* Cambridge Univ. Press Cambridge (1981).

from which one can escape are outside, and those from which one cannot escape are inside. Other analysts have enlarged and built upon this initial drawing of the boundary.

The functional differentiation of inside and outside comes most clearly from Freud's statements (1938) on identification: "A portion of the external world has been abandoned, at least partially, as an object and instead, by identifications, has been taken into the ego and has thus become an integral part of the internal world. This new psychical agency continues to carry on the functions which have hitherto been performed by people in the external world [p. 205]." Here we see the familiar taking over in performance, which currently is stressed by Kohut in his work on transmuting internalizations, wherein one assumes functions previously performed by the selfobjects. This is the inner agent.

The taking over of functions, as well as the positioning of the outside things on the inside, then leaves the last usage suggested by Schafer: the consideration of one's self as an object. Freud was clear in indicating that the ego/nonego was equivalent to internal/external (1915). The position of oneself on the outside makes it no longer you. However, this is a developmental achievement of momentarily being able to consider oneself as if you were someone else. The capacity to see oneself or to stand apart and scrutinize *as if* one were two individuals is a process that can be seen on a continuum from the schizophrenic sense of alienation to the analysand's development of an observing ego. Here again, one confronts the varied meanings of internalization that permeate our language and thinking.

My reexamination of the inner–outer dichotomy pursues a somewhat different course than Schafer's outstanding, extensive discussion, which notes and supports the three-part stance just outlined. My three parts are concerned with a different form of inner experience: the problems of ownership, privacy, and representability. By themselves they may not resolve the problem of an alternative to internalization, but together they may allow us to see clinical data a little differently. They also may serve to highlight what has heretofore been a subtle shift in the field of psychoanalysis: a shift from the study of the mind to that of the person, from a concentration on the contents of an apparatus to one on the relationships of individuals (Goldberg, A. 1980).

OWNERSHIP

Extending the arena of individuality beyond its physical confines enables us to declare just what and who we feel to be a part or parts of ourselves. People usually include at least their clothing as a part of their self, and yet analysts and self psychologists in particular contend that one can extend a functional consideration of selfhood to other persons via selfobjects. Thus, internalization expands to the realm of what is felt to *belong* to a person. The position of ownership thereby can newly determine and thus substitute for the line between inner and outer.

The beginning of a developmental study of owning usually focuses on the child's use of a transitional object, an object employed to cover the border of inside–outside and one which carries the peculiar property of shared ownership as well as indestructibility. The transitional object is: "the first not-me possession" and "not part of the infant's body," yet not fully recognized as belonging to external reality (Winnecott, D. W. 1951). Such a descriptive categorization betrays a bias that has seemingly led to much confusion in psychoanalytic discussions of the transitional object or phenomenon, namely, that "belonging" remains connected to the body and that separation has something to do with physical presence.

To say that something is mine is a process of development that entails putting one's stamp on something; it extends from the body, to the family, to the world of things and ideas. Thus, the ownership struggle that seems to go on over the child's blanket need not reflect a boundary problem of delineating one's own body as much as a capacity to claim the rights of owning. In a study of language we see both cultural differences in the words that entail ownership as well as developmental differences that do not necessarily parallel a line from union to autonomy. In some languages the phrase "my head" is rendered differently to distinguish the head on one's shoulders from the head being held in one's hand after a victory over a rival. In normal growth the child's claim to what is "mine" has no single direction as, for instance, from the whole world to a small arena of ownership; it moves back and forth. Boundaries are variable and of diminished significance.

How should we define ownership? Schafer (1968) states in his discussion of self-regulation: "Stimulation and impact of the regulation does not depend on the actual presence, action, or emotional position of the external object that was one part to the original interactions. Inner indicates that the subject locates the previously external regulatory agents within some self-boundary [p. 10]." Clearly, at that time, he still was involved with spatial problems. Yet we can easily envisage a child assuming a function that was previously performed by a parent by a claim to its being his, that is, under his control or belonging to him without it being accorded a niche in his brain or body.

This then becomes the differentiating point for ownership, that is, one has the process under his or her own control. You own something that you do with as you please. This is not meant to be read in the sense of casualness but rather that ownership, control, and belonging together are used to signify that something is a part of someone. Now the added feature of ownership can be seen to cover functions as well as things. As a child learns to read, to remember, or even to recognize others, these all become *capacities* that bear the stamp of that child. As they belong to the child, they have no need of a place to reside.

A telling example of the advantage of the use of an ownership model over a spatial model presented itself with a patient who was discussing a painting in his art collection. This particular work was a highly prized representative of a certain historical period and was therefore always on loan at one or another museum throughout the country. My patient, the owner, had not seen it in years. He was approached about its sale, and as he was considering it, he became depressed and agitated. He said to me that regardless of whether or not he ever saw the painting again, it made all the difference in the world whether it was his or not. It was the very fact that it belonged to him that was important. He then contrasted this to a feeling in another situation with which he was also quite familiar having to do with stolen paintings in one's possession which could never be put on display or declared as one's own. He said that they had to be viewed in dark basements with no one around, but this in no way diminished the pleasure of having them. He knew of many people who had large collections of this sort.

I think a psychoanalyst listens to this material of narcissistic investments with several forms of comprehension: those that have to do with exhibitionist fantasies, others that deal with dominance and power, still others that relate to secret masturbatory episodes, and so on. Yet the model of an inner world of things and relations seems to be a less powerful intellectual aid than one of ownership and possession. The latter allows us to reach across the confines of the individual to the limitless expanse involving untold others and back again to the most minute reveries that exclude everyone else.

As we range over a variety of events, such as from a child being read to, to learning to read, all the way to the adult who enjoys being read to and/or who needs to be read to, we can see how the variety of ways to make something one's own becomes paramount and, for some individuals, even crucial. Each of us declares what we can lend to someone else and what we must continue to hold fast. At times during a conversation or a scientific exchange, an idea may issue forth which momentarily is either without ownership or is truly shared. The matter may remain suspended as such or may become resolved—usually on the basis of who first thought of it, who was the initiator. In the matrix of communication, the owner is the sender. In the matter of material things, the owner has his or her name on it. It is a personal decision based on how one experiences something as being his (i.e., within his control, emanating from him, or decided by him). That this is so can be further demonstrated in situations where multiple ownership can exist without controversy. A good learning situation can lead to a number of students laying claim to knowledge with no hint of a fixed amount of this knowledge needing to be equally divided. A good analytic hour often is paced by the analysand who will accomplish up to a particular point and then require an assimilation of the accomplishment over a defined time period. Every analyst soon learns the times and occasions for allowing the analysand to take over the analysis by the appropriate steps toward self-analysis (another instance of the self- prefix reflecting who owns the function). Yet ownership need not enter a problem area of something being either mine *or* yours, because personal control is a larger domain than merely competing for a thing like the familiar transitional object.

At another end of the spectrum the vexing problem of projection and its kin of externalization can be fruitfully reexamined in the light of claiming ownership. The paranoid individual claims an impulse belongs to another. The road from such disclaimers to that of assuming responsibility for negative thoughts as well as actions is part of the road to maturity. When one projects an idea or wish onto another person, we are employing a particular form of illustration involving a movement from one site to another. It is no secret that psychoanalysis has troubled over the difficulty that develops when this defense mechanism is posited as arising very early in life, perhaps even before the cognitive differentiation of self from object. It may be that the model or metaphor employed for this explanation does not allow the data to be accurately understood. If we shift to a model of ownership and responsibility, there may be greater flexibility in our capacity to comprehend how an idea is assigned to someone else without a concern for the issue of a firm boundary of differentiation and the concomitant move from inside to outside. We can begin to note the developmental requirements for a claim of ownership, which do not belong merely to self and object differentiation and separation. Rather, they depend on a feeling about one's self, a capacity to manage or control an idea or a function, and a willingness to assume responsibility for it residing in one's own domain.

As another clinical example we may turn to the very common problem of the missed hour and the patient's reaction to it. No treatment seems to merit its name until and unless one can study a patient's handling of a miss in terms of anticipation, acknowledgment, and resolution. The multiple meanings of the missed hour are also legion, and they range from absent body parts to competitive struggles over oedipal issues. Not infrequently the issue can be seen in terms of just whose hour it is. I recall one patient whose dreams heralded an approaching holiday long before the calendar seemed to indicate it and for whom the initial acknowledgment of the lost hour was always a devastating humiliation. Although he often chose to speak of his rage and curiosity over what I would be doing and where I would be during these times, there seemed to be little relief experienced from this discussion when the next one rolled around. As we worked through the issue of his rights to the hour we continually came back to his intense childhood anger at his psychotic maternal grandmother who greedily laid claim to most of his mother's attention. The patient was a homosexual who was beginning to think about heterosexual relationships. He had recently found himself equally enraged at an attractive woman who liked him and wanted to be with him. He had a dream of the beautiful blond floors in his apartment being permanently marred by visitors, and we both recognized that this had to do with this woman moving into his life. He recalled with equal rage how he had been dressed in girl's clothing when he was 4 years old and how his sister and mother had laughed at his penis. Every attempt to express his masculinity had met with hurt and rejection, and so he retreated to some sort of neutral and pure or nonsexual view of his body. Now, as the analysis allowed a developmental path to reestablish itself, he again felt himself offering his sexual and masculine aspects for confirmation and acceptance. In a very encapsulated form the missed hours were like the parts of his body, which were wrested away from him before he could quite lay claim to them. The child needs a gradual and flexible grasp of his newly found capacities, functions, and parts before he can feel able to share and allow someone else to use them. First he needs his claim to be substantiated by confirmation of another. The development of owning involves the sequence of one laying claim to something as mine and then extending this to a free interplay in the relations with others. The metaphor of owning allows us to study this area of exchange between and among persons.

PRIVACY

The fact that one can have a secret is learned fairly early in life. Kohut (1971) notes that the first undetected lie allows for a change in the child's perception of the all-knowing idealized parent. The having of private thoughts, images, and ideas extends to being able to maintain one's private mental life regardless of someone else's attempted intrusions into it. We know that others usually cannot tell what we think, and we know that we can pretty much determine just how much we want them to know.

The foregoing is qualified by our recognition that the availability of a private mind is a developmental achievement; the feeling that others can read one's thought remains with us in schizophrenia, as well as via our empathy. Nowhere is the metaphor of a special arena or place better seen than in the "privacy of one's mind," although some poets prefer the site to be the heart (or perhaps a vaguer area in the chest or thorax). It should be clear that bodily confines for the world of privacy are literary devices that enable one to have a feeling of separation with a barrier, but the barrier is breached by communication. This simple fact is compounded and yet clarified by the psychoanalytic knowledge that a whole host of barriers are constructed in one's mind, for example, between the unconscious and the preconscious, between the preconscious and the conscious, and between the disavowed and the acknowledged.

To say something is private means that you decide what someone else can know. The movement across a line of privacy is an intrusion, and although such lines are sometimes physical barriers that mark off and protect private property, at other times they are psychological barriers that similarly prohibit the intrusion of another. Privacy really has to do with access. We know that much of mental life is readily accessible, but much more is seemingly out of reach. In analysis the out of reach is hidden, and the goal of psychoanalysis is to make more of what is hidden manifest. Freud cautions his readers to recognize that the separate areas of unconscious, preconscious, and conscious are qualities, attributes, or properties of mental life and not places of residence. The change from one locale to another essentially is a change of certain properties occasioned by communicability. In a like manner the communication or exchange between two persons removes the realm of the private to that of the social, and so, discourse becomes the key to the boundary. This feature allows one to see that private issues are drawn or delineated by arbitrary and individual decisions. Such lines often have to do with the physical or bodily limits of a person, but more often they have to do with personal decisions about the extent of one's mental operations to be communicated or revealed.

We are usually satisfied with the feeling of a private mind. However, in one sense, we sometimes do not know our own thoughts until we speak them, and in another sense, an empathic observer might be better equipped to tell us how and what we think and feel. This leads us to the issue of sharing. We not only share incidents of mental life, such as a single perception, but we soon inhabit a world of shared meanings. The fact that some people understand others ranges from an immediate "connection" with a stranger to a wide range of unspoken and never explained phenomena noted in many closely knit families. A similar state is sought in a psychoanalytic setting wherein the state of being understood, of sharing one's mind with another, is the *sine qua non* of effective treatment.

Privacy as an asepct or form replacing internalization can be used to highlight and illustrate the indefinite and arbitrary nature of the delineation of one person (be that body, or mind, or both) from another. We must remind ourselves that the concept of an inner mind is a metaphor employed to handle the lack of a firm entity of sensory observation.

In psychoanalytic treatment, as well as in normal development, we can follow the maturation of the privacy issue. Certain modes of thinking, such as the repressed and disavowed heretofore seen as inaccessible, should with treatment become available and should participate in communication within our self. Likewise, a strengthening of the borders of the overall feeling of the private may be a notable feature. Perhaps more importantly, an increased capacity for sharing or empathy becomes manifest. The extremes of privacy also can be seen as an indication of abnormal psychological function, as is obviously noted in individuals who are so private that they are restricted in normal exchange, as well as in those for whom the limits or controls of revealing to others are weak or lacking.

One clinical illustration of this phenomenon concerns an analytic patient for whom analysis was a periodically threatening situation because it forced him to think about and talk about a variety of ideas that he continually was putting to rest. Thoughts and feelings came tumbling out as he lay on the couch, and he longed for the opportunity to "relax," to stop the thinking and obsessing. He periodically felt he had effectively warded off his upsetting thinking, only to have the equilibrium upset and destroyed in the analytic hour. He so wanted to keep things to himself in order to achieve this longed-for state of relaxation and peace. Unfortunately, his barriers tended to collapse in the analytic hour, and as he would speak of some particularly strong set of feelings, usually those of profound hostility and competition toward one or another opponent, his agitation and accompanying guilt or shame would accelerate correspondingly. As his roadblocks diminished and as he spoke more heatedly and in greater detail, more often than not the quieter voice of the opposite set of feelings would begin to be heard. He usually would need help to gain some awareness of the ambivalent nature of his feelings, which was kept in check by a seeming other and different set of barred entries. Yet the mingling and expression of thoughts and feelings shared in the analytic setting could, on occasion, lead to a greater sense of equanimity and calm. Clearly, the concepts of things moving from one place to another, of ideas shared, and feelings allowed the freedom of expression all combined to play out the privacy metaphor and allow us to recognize the main issue as being one of access and communicability.

Most of us are familiar with patients for whom noncommunication becomes a protective mechanism. In most cases this takes the form of a more or less benign phobia: a simple task of avoidance. One patient, who had been divorced for over 15 years, told of the elaborate system that he devised in order to avoid any contact, knowledge, or casual comment with or about his ex-wife. Her presence continued to cause him extreme anxiety and agitation, and he had even arranged never to be forced to see or sign the monthly alimony checks that were mailed to her. Although such extreme as well as simpler forms of nonspeaking are thought of as a defense against inner arousal related to internal but unconscious images of anxiety, it is also true that they can be realistic carriers of fearful reactions. This patient's fear of his ex-wife is not able to qualify as a phobia, per se, because it contains both rational and irrational elements.

So-called external barriers aid in psychological adjustments as much as do the supposed internal ones, and we all construct such barriers both wittingly and otherwise. Likewise, considering the analyst as a neutral or external screen for the projections of the patient posits a different form of observational material than one that considers an empathic failure (i.e., an introspective position on the analyst's part), leading to an upset in the patient. The first model suggests a sharp boundary and difference; the second requires a communicative link, which is broken. One analytic patient was most difficult to listen to because he had perfected a style of being able to speak about one topic while preoccupied with another. Of course, he ultimately would get caught up in his preoccupations and would lapse into silence, but his explication of these silent periods would be amazingly disparate from what seemed to be the topic of the moment. Over the course of the analysis we had learned to recognize just when he was involved with something else, and often we would connect it to some problem in the transference, which forced him to keep things to himself. His childhood environment of a preoccupied mother and a precocious capacity of his own to regulate just what she could respond to and just when he had to restrain himself were markedly and vividly reenacted in the analysis, and in equal vividness they aroused strong countertransference feelings of exclusion and dismissal.

One day he reported a dream of his wife entering into an analytic session, lying down on the couch, and announcing that this would now be joint therapy. He angrily responded that he resented such an arbitrary decision, and *he* would be the one to determine just what to make of his analytic hour. He had no doubt that his dream resulted from a decision with his wife about finances and a suggestion (from him) that perhaps he should drop his analysis. The hour was characterized by an excessive amount of this halting or third person speech, and we agreed that something else was on his mind. He was an academic involved in a research project, and lately he had been rather excited about some new finding by one of his doctoral students. The student wanted to finish up a dissertation; the patient felt that more experiments were needed, but he wanted to be seen as a benevolent and understanding advisor. It was also clear that he felt the ideas for this new scientific advance were entirely his own, and he resented any hint that the student would lay claim to originality. It became clear that the patient was loathe to communicate his excitement and his own megalomanic fantasies to me or to any others who might consider him as selfish and/or self-centered.

The fierce competition with the wife and student derived from the birth of a sibling when he was 2 years old, which further strained the attentive capacity of his mother. The patient's wish to conceal or keep private these hidden narcissistic fantasies repeated his childhood setting of attentiveness to his younger sibling as he struggled to keep his own wish for center stage in obeyance. His analytic work allowed him to expose his fantasies for recognition to another person and thus to modulate and regulate them. These were not readily seen to operate as a form of drive expression, but rather as a need for another, a selfobject, to aid in the experience. The metaphor of sharing a private thought allowed for a much more compatible way of considering this hour than would one of two distinct individuals in opposition. The concept of sharing or bridging separateness by a communicative link seems much more congenial to that of the self-selfobject unit than does the idea of a drive being gratified. The latter is really the province of object relations theory, which focuses on such discrete entities, whereas the metaphor of self psychology and privacy concerns itself with the intermediate area between and inclusive of both self and object.

The difference between the uses of the metaphors of ownership and privacy may serve to highlight a difference between self psychology and object relations theory in yet another way. Self psychology studies the developmental story of the lasting connection between the self and selfobject as a unit. Object relations theory stresses the internal workings of those external phenomena *between* people as if reenacted in a internal replica within the mind. I cannot at the present time detail the third change in metaphor that I feel is needed, but it is one that concerns itself with the whole issue of internal representation, one suggesting that the inner world is some sort of miniature theater of the external world. I think there are worthy alternatives to this viewpoint—those that will allow us to see our models as concerned with relationships or linkage rather than of discrete entities in opposition.

To extend this idea for a moment, we can readily reexamine the common analytic usage of the self as self-representation. To begin with, it is by no means reducible to the particular image one may have of oneself, nor can it be portrayed as that person in opposition to other people (i.e., the self vs. the object representations). Rather, it is one's idea of oneself or one's meaning of one's self. This forces a study of the very complex sets of relationships by which one defines and delimits one's psychological world. It needs to be emphasized that this accordingly is multidimensional and arbitrarily drawn. It necessitates the usual psychoanalytic stance of introspectively ascertaining the particular meanings of the varied relationships and can only be considered in the shorthand of the printout (i.e., the representation with this in mind).

IMPLICATIONS

The thesis against internalization need not lead to the conclusion that one cannot consider an inner world based upon the subject as agent, object, and place. Rather, these must be seen as devices of conversation and explanation, and they must be restricted as to their applicability. Psychoanalysis, in particular, has so emphasized the discrete separation of people that it has spawned a variety of theories based on independence as an end point. Unfortunately, independence is enlarged to become self-sufficiency and, therefore, the state of doing without others. Thus, internalization has become a virtue with a logical end point of having enough inside so that nothing is needed outside. Because this is so patently outrageous, we must either modify our theory in terms such as mature dependence, or else we must discard part of it to recognize the fact that although our relationships with others change, this never is in the direction of dispensing with them.

Therefore, internalization must be recast. It is not a matter of emphasizing the discrete boundary between people but, rather, the expansion of self-control. As we grow and develop, we extend ourselves to increasing relationships, which are ideally characterized by flexibility and freedom. The child is *not* now able to allow the mother to leave the room because of the presence of an image of mother in his or her head. The orchestra conductor is not conducting a miniature orchestra in his or her head. The proper study of the child's increasing independence is in his or her changing relationship with mother. So, too, does the conductor have a continual and viable relationship with the orchestra. The mind is the sum and substance of these relationships. But relationships are always those units of persons or minds that expand as one grows. Thus, independence and autonomy are mistaken words for the goal of maturity. Only the nature of relationships reflects that quality, not the absence of them.

A reconsideration of internalization may suggest a similar treatment of the many issues surrounding the problem(s) of separation. This would include reexamining the movement from one stage of development to another, the work of mourning as it may focus less on the holding onto the lost object and more on the gaining of a replacement, and the study of the termination phase of psychoanalysis as a taking over of functions with no necessary aspect of trauma involved.

If one reconsiders and reorders the concept of internalization, it necessarily follows that a similar reconsideration of structure and structuralization is called for. Psychoanalysis treats the process of internalization as leading to the formation of psychological structures. This structure is considered to be the groundwork for the strength and stability of the psyche and can be thought of as either a near-physical substance or as a set of "enduring functions." If we now see structure in terms of the initial positions previously outlined, we can see it in the perspectives of access or communicability, control or regulation, and representability or capability of being thought about. Our mental structures are capacities. They allow us to communicate with ourselves and with others. They enable us to fix the boundaries and limits of ourselves. Finally, they allow us to participate in the world of symbols or meanings uniquely relevant to humans. Such an alternative view of internalization and structure may enable us to see growth and development in terms of the maturation of relationships that depend on these standards of communication, self-control, and shared meanings and less in the sense of autonomy, independence, and self-sufficiency. The task ahead is one of detailing these developmental steps, which will serve to increase and enhance one's interdependence or enlarge and deepen the shared matrix of human endeavors.

In summary, the new findings of self psychology seem to tax the limits of classical psychoanalystic theory. This is not a cause for despair, nor is it a call to arms. Certainly, no one felt that psychoanalysis was a finished science. What is needed is an effort of clinical practice, which uses new models and theories, to carry us even further along until that day in the future when a conference will convene and declare that the theories of self psychology seem unable to handle the new data that are emerging.

26

Self Psychology and "Classical" Psychoanalytic Psychology—The Nature of Their Relationship: A Review and Overview

Robert S. Wallerstein, M.D.

It is over a decade now that psychoanalysis has been explicitly confronted with the contributions to its theory and its technique offered by Heinz Kohut and his many collaborators first under the rubric of concern with the problems of narcissism and more recently under the declaredly more encompassing rubric of the psychology of the self. The two major landmarks in this progressive unfolding have been Kohut's first book (1971), *The Analysis of the Self*—subsequently declared to be the expression of the psychology of the self in the narrower sense, of self as content of the agencies of the mental apparatus, that is, as mental representations *within* the ego, id, and superego—and then Kohut's second book (1977), *The Restoration of the Self*—the elaboration of the psychology of the self in the declaredly broader sense, of self as a *supraordinate* constellation, with the drives and defenses (the central ingredients of the classical psychoanalytical conceptions of psychic functioning) subsumed as constituents of this self. This is the view of what has come to be called the bipolar self with, in its maturation, the crystallization of normally self-assertive ambitions as one pole and attained ideals and values as the other. The two poles are then connected by a tension arc of talents and skills.

As one of the participants in the first panel by the American Psychoanalytic Association on the Bi-Polar Self, held in New York City in December 1979 (Wallerstein, 1981), I developed at some

An expanded version of this chapter was published in *The Future of Psychoanalysis* (Arnold Goldberg, ed. International Universities Press, 1983) and also in *Psychoanalysis and Contemporary Thought* (1983). This version was read at the Boston symposium.

313

length my *clinical* perspectives on the nature of the contributions of the self-psychological approach. I now welcome the opportunity to articulate a more *theoretical* critique of this most significant—and most controversial—new development in the psychoanalytic corpus offered by Heinz Kohut and his followers.

Let me begin with a schematic statement of what I see to be the essence of Kohut's contribution to the body of psychoanalytic concept and endeavor. It is, to me, most simply and directly what Kohut took as his own clinical starting point: the focusing of our psychoanalytic awareness on the psychological as well as the psychopathological phenomena of narcissism as representing a most central aspect of the psychological functioning, normal and abnormal, of *all* people. Previously, this aspect was not regularly and systematically conceptualized and explicated, and it is an aspect of overriding clinical importance with some particular people, the so-called narcissistic personalities or narcissistic characters.

By this I do not mean the proposal of the concept of a separate developmental line for narcissism apart from that for object-relatedness and object-love, as a splitting apart and an expansion of Freud's original conceptualization of the line of developmental stages proceeding from autoerotism, through narcissism, and on to object love, though this proposal was clearly set forth in Kohut's first book (1971) as the centerpiece of his new views on narcissism. Though some theoretical controversy did arise around Kohut's strong statement for separate developmental lines, this is not where the most searching critiques of self psychology have rested their main case. Rather, I have sensed widespread agreement among analysts with my own view that this particular aspect of Kohut's formulations is neither that new nor, by itself, that important. As I stated at the New York panel, in terms of both the clinical and theoretical conceptualization of the phenomena with which psychoanalysis deals, I *have* found it eminently useful to see narcissistic investments and object-related investments as parallel, complexly interrelating developmental processes each originating in the most archaic mental dispositions and each being successively transmuted in the crucible of life experience into more matured, ego syntonic, and socially valued mental states and propensities.

But I also stated that by the same token I did not regard this aspect of the formulation of Kohut's self psychology to be as revolutionary a contribution as Ornstein (1981), for example, implied. I said that in principle it was no different than Anna Freud's (1965) longtime work in separating out great varieties of developmental lines along many drive- and ego-related axes, as well as Mahler's (1975) similar focusing on the developmental axis from the autistic, through the symbiotic, and onto the separation-individuation unfolding. Of all this, I (Wallerstein, 1981) said: "psychoanalytic thinking has long transcended its initial formulations by Freud that had assumed the unitary centrality of the psychosexual developmental ladder as a comprehensively satisfactory framework within which to view life course and development, the influence of past on present, or said for different purpose, the incremental transformation of past into present [p. 381]." And I went on to state that psychoanalysts today, including Kohut himself, more in the spirit of his second book, are in general accord with a conceptualization of a unitary-ness and a togetherness of development within which for purposes of heuristic highlighting we can in turn focus on varieties of drive-, ego-, and object-related developmental line and axes. Division among us would be much more on the question of the specific value of Kohut's particular conceptualization of the *self* as the supraordinate unifying perspective on the personality.

Nor do I regard as the major importance of Kohut's formulations on narcissism the clear emphasis on the primacy of the libidinal over the aggressive component in emotional interaction and development. This issue has of course been one major focus in the theoretical differences with Otto Kernberg who has so consistently called attention to the deemphasis in Kohut's "empathic" and "soothing" clinical approach to the pre-oedipal transferences, the deemphasis there of the role of primitive aggressive drives, of the hateful, pre-oedipal maternal transference imagos, and of the vicissitudes of infantile oral envy and rage (Kernberg, 1974; also, 1978). In fact, Kernberg (1974) talks about a failure of "a basic resolution of what I consider the pathological structure of the grandiose self [p. 238]," which he feels (Kernberg, 1978) to be the inevitable consequence, if not the intent, of helping patients rationalize their aggressions as "a natural consequence to the failure of other people in their past [p. 17]."

Yet here too, I do not regard this issue as the most central to the nature of the contribution to (or the departure from) the theory of psychoanalysis in Kohut's proffered formulations on narcissism. Rather I look at this as the kind of temporary one-sidedness that seems almost inevitably part of any new conceptual position, one that gradually becomes moderated over time to a more accommodating and consensually agreed upon return of the pendulum to a more central conceptual resting place.

Given these disclaimers, where then do I center my main statement of the nature of Kohut's central contributions to our psychological understandings? They are to me most importantly in the *clinical* realm of the specific and careful delineation of the significance and meaning within the psychoanalytic situation of the interactional modes called first the narcissistic transferences (Kohut, 1971) and subsequently the selfobject transferences (Kohut, 1977)— as well as the counteractive and countertransference responses that they can characteristically evoke. Here again there is widespread agreement in the psychoanalytic world, even among those who have been most sharply critical of Kohut's formulations (see, e.g., the book review by Martin Stein, 1979).

Of course not all, or perhaps even not many, would follow Kohut all the way in the overriding centrality that he accords these formulations as explainers of human psychological functioning, as when he stated (Kohut, 1980) at the Chicago Conference on the Psychology of the Self in 1978: "In the view of self-psychology man lives in a matrix of selfobjects from birth to death. He needs selfobjects for his psychological survival, just as he needs oxygen in his environment throughout his life for physiological survival [p. 478]." This extreme and somewhat fanciful metaphor aside, I think almost all of us in analysis can agree that Kohut's clinical formulations of the selfobject transferences, the varieties of mirroring and idealizing transferences and their characteristic colluding countertransferences, and the elegant delineation in the beautiful outline presentation by Kohut and Wolf (1978) of psychopathological types and the behavioral typologies into which they sort themselves considered from the standpoint of selfobject transference formulations are indeed significant and enduring additions to our psychoanalytical vistas and our therapeutic armamentaria.

Thus far, I trust that I have traced a path that can be broadly traveled together by both the proponents and the critics of the new self psychology that is evolving within psychoanalysis. At what point, then, does our consensus part and do I myself offer a different and critical perspective on the nature of the ultimate place of the self psychology addition in relation to the tenets of classical and traditional psychoanalysis? It is, most briefly put, at the point of translation of broadly clinical into broadly theoretical contribution, perhaps marked at the point of transition from the psychology of the self in the narrower sense—the retrospectively described perspective of Kohut's first book, of the self as *contents* of the mental apparatus, representations within the classically established mental instances of id, ego, and superego—to the (by contrast) described psychology of the self in the broader sense—the perspective of the second book, a psychology in whose theoretical framework the self occupies *the* central encompassing and supraordinate position, with the drives seen in their expression as *breakdown products,* emerging under fragmenting pressures stemming from improper and "disempathic" interactions, rather than as primary component manifestations of the malfunctioning psyche whose unconscious *meanings* are surfacing for exploration and elucidation. This is what Ornstein called (in Kohut, 1978; Ornstein, 1981) the "revolutionary" step to the third paradigm of psychoanalysis, that of self psychology as the successor to its two prior paradigms (both created by Freud) of first drive psychology and then ego psychology.

Here I would like to elaborate my position of difference beginning with my use of the word "paradigm" in the sense propounded and given its wide currency by Kuhn (1962). In that sense, psychoanalysis clearly has had and still has but one basic paradigm of how the mind works: the paradigm devised by Freud, which rests on the fundamental postulates (as underlined by Rapaport, 1967, see The Scientific Methodology of Psychoanalysis, p. 165–220, 1944) of psychic continuity and of unconscious psychic processes. I therefore explicitly do *not* use the word paradigm in the sense that I feel was trivialized by Eissler (1969) in his paper on the present and the future of psychoanalysis in which he practically equated each conceptual advance by Freud with the addition of yet another paradigm.

In my sense, I feel that we are not dealing with a new paradigm at all, but rather with a substantial addition to our clinical insights into psychoanalytic phenomena having to do with the play of narcissistic or selfobject transferences and their counterpart countertransferences. This most impressive clinical contribution can be incorporated into the main body of classical psychoanalysis without the need for either new or separate theory, whatever the ultimate usefulness of the particular theoretical accents devised by Kohut such as the concept of the bipolar self with the twin poles of normally self-assertive ambitions, and attained ideals and values connected by their tension arc of talents and skills. Indeed these may prove to be useful, *additional* conceptualizations to our classical conceptualizations of the mental apparatus.

I begin the thread of my main argument and my own counterposed perspectives by picking up what I feel are some surprisingly overlooked internal inconsistencies within the formulations by Kohut and others of the new psychology of the self, beginning with a statement by Ornstein (1980) from the 1978 Chicago Conference in which he emphasized Kohut's call that psychoanalysis should "expand its border and place the classical findings and explanations within the *supraordinate* framework of a psychology of the self [p. 145, italics added]." Ornstein went on to note: "He [Kohut] has put self psychology side by side with ego-psychology in a *complementary* relationship and demonstrated that the new paradigm of self psychology can *encompass* certain aspects of mental health and illness that could not be adequately accounted for within the previous paradigm [p. 157, italics added]."

The inconsistency that I see here is the simultaneous, vigorous thrust within self psychology into two incompatible directions. The first is the formulation of self psychology in the broader sense as the *supraordinate* and more *encompassing* framework that can enable us to do better in explanatory and therapeutic power by the narcissistic personality disorders upon the treatment of which its claims were first built. It then can presumably also enable us profitably to reconceptualize many if not most of our heretofore most central classical metapsychological formulations (e.g., the nature and the position of the Oedipus complex in human mental development). In addition, it even extends the claim, as an issue for open-minded empiric scrutiny, that the treatment of classical neurotic conflict as it evolves within the transference neurosis in classical psychoanalysis can also be enhanced in range and effectiveness when considered within the more encompassing self psychological framework. The other and incompatible thrust is that of *complementarity,* meaning separateness and dichotomization. Within this thrust Ornstein (1980) can ask: "Do these . . . observations, therefore, not suggest that integration of conflict psychology within the new paradigm of self-psychology is the logical next step in psychoanalysis? The answer to this question is a decisive no [p. 145]."

Rather than an integration, which should not be forced, Ornstein opts for "Leaving them unintegrated—and maintaining thereby the duality of 'Guilty Man' and 'Tragic Man' . . . [because] . . . the complementary [i.e., separate] use of conflict psychology and self psychology is closer to the available clinical data [p. 145]."

Here is where I feel that the theorists of self psychology have created an unnecessary inconsistency and a specious dilemma. Against the dichotomization that devolves from the framework of complementarity of psychologies, there is my position (Wallerstein, 1981) that, most simply put, states we are not dealing with an either/or situation but rather a both/and. Granted that Kohut's central clinical contribution may well lie in seeing so many aspects of the psychopathology of pregenital development not as regressive defenses against the emergence of oedipal transferences *alone,* but centrally also as re-creations of deficient and impoverished childhood constellations within mirroring and idealizing selfobject transferences. Granting this, it is the word *alone,* which is my inserted qualifying word, that is to me the crux of this particular issue. For in the flow and flux of analytic clinical material we are always in the world of both/and. We deal constantly and in turn with both the oedipal (where there is a coherent self) and the pre-oedipal (where there may not yet be), with defensive regressions and with developmental arrests, with defense transferences and defensive resistances and with re-creations of earlier traumatic and traumatized states, and so forth.

Of course, all this is not new. It is simply the application once again of the psychoanalytic principle of overdetermination and in Waelder's (1930) terms of multiple function. And this has been a central point made in several of the critiques of self psychology offered to this juncture. Segel (1981), for example, decried what he called Kohut's setting up the self as a "separate kingdom" as against what is rather "the constant interrelatedness developmentally of a sense of self-identity and of object constancy [p. 470]." Rather than two psychologies—a psychology of the self, where empathy prevails, and a psychology of drive and structure, where conflict prevails and where interpretation of transference and resistance is the vehicle—Segel stresses that these realms of self and of structure, of pre-oedipal and of oedipal, are continuous with one another and that psychic phenomena need to be looked at not in terms of one framework or the other, of defect in self or of conflict, of pre-oedipal or of oedipal, of developmental arrest or of defensive regression, but from both (and all) perspectives at the same time for what each contributes at the particular time. Including the now added self-psychological perspective just constitutes an enlargement to our familiar metapsychological way of thinking from multiple vantage points simultaneously. With clinical references Segel pointed out that, after all, narcissistic reactions may well represent regressive resistances to oedipal conflicts, especially in developmental histories where an overly stimulated child has been unbearably and painfully deflated by traumatic primal-scene experiences. Regressive attempts at solution of the thus engendered anxieties could well take the form of compensating grandiose, exhibitionistic wishes or intense, narcissistic rages. I would add that this view of multiple and shifting vantage points from which to direct the analyzing instrument, as the clinical material shiftingly surfaces and resonates with our empathic and introspective capacities, can allow the harmonious reconciliation of the many solid advances in our therapeutic work from within the new framework of self psychology with the established clinical wisdoms from within the framework of classical analytic psychology to indeed take place.

This discussion of separateness versus relatedness, of distinct psychologies—self psychology and classical psychoanalytic conflict psychology, each with its separate domain of transcendent explanatory power and therapeutic applicability—as against the effort to conceptualize the continuity of and the explanatory trafficking between the phenomena of both the earlier and the later childhood developmental phases leads directly to what I consider the heart of the challenge posed by self psychology to our heretofore classical psychoanalytic metapsychology. This has to do with the posited distinction between self psychology as a theory of psychological formation born not out of conflict but out of states of psychological deficiency as against classical psychoanalysis, which has always been prototypically a psychology of conflict.

In Ernst Kris' (1947) famous—and terse—aphoristic definition, the subject matter of psychoanalysis was defined as nothing but "human behavior viewed as conflict [p. 6]." Brenner (1979) gives a more current and more elaborated statement of the same basic and quintessentially psychoanalytic theme: "the goal of psychoanalysis is to alter conflict . . . both the normal and pathological arise from psychic conflicts that originate in the same childhood instinctual wishes. . . . [p. 562]." These words stress a broad consensus among most practicing psychoanalysts about the centrality of conflict as a (or as *the*) explanatory principle governing psychopathology and its psychoanalytic treatment.

By contrast, Ornstein in a personal communication properly pointed to why *The Restoration* is more revolutionary or more explicitly revolutionary than *The Analysis of the Self:*

> This is because *The Restoration* introduces the new paradigm of the bipolar self that is *not* born out of conflict. Psychoanalysis has been a conflict psychology par excellence, as derived from the neuroses and neurotic character disorders. That has not changed. We will have to maintain it, side by side, with a self psychology, born out of our new understanding of primary self-pathology, based not on conflict but on psychological defect or deficiency. The empirical question then is whether concepts and theories of self-pathology, first and foremost among them the concept of selfobject and the selfobject transferences, offer us a better therapeutic handle for the treatment of nonneurotic conditions or not.

I have summarized this juxtaposition of psychological perspective (Wallerstein, 1981) as follows:

> Kohut and his followers propound as their major clinical insight that in contradistinction to the neurotic problems that stem from the intrapsychic conflicts of the developmentally more structured personalities, where attention to the opposition of drive and defense, i.e. to *conflict,* and to the attendant regressive neurotic transference is the key to resolution and cure, with the narcissistic problems of those with unintegrated selves vulnerable to fragmenting pressures under stress, it is attention to the unfolding of selfobject transferences that stem from more archaic (more undifferentiated) experiences of failure of parental empathy, i.e. experiences of emotional *deficit,* that becomes the central key to analytic amelioration—and *restoration* (p. 382–383).

Which brings me to the very crux of my argument, the usefulness of this distinction between deficit and conflict which I regard as the very centerpiece of the claim of self psychology to be a different psychology, alongside of, complementary to, but not (or not yet anyway) to be integrated with so-called "classical" psychoanalytic metapsychology (which is avowedly centered on conflict)—albeit the self psychologist theorists do also confusingly at the same time claim the one framework to be supraordinate to the other and able to encompass and subsume it as I have already discussed.

Here I take my point of departure in the formulations advanced by Sandler in recent statements of a modern and broadened psychoanalytic conceptualization of conflict (1974, 1976). Basically his thesis (Sandler, 1974) is that what is essential to conflict is what can be called the "unconscious peremptory urge [p. 53]." Such urges are not to be confined to or equated with the id, the instincts, the drives, nor to conflict just with superego standards or the sense of reality. There is such intersystemic conflict (between established and consolidated psychic instances), but there is also intrasystemic conflict as between different instinctual tendencies (heterosexuality and homosexuality, activity and passivity, love and hate, etc.) or between conflicted ego impulses. More broadly, Sandler goes back to the logical development of Freud's (1894/1962) original statement of the individual's need to defend against any incompatible idea. For example, he (Sandler, 1974) brings within this orbit our now familiar ideas about "defenses against defenses [p. 60]" and "conflict over previous solutions to conflict [p. 57]." In fact, he includes as conflict any opposition between any kind of peremptory urge and any impulse to delay, involving any aspect of psychic functioning in any form. He specifically rejects "the equation of the idea of 'peremptoriness' with drive impulses in one form or another in the structural theory . . . [as but] a legacy of earlier phases of psychoanalysis" in favor of the statement that: "Peremptory impulses are not always the manifestations of instinctual wishes alone, but may arise as a consequence of stimuli from any part of the mental apparatus or from the outside world [p. 60]." In his 1976 paper Sandler summed up simply that "we can regard all conflict as being a conflict of *wishes of one sort or another* [p. 61, italics added]."

Given such conceptualization of the nature of conflict, how can we view the self-stated revolutionary claim of self psychology that it is a psychology and yields a therapy that is born not of conflict but rather of deficit. In my presentation in New York (Wallerstein 1981), it was the effort at just this distinction that I called "puzzling and to me fundamentally unhelpful [pp. 388–389]." Let me elaborate what I mean from the writings of self psychological theory, starting with the excellent summary paper by Kohut and Wolf (1978). The authors state there that the firm and consolidated self develops, out of optimal interplay with the selfobjects, into three major constituents: "(1) one pole from which emanate the basic strivings for power and success; (2) another pole that harbors the basic idealized goals; and (3) an intermediate area of basic talents and skills that are activated by the tension-arc that establishes itself between ambitions and ideals. Faulty interaction between the child and his selfobjects result in a damaged self—either a diffusely damaged self or a self that is seriously damaged in one or the other of its constituents [p. 414]." Here I would begin by underlining that "tension-arc" and "faulty interaction" to me do connote, in some fashion, the concept of something out of kilter (i.e. conflicted).

But let me follow further the argument of Kohut and Wolf as they address the (normal) developmental process: "The self arises thus as a result of the interplay between the new-born's innate equipment and the selective responses of the selfobjects through which certain potentialities are *encouraged* in their development while others remain *unencouraged* or are even actively *discouraged* [pp. 416–417, italics added]." And in this context the authors speak constantly of optimal (i.e., minor and nontraumatic) failures in maternal empathic response, that is, frustration, and side by side, of optimal gratification. And it is "Such optimal frustrations of the child's need to be mirrored and to merge into an idealized selfobject, hand in hand with optimal gratifications, [that] generate the appropriate growth-facilitating matrix for the self [p. 417]." Again, one can wonder how all this is essentially different from the parental response to the play of impulse, of affect and drive (both libidinal and aggressive), in terms of allowing and thwarting, of setting the parameters and the requirements for accommodation or amelioration. Or put differently, isn't this what conflict is all about and what makes the one, then, a psychology to be understood in terms of conflict and the other not?

And now, in even more explicit support of this main point that I am making vis-à-vis self psychology from the position of the paradigm of classical psychoanalysis as a conflict psychology, I want to quote Ornstein (1980): "The point is that our usual interpretive focus on the compromise formations made necessary by the unresolved conflicts now has to be extended to a consideration of how such conflicts hamper the expression of ambitions, talents and values as conceptualized from the standpoint of the bipolar self [p. 151]." In the very final sentence concluding the paper Ornstein writes: "With the introduction of the bipolar self as a supraordinate constellation and especially with the differentiation of *primary, defensive,* and *compensatory* structures within it . . . [pp. 157–158]." Here again, should one not see this as a statement of conflict, and conflict compromise and resolution, within the "structure" of the self, just as ambitions, values and ideals, and a tension arc between of skills and talents can also be read as a structured delineation within which conflict is necessarily of the essence?

I hope that I have by now in the discussion of this fundamental issue of conflict versus deficit sufficiently elaborated two main points. The first is the counterposing of a broadened construction of what is meant by the concept of conflict in psychoanalysis as against an overly narrow reading of the concept by the self psychologists, which I think set the stage for the unfortunate division between the notions of conflict and deficit. A corollary to this is the obligation to conceptualize the terms of the conflict at each developmental level within the array of disparate or opposed needs and fulfillments that are crystallized and expressed at that developmental stage. The second point is that conceptualizing conflict in this way renders unnecessary the dichotomization and the opposition (with all that flows from it) of the realms of deficit as against the realms of conflict.

In fuller statement of my position (Wallerstein, 1981) on this centrally important issue I wrote:

> I rather see the life course as one of the successive facing and the adequate resolution—or not—of a sequence of phase-specific developmental tasks, in each phase and in each instance, a task created by the unique conjunction of the innate maturational unfolding of capacities and readinesses, together with the phase-linked normative societal expectations within that culture at that historic moment, and added to by the happenstance and timing of more or less traumatic and adventitious life experience. Seen this way the task (or *a* main task) of the earliest developmental phase in accord with the tenets of self-psychology is the development of a coherent and consolidated self-organization as an ultimately emerging "independent center of initiative" (Kohut's words) and the task in the later psychoanalytic treatment of disorders of the self that come out of the failures of this stage is that of completing an arrested or derailed development of such an integrated self, consolidating its cohesiveness and/or restoring its vitality. *Pari passu,* the task (or also *a* main task) of the oedipal developmental phase is the appropriate and ego-syntonic mastery of the inevitable vicissitudes of triangular and all

multilateral human relationships within the context of the innate human propensities for ambivalence. And of course the task in the later psychoanalytic treatment of the structured neurotic disorders that come out of the failures of this oedipal stage is that of the resolution of the attendant intrapsychic conflicts that represent the structural embedding within the psychic agencies of the earlier pathological oedipal resolutions.

At both levels, that of the earlier arena of primary development of the self and that of the later structuring of the personality under the impact of the emergence and resolution of the Oedipus complex, severe anxieties and other attendant dysphorias can arise that must be coped with to the best of the ability of the immature ego, or self, of that stage, given the resources, defenses and coping mechanisms available to it within, as well as the empathic support and material and psychological nutriments available to it without. This coping will then have a more or less healthy *vis-à-vis* a more or less pathological outcome in specific character formation or deformation. I do not therefore really see how it is therefore any more or any less a matter of developmental task or dilemma, of attendant anxiety and of its management, in short of psychic conflict, and its more or less healthy or pathological resolution, in either case (p. 389–390).

At this point I want to turn to the related and equally vital issue of the unnecessary confusion introduced by the overly narrow usages within the self psychology literature of the concept of conflict. There is a concomitant, serious confounding of the distinction between conflict and pathology—conflict, which is the universal fundament of the human condition, and pathology, which is its centrally untoward outcome. Kohut (1977) and his followers may be correct in their assertion that the *pathology* of the oedipal phase, which eventuates in the various disorders known to us from classical psychopathology, may not be as basic and as ubiquitous in human psychic functioning as many of us may have thought and may, to a considerable and perhaps heretofore somewhat unappreciated extent, be a consequence of or rest upon the kinds of earlier developmental failures to which they have so convincingly drawn our attention.

But to see the extrapolations to which this viewpoint has been drawn, let me turn to Ornstein's paper (1980) where he talks of the contribution of self psychology toward a "decisive shift of emphasis away from a preoccupation with the pathological and toward a focus on the potentially healthy or more adaptive aspects of the personality [p. 137]" and of Kohut's intent from the first to correct a widespread "negatively toned evaluation" of narcissism, to focus from the start on the contributions of narcissism to "health, adaptation and achievement [p. 138]." Ornstein (1980) speaks of the functional freedom of the healthily developed or the rehabilitated self "in which ambitions, skills and ideals form an unbroken continuum that permits joyful creative activity [p. 144]." All this is then extended to what is called a "reassessment of the form and content of the Oedipus complex [p. 147]," the evolution in normal development of a joyful Oedipus complex as a maturational achievement marked by "the essentially healthy and adaptive aspects of the oedipal period [p. 147]."

However, and here Ornstein further extends the ground to where the confounding of conflict and pathology becomes clear, he goes on to say that in classical theory "the positive qualities acquired by the psychic apparatus during the oedipal period were seen as the *result* of the oedipal experience and not as a *primary intrinsic aspect of the experience itself.* (Kohut, 1977, p.229). The contrast between the two theories is evident [p. 147]." That is, classical theory "could only conceive of health and the capacity for adaptation emerging out of pathology, i.e., out of the resolution of infantile oedipal conflicts. In self psychology, conversely, the potential for health and adaptation is seen as present *a priori* in any given empathic self-selfobject relationship [p. 148]." Here the straw man argument has been made explicit. It is infantile conflict and not infantile neurosis or pathology that classical theory calls universal and ubiquitous. And health clearly grows out of effective mastery of conflict; it does not arise of necessity out of the bedrock of pathology and neurosis, the perspective given to classical theory in these writings of self psychology, an imputed error from which self psychology then feels that it rescues psychoanalysis.

Ornstein (1980) goes on to say finally: "In this connection it should be stressed that it is quite likely that the customary view of the infantile Oedipus complex as highly conflict-laden and ubiquitously pathological [again, cf. the automatic equation of conflict-laden with pathological] is an artifact of erroneous reconstructions from the transference neurosis [p. 149]." At this extreme we do indeed have a recasting of our classical formulations of the ubiquitous Oedipus complex as the universal psychological nodal point of the human developmental drama into the happenstance of traumatic and particular psychopathological outcomes and/or the "artifacts" created out of "erroneous reconstructions," again from the pathological outcomes of the adult neurotics in our consulting rooms.

At this point Freud's fundamental insight into the basic nature and the ubiquity of oedipal *conflict* as an inevitable central part and parcel of the vicissitudes of normal human development has been unacceptably shaded. By this I mean the central teaching of psychoanalysis that central to healthy development is the appropriate mastery within the oedipal phase, and to be recurringly reworked over all the successive phases of the life cycle, the mastery of all the inevitable conflicts in human triangular relationships within the context of the innate human propensities for ambivalence. The fact that such oedipal *conflict* (not necessarily pathological outcome) retains its central role as basic and ubiquitous in proper psychic development—even if the particular outcome be, in Kohut's words, joyful and creative—is exactly what I feel gets lost in recent writings in self psychology.

As a logical corollary to this effort at major reconceptualization by self psychology of the oedipal drama as not necessarily conflicted and therefore not necessarily problematic or "traumatic" as a developmental task, there is a curious concomitant deemphasis altogether on the role of "gross events" or traumas in psychic development. This was first noted by Segel (1981):

> It is also difficult for me to believe with Kohut (1977, p. 187) that 'psychoanalysis will move away from its preoccupation with the gross events in the child's early life' towards the preeminence 'of the child's needs to be mirrored and to find a target for his idealization'. The difficulty stems from the inclusion as 'gross events' of such things [all taken from the same page in Kohut's text] as births, illnesses, and deaths of siblings, the illnesses and deaths of parents, the breakups of families, the child's prolonged separations from significant adults, his severe and prolonged illnesses, observations of parental intercourse or sexual overstimulation [p. 470].

Kohut and Wolf (1978) make this same point central:

> Psychoanalytic case histories tend to emphasize certain dramatic events—from the child's witnessing the "primal scene" to the loss of a parent in childhood. But we have come to the opinion that such traumatic events may be no more than clues that point to the truly pathogenic

factors, the unwholesome atmosphere to which the child was exposed during the years when his self was established. Taken by themselves, in other words, these events leave fewer serious disturbances in their wake than the chronic ambience created by the deep-rooted attitudes of the selfobjects, since even the still vulnerable self, in the process of formation, can cope with serious traumata if it is embedded in a healthily supportive milieu [p. 417].

What is troubling in all of this is the one-sidedness, the not so subtle devaluation of the conceptual importance of the kinds of life circumstance that we have on the basis of cumulative clinical experience come to consider developmental organizing foci, and again the either/or quality, the counterposing of "grossly traumatic events" against "unwholesome atmosphere" and "chronic ambience."

And yet, curiously, Kohut and self psychology can be paradoxically charged with a simultaneous overvaluation of the external event (external trauma?) for the healthy unfolding of the self in their insistent deep and one-sided emphasis on the role of maternal empathy (which is what they basically mean by ambience and milieu) in the proper fulfillment of the developmental potential. There are many aspects to the issues of the role of empathy. Certainly, all agree on the powerful corrective emphasis that Kohut has given to *empathy* and *introspection* as central vehicles of the psychoanalytic endeavor, initiated by his most important 1959 essay on that subject that Ornstein properly declares to be "the first nodal point" (Kohut, 1978, p.27) in the evolution of self psychology theory. And of course the emphasis on the role of empathy and introspection in the psychoanalytic undertaking is the counterpart of the emphasis on the role of parental empathy in the promotion of a healthy development and consolidation of a cohesive self.

However, Kohut's emphasis on empathy (and introspection) as vital components of the psychoanalytic process is neither that new nor that unique to self psychology theory. Certainly, there was arising at the same time a number of converging strands of psychoanalytic emphasis on the closely related issue of the nature and quality of the psychoanalytic relationship as a major factor in the mutative process in analysis. These ranged from Alexander's (1946) strong but misguided emphasis on the importance of the "corrective emotional experience," to Zetzel's (1956) elaboration of the concept "therapeutic alliance," and Greenson's (1967) elaboration of the closely related concept "working alliance," as elements vital to the matrix within which a successful psychoanalytic resolution becomes possible, through to Loewald's (1960) most influential article "On the Therapeutic Action of Psychoanalysis" with its conceptualization of the empathically crafted "integrative experience" as a condition of, or explanation of, change in psychoanalysis, of at least equal import as the process of interpretation leading to insight.

True, many within analysis feel that Kohut has gone overboard in this emphasis with a concomitant unnecessary downgrading of the (at least equally vital) role of interpretation and insight, and this has been central to the criticisms of Kernberg (1979) and others. Kernberg (1979) wrote:

> The misinterpretation and overgeneralization of these findings imply that, for patients in regression, it is the therapist's empathic presence—rather than his interpretation—that is really helpful; that it is the patient's identification with this mothering function—rather than his coming to terms with his intrapsychic conflicts—that is important. . . . An empathic and concerned attitude on the part of the analyst is a necessary precondition in all cases of psychoanalysis. . . . Empathy is a prerequisite for interpretive work, not its replacement [p. 231–232].

But overemphasis on one's own perspective is not a major fault, and time will no doubt correct this as it has corrected so many other fashions and accents within our field. Of greater concern to me in this highlighting of the dominating role of empathy and introspection to the analytic endeavor is a variety of other considerations that I now present in some order of ascending significance. First, empathically derived knowledge can be quite wrong, for as Jacobson (1978) stated in his discussion of Segel's paper: "while empathic use of our inner selves in psychological therapy has on this score highest value, opening us to the possession of incredibly intimate knowledge of the workings of the mind of another person, it harbors at the same time the potential of opening us to the most grievous errors; errors where while we think we are grasping a fundamental aspect of the patient, we may in fact be grasping a fundamental aspect of ourselves, of some object from our own history, or of a cherished belief [p. 7]"—that is, all the well-known risks of wild analysis.

A second, even greater, danger in the self psychology elevation of empathy and empathic failure as guiding explanatory concepts in understanding the possibilities for change in analysis rests in the implications for technique and for the understanding of the theory of technique in analytic work. This is the serious issue raised by Segel (1981) of a not so subtle shifting of the responsibility (and the blame) for therapeutic difficulty unfairly (i.e., one-sidedly) onto the interfering countertransferences of the analyst. At least that *can* be the consequence of analytic progression being held to be dependent on as near perfect as possible analytic empathy and analytic setback held to be characteristically reflective of analytic empathic failure. According to Segel (1981): "We might even be tempted to raise the question of whether the pendulum may now have reversed itself partially so that instead of punishing our patients, some self-flagellation is even subtly evident. I am referring to the widespread use of terms like 'empathic failure' of the therapist even where the demands of the patient, verbal and non-verbal, seem impossibly excessive, even when directed towards experienced therapists [p. 469]." In summarizing this point, Segel quotes Kohut as stating that our unavoidable failures of empathy should not produce *undue* guilt in us. Segel (1981) finds this terminology pejorative and unfairly critical: "It is striking to me that while removing the demeaning label from the narcissistic patient, Kohut seems to have shifted it on to the parents and the therapists [p. 469]."

As the third concern that I want to raise as a consequence of the particular kind of overemphasized position of empathy in Kohut's work, I wish to shift from the implications for analytic technique to the wider implications for analytic theory, and to shift the ground of concern from the conceptualization of the role of (analytic) empathy in psychoanalysis to the role of (maternal) empathy in psychic development. Earlier I referred to this as the curiously paradoxical overvaluation of the external event for the healthy development of the self. This issue was central to Stein's (1979) critical review of Kohut's second book: "The impact of Kohut's work is, paradoxically, far more literally deterministic than that of Freud, since it tends to ascribe an extremely complex set of disturbances and developments to what is essentially a single etiological factor: defects of maternal empathy [p. 673]." The point is a vital one. It is the danger of theoretical reductionistic oversimplification that psychological explanation can all too readily be prone to, and that it is part of the overdetermined complexity of psychoanalytic explanation to guard against.

However, now I would like to turn to statements from the proponents of self psychology itself to illuminate what I feel is the most fundamental issue for our conception of what psychoanalysis is all about, raised by self psychology theorists around the conceptualization of empathy and its role in analysis. This is essentially a matter of the redefinition of analysis or at least of its determining parameters, which self psychology arrives at. Freud's well-known and simple statement that whatever deals with the phenomena of transference and resistance can properly call itself psychoanalysis, though requiring considerable amplification and qualification, has nonetheless stood the test of analytic usage over time well. It is this fundamental conceptualization about the essence of psychoanalysis that Kohut's evolving views on the role of empathy in psychoanalysis have asked us to reconsider. Kohut (1977) asks the question: "What Is the Essence of Psychoanalysis?" [p. 298–312], and his answer is consistently and single-mindedly: "the essence of psychoanalysis . . . [is] the fact that its subject matter is that aspect of the world that is *defined* by the *introspective stance* of the observer [p. 303, italics added]." Furthermore: "Empathy is not a tool in the sense in which the patient's reclining position, the use of free associations, the employment of the structural model, or of the concepts of drive and defense are tools. Empathy does indeed in essence *define* the field of our observations [p. 306, italics added]."

That this redefinition *can* indeed lead ultimately to the discarding of Freud's definition of the essence of psychoanalysis is a potentiality that Kohut does make explicit: "I am not able to imagine how analysis could *at this time* do away with the two concepts—transference and resistance . . . I would still insist that some future generation of psychoanalysts might discover psychological areas that require a novel conceptual approach—areas where even in the therapeutic realm these two now universally applicable concepts have become irrelevant [p. 308]." The truly idiosyncratic, as well as radical, nature of this definitional transformation of psychoanalysis has been made most explicit in Schwaber's (1979) article, in which she redefines empathy itself in specifically self-psychological terms: "The object's inability, for whatever reason, to serve as the needed self-object supplying the missing structure or function, is experienced as a 'failure' in empathy. Empathy is here implicitly understood as the provision of a *self-object use* [p. 469, italics added]." And then even more explicitly: "It is such a perspective that is considered to be the intrinsic aspect of what is meant by empathy. Empathy is herein viewed as an introspective awareness arising within the context of a *self-object phenomenon* [p. 477, italics added]."

By this point, both psychoanalysis and empathy have been redefined and equated and made into self psychology theory. Thus, it is perhaps fair to say that not just empathic failure as an explanation for difficulties in technique in work with narcissistic (and other) patients, but much more comprehensively, *empathy* as a central explanatory key to the understanding of the essence of our subject matter is as much a fundamental building block at the core of the development of self psychology as a theory as is the more widely focused upon and appreciated concern with the phenomena of narcissism. It is these conceptualizations of empathy and narcissism that have coalesced and expanded into the new psychoanalytic psychology of the self. In the process psychoanalysis has potentially been seriously altered.

It is the positioning of empathy in self psychology, as a central explanatory construct as well as a central technical tool, that also raises a number of related questions about the therapeutic results achieved that can be considered under a variety of headings of therapist style and/or personality and/or experience. These questions have arisen most pointedly around discussion of the fullest case description ("The Two Analysis of Mr. Z", 1979) in which Kohut has laid out two periods of his analytic work with the same patient, each period about 4 years in length with an intervening 5 years without treatment. The first analysis was conducted by Kohut in terms of his understanding of classical theory and technique. The result achieved seemed satisfactory enough at the time to both Kohut and his analysand. The patient returned after some 5 years with familiar symptoms reawakened by new life pressures. The second comparably long period of analysis was in terms of the newly evolved understandings of self psychology. The case report is a side by side discussion of the analytic issues in the first analysis, the kinds of understandings reached about them, the limitations that Kohut subsequently discerned in those resolutions, and the new understandings of the very same issues that were arrived at in the second analysis with the sense of a far more substantial and enduring analytic result. Needless to say, the patient suffered from severe narcissistic problems.

How is the more thorough analytic cure that was finally achieved to be understood? To Kohut, this is clearly an issue of the more appropriate theoretical perspectives of self psychology, with their derived technical implementation, to the dominant narcissistic problems of the patient. In my own review of this case material (Wallerstein, 1981), I compared in some detail the description of six critical configurations, contrasting Kohut's earlier understanding and interpretive endeavor with his later endeavor. His format (Kohut, 1979) was in all cases the same: "In the first analysis, I saw it thusly (basically, as defensive against oedipal pathology) . . . but in the second analysis, I came to see it thusly (basically, as analytically valuable reenactment of childhood constellations revived in the selfobject transference)." My own main point was that Kohut put all this in terms of either/or—and, by implication, correct/incorrect. On the other hand, to me it was a matter of both/and, the application once again of the principles of overdetermination and multiple function. I felt that *each* of the explanatory perspectives adduced by Kohut in relation to each of the various aspects of the analytic material (as well as probably still other perspectives not mentioned) could play its appropriate role in the overall understanding of the total psychological picture and therefore have its place as part of the total analytic work. Where, at what point, with what emphasis, and how, would then become matters of tact and timing as well as clinical judgment, matters, that is, of the appropriate employment of the tools of empathy and introspection that Kohut has been at the forefront in making self-consciously central to our clinical (and also theoretical) undertaking.

It is considerations such as these that have led different observers to wonder how much the more substantial and more enduring result that eventuated from the second analysis of Mr. Z was indeed a matter of new and better theory, and how much a matter of better empathy, guided perhaps by the enlarged perspectives for understanding that derived from the conceptual additions of the psychology of the self. Some have seen in this issues of style and personality. Was Kohut's style more heavily authoritative in the first analysis, more benignly empathic in the second?

The overall point is to raise as legitimate the question: How much of what Kohut takes issue with clinically in the work of others (or, as in the case of Mr. Z, in his own work at an earlier time) is truly an issue of differing conceptualization and how much a quarrel with faulty (i.e., unempathic) technique? Let me quote at two points from the paper by Kohut and Wolf (1978): "If the analyst responds to these [narcissistic] demands by *exhortations* concerning realism and emotional maturity, or, worse still, if he *blamefully interpets* them as the expression of their insatiable oral drive that needs to be tamed or of a primary destructiveness that needs to be neutralized and bound by aggression-curbing psychic structures, then the development of the narcissistic transference will be blocked [p. 423, italics added]." This is then contrasted with: "If, however, the therapist can *explain without censure* the protective function of the grandiose fantasies and thus demonstrate that he is in tune with the patient's disintegration anxiety and shame concerning his precariously established self, then he will not interfere with the spontaneously arising transference mobilization of the old narcissistic needs [p. 424, italics added]."

Clearly, many will see this not as an opposition between interpretation, declared to be misplaced or inappropriate, as contrasted with (more properly) empathic acceptance of unfolding transference positions, but rather as an opposition between bad technique, exhortation and blameful interpretation—and appropriate technique, explanation without censure. And again, one could ask: Why is a dichotomy being set up between "blamefully interpreting" the libidinal and aggressive drives (clearly not okay) and "explaining without censure" the narcissistic needs (clearly okay)? Can we not rather agree that Kohut is placing here an appropriate emphasis on the proper empathic posture in relation to all drives and all needs, an emphasis that we all do share, albeit he has indeed made us more mindful of it? In this same sense, then, perhaps the advocates of self psychology can in turn agree with the unifying view of both/and, of overdetermination and multiple functioning, that I have been offering from within the perspective of the classical analytic position, which in Rangell's words (1981) on the same issue from within the same perspective: "'The Two Analyses of Mr. Z.' reported by Kohut should have comprised one total classical analysis [p. 133]."

It is this emphasis on "one total classical analysis" that brings me back to the statement of my own central theme in this effort at review and overview of the contribution of self psychology to the theory and technique of psychoanalysis. It is that of the wholeness of psychoanalysis within its one (Freudian) paradigm, dealing with its phenomena—complex mental states—in overdetermined perspective, from multiple (metapsychological) points of view, according to the unifying language and thought conventions of both/and, rather than the splitting and dichotomizing thrusts of either/or.

And in this context I can, in summary, state my own view of the nature of Kohut's contribution to our science and its fit within the total psychoanalytic corpus. It is I feel at the point stated at the beginning of this review, in the *clinical* realm of the much more precise than heretofore specification and delineation of the narcissistic phenomena as discerned in the specific narcissistic (or self-object) mirroring and idealizing transferences emergent in the psychoanalytic process, as well as their counterpart, the specific countertransferences that are characteristically evoked by them. Kohut (1977) has also stated this very major contribution typically in terms such as: "it is possible, from the viewpoint of the psychology of the self in the narrower sense—i.e., from the standpoint of a theory that considers the self as a content of the mental apparatus—to enrich the classical theory by adding a self psychological dimension [p. 227]." It is indeed just this most salutory impact on our field of this new focus on the self, on the psychology and the pathology of the self as revealed in the selfobject transferences and countertransferences of the psychoanalytic situation, the impact of the focus on all of this as a central dimension of our understanding of mental functioning, that I do want very much to acknowledge.

By the same token, I have yet to be convinced that such enrichment in the clinical realm requires a new theory, a new metapsychology, all the ramifications of the psychology of the self in the broader sense, the theoretical reifications in the conceptions of the bipolar self and the special and separate new psychology of Tragic Man. It is the controversy that I feel has been generated in this metapsychological theoretical realm that has tended to obscure somewhat our-fullest appreciation of so major a set of additions to our clinical wisdom and our clinical capacities as has been offered to us by Heinz Kohut, his collaborators, and their appropriate integration within the ever growing mainstream of classical psychoanalysis.

REFERENCES

Alexander, F. & French, T. M. (1946). *Psychoanalytic Therapy: Principles and Applications.* New York: Ronald Press.

Brenner, C. (1979). The components of psychic conflict and its consequences in mental life. *Psychoanal. Q.* 48: 547–567.

Eissler, K. R. (1969). Irreverent remarks about the present and the future of psychoanalysis. *Int. J. Psychoanal.* 50: 461–471.

Freud, A. (1965). *Normality and Pathology in Childhood: Assessments of Develop-ment*. New York: Int. Univ. Press.

Freud, S. (1894). The neuro-psychoses of defense. *S.E.* 3: 41–68, 1962.

Greenson, R. R. (1967). *The Technique and Practice of Psychoanalysis* (Vol. 1.) New York: Int. Univ. Press.

Jacobson, J. G. (1978). Discussion of Nathan Segel's paper: Narcissism and adapta-tion to indignity. *Newsletter, the Denver Psychoanalytic Society* 5: 5–8, Fall.

Kernberg, O. F. (1974). Further contributions to the treatment of narcissistic person-alities. *Int. J. Psychoanal.* 55: 215–240.

———— (1979). Some implications of object relations theory for psychoanalytic tech-nique. *J. Amer. Psychoanal. Assoc.* Supp. Vol 27: 207–239.

———— (1978). *Contemporary Psychoanalytic Theories of Narcissism*. Symposium at Columbia Univ. Coll. of Phys. and Surg., Dept. of Psychiatry and Center for Psychoanalytic Training and Research, New York.

Kohut, H. (1959). Introspection, empathy, and psychoanalysis: An examination of the relationship between mode of observation and theory. *J. Amer. Psychoanal. Assoc.* 7: 459–483.

———— (1971). *The Analysis of the Self: A Systematic Approach to the Psychoanalytic Treatment of Narcissistic Personality Disorders*. New York: Int. Univ. Press.

———— (1977). *The Restoration of the Self*. New York: Int. Univ. Press.

———— (1978). *The Search for the Self: Selected Writings of Heinz Kohut: 1950–1978*, P. H. Ornstein, ed. New York: Int. Univ. Press.

———— (1979). The Two Analyses of Mr. Z. *Int. J. Psychoanal.*, 60: 3–27.

———— (1980). Reflections on advances in self psychology. In *Advances in Self Psy-chology*, A. Goldberg, ed. New York: Int. Univ. Press, pp. 473–554.

———— & Wolf, E. S. (1978). The disorders of the self and their treatment: An out-line. *Int. J. Psychoanal.* 59: 413–424.

Kris, E. (1947). The nature of psychoanalytic propositions and their validation. In *The Selected Papers of Ernst Kris*. New Haven, Conn.: Yale Univ. Press, 1975, pp. 3–23.

Kuhn, T. S. (1962). *The Structure of Scientific Revolutions*. Chicago: Univ. of Chicago Press.

Loewald, H. (1960). On the therapeutic action of psychoanalysis. *Int. J. Psychoanal.* 41: 16–33.

Mahler, M. S., Pine, F. & Bergman, A. (1975). *The Psychological Birth of the Human Infant: Symbiosis and Individuation*. New York: Basic Books.

Ornstein, P. H. (1980). Self-psychology and the concept of health. In *Advances in Self Psychology*, A. Goldberg, ed. New York: Int. Univ. Press, pp. 137–159.

———— (1981). The bipolar self in the psychoanalytic treatment process: Clinical-theoretical considerations. *J. Amer. Psychoanal. Assoc.* 29: 353–375.

Rangell, L. (1981). From insight to change. *J. Amer. Psychoanal. Assoc.* 29: 119–141.

Rapaport, D. (1967). *The Collected Papers of David Rapaport*, M. M. Gill, ed. New York: Basic Books.

Sandler, J. (1974). Psychological conflict and the structural model: Some clinical and theoretical implications. *Int. J. Psychoanal.* 55: 53–62.

———— (1976). Actualization and object relationships. *J. Phila. Assoc. for Psycho-anal.* 3: 59–70.

Schwaber, E. (1979). On the "self" within the matrix of analytic theory—Some clini-cal reflections and reconsiderations. *Int. J. Psychoanal.* 60: 467–479.

Segel, N. P. (1981). Narcissism and adaptation to indignity. *Int. J. Psychoanal.* 62: 465–476.

Stein, M. H. (1979). Book Review: The Restoration of the Self. *J. Amer. Psychoanal. Assoc.* 27: 665–680.

Waelder, R. (1930). The principle of multiple function: Observations on overdetermination. *Psychoanal. Q.* 5: 45–62.

Wallerstein, R. S. (1981). The bi-polar self: Discussion of alternative perspectives. *J. Amer. Psychoanal. Assoc.* 29: 377–394.

Zetzel, E. R. (1956). Current concepts of transference. *Int. J. Psychoanal.* 37: 369–376.

27

Discussion of Papers by Drs. Goldberg, Stolorow, and Wallerstein

Paul H. Ornstein, M.D.

The three presentations that I discuss in this paper are wide ranging and thought provoking. Drs. Goldberg and Stolorow offer some specific ideas on how to expand further the domain of self psychology and how to improve its conceptual language and its experience-near theories. Dr. Wallerstein offers his views—directly and forcefully stated—on where the central clinical contributions of self psychology fit into classical psychoanalysis, in what way these have significantly expanded the field, and where self psychology had gone too far in its theoretical claims. Each of these three major papers deserve a lengthy, separate, and detailed appreciation and critique. But because I agree with the main thrust of Goldberg's and Stolorow's ideas, I only comment briefly on their contributions and then turn my attention to some selected core issues raised by Wallerstein.

Both Goldberg and Stolorow suggest ways to bring self psychology into line with other contemporary efforts at leaving the remnants of earlier, positivistic, mechanistic-spatial, and anthropomorphic language behind (although Stolorow, in his own language, does not go as far as Goldberg does in this direction). However, neither of them asks us to clean up our language merely to conform to present-day philosophic-epistemologic trends, which is the lesser of their concerns, but in order to encompass more adequately certain clinical observations that might otherwise either remain unnoticed or, even if recognized, would not be sufficiently understood and explained.

It is the areas of further study to which Goldberg and Stolorow are able to point—each from his own particular vantage point—that I consider to be their most significant merit. Interestingly enough, some of these areas turn out to be identical or overlapping in the two contributions, such as the processes of transmuting internalization with a detailed developmental study of the structuralization of the self, the nature of the analyst-patient relationship as it affects the observational data, and so forth. Indirectly, and certainly not by design, both contributions also answer many of Dr. Wallerstein's challenging questions and simultaneously, again indirectly, challenge many of his assertions. In this paper I can only point to some of these.

Arnold Goldberg proposes to reexamine, from a clear and compelling epistemologic position, what is "self" and what is "other." In this effort he finds the spatial concept of boundary—some artificial demarcation that is imagined to exist in physical or mental space; a line of demarcation between internal and external, between self and other—a hindrance to the analyst's attempts to capture the essence of varied self-experiences. According to Goldberg once the idea of boundary and the metaphors of external and internal are abandoned, it is clear that the key concept of "internalization"—the mode of acquisition of psychic structures—needs recasting. Goldberg maintains that self psychology aids in this process of reformulating the notion of internalization, and he demonstrates that once this is undertaken a number of other related concepts such as "structure" and "structuralization" also have to be revised (see also Stolorow's ideas in this same direction).

Goldberg aptly chooses a central clinical-theoretical problem to illustrate the necessity for new theoretical models. He calls attention to Kohut's recent finding that our need for selfobjects is enduring—that we live in a matrix of maturing self-selfobject relations from birth to death—"that people maintain lasting selfobject relationships throughout life as part and parcel of normal growth and development." He then cogently points to the fact that such a view cannot even be conceived ". . . with our present concepts of internalization, which posit that continuing growth and structuralization lead to adult positions of independence and autonomy (Mahler)."

In an attempt to deal with these mutually contradictory ideas—lifelong need for selfobjects (from archaic to mature) versus independence and autonomy as the expected end points of normal development in the adult—Goldberg opens the door for a creative leap (very much in line with the tradition Kohut established) when he says: "Let us, for the moment, resist the temptation to tamper with and modify our classical theory further and test whether alternative theoretical models might help to extend our vision of clinical material and thus ultimately lead to major restructuring of psychoanalytic theory."

We have, of course, tampered with and modified classical theory all along, in *piecemeal* fashion—sometimes in relation to one or another isolated or even broader clinical issue, which demanded new conceptualization, but other times in relation to some dissatisfaction with this or that aspect of the theory itself, stimulated by other than clinical problems. Regarding the piecemeal modifications in relation to clinical issues the limiting circumstance has been the need to retain the overall conceptual framework—the basic paradigm—at all cost. Regarding the piecemeal modifications in relation to purely theoretical issues the stimulus either came from the gradual loss of the heuristic value of an aspect of the theory or from newer findings in related or neighboring fields that seemed to require corrections in some of the theoretical assumptions or basic models (e.g., infant-mother observations, ethology, linguistics, shifts in certain assumptions of biology and physics, the transcendence of positivism in philosophy, etc.). But here, too, the need to retain the overall theory and to remain compatible with it served as distinct limitations. As an example, the ongoing battle in psychoanalysis regarding the relevance of classical metapsychology—where the arguments range from highly relevant (with minor modifications) within the existing paradigm at one extreme, to utterly irrelevant at the other extreme, to the need for a metapsychology with updated scientific concepts and models in the middle—has generally suffered from the inability to break out of the confines of a limiting theoretical framework in response to new clinical findings and from the decision to patch it up rather than to change it. The fact that what we refer to so freely as the "basic paradigm" has never been fully articulated, nor generally accepted (except implicitly), adds to the difficulties of such a discourse.

Thus, when Goldberg asks us to cease tampering with and modifying classical theory, I believe, he also has a message for Wallerstein and for some of our other critics, which says that a psychology based on the concept of archaic and mature selfobjects is not compatible and therefore cannot be integrated with a psychology that sees independence and autonomy as its—even if only theoretical—end points. (I return to this issue once more in discussing Stolorow's recommendation for a terminological change that involves just such an incompatibility.) The idea of *relative* independence and *relative* autonomy as efforts at a compromise solution to accommodate the clinical facts will not do, because simply adding the adjective "relative" does not specify what the relativity consists of (quantitatively or qualitatively) and what the area of psychic functioning is in relation to which independence and autonomy are the expected norms.

Instead of integrating, then, ideas that essentially cannot be integrated, Goldberg suggests the exploration of new models. He takes a fresh look at what is "self" and what is "other" in order to find an alternative language (i.e., new metaphors) for the customary, deeply ingrained, "inner agent," "inner object," and "inner place"—all references to an "inner mind" as if it were a space-occupying location.

As an alternative, Goldberg introduces the concepts of *ownership, privacy,* and *representability:* (1) in order to enable us to grasp certain self-experiences (including the varied and forever-changing relations of self and other) without being limited by spatial metaphors and physical boundaries; and (2) in order to avoid having to account for the acquisition of certain functions via the unfolding and development of inner capacities with the imagery that these functions have to change geographic location, move inside from the outside, and thus become "internalized" within the well-demarcated bodily or physical confines of an independent and autonomous self.

Goldberg is cautious here and recognizes that the concepts of ownership, privacy, and representability may not yet be fully adequate alternatives to the broad concept of internalization. Yet, these three vantage points together illuminate clinical data "a little differently"—he modestly says—and "highlight what has heretofore been a subtle shift in the field of psychoanalysis: *a shift from the study of the mind to that of the person, from concentration on the contents of an apparatus to one on the relationships of individuals* [italics added]"—and I might add: to the impact of these relationships on the development and sustenance of the bipolar self. Goldberg not only documents this fundamental shift, which is decisively and consistently promoted by self psychology, but he also creatively enhances it. In this process he further delineates self psychology from object relations theory and from drive psychology.

Goldberg is most persuasive regarding the value of his conceptualizations in his presentation of the many brief, well-chosen, illustrative clinical and everyday problems. In these examples he shows us the results of replacing the theory that describes what goes on *in* people and *between* people, from the vantage point of conceiving them as *discrete units*, with a theory that views the same experiences from the vantage point of *self-selfobject units*. In so doing he elegantly avoids polemics by simply juxtaposing the clinical-theoretical yield with one language as compared and contrasted with the other.

I cannot convey in these few remarks enough of a sample of the expanded and enriched meanings of those clinical and everyday experiences that Goldberg chooses to illuminate through his new metaphors; only a sustained empathic immersion would fully disclose them or yet reveal unexpected meanings. But there is one basic feature to all of his new metaphors to replace internalization that I wish to underscore: Ownership, privacy, and representability are well suited to make our observations entirely and consistently from the vantage point of the experiencing self. Goldberg has chosen a language that is exquisitely tailored to the empathic observational stance—the method *sine qua non* of self psychology.

Under *ownership* Goldberg discusses the capacity to claim possessions; the feeling that something belongs to us and that we are either able or unable to share it; the transitional objects' role and functions; the development of personal control over possessions and the responsibility of ownership, that is, of owning up to something or its opposite, not owning up to something (as in "projection" and "externalization"). In comparing the model of the inner world of things and relations to the model of ownership and possession, the advantage is that "the latter allows us to reach across the confines of the individual to the limitless expanse involving untold others and back again to the most minute reveries that exclude everyone else."

Goldberg is aware of the fact that by shifting to the new metaphors he suggests, we now have to study the development of how we get to own, to possess; how something gets to belong to us; how it gets to be under our control and what leads to the achievement of our ability to claim it. These are tasks that demand a reopening of the conception of transmuting internalization for renewed developmental and clinical scrutiny, for which he supplies a new language.

Under *privacy* Goldberg discusses secretly held thoughts, images, and ideas—"the private mind as a developmental achievement"—and the capacity to share them or to withhold them; to allow access to them or to bar their communication. Access to and communication of thoughts are more useful metaphors than their changing locale when they emerge from their unconscious or preconscious state to awareness. Here the issue of the capacity for sharing and the acquisition of "the world of shared meanings," leads to the consideration of empathy in psychoanalysis, "wherein the state of being understood, of sharing one's mind with another, is the *sine que non* of effective treatment." In other words, this sharing becomes a significant analytic achievement and a vehicle in the process of cure.

Under *representability* Goldberg touches only briefly on self-experiences that are capable of being thought of and have usually been considered under the heading of "internal representation"—"one suggesting that the inner world is some sort of miniature theater of the external world." He prefers here the models that portray "relationships or linkages" and not "discrete entities in opposition" and calls for a reconsideration of the usefulness of the conception of self-representations versus object representations in an inner world.

In his focusing on relationships rather than on discrete entities, Goldberg can further articulate the implications of the shift he is both documenting and enhancing in his work by saying: "The mind is the sum and substance of . . . relationships. But relationships are always those units of persons or minds that expand as one grows. Thus, independence and autonomy are mistaken words for the goal of maturity. Only the nature of relationships reflects that quality, not the absence of them."

It shows how widely Goldberg casts his net to collect the metaphors that should be replaced when he suggests that once internalization is reformulated so as to focus on "the expansion of self-control" (i.e., an aspect of self-regulation), rather than on the "discrete boundary between people," issues related to separation, mourning, and termination of analysis, to name only a few, may be profitably reexamined for new findings.

One of Goldberg's many stimulating ideas—all of which will undoubtedly serve to guide us to new insights in the next phase of progress in self psychology—should be singled out again for a final comment, because it clarifies some basic distinguishing features of self psychology that are so difficult to comprehend from within alternative vantage points and often lead to unproductive discussions. Goldberg talks about two different models for viewing the analytic relationship and their respective implications for the data obtained. In one model the analyst is considered as an external, neutral screen for the patient's "projections"—here we are dealing with a sharp boundary, with discrete units or entities in opposition—obviously determining the nature of the observational data that are seen as emerging against "resistance." The other model focuses on relationships and linkages. Here the introspective observation of the analyst's empathic failures leads to the recognition of disruptions in the relationship—the communicative link may be broken—resulting in functional disturbances in the patient, known as the various signs of fragmentation and enfeeblement. In this second model, when the sharp boundary and the opposition of discrete units are replaced and Goldberg sees ideas, feelings, wishes, and fantasies changing (ideally) freely and flexibly from being unacceptable to the self (unconscious), to being acceptable and safe (preconscious), to being shared (when verbally expressed), he has essentially redefinied "resistance."

In bringing to the fore the issue of the relative merits of each of these models with a clinical example from an analytic session, Goldberg introduces into this discussion the pivotal methodological issue of the extrospective versus the introspective observational stance in psychoanalysis. I found his comparison of the two models and their clinical illustrations illuminating, because I hear this also as a prescription for how to approach, on a broader scale, the study of competing or alternative conceptualizations.

Robert Stolorow introduces his view of self psychology "as a [new] scientific paradigm" in the context of a brief survey of the main steps in its evolution. On precisely those issues on which Wallerstein faults self psychology, Stolorow thoroughly approves of it and joins it—namely, on its distinctive features as a psychology, underscoring Goldberg's similar contention. Stolorow undertakes, in this paper, to remove the last vestiges of classical metapsychology from the concepts and theories of self psychology, utilizing the works of G. Klein (1976) and Schafer (1976) to accomplish this task. He then defines self psychology as a "structural psychology," which he describes in essence as *"a developmental phenomenology of the self* . . . principally concerned with the ontogenesis and structuralization of self-experience. . . ."* (p. 287). He further spells out the advantages of this new outlook as based on "a conceptual shift from the motivational primacy of instinctual drives to the motivational primacy of self-experience. . . ."* (p. 288). It is this conceptual shift that Stolorow rightly depicts with a few well-aimed brush strokes as the source of the specific clinical and theoretical advances of the psychology of the self in the broader sense—in stark contrast to Wallerstein's views. Stolorow considers self psychology as meeting Klein's criteria for being a *clinical* psychoanalytic theory, which ". . . asks 'why' questions and seeks answers in terms of personal reasons, purposes, and individual meanings" and can dispense with a metapsychology, which ". . . asks 'how' questions and seeks answers in terms of impersonal mechanisms and causes."

Although I, too, value most highly the experience-nearness of the central constructs of self psychology and their direct derivation from the clinical (transference) situation, I also think that we cannot and should not dispense with its more experience-distant derivatives— the level on which we can communicate with other disciplines and on which we can apply psychoanalysis to nonclinical problems. On this level the selfobject has become an enormously significant bridging concept (Ornstein, 1978). But the more significant issue here is whether these experience-distant concepts and theories—call them metapsychologic or not—are essentially of the same cloth. To be sure, these experience-distant concepts and theories are not *directly personal,* but they are at least *personalistic* rather than mechanistic and are therefore close to experience even on this more abstract level.

Take, for instance, the concept of the selfobject, which Stolorow aptly regards as "the foundational construct upon which the theoretical framework of self psychology rests." (p. 289). This construct has a history of a progressively expanding development within self psychology. The archaic selfobject (Kohut, 1971) was first and foremost an experience-near clinical construct. It encompassed the new observations and meanings of the transference experiences (hence, later called selfobject transferences) of patients who suffered from narcissistic personality and behavior disorders. A more experience-distant formulation, but still relatively experience-near, was the archaic selfobject as a developmental structure. Kohut viewed this archaic selfobject as the carrier of, or as the continuation of, early reality. In this role the archaic selfobject, as a precursor of psychic structure and as the agent that brings about structuralization, is already a more experience-distant theoretical construct. However, the roots of it are very clearly discernible in the experiences of infancy and childhood and later on in analysis. Perhaps on the level of its role in structure building, the selfobject, with its attribute of a more impersonal "function," is already a metapsychologic concept, but naturally fitting into a personalistic framework. It is certainly not the kind of metapsychologic concept that is grafted upon the clinical concepts from an unrelated field, such a physics.

We must add here to Stolorow's exposition that the concept of the archaic selfobject, to which he restricts his observations, expanded in recent years, through the recognition of its later developmental stages—notably, the oedipal selfobject (with its specific, phase-appropriate functions), the adolescent selfobject (with its specific, phase appropriate functions), and finally the mature selfobject (with its lifelong, changing functions). It was precisely the realization by Kohut (1978) of the need for selfobjects from brith to death, as you recall, that Goldberg pointed to as the clinical data that necessitated new conceptualizations and that Wallerstein could only view as an "extreme . . . and somewhat fanciful" proposition.

I fully subscribe to Stolorow's assessment that "the concept of a selfobject radically alters our understanding of the meaning of patient's experiences in the analytic situation." I only wish to propose that we now state explicitly that this assessment not only applies to the archaic selfobject, but is equally valid regarding those on more advanced developmental levels (i.e., to *all* of a patient's experiences in analysis), a view that is then even more radical than Stolorow envisioned.[1]

---

[1]The question cannot be dealt with extensively here as to what we mean now in self psychology when we speak of a self as a well-demarcated and firmly consolidated structure with its own independent center of initiative and what we mean by the recognition of the well-demarcated separateness and the well-consolidated, independent center of initiative in the other. Does the latter qualify as a "true object" or a "love- and hate-object" to be contrasted with a selfobject? Suffice it to say that to whatever extent the separateness and independence of the other is recognized (perceptually or cognitively, which is not the issue here), from the vantage point of self-experience—and therefore also from the vantage point of the empathic observer—the other is always a selfobject, whether archaic or mature. This view is the result of placing self-experience consistently at the center of psychoanalytic inquiry and asking how a person experiences the other rather than taking the position of an external observer and speaking of "whole object" or "part object" (see E. Schwaber, 1978 [1980], p. 215 in this connection).

This has far-reaching clinical and theoretical consequences, which justify our view of self psychology as a new paradigm, and it suggests different solutions for some of the specific problems discussed by both Stolorow and Wallerstein. Another way to describe this advance is to say that the domain of self psychology is no longer restricted to primary self-pathology, but that it now also includes secondary self-pathology. It encompasses clinically the entire spectrum of psychopathology and developmentally the whole life cycle. Thus, it is no longer valid to view Schafer's action language as addressing an empirical domain *fundamentally different* from that of self psychology, which only addresses the clinical-theoretical issues that relate to "missing, vulnerable, fragmentation-prone psychic structure" and where "the self-as-agent has remained undeveloped or atrophied as a result of developmental interferences and arrests."

If self psychology can truly encompass *both* domains and make them into one, as we now claim (I deal with Wallerstein's objection to the idea of *two* domains later), I believe we should hold off introducing "the concept of *the person* when referring to an 'agent' who initiates actions . . . and reserve the term *self* when referring to the 'structure' of self-experience." I agree with the idea that self psychology is a structural psychology in the sense in which Stolorow defines structure as having a "characteristic form and enduring organization." But he only points to Kohut's early discoveries to justify his view and his terminological change, whereas I believe that we also need to take the later concept of the bipolar self into consideration to see if the suggested change is still warranted. Although I share Stolorow's view that self psychology is a structural psychology—that is, indeed, what it was meant to be—I consider his terminological choice of separating "person" and "self" unnecessary and certainly premature.

At this point I would prefer to retain the bipolar self as representing *both* structure and agent, rather than separate them conceptually in order to give ourselves a chance to see whether that separation is, indeed, necessary and advantageous and to see what will grow directly out of the soil of self psychology itself as a result of further clinical experience. But, in addition to this general principle of preferably using indigenous rather than transplanted concepts, there is a specific reason why we should not graft onto our theories even such a logically fitting and seemingly compatible one as "the person as agent." This reason should now be obvious: Stolorow himself suggests that Schafer's action language is restricted to the domain of intrapsychic conflict in well-demarcated persons with an abiding, independent center of initiative. Thus, "the person as agent" cannot be successfully transplanted into the theoretical context of the bipolar self, which grew out of the concept of the self-selfobject matrix.[2] Within this matrix, as Goldberg clearly notes, we focus on "relationships and linkages" and not on "discrete units"— on "two distinct individuals in opposition." The concept of the bipolar self includes the self as organized and as capable of initiating action, as well as the self that is insufficiently or faultily organized and is thereby hampered in purposeful action.[3] In addition, the bipolar self also has characteristics (capacities and functions) beyond its form and enduring organization, namely, the contents of its self-assertive ambitions and of its specific values and ideals; its feminine or masculine features; its nuclear design or program of action, which it will always try to bring to fruition. I do grant that all these could, of course, be subsumed under the heading of "enduring organization" as part of the structure of the self, but then is not "the person as agent" an intrinsic part of that higher level organization we now call the bipolar self? What I am suggesting is that the conceptual separation of *person* and *self* not only offers no clinical or theoretical advantages I can see, but instead continues the very separation of our field into two domains that we are now trying to unify.

Because the bipolar self contains all that I just described, I consider it a supraordinate constellation in the sense that it has been conceptually placed into the very center of the personality; It is

---

[2]"The person as agent" may well be—in fact, I think it is—an improvement over metapsychologic formulations *within* classical conflict psychology. But Schafer's innovation did not aim at expanding the field of analysis, nor did it aim at improving its therapeutic leverage. Schafer himself claims that action language left the clinical theories and the technique of psychoanalysis essentially intact. "The person as agent" is an experience-near theoretical construct that fits well into the theory of action language, but it cannot be lifted out of there without a redefinition of its new context, namely, the concept of the bipolar self.

[3]Schafer may, of course, argue that his concept of "disclaimed action" covers the territory claimed for self psychology by Stolorow. The fact that action language per se had no special contributions to make to the understanding and treatment of narcissistic disorders favors Stolorow's view that "psychological configurations that are remnants of developmental voids or traumatically aborted developmental thrusts cannot be fruitfully conceptualized as purposefully performed but disclaimed actions."

what gives the person or personality its depth-psychological dimension. Without the concept of the bipolar self, the person or personality does not have an indigenous (i.e., metapsychologically definable) structure. Herein lies, I believe, the ultimate solution to the vexing problem of complementarity (Kohut, 1977), to which I now turn.

Stolorow and Wallerstein, each from his own vantage point, singled out the issue of complementarity for criticism. I have chosen to respond to both of them separately (to Stolorow here only in passing), because I feel that the basic principle of Kohut's use of the concept of complementarity has been widely misunderstood. Stolorow proposes to revise the "conception of complementarity between self psychology and mental apparatus psychology" by dispensing with the mental apparatus concept altogether and considering "the essential complementarity," the only really possible or true complementarity, "between a psychology of conflict-ridden but firmly consolidated psychic structures and a psychology of missing, precarious, and disintegration-prone psychic structures." Thus, although true to his basic aim of clearing away outmoded, mechanistic-physicalistic models—an endeavor in which I join him—the solution Stolorow offers is again problematic. He offers the same solution many of us have lived with for some time, but we now have reasons to question its validity. Wallerstein is sharply critical of this complementarity; his criticism is, in fact, connected with his main objection to self psychology as a theory.

The problem with the "true" complementarity of conflict psychology and deficit psychology (as against mental apparatus psychology and deficit psychology), as Stolorow envisions it, is that the difference is not as radical as it might seem, albeit the language is more congenial. We would have to ask: What is conflict in this formulation if not a clash of forces? How could a psychology based on the concept of a clash of forces be any more truly complementary to a psychology of deficit than a mental apparatus psychology can, which is thought of as driven by those very forces that create the conflict? In other words, changing from mental apparatus psychology to conflict psychology is merely cosmetic, unless we also redefine what we mean by conflict, which is precisely what Wallerstein has done.

But while we have lived with this idea of a complementarity between conflict psychology and deficit psychology as something tentative and temporary, Stolorow's proposed solution sounds too definitive and final. I return to this point in connection with Wallerstein's critique, where I use my earlier expressed view of the supraordinate position of the bipolar self to suggest a solution.

Stolorow completes his study by pointing to the need for reconceptualizing "transmuting internalization," *the* key issue of the process of structure building by any name. He offers a step by step consideration of what he sees as divided into "two closely interacting but conceptually distinguishable developmental processes": *internalization* (the acquisition of certain functions or self-regulatory capacities, such as soothing, comforting, mirroring, etc.) and *structuralization* (of self-experience, such as self-articulation, self-demarcation, and the further differentiation of the self-structure). As you recall, Goldberg spoke in the same connection of "capacities" instead of "structures"; and albeit in a different language, I believe, Stolorow essentially moves in the same direction. In this context he recognizes the value of Kohut's idea that narcissism has its separate line of development as an invitation for "the construction of a *detailed* developmental psychology of self-structure, fleshing out his broad descriptions of the child's early ties to mirroring and idealized selfobjects [italics added]."

I believe that Stolorow, like Goldberg, rightly points to the further study of transmuting internalization during development and in analysis as a most important avenue of further progress in self psychology, a progress to which he himself has here and elsewhere already contributed a number of significant steps.

Robert Wallerstein appropriately set the stage for his detailed appraisal of the clinical and theoretical contributions of self psychology by explicitly defining his own vantage point. Succinctly stated, he believes, that "psychoanalysis has had and still has but one basic paradigm of how the mind works, that devised by Freud which rests on the fundamental postulates . . . of psychic continuity and of unconscious psychic processes." From this very broadly based platform Wallerstein then states that self psychology does not represent a ". . . new paradigm at all, but rather . . . a substantial addition to our clinical insights . . . having to do with . . . selfobject transferences and their counterpart countertransferences. . . ." He goes on to say: "This most impressive clinical contribution can be incorporated into the main body of classical psychoanalysis without the need for either a new or separate theory . . ." He then, true to the depth and breadth of his scientific attitude toward psychoanalysis, leaves the judgment regarding the ultimate usefulness of the concept of the bipolar self open, granting that it, too, may prove to be a useful *additional* conceptualization.

This stage-setting through the careful definition of the basic theoretical outlook that guides Wallerstein in his critique has to be kept in mind in order to appreciate his position and to understand his differeing response to the clinical as against the theoretical contributions of self psychology. Wallerstein includes in this stage-setting a few disclaimers: comments regarding a number of important steps in the evolution of self psychology, which he considers both less radical and also less central to the controversies surrounding self psychology than I have claimed them to be. Some of these disclaimers relate to the proposition of a "separate developmental line for narcissism apart from that for object-relatedness and object-love"; others relate to "the clear emphasis on the primacy of the libidinal over the aggressive component in emotional interaction and development"; and finally, some relate to aspects of the concept of the selfobject. I am mentioning these disclaimers in passing here, and I return to them later. As you may have already noted, these disclaimers include issues even from those areas of self psychology that Wallerstein can enthusiastically accept, such as the selfobject transferences. He thereby consistently remains within his broadly formulated, basically unalterable, but only expanding, paradigm. It is on this basis then, as I see it, that Wallerstein can, and apparently prefers, to accommodate some of the fundamental clinical contributions of self psychology as *additions* to classical analysis. And it is apparently on this basis that he prefers to divorce so sharply the clinical from the theoretical contributions. I consider such a divorce thoroughly unwarranted, first, on the general grounds that there is always an inseparably close relationship between the clinical method, the data, and the theory; second, and more specifically in this instance, because of the relative experience-nearness of the central theoretical formulations of self psychology.

The main thrust of Wallerstein's *theoretical argument* has to do with his questioning the usefulness of the sharp distinction between conflict and deficit. Hence he also questions the validity of a distinction between conflict psychology and self psychology. The latter, he maintains, cannot claim to be a separate psychology. This argument is buttressed by a comprehensive redefinition and broadening of the concept of psychic conflict, to a point, perhaps, of blurring its erstwhile specificity.

The main thrust of the *clinical argument* is that whatever the valuable additions self psychology has brought to psychoanalysis, they can and should be incorporated into the clinical method in a "both/and," rather than in an "either/or" fashion. This argument is buttressed by the concept of overdetermination or multiple function.

I propose to examine some of these arguments as a way to respond to the challenge that Dr. Wallerstein has presented. I do this with the explicit purpose of clarifying our respective claims, the seeming inconsistencies or contradictions, even as new clinical problems and theoretical expansions continue to change our own perspectives. First I wish to return briefly to the disclaimers Dr. Wallerstein introduced in connection with his appraisal of the psychology of the self in the narrower sense:

1. The postulate that narcissism had a developmental line separate from that of object-love expressed, in this relatively experience-near abstraction, the clinical finding that the salutary results with patients who suffered from narcissistic personality or behavior disorders were accomplished analytically *without the working through of an infantile Oedipus complex*. The postulate thus simply translated this important and far-reaching clinical observation into a theoretical statement, which called attention to the transformation of narcissism from archaic to mature forms, rather than its direct transformation into object-love, and thereby also underlined the healthy, permanent psychological significance of narcissism. I would still say that the implications of these reformulations were very far-reaching indeed, because they already contained the nucleus of what was to be made explicit in subsequent contributions.

This proposition gave theoretical underpinning to the notion that what was narcissistic was not always primitive; but most importantly, it was not always a regressive defense against oedipal anxieties. This observation led to the recognition that henceforth the term "object relations" covered *both* object-love experiences *and* the narcissistic or selfobject experiences. This important differentiation, in turn, enhanced the perception of certain qualities in the transference, rather than maintaining earlier notions of the absence of transference in people who did not treat the analyst as a "true" object, with an independent center of initiative (see my footnote 1 in this connection).

The postulate of the separate lines of development for narcissism and for object-love never questioned the unitary-ness of experience, of the developmental interrelatedness with other psychological trends, the same way that A. Freud's or Mahler's focus on the study of other developmental lines never meant to disavow that unitary-ness. But by the same token, neither A. Freud, Mahler, nor any other analyst dealt specifically (and in this same fashion) with *this* particular developmental line. The new clinical findings, which were summed up by Kohut's postulate at the time it was first articulated, and the potential it contained for further expansion of our knowledge—which has since come to fruition—justify our view of it as a revolutionary step. (I believe this is still true, even if the central significance of this postulate has since shifted as a result of the proposition of the concept of the bipolar self.)

2. The observation (or old charge) that self psychology overemphasized the libidinal aspects of narcissism and deemphasized aggressive-destructiveness and primitive rage has long been answered. I want to respond to it again at this point only to comment on a methodological or epistemological error that comes up over and over again in relation to the whole idea of conflict (which I return to later on). The problem is that from the vantage point of another paradigm it may indeed seem as if we overemphasized or deemphasized one or the other clinical manifestation, when in fact we have attributed a different meaning or a different significance to it and have adequately responded to it analytically (i.e., with understanding and interpretation) from our own vantage point. Perhaps we may describe criticisms of this sort as stemming from what I would call a "positivistic fallacy," in which observers assume that what are data from within their own theoretical viewpoint must also be exactly the same kind of data from within the other point of view. I am reminded of a case in point from a dialogue with Otto Kernberg, in which he asked how it was possible that self psychologists did not see the Oedipus complex in the narcissistic disorders (which were on a higher developmental level) when he saw it in borderline conditions (which were on a lower developmental level). I responded by saying (though only his question has appeared in the literature so far; my answer hasn't) that neither he nor we *saw* the

Oedipus complex. *He* simply decided to use that clinical construct to order his data, I said, whereas *we* chose a different clinical explanatory construct to order our observations. Are there no data, then, that we could all see? Of course, in a sense there are; for instance, the intense, often perverse, and isolated sexuality, aggression, sadism, and so on may be seen by all. These may have *oedipal content*, but in the absence of a cohesive, firmly established self, their meaning and significance—and *therefore* our interpretations of them— differ greatly. Our interpretations of these intensified and isolated drive manifestations as breakdown products of the self cannot be accurately described as neglect, deemphasis, or suppression in a soothing climate, as is frequently done. The proper assessment of the clinical-theoretical validity and usefulness of the analytic approach suggested by self psychology demands extensive and intensive clinical trials. Such trials involve the prolonged immersion of the clinician in the patient's transference experiences, with the understanding and interpretations offered by self psychology freely available to the clinician, alongside his or her classical analytic knowledge. Only the systematic and prolonged application of the new understanding will allow the clinician sufficient opportunity to make a valid comparative clinical study.

3. The third and last disclaimer I want to comment on may seem minor, but it belongs to a particular area that is of considerable interest to self psychology at the present time. It is the further extension and expansion of the concept of the selfobject as I already indicated in connection with Stolorow's focus upon the archaic selfobject. Wallerstein questions Kohut's (1978) statement, which contains this extension and expansion, as follows: "In the view of self psychology man lives in a matrix of selfobjects from birth to death. He needs selfobjects for his psychological survival, just as he needs oxygen in his environment throughout his life for physiological survival [p. 478]." I think I understand why Wallerstein has found this epigrammatic formulation somewhat extreme and fanciful, as I have already quoted him before: If from within his vantage point one should move developmentally beyond the need for selfobjects to separate and independent "true objects," then the idea of such a persistent need throughout the life cycle does not seem to make good theoretical sense. One might question the claim not only from the classical viewpoint, but also on the basis of earlier formulations within self psychology, when the focus was explicitly upon the need

for *archaic* selfobjects. It should therefore be stressed here again that the concept of the selfobject now clearly conveys that even when the other is already recognized perceptually and cognitively as another, the need for the supply of certain functions (archaic or mature) from the other makes that other experientially a selfobject on *any* level of development (see my footnote 1).

Let me now add a disclaimer of my own: It is not my *main* contention in these remarks that self psychology in the broader sense is a new paradigm. Both Goldberg and Stolorow, in their different ways, express that claim and document its validity. I am merely restating it now because Wallerstein has marshaled his central arguments essentially against that claim, and I find it a convenient way to discuss some of the controversial issues raised in this discussion, especially because he clearly stated what basic paradigm directed his own evaluation of the place of self psychology within psychoanalysis.

Claiming that self psychology *is* a new paradigm in Kuhn's sense simply means that I think we have a comprehensive set of theories, explicitly and systematically formulated, which help us define our crucial scientific concerns *and* determine the ways we may be able to deal with them. Viewed in this light (admittedly schematic and simplified for this discussion), a paradigm can be so broadly formulated that it does not clearly define the central scientific issues of our field and does not clearly prescribe methods for their study. Such a formulation could not be helpful to us, because it would not allow us to detect the anomalies of our paradigm—that is, those areas in our field that the paradigm could not adequately encompass. Such a broad formulation, then, could easily deprive us of being able to direct our attention to remedying our clinical or theoretical anomalies. And we may then also proceed in our work as if all was well within our existing, entrenched paradigm. But it would indeed be difficult to discover what is new and what is old; what is helpful and what is not; what fits under the umbrella of the old paradigm and what demands the setting up of a new one. In other words, leaving the paradigm too broadly formulated and hence full of anomalies—detected or undetected, admitted or denied—might lead us to include everything under the old umbrella. But how could that really advance our field? In the sense, then, in which I use the concept of a paradigm here, agreeing that it not be trivialized, Wallerstein's claim that Freud's "fundamental postulates . . . of psychic continuity and of unconscious processes" still constitutes the only valid psychoanalytic paradigm is, at best, incomplete because it no longer adequately defines contemporary psychoanalysis. At worst, although Freud's basic paradigm as proposed by Wallerstein remains broadly valid, in its stated form it obscures, rather than illuminates, our present discussion. Its very breadth is the problem because, as formulated, it no longer spells out clearly and unambiguously—as it did originally and until fairly recently—what is to be considered the central content of that "psychic continuity" and of those "unconscious processes" to which the paradigm refers.

As I see it, we now have two competing basic hypotheses regarding the origin of psychic development, within each of which we can specify the contents of psychic continuity and of the unconscious processes:

1. Freud's hypothesis derives psychic development from the clash of forces of the primary drives with the socializing demands of the parental imagos as the earliest representatives of the social environment. A psyche that is conceived as developing out of such a matrix is, *by definition,* full of *primary* conflicts. Thus, the notion of psychoanalysis as a conflict psychology *par excellence* is thereby built into our view of human development.

This view has repeatedly been amended, expanded, and reformulated by ego psychologists (within the mainstream of psychoanalysis) and by object relations theorists (close to the mainstream).[4] The details of the amendments, expansions, and reformulations, however, are not immediately relevant to my argument, because *all* of them have essentially retained the primacy of the drives in their conceptualizations.

2. Kohut's hypothesis derives psychic development from within the self-selfobject matrix, where the relation between the rudimentary self and its empathic selfobject constitutes the primal unit of psychological experience. Expectably, nontraumatic disruptions of

---

[4]Wallerstein frequently calls attention to these changes in theory to claim that self psychology sets up straw men by referring to earlier theoretical formulations, without due regard for the many advances introduced by an ever-expanding ego psychology and object relations theory, which can, for the most part, be accommodated by the unaltered, one basic, paradigm, without the need for a new psychology. I examine this claim in the main portion of my reply to Wallerstein, which is to follow.

the empathic bond between self and selfobject (optimum frustration) lead to structure building through transmuting internalization. Thus, there is here, *by definition,* no built-in primary conflict in the psyche. Traumatic disruptions, on the other hand, lead to defects or deficits in structure building, which, in turn, lead to *secondary* conflicts.

In both of these basic hypotheses psychic structure is built up as a result of optimum frustration. But in Freud's hypothesis optimum frustration involves (basic or primary) *drive-related needs and wishes,* whereas in Kohut's hypothesis optimum frustration involves *nondrive-related,* developmental (*mirroring and idealizing*) *needs and wishes.* The drives are in this context building blocks or integral components of a cohesive self and appear in isolated, intensified, pathological forms only upon a transient or protracted breakdown of the cohesiveness of the self.

A paradigm that cannot help us with sorting out the many, far-reaching clinical and theoretical implications of these differing hypotheses and cannot aid us in discovering their compatibilities or incompatibilities is no longer up-to-date and useful enough. It needs to be replaced, therefore, by a new paradigm, which is at once more encompassing and more specific, and which should not only retain what has remained clinically and theoretically valid, but should also account for and lead us toward new observations that could not be made within the confines of the previous paradigm.

These general remarks should now be followed by a more detailed examination of some of the major issues highlighted by Wallerstein's critique around questions related to: (1) the complementarity between conflict psychology and deficit psychology; (2) the selfobject transferences and the developmental concept of the selfobject; (3) empathy in the psychoanalytic process and in theory formation; and finally, (4) method of criticism.

1. The Complementarity Between Conflict Psychology and Deficit Psychology.   To proceed to Wallerstein's main point of argument, we have to take up again the issue of complementarity where we left it off in discussing Stolorow's suggested solution to this problem. As you recall, Stolorow argued for replacing the complementarity between an outmoded mental apparatus psychology and deficit psychology with the clinically and theoretically more appropriate "true" complementarity between conflict psychology and deficit psychology. This is precisely what Wallerstein objects to. He proposes to eliminate the unsatisfactory state of affairs of complementarity—the separation of conflict versus deficit into two psychologies—by integrating the concept of deficit under the concept of conflict and thereby maintaining a unified psychology under the old "classical" paradigm. Can he really accomplish this unification successfully? In fact, he cannot. In order to attempt it Wallerstein first has to revise classical conflict theory and turn it into what he calls "modern and broadened psychoanalytic conceptualization of conflict," based on Sandler's not yet fully appreciated formulations (Sandler, 1974, 1976, and 1979, which Wallerstein did not include and where Sandler further expanded his object relations theory).

In order to examine whether Wallerstein is able to integrate deficit psychology under this revised conflict theory, let us briefly review its essential elements, along with the theory of deficit offered by self psychology. Both Sandler's original formulations and Wallerstein's further elaboration of them here would deserve a more thorough and careful study. Sandler's reformulation of conflict theory (ultimately linked to his evolving object relations theory) is more of a sweeping critique of Hartmannian ego psychology and classical psychoanalysis as a whole than his presentations of it—*sotto voce*—might at first have revealed. The implications of Wallerstein's adoption and present use of this revised conflict theory almost overshadow his critique of self psychology, because, in fact, he thereby buttresses—I believe—many of the claims of self psychology that he explicitly rejects.

Sandler (1974) noted, compelled by clinical evidence, that "Freud emphasized *intersystemic* conflicts (conflicts between the different structures) at the expense of the idea of *intrasystemic* conflict [p. 55]." He concluded that "from the point of view of clinical practice and technical procedure, the idea of conflict between the various psychic agencies in the structural model ha[d] very definite limitations [p. 57]." He put this even more strongly when he stated: "The usual distinction between id on the one hand and ego on the other fails to account for our clinical data when conflict is being considered [p. 60]." According to Sandler, *any* "unconscious peremptory urge," be it drive-related or nondrive-related, may lead to intrasystemic or intersystemic conflict. The crucial, perhaps even daringly innovative statement here is, that "peremptory impulses are not always manifestations of instinctual wishes alone, but may arise as a consequence of stimuli from any part of the mental apparatus or from the outside world [p. 60]."

Hence, Sandler considered the "need to reconceptualize conflict in terms of the *whole* mental apparatus . . . [p. 60]." He particularly emphasized the importance

> of the analysis of conflict in regard to previous adaptations which have later in development become ego-dystonic, i.e., have come into conflict with the ego's need to maintain its self-esteem, sense of well being, feelings of harmony and safety, and its relations to its objects, internal or external. Conflicts of this sort need to be interpreted as such, and *it is a major and misleading oversimplification to consider them simply as conflicts between the ego and the other major agencies of id, superego and reality* [p. 60, italics added].

Sandler (1976) follows this with a statement that "we can regard all conflict as being a conflict of wishes of one sort or another [p. 61, italics added]."

Wallerstein carries this even further, as he chooses to see conflict where we see deficit, when he quotes Kohut and Wolf (1974): "Faulty interaction between the child and his selfobject results in a damaged self" and then states that faulty interaction for him *"connotes, in some fashion, the concept of something out of kilter, i.e., conflicted* [p. 323, italics added]."

Where does such an all-encompassing, radically revised conflict theory lead? No wonder that Wallerstein can now, at least by definition, include what we call deficit or defect into his updated conceptualization of conflict. But what clinical or theoretical advantage is there in redefining "deficit" through that very general and imprecise concept of "something out of kilter"—out of order or adjustment; out of balance or alignment—as a "conflict?" Has Wallerstein not, thereby, blurred the psychoanalytic specificity of *both* conflict and deficit?

His redefinition of conflict, which should now encompass deficit, has thereby not done away with the specific meaning of defect or deficit in self psychology. *Developmentally,* deficit refers to the inadequate or insufficient availability of those emotional nutriments in the self-selfobject matrix that are the *sine qua non* for the attainment of a functionally competent bipolar self. *Genetically,* deficit refers to the very specific idiosyncratic configuration of the countless variety of empathic failures by the mirroring and/or idealized selfobjects. These empathic failures may arise in an infinite number and form of omissions and commissions on the part of the selfobject environment. Coupled with the innate propensities of the infant or child, these will lead to the unique deficit, which can only be reconstructed as to its specific configuration, etiology, and pathogenesis, through the selfobject transferences. It should be noted here explicitly that the concept of the empathic failures of the selfobjects permits as rich and as complex a view of etiology and pathogenesis as we have ever had in psychoanalysis, if not even more so. Statements to the contrary by some of our critics, who perceived the concept of empathic failure (especially defects in maternal empathy) as a *single* etiologic-pathogenetic factor, have entirely missed the point I am emphasizing (Stein, 1979). We may wonder why. *Dynamically,* deficit refers to those nondrive-related mirroring and idealizing needs that clamor for belated recognition of and responsiveness to the thwarted urge to complete development, in everyday life and—more particularly and intensely—in the transference. It is here that the analytic observer can study directly the role and function of empathic failures, their immediate consequences, long-term effects, and their etiologically and pathogenetically significant genetic antecedents. It is in the selfobject transferences, mobilized by the structural deficits resulting from an incomplete, arrested, or derailed development, that the meaning and significance of drive-related and nondrive-related needs and wishes can be most fruitfully examined. It is here, then, that the *relationship* of these two groups of needs and wishes at the heart of our present controversy can best be studied as to the *primacy* of one versus the other in development and in symptom formation. *Structurally,* deficit refers to those missing components of the bipolar self that lead to its functional insufficiency in the pole of self-assertive ambitions, and/or in the pole of values and guiding ideals, or in the intermediate area of innate skills and talents. Again, the configuration of the deficit and its consequences can only be understood and explained in genetic-dynamic terms through reconstructions within the transference. The difficulty many of our critics have had with the concept of deficit, which may not be the most felicitous designation, may in fact have to do with the idea that what we see directly is not a void, but a complex set of hierarchically layered defenses (motivated according to different contemporary views by drive-related, and/or object-related conflicts, or selfobject-related deficits) that require painstaking analysis. These same critics have apparently not appreciated Kohut's (1977) description of *primary, defensive,* and *compensatory* structures. Defensive structures do indeed develop to cover over the void, to fill in the defects with more or less (usually less) lasting success. Compensatory structures, on the other hand, may be successful in filling in for what has not been acquired in the primary self-selfobject matrix in the form of primary structures.

The pathognomonic regression, however, and its working through in the transference, ultimately remobilizes and thereby frees the thwarted developmental thrust to grow, and the patient may then acquire the missing psychic structures through transmuting internalizations. Thus, the analysis penetrates *below* the surface defenses (which sometimes occurs relatively easily and quickly, but other times is more difficult and requires a prolonged period of working through) to bring the *unconscious, infantile configurations* within the purview of the transference.

It is remarkable how consistently this last point is overlooked by many of our critics. The recognition of elaborate defensive structures apparently obscures the "deficit" (whose presence powerfully emerges in the transference) for those who focus their attention and their therapeutic approach onto these *secondary elaborations.* A case in point, which Wallerstein quotes without questioning, is Kernberg's claim that Kohut's " 'empathic' and 'soothing' clinical approach to the preoedipal transferences" (whatever that characterization may mean in the context of an analysis?!) fails to resolve the "pathological structure of the grandiose self." In fact, the "grandiose self" described by Kohut is a repressed (unconscious) infantile (more or less phase-appropriate) constellation, which can only be remobilized in an analytic process characterized by optimum frustration. Kernberg's use of the term "grandiose self" seems to designate behaviorally manifest, defensive, personality features, with intense (again manifest) primitive aggression. The clinical question of how to engage patients optimally with such pervasive surface defenses, while at the same time aiming toward mobilizing the repressed and/or disavowed infantile structures in the transference, cannot be fruitfully addressed by using the same term for such vastly different psychological configurations. Kernberg assumes, furthermore, that Kohut's approach fails to achieve "a basic resolution . . . of the grandiose self" and then attributes this failure to the help patients obtain in rationalizing their aggressions as "a natural consequence to the failure of other people in their past." This assumption on Kernberg's part indicates to me that we have not yet reached the level of successful interchange where understanding and taking each other seriously as analysts is a minimum requirement for a mutually beneficial critical discourse.

The preceding references to conflict and deficit should now carry us further along toward understanding the substantive issues that preclude the integration of deficit even under the modified and expanded conflict theory.

What did Sandler essentially accomplish with his revision and expansion of what he considered to be a narrow perspective on conflict in the widely held, dominant structural theory or the tripartite model? A comprehensive response to this question is not possible in this context. Suffice it to say for our present purpose that Sandler accomplished the following: (1) he recognized that a wide variety of potentially pathogenic peremtory urges, emanating from *anywhere* in the mental apparatus or any of its agencies, could not be accounted for in terms of intersystemic conflicts alone; (2) in reaffirming the potential pathogenicity of intrasystemic conflicts (to undo the near-exclusive emphasis—at least theoretically, if not clinically—on intersystemic conflicts since 1923), he cogently called for a reconceptualization of conflict within the *whole* mental apparatus and not only between its agencies; and finally, perhaps even more importantly for the issues at hand, (3) he raised nondrive-related conflicts to the same level of clinical and theoretical significance (e.g., regarding their pathogenic role) as the drive-related conflicts had occupied.

In this connection Sandler explicitly stated that the need to find a place for nondrive-related conflicts side by side with drive-related conflicts arose, in part, on the basis of clinical experience with narcissistic disorders. Certainly his emphasis on the importance of focusing on the vicissitudes of self-esteem regulation, the attainment and maintenance of a sense of well being along with feelings of harmony and safety, has for some time drawn his clinical attention to these fundamental nondrive-related issues, for which—in his reformulation of conflict theory—he has also been trying to account theoretically.

Thus, although Sandler has established what I would call a *de facto* complementarity between drive-related and nondrive-related peremptory urges on the clinical level (i.e., where a view of conflict as either drive- or nondrive-related complements each other in an effort to encompass all clinical data), I question whether he accomplished a true integration on a theoretical level by merely juxtaposing the two kinds of urges under the widened concept of conflict.

One of the many reasons for my questioning this has to do with Sandler's (1974) own recognition that "painful feelings other than anxiety [I assume Sandler means drive-related anxiety] can also prompt peremptory impulses or responses. This ha[d] become more evident with the increase in our knowledge of narcissistic character disorders [p. 60]." To buttress his claim, Sandler offers some very perceptive, brief, but complex clinical vignettes and states: "Although it could be argued that patients are, in all these instances, defending against instinctual wishes, *these did not appear to be the crucial dynamic factors at the time* [p. 60, italics added]."

I see a central methodological problem here. Decisive clinical experiences remain somewhat ambiguous regarding their theoretical significance, because they are not permitted to carry their considerable weight in bringing these nondrive-related needs into their proper place of *primary* role in pathogenesis. Sandler frequently affirms (clinically) throughout his writings the more fundamental significance of nondrive-related urges and needs over the sexual-aggressive concerns or conflicts of this or that patient, but he has consistently refrained from making the necessary theoretical adjustments as a result of such observations. I see his paper on conflict theory, along with his emerging object relations theory (into which his new conflict theory will ultimately have to be more systematically embedded) as an effort in that direction. Any conflict or deficit theory, including any attempt to unify the two, will have to be part of a comprehensive developmental theory. Here, at present, the choices are either in object relations theory or in self psychology.

I see the clinical results of Sandler's reformulation of conflict as in many ways compatible with (certainly as not contradictory to) the clinical-theoretical claims of self psychology. But I view these reformulations: (1) as falling short of consistently evolving the clinical changes from the specific configuration of the transferences (as is pursued in self psychology); and (2) as falling short in raising these clinical observations to the level of clinical theory and metapsychology (as is pursued in self psychology). What, then, has Wallerstein accomplished by further elaborating Sandler's conflict theory, with explicit reference to the issue of conflict versus deficit, which Sandler bypassed?

Again, I am not able to offer a comprehensive response to this question in this context, but I can selectively focus on those elements that show the inadequacy of a conflict theory that simply combines drive-related and nondrive-related conflicts under one umbrella and reveals their incompatibility when the attempt is made to fit the latter into the former by essentially collapsing the two into one expanded and revised theory. The inadequacy and incompatibility reside in the fact that in a drive-related conflict theory the primacy of unresolved conflicts has often been invoked as leading to secondary defects or deficits in psychological structures, whereas in relation to primary, nondrive-related, unmet, developmental needs, defects or deficits arise, which lead to secondary conflicts. A theory that does not clearly articulate the clinical and theoretical reasons for the primacy of conflict over deficit or of deficit over conflict is incomplete and inevitably contains incompatible theoretical assumptions. Such a theory is not able to account satisfactorily enough for how and why "normal" conflicts may become pathological and pathogenic. But because Wallerstein holds self psychology and my own writings in particular responsible for some of the confusion related to these issues, I return to this point once more shortly. To anticipate here the direction of my argument, a very different situation arises when we attempt to fit drive-related conflicts into a self psychology, because we can then account both for the deficits and for the conflicts—including the pathological and pathogenic conflicts—without needing to blur the differences between them.

What Wallerstein accomplished with his reformulations can be summarized as follows:

1. In explicitly focusing on the issue of deficit, even if he had to translate it into a broadened and not yet widely accepted definition of conflict in psychoanalysis, he was able to accept and include much of the essential contributions of self psychology in the narrower sense into his conception of psychoanalysis.

2. In explicitly focusing on a both/and rather than on an either/or view regarding the two kinds of peremptory urges, he has brought the clinical-theoretical issues related to this blurring of fundamental differences into sharper relief. His insistence that both kinds of peremptory urges can be accommodated within the new conflict theory should ultimately be more productive, because at least it confronts us with the existence of two different kinds of

peremptory urges, even if we consider their present juxtaposition as short of integration on the theoretical level.

3. In the process of this effort, Wallerstein was able to spell out more clearly and unambiguously his ideas of what normal and pathological or pathogenic conflicts are—especially those related to the oedipal phase of development—than is to be found in the psycho-analytic literature. Here again, he sharpened our awareness that these were essentially unsettled, or at least not very satisfactorily settled, issues in psychoanalysis.

What, then, is my response to Wallerstein's critique of the complementarity between mental apparatus or conflict psychology on the one hand and deficit psychology on the other? A glance at the evolution of self psychology at that moment when Kohut proposed the complementary use of the two theories should facilitate the necessary clarification. In 1977 Kohut had just expanded the psychology of the self in the narrower sense (with the self as the content of the mental apparatus and its agencies) to the psychology of the self in the broader sense (with the bipolar self as a supraordinate constellation). This new and expanded concept of the self was viewed as supraordinate to the mental apparatus, its agencies, and constituents, such as the drives and defenses.

Wallerstein correctly perceived that there were two—according to him incompatible or antithetical—implications in this proposition. On the one hand, the bipolar self was raised to a supraordinate position within the new psychology of the self; simultaneously, on the other hand, the claim was put forward that mental apparatus psychology (or conflict psychology) was also to be retained side by side with the bipolar self in a complementary fashion until further empirical data warranted a different conception of their relationship.

Yes, indeed, these are two, empirically-pragmatically justified, but theoretically divergent propositions. Kohut had not yet fully extracted at that point from his clinical experiences with the neuroses and from his newly formulated proposition of the bipolar self a way to integrate the two psychologies. He explicitly stated, however, the direction into which his emerging data and his evolving theories carried him: an integration of drives and conflicts into the psychology of the bipolar self, rather than into the opposite direction, which Wallerstein favors. He preferred to leave the two theories *unintegrated* for the present, to maintain the creative tension between them, to keep the road open for further progress, and to allow time for the kind of integration that would emerge under the impact of new clinical data, obtained from the vantage point of the bipolar self.

Wallerstein's suggestions for an immediate integration of self psychology in the narrower sense, under the umbrella of a broadened and revised conflict theory, are premature. Not only does this integration leave out the psychology of the self in the broader sense, which cannot be so lightly dismissed, but even the integration of self psychology in the narrower sense cannot be adequately accomplished without articulating the new conflict theory more broadly within the psychoanalytic process, because it is within the psychoanalytic process that we are able to study what is primary and what is secondary. And it is within a developmental theory that we are able to account for the significance of nondrive-related needs in structure building as well as for the consequences when these needs are not met, inadequately met, or erratically met in the course of early and later development. Furthermore, redefining deficit as conflict sidesteps the fact that there has always been a kind of deficit psychology side by side with a predominant and central conflict psychology in psychoanalysis. A primary deficit or defect as an outgrowth of inadequate emotional nutriments was assigned to the ego in the psychoses. A less clear-cut assumption was made about ego alterations in certain severe personality disorders. In some of these, unresolved conflicts were assumed to lead to secondary ego alterations; in others (i.e., those closer to the psychoses), deficits were thought to lead to the more severe ego deformities. In the neuroses, however, unresolved conflicts and the defensive compromises mobilized to deal with them were considered responsible for secondary ego weaknesses.

Thus, the issue of deficit was known and explicitly acknowledged in psychoanalysis. Why was this *de facto* complementarity silently accepted? Why is Kohut's tentative, tactical, and pragmatic complementarity so unacceptable? I believe that the answer lies, at least in part, in the fact that most analysts had considered only patients with a psychopathology based on conflict (the neuroses and neurotic personality disorders) analyzable, whereas patients with a psychopathology based on deficit (the psychoses and severe personality disorders) were considered unanalyzable. It was the issue of analyzability that turned most analysts off from "deficit-disorders." Some even went so far as to conceptualize structural deficits throughout the spectrum of psychopathology as secondary and spoke of efforts to analyze psychotic conflicts as they analyzed neurotic conflicts, with the hope of undoing the secondary deficits in that fashion. Others viewed patients with structural deficits as becoming analyzable after some preparatory, so-called structure-building psychotherapy, after which such patients might then be able to respond to a classical analytic approach.

I cannot dwell in greater detail on the history of these antecedent theories of deficit and conflict in child and adult analyses. Nor can I examine more closely the various prior clinical and theoretical solutions analysts sought in order to deal with the *real* differences inherent in the two kinds of psychopathology. However, I hope to have demonstrated: (1) that the conflict-deficit complementarity has always been present in psychoanalytic nosology (although deficits were thought not to be treatable by analysis); and (2) that the premature integration Wallerstein advocates does not resolve our clinical-theoretical problems.

Further consideration has to be given, however, to Wallerstein's claim that a both/and, rather than an either/or, view of psychological processes within the transference encompasses *all* available interpretations from *all* possible metapsychologic points of view within the classical paradigm. The generally accepted notion of "overdetermination" (Freud) or "multiple function" (Waelder) serves Wallerstein as a compelling conceptual underpinning for his integrative efforts. Turning briefly to the selfobject transferences and to the developmental concept of the selfobject should aid in further examining the clinical and theoretical advantages or shortcomings of Wallerstein's proposed integration.

2. The Selfobject Transferences and the Developmental Concept of the Selfobject. Expectations based on classical theory have focused ultimate analytic attention exclusively on the *transference neurosis* for quite some time. Within this transference neurosis the repressed *infantile neurosis* was to be remobilized, containing at its core *the infantile Oedipus complex.* In spite of the fact that clear-cut, uncomplicated examples of such a transference neurosis were rare, this remained not only the theoretical ideal but also the practical-clinical standard against which analysts could judge whether an analytic process developed or not in a given clinical situation (compare the Ratman and the Wolfman in this regard, in Eissler, 1953, and in Tolpin, 1970). Clinical experience finally led to the assumption that the regressive emergence of pre-oedipal issues in the transference blurred the sharpness, clarity, and the well-delineated structure of the transference neurosis—at times to such an extent that the analyst searched for its very appearance in vain. When continued hope for the interpretive undoing of the supposed regression did not bring forth the expected transference neurosis, the presence of pre-oedipal fixations, with accompanying ego alterations, were thought to necessitate the use of parameters to make a classical analysis possible. From among the many, varied, and significant efforts by ego psychologists and object relations theorists to deal with these expansions of psychoanalysis beyond the neuroses and neurotic personality disorders, I select only one here, in transition to my remarks about selfobject transferences.

In what was then a landmark contribution, a deeply penetrating study, Eissler (1953) called attention to the technical problems in patients with structural defects in the ego: "it is not so much the particular combination of symptoms and defenses—that is to say, the structure of the symptom—which necessitates the specific technique [of the use of parameters] but the ego organization in which the particular symptom is embedded [p. 117]." He further recognized that the symptoms or behavior deviations did not, in and of themselves, necessarily betray the true structure of the ego organization. He then deplored the fact that: "Unfortunately we do not yet have an adequate conceptual frame of reference to describe these ego modifications although we are constantly struggling with them in most patients who now come for analysis [p. 133]."

In the absence of an adequate conceptual frame of reference and by fully maintaining the drive-defense model, Eissler used "the basic model technique of analysis" as his fixed point, in relation to which he focused on the patient's ability either to use interpretations exclusively or not (in which case parameters had to be introduced) to detect the presence or absence of flaws in the organization of the ego. It was at this point that Eissler, with his attention focused on the ego matrix and not on the structure of the symptom or behavior, was on the verge of truly new ideas regarding the nature of psychopathology and the psychoanalytic treatment process. What blocked his road to new discoveries? He seems to have posed the question: What is the nature of the ego matrix in those patients who cannot use the basic model technique? This question is oriented toward the specific psychopathology of the ego organization *wthout reference to a specific transference,* and it also assumes that the interpretation of drives and defenses (supposedly responsible for this alteration in ego organization) is correct and applicable. Therefore, something must be the matter with the patient, if he or she cannot make use of the analyst's interpretations. Had Eissler asked himself what his patients attempted to revive in the transference and what they conveyed about themselves to him with the expression of these needs, he might have discovered the narcissistic transferences. In other words, had Eissler's questions been oriented toward the discovery of the specific nature of the transferences that his patients with ego defects tried to mobilize in the analysis, he would have opened the road to new insights. It would have been especially useful if he could also have asked about the interpretations themselves—their focus and content—which his patients could not use. He might then have discovered that the usual drive-defense interpretations did not address the basic issues in these transferences. And he could also have been alerted to the primary pathogenic significance of unmet, nondrive-related developmental needs in his patients and could have come upon the discovery of those deficits or defects that give rise to the selfobject transferences.

Eissler's careful and meticulous approach to the clinical-theoretical problems of what we would now call self pathology teaches us an important lesson: Analysis can only make lasting, major leaps ahead regarding any treatment problems through a deeper comprehension of the nature of the transferences and their working through. In retrospect, we can now see how Eissler's then creative use of the idea of parameter (to delineate the basic model technique) deflected his attention from what his patients were striving to revive with him in the analytic situation. Instead, he aimed at specifying the nature of the ego pathology, which—as he stated—could not yet be accurately described without an adequate conceptual frame of reference. Focusing on his patients' reactions and behaviors in relation to the "fixed" basic model technique, Eissler seemed more concerned with preserving *it* than with finding a fundamentally more suitable analytic (i.e., interpretive) approach if that entailed altering the classical paradigm. It is easy to see with hindsight that the use of parameters blocked substantive new discoveries precisely at those points where parameters were applied. Such moments in an analysis provide opportunities for finding new interpretive approaches as well as new configurations of psychopathology by not rushing in with parameters.

Kohut's contributions, slightly more than a decade later, began with a fresh approach to patients who were coming to him for analysis. His systematic delineation of the selfobject transferences and his reconstruction of the selfobjects' specific role and function in development from the working through of these transferences successfully addressed the clinical-theoretical problems related to his patients. Kohut described the manifestations and specific configurations of these transferences on the basis of empirical data, gained in the process of using his newly discovered interpretive approach, focusing on the mirroring and idealizing needs of his patients and their vicissitudes (including the resistances against their emergence) in the analytic situation. He described the spontaneous clustering of the significant themes in the analysis around the issues related to the two main lines of development in the self. In other words, the predominant and significant traumatic experiences— leading to an arrest or derailment in the development of the grandiose self (mirror transference) or in the development of the idealized parent imago (idealizing transference)—are always reflected in their singular or sequential emergence in the transference. These empirical findings—their claimed "purity," as against their regular and anticipated mixture with object-instinctual transferences in the same analytic process—could only be confirmed or disconfirmed with the application of the same method.

Kohut was fully aware of the "logic" of his critics in this area, most clearly expressed by Wallerstein, when he said: "For in the flow and flux of analytic clinical material we are always in the world of both/and. We deal constantly, and in turn, with both the oedipal where there is a coherent self and the preoedipal where there may not yet be, with defensive regressions and with developmental arrests, with defense transferences and defensive resistances and with re-creations of earlier traumatic and traumatized states, etc. [p. 319]." It is here that Wallerstein considers the principle of overdetermination or multiple function as the appropriate concept, justifying a both/and rather than an either/or view.

There are some problems with this claim. The concept of overdetermination is logically untenable, if it means that a particular symptom, behavior pattern or dream image, etc., is simultaneously or sequentially determined by more than one dynamic-genetic motive. If one of these motives is enough to determine the presence of a symptom, a behavior pattern or a dream image—it would be impossible to demonstrate convincingly that more than one determining factor was necessary to bring forth any of them. Waelder resolved this logical dilemma by reformulating the concept essentially thus: each psychological event or pattern might be used as a vehicle for the expression of many different dynamic-genetic motives, simultaneously or sequentially—and that each of these psychological phenomena may, therefore, generally serve *multiple functions.* Another way to say this is that the psychological phenomena under consideration would be able to express many, varied and developmentally layered sequences of meanings. This concept is *not* related to the different metapsychological points of view, which might be used to describe any *one* of these psychological events and any *one* of the meanings each might convey, from different vantage points. The different matapsychological points of view would not offer different meanings for the same experience; they would only offer different vantage points from which to describe them.

Based on the concept of multiple function *in isolation* one could claim validity and relevance for any meaning or any variety of meanings, as fitting into the same context. Many incompatible or even contradictory meanings could be viewed as simultaneous possibilities, if we had no further guide-lines to sort them out and to discard those found irrelevant or untenable in a particular clinical situation.

Based on the concept of multiple function *within the transference,* however, we would have a way to determine the relevant and tenable meanings which *do* fit into the same context. With recourse to the dynamic-genetic reconstruction in the transference we could sort out from among the many *possible* meanings those that are compatible with, or contradictory to, the overall clinical context.

For example, the transference of a patient with an incompletely structuralized psyche would reveal central concerns with issues related to self-regulation (self-soothing, self-calming and the efforts at channeling and containing peremptory drive-needs or using them to maintain or to re-establish the precarious cohesiveness of the self, etc.). An archaic idealizing transference would crystallize around these issues and would serve as the red thread to guiding us to the various *related* meanings in the patient's experiences. In the process of a sustained, cohesive, archaic idealizing transference the *content* might, for instance, frequently be manifestly sexual, but its meaning would still be related to issues of self-regulation and not to oedipal or post-oedipal sexuality.

Wallerstein, on the other hand, claims that in the flow and flux of analytic material we would regularly encounter oedipal issues where there is a coherent self, side by side with preoedipal issues, where there may not yet be a coherent self. Our thesis is—not refuted by anything Wallerstein presented so far—based on our clinical approach, that the not yet structuralized part of the psyche, if extensive, would manifest itself in a cohesive selfobject transference, in which the issues of self-regulation would be paramount (depending on how early development had been arrested or derailed). Oedipal issues—*as content*—in such a situation may, of course, enter into the selfobject transference and would show that these were "used," with some urgency and even compulsion, for self-stimulation. The appearance of oedipal content may, as it often has, mislead us regarding the central pathognomonic transference. (Note that Wallerstein was not talking here about regression from oedipal issues, side by side with the oedipal issues themselves, but about fixations at prior levels, where there is not reliable cohesiveness of the self as yet.)

How could we have a both/and view of the oedipal and pre-oedipal issues here, when we see the centrality of self-pathology in the transference and consider the oedipal issues as expressions of self-healing efforts that are bound to fail, until belated structuralization becomes possible? A both/and view would only make sense from our vantage point if a *genuine* Oedipus complex manifest in the transference neurosis could be observed side by side with prestructural issues severe enough to mobilize an archaic, cohesive selfobject transference within that same analytic process.

An analysis characterized by the emergence of an archaic idealizing transference could still be very rich in content and yet essentially revolve around the working through of the pathognomonic transference, which would lead to the belated acquisition of missing self-regulatory functions.

The "flow and flux" discussed by Wallerstein, which seems to contain so much, from so many different developmental levels, and with different degrees of structuralization, seems to overlook the clustering that Kohut first described and was subsequently noted by many of us. The idea of looking for such a clustering was not new, because the transference neurosis also represented a clustering of themes within a defined structure. Inasmuch as there was only one such transference structure available to us for so long, it seemed to be inclusive of everything we might observe in an analysis, and we used to think that it was either mobilized, partially mobilized, or not mobilized at all (in which case there was to be no analytic engagement or analytic process). This all-inclusiveness may well have been one of the reasons why, with time, the transference neurosis became a less and less sharply delineated configuration, and this paved the way for the discovery of the selfobject transferences.

Kohut's view that we are empirically—even if this is illogical from the vantage point of previous conceptualizations—in the world of either/or is not shaken by invoking the principle of multiple function in isolation. Neither is it shaken by simply registering, phenomenologically (i.e., in terms of their appearance in the content), the "flow and flux" or varied analytic material. Their relationship to each other in terms of the specific form of psychopathology, its correlated central transference constellation, and the developmentally significant issues that are revived in it can aid in assigning primary significance to some and secondary significance to other manifestations of the transference. Another way to say this is that a variety of contents (in an incompletely structuralized psyche), from any level of human experience, can be used to express the efforts at belated structure building through transmuting internalization.

How these specific efforts are reflected in the process and content of the analysis certainly needs further study. The selfobject as a developmental construct, however, because it is closely tied to the selfobject transferences that gave rise to it, puts the treatment process more firmly within a developmental context, within which ultimately analytic cure and how to obtain it will also be more clearly articulated. In the meantime, I can only say that the either/or view—even if it will have to be modified later on—is at present still of greater heuristic value than the more weakly supported, albeit logical, both/and approach, for which the concept of multiple function lends no compelling support.

Thus far I have argued that deficit psychology cannot be integrated even into a broadened conflict theory without considerable loss. Furthermore, the concept of multiple function in isolation (i.e., without reference to the pathognomonic transferences) cannot forge a reliable bridge between certain incompatible meanings (which emerge in distinct transferences), and we cannot combine them under one conceptual umbrella in the manner suggested by Wallerstein. However, I have indicated, as Wallerstein himself noted, the direction in which Kohut envisaged that such an integration might ultimately be possible: an integration under the broad concept of the supraordinate bipolar self.

What still remains to be discussed, however, is the role and function of empathy, which continues to be misunderstood and therefore unnecessarily complicates our dialogue. I can only deal here, rather briefly and narrowly, with those aspects of empathy that Wallerstein chose to focus on in his critique.

3. Empathy in the Psychoanalytic Process and in Theory Formation. The preceding discussion, stressing deficit psychology and the preference for the temporary, tactical maintenance of a *de facto* complementarity, requires further support by addressing an aspect of the method of psychoanalysis that Wallerstein considers to have been overemphasized or altogether one-sidedly considered in self psychology: the issue of empathy—maternal, or more generally, parental empathy and analytic empathy.

Let me reiterate that empathy had, indeed, always been considered an essential aspect of the psychoanalyst's approach to patients. This had frequently been acknowledged, albeit often only in passing. Even though the process of empathy and its precise definition eluded us, its importance has not. Wallerstein is right in stressing the fact that its importance has preceded the development of self psychology. Even in Kohut's own work, the clinical use of empathy and its various deepening and broadening definitions emerged gradually. In his first contribution to the subject, Kohut "simply" delineated the field of psychoanalysis against biology on the one hand and against social psychology on the other. He circumscribed psychoanalysis as a field of knowledge characterized by what is empathic-introspectively graspable or potentially graspable. This put psychoanalysis as a "pure" psychology, rather than as a biologically anchored psychology, on the map—along with many other attempts to see it within that framework. The most prevalent definition of empathy was then still a narrow one. Empathy was considered to be, as its German term "Einfühlung" indicates, an approach to the feeling-states of others,

an avenue to the inner world of feelings. In its later expansions in the
work of many analysts and nonanalysts—including Kohut's own
work—empathy encompassed feelings *and* thoughts, and it was *the*
most direct avenue for the observation of the complex inner life of
humans. It was conceived as the capacity for *feeling* oneself into and
thinking oneself into complex mental states; a mode of cognition, an
observational vantage point *sine qua non,* for the psychoanalytic
study of people. There is no contradiction of any note, in the recent
literature, that would question the definition just given. Psychoanalysts of all persuasions share it, although some would not consider empathy in a central position in psychoanalysis, and some would
be more preoccupied with the potential errors in understanding that
empathy might lead to, namely, to "well known risks of wild analysis" (p. 329). Though there is broad definitional agreement, there are
diverse ways in which analysts consider the importance of empathy
and its application in the clinical situation, that is, in its actual use.
Wallerstein, in recognizing "empathy (and introspection) as vital
components of the psychoanalytic process," claims that stressing it
"is neither that new nor that unique to self-psychology theory."

I continue to feel that Kohut's first use of introspection and empathy to define our field and to define our analytic observational
stance—acceptable or unacceptable as these definitions may be—is
not only novel but revolutionary. The latter aspect could not be
appreciated in 1957 [1959], but with hindsight none of us could miss
it. All of Kohut's work is a sequel to it.

Wallerstein, on the other hand, proceeds to claim that "a number
of converging strands of psychoanalytic emphasis on the closely related issue of the nature and quality of the psychoanalytic relationship as a major factor in the mutative process in analysis" have
emerged at about the same time, and he places Kohut's emphasis on
empathy into the same broad and diverse trend. When he then lists
Alexander's "corrective emotional experience," Zetzel's "therapeutic alliance," Greenson's "working alliance," and Loewald's "integrative experience" (which Wallerstein terms "empathically crafted") as "closely related issues," it is clear that his focus on "the
nature and quality of the psychoanalytic relationship" misses the
essential points regarding introspection and empathy. None of those
concepts Wallerstein listed are even remotely related to what we
consider to be the empathic (introspective) observational stance, the
scientific use of empathy. They seem to be more closely related

(except for Loewald's concept) to such notions as tact, personal warmth, and the expressions of caring—as if these could or should be made a part of technique, rather than remain in a natural part of any good analytic ambience. (Loewald's concept is an exception in that context; his ideas on the role of empathy are, in some respects, more akin to ours.)

There is then the added misconception that in self psychology empathy is used *instead* of interpretation, when in fact Kohut consistently spoke of empathic understanding as an obligatory precursor of interpretation. Understanding and interpretation are the key issues in any analysis, and he clearly restated, further articulated, and explicated the details of this process.

Could empathy as a mode of observation be regarded as overemphasized? I imagine it could if there occurred simultaneously a real underemphasis of interpretation. But this is definitely not the case, certainly not in principle and certainly not as an ideal to approximate. What the patient makes of the analyst's efforts at empathic understanding, how he or she experiences it, is another issue. But isn't the patient "entitled" to use the analyst's interventions, in the transference, in terms of his or her own needs, wishes, demands, and fantasies—which are ultimately analyzed?

Of course, empathically derived knowledge can be wrong. The empathic stance by itself does not guarantee accuracy or validity; the transference context, the patient's associations, dreams, and the like help us sort out and verify the validity of our observations. But the extrospective stance does not automatically guarantee accuracy or validity of observations either. Some scientists (e.g., Polanyi) and historians (e.g., Collingwood, Tuchman) are further along in their appreciation of the role and function of empathy as a mode of observation than are some psychoanalysts, who view the method of empathy (introspection) with greater suspicion.

Not only can empathic observation be incorrect, it can also be used against our fellow men—Kohut knew that and wrote about it before his critics argued about its potential misuse. We should more even-handedly recognize that extrospective, as well as introspective observations, if unchecked, could lead to "grievous errors" and "wild analysis."

Maternal empathy (or the empathy of the selfobject milieu in general) is another subject in need of extensive further exploration in this context, since it is the developmental precursor of analytic empathy (which is different, even if it springs fundamentally from the same source). Putting the selfobject's empathic attunement and responses and their failures into the center of etiologic and therapeutic concerns, is by no means a "theoretical reductionistic oversimplification" if its complexities are truly perceived.

Maternal empathy and the "empathic failures" of the analyst-selfobject are also misunderstood and tendentiously portrayed by the critics Wallerstein quotes, without in turn critically examining their assertions. Empathic failure is an observable, verifiable fact in the analytic situation. How it arises and what its consequences are, can be studied microscopically within the process of analysis. Why such failures lead to disruptions in the transference; what their genetic precursors were, tell us a great deal about the reasons why patients react to them the way they do. Their role—if not traumatic—in belated structure building is another aspect that can be studied, if we don't dismiss such considerations a priori as parent-blaming or analyst-blaming. Of course, failure in treatment outcome is a complex issue. The nature of the patient's psychopathology, countertransference reactions of the analyst, inadequate skills, and so forth have all been studied more extensively as to their contribution to therapeutic failures. The specific issue of empathic failures (chronic empathic failures especially) are of enormous, as yet not fully appreciated, significance in analytic stalemates and dropouts, whereas nontraumatic, expectable, and inevitable failures are part of the structure-building process during development, as well as during analysis. Why is a focus on expectable, nontraumatic empathic failures more analyst-blaming than Freud's dictum that an analyst can only take his patient so far in the analysis, as he himself was able to go in his own analysis? Has anyone ever attacked Freud on that point?

Wallerstein correctly links the place self psychology accords empathy in the clinical situation and in theory formation to his concern with whether this does not radically alter our current notion of psychoanalysis as a science and as a treatment process. To elaborate on that concern here would require more space than I have at my disposal. Instead, I would just indicate that we, as clinicians and as scientists, ought not fear radical alterations in our clinical or theoretical approach if they are warranted by offering us increased explanatory and therapeutic power because, if they in fact do not, they will ultimately wither away on the vine. Furthermore, should we not rather feel liberated by the thought that even some of our more cherished concepts—those which we cannot at this point imagine being able to do without, as Kohut said—might someday be replaceable? Is it not this particular stance that lends additional validity to the claim that psychoanalysis is a science?

How is all this related to the issue of complementarity, the both/and rather than the either/or view, and the supposedly deciding principle of multiple function? First, it should now be clear that vague, quantitative statements involving *more* empathy or *less* empathy do not address the issues related to empathy as an observational stance, as a mode cognition. Such statements use the term in its reference to tact, warmth, giving and caring attitudes, and so on rather than in its scientific sense.

Second, it should also be clear that this observational stance naturally leads to different kinds of data about the patients' subjective inner world and that, based on such data, more experience-near theories had been constructed to explain health and illness. From the outset, Kohut stressed the inseparable relationship between mode of observation and theory.

Third, empathy was, of course, not introduced into psychoanalysis by self psychology, as I noted earlier. Kohut had not yet even embarked on his work on narcissism when he considered introspection and empathy as the central method *and* as the definer of our field. Has self psychology subsequently and unfairly appropriated psychoanalytic empathy and claimed a superior usage of it as some of our critics charge? In other words, have self psychologically informed analysts claimed to be more empathic than their colleagues? Not at all. Their references had never been to a "more" or to a "less," but to the deliberate, systematic, prolonged, and sustained use of empathy as an observational attitude or the nonuse of it in this manner. To the degree that method of observation and resulting theories are inextricably intertwined and, furthermore, to the degree that the development of empathy could now be studied in the analytic process as a transformation of archaic narcissism and that the analyst's use of it and his expectable, recurrent failures could also be observed, more knowledge has been gained in relation to its development, role, and function in the curative process of analysis. To this degree and in these areas it has, indeed, become more closely linked to the clinical approach and to the theories of self psychology.

All this brings me back to "The Two Analyses of Mr. Z." It is decidedly not a matter of "less empathy" in the first analysis and "more empathy" in the second that improved the results of the second analysis. One might argue about less correct or more correct observations as a result of the effort at empathy. Whatever criticisms we may now have of the first analysis—that it was conducted in an authoritarian climate, that the analyst pushed interpretive interventions too strongly, that he missed some significant pregenital issues related to the mother, and so on—none seem to me decisive, even if correct. Both patient and analyst were reasonably satisfied with the work accomplished, which might indicate that at least the analytic ambiance was reasonably good. Patients usually do not return to the same analyst for a second analysis, if they felt that something was lacking in the earlier ambiance. Not having felt fully understood—though extremely important—is often of less significance in such decisions, if the analytic climate, on the whole, was reasonably good.

No one who has actually tried the approach illustrated by Kohut in his second analysis of Mr. Z could miss the significance of the remobilization of the mirror transference and the idealizing transference—squelched in the first analysis to a significant degree, because it was not recognized—in the attainment of the results of the second analysis. Although Wallerstein does not seem to be sufficiently impressed by it, viewing the mirroring and idealizing needs as expressions of selfobject transferences rather than as defenses against object-instinctual demands made all the difference. The new theories seemed to offer a better guide for the analyst's empathic observations and interventions. The outcome, including the richness of analytic material in the process, could not be ascribed to an improved ambiance.

Rangell's idea that the two analyses of Mr. Z together "should have comprised one total classical analysis" is an inexplicable claim. How the conception of the mobilization and working through of the selfobject transferences can be both Kohut's significant addition to classical analysis (Wallerstein) and simultaneously be considered an integral part of a total classical analysis (Rangell) is beyond my comprehension.

But what is more important in the long run is the fact that most critics of self psychology who focused upon the issue of empathy before they had a chance to test its application in the manner suggested by Kohut and others in self psychology (Ornstein, 1979) could therefore not yet offer us substantive criticisms of the actual use of empathy from within the vantage point of the prolonged empathic-introspective immersion into the transference experiences of their patients and thereby meet us on the same level of discourse. This last point brings me to conclude this discussion with some reflections on Wallerstein's overall message and his method of critique.

4. Some Reflections on Wallerstein's Overall Message and His Method of Critique. Wallerstein has thus far offered what is undoubtedly a most comprehensive and most balanced critique. His acceptance of and efforts at integrating the psychology of the self in the narrower sense into his redefined brand of psychoanalysis and his leaving the door open for the possible usefulness of the concept of the bipolar self within his own broadened and considerably altered (yet still classical?) basic paradigm have all created an ambiance conducive to a fruitful (and I hope ongoing) scientific dialogue.

In his overall message Wallerstein gently admonishes us for what he considers our devisive language of either/or; somewhat less gently, he admonishes me in particular for insisting that self psychology deserves to be considered the third paradigm in psychoanalysis and for insisting that an integration of self psychology into classical analysis is at best premature and at worst not really possible. Let me remind you of a historical parallel: Ego psychology could not possibly have been integrated into id psychology, whereas id psychology could—in time and with certain transformations—readily be integrated into ego psychology.

Wallerstein's ardor for integration is admirable, but its intensity may have obscured his vision from recognizing certain methodological obstacles in its path. It is not a matter of psychoanalysts being friendly, ecumenical, and mutually supportive. That, I believe, we should always be, and most of us are in any case. But for the sake of possible further advances in our field, we should accept with a greater degree of tolerance and good will various attempts to struggle with the very real clinical and theoretical problems at hand. In this spirit, then, why should we not recognize the presently maintained complementarity as a clear-cut, legitimate difference of opinion and, rather than counseling moderation or accommodation, accept the heuristic value of sharply divergent formulations and leave the decision about integration to the arbitrating influence of further clinical-empirical observations.

I do not underestimate the powerful elements of group psychology in needing the support of like-minded people to carry on with the lonely task of analytic practice, and therefore the legitimacy of striving for consensus and for avoiding unnecessary conflicts. But could we not support each other more explicitly in the endeavor of finding new solutions for widespread clinical-theoretical problems, thereby strengthening ourselves for facing the necessary and inevitable conflicts on the scientific plane?

Turning to this scientific plane, what is Wallerstein's method of critique? His method could best be described as extrospective and comparative; he views our clinical data and theories from within his own expanded and revised point of view and from the vantage point of his own clinical experience, which he accumulated within his own stated frame of reference. Within this approach, he appropriately compares our clinical data and our theories with his own and arrives at certain judgments regarding their novelty in relation to, and compatibility or incompatibility with, his own frame of reference, along with the judgment of whether even the new propositions can be properly accommodated within the old. Wallerstein certainly does not remain a *distant* external observer. He does not do what most of our critics do—shout across to us from a gaping divide; rather he comes over to our side and takes his measure of our clinical and theoretical contributions from up close. He is a friendly, broadly knowledgeable, and helpful critic, but an extrospective one nevertheless.

This extrospective observational stance is not the most effective form of psychoanalytic criticism, as is demonstrated by the fact that it made it necessary for Wallerstein to translate some of our concepts first into his own (e.g., deficit into conflict) before he could finally accommodate or reject them. It was apparently the same observational stance that made it necessary for him to blunt the edge of Kohut's "strong statement" regarding a separate developmental line for narcissism or the "extreme" and "fanciful" metaphor of needing selfobjects from birth to death for psychological survival, as much as needing oxygen for physiological survival. By attempting to attenuate so-called strong statements and modulate or moderate those that seem to him to be extreme or fanciful, Wallerstein transforms basic concepts of self psychology into his own by mere rhetoric. Whether a statement is "strong" or "weak" is of minor significance compared to *what* it states. One either views the developmental line of narcissism as separate, with all of the clinical and theoretical consequences of such a view, or one chooses not to view it as separate, with all of its consequences. Quantitative statements of this sort only obscure the point. One could more appropriately argue about the clinical or theoretical consequences of one view as against the other, but attenuating or modulating efforts do not seem to me to be of help. The same applies to Kohut's relatively newly formulated claims regarding archaic and mature selfobjects. One either needs selfobjects throughout life, or one does not. Can one claim such a need if one views the selfobject as life-sustaining throughout the life cycle (albeit with changing functions) by comparing this to the need for oxygen? Would omitting the oxygen metaphor make this statement "less extreme?" I doubt it. Again, we either do or do not need selfobjects throughout the life cycle, and each view will have its clinical and theoretical consequences, which can be critically studied within the psychoanalytic situation.

Without first attempting to translate our concepts into his, or simply to compare them, Wallerstein might have moved *inside* our frame of reference entirely—even if only temporarily and experimentally—to gain an insider's view and to offer his critique from that internal vantage point. Our claim remains that the "inside view" is different.

I realize that asking Wallerstein to enter our frame of reference is no small task; perhaps, it is an impossible expectation. However, as analysts, we cannot work with "alien" understandings but only with those that we have finally made into our very own—those that we had been able to digest and metabolize, the way we digest and metabolize foreign protein and assimilate it into a constituent of our own body.

On balance, and leaving many other topics for future discussions, I am deeply indebted to Dr. Wallerstein for his scholarly and outspoken critique. We shall live with his challenge for some time to come, and in our ongoing work we shall continue to address the issues he raised, hopefully with greater clarity and on the proper scientific plane.

REFERENCES

Collingwood, R. G. (1946). *The Idea of History*. Clarendon Press.

Eissler, K. R. (1953). The Effect of the Structure of the Ego on Psychoanalytic Technique. *J. Amer. Psychoanal. Assn.* 1: 375–451.

Klein, G. (1976). *Psychoanalytic Theory: An Exploration of Essentials*. New York, Int. Univ. Press.

Kohut, H. (1971). *The Analysis of the Self—A Systematic Approach to the Psychoanalytic Treatment of Narcissistic Personality Disorders*. New York, Int. Univ. Press.

—— (1977). *The Restoration of the Self*, New York, Int. Univ. Press.

—— (1978). Reflections on advances in self psychology. In Goldberg, ed. *Advances in Self Psychology*. New York, Int. Univ. Press.

—— & Wolf, E. (1978). The Disorders of the self and their treatment: An outline. *Int. J. Psychoanal.* 59: 413–425.

Ornstein, P. H. (1978). Self psychology and the concept of health. In Goldberg, ed. *Advances in Self Psychology*. New York, Int. Univ. Press, pp. 137–159.

—— (1979). Remarks on the central position of empathy in psychoanalysis. *Bull. The Assoc. of Psychoanal. Med.* 18: 95–108.

Sandler, J. (1974). Psychological conflict and the structural model: Some clinical and theoretical implications. *Int. J. Psycho-Anal.* 55: 53–62.

—— (1976). Actualization and object relationships. *J. Phila. Assoc. for Psychoanal.* 3: 59–70.

—— (1978). Unconscious wishes and Human Relationships. University College London. Freud Memorial Inaugural Lectures. (Pamphlet).

Schafer, R. (1976). *A New Language for Psychoanalysis*. New Haven: Yale Univ. Press.

Stein, M. (1979). Book Review: *The Restoration of the Self. J. Amer. Psychoanal. Assn.* 27: 665–680.

Tolpin, M. (1970). The infantile neurosis: A metapsychological concept and a paradigmatic case history. *The Psychoanal. Study of the Child* XXV: 273–305.

Tuchman, B. (1981). *Practicing History—Selected Essays*. New York, Alfred A. Knopf.

Polanyi, M., 1974. Personal Knowledge.

VI THEORY

28

Selected Problems of Self Psychological Theory[1]

Heinz Kohut, M.D.

I

Having carefully read the contributions to this volume of Arnold Goldberg, Robert Stolorow, and Robert Wallerstein, along with Paul Ornstein's thoughtful discussion of these papers, I realize that I can hardly do justice in these remarks to all the fascinating ideas that have been expressed. I have decided, therefore, to limit myself to only the most challenging ideas and, furthermore, to those ideas about which I can comment meaningfully in a relatively brief essay.

Let me start with the question that is foremost in the minds of many analysts trying to understand the viewpoint of self psychology: How does the psychoanalytic self psychologist view the Oedipus complex? In addressing this question I must first say that I deal with this issue at length in a forthcoming volume on the concept of the analytic cure and that the following remarks can do no more than briefly preview some of the principal conclusions I reach in that study. Let me say first of all that I have found it useful to differentiate

[1]My original extemporaneous discussion was recorded, transcribed, and then carefully preedited by Dr. Arnold Goldberg. It is the transcript as edited by Dr. Goldberg that provided the basis for the following reflections. Dr. Paul Stepansky's editorial work in the early preparation of this manuscript is gratefully acknowledged by the editors. See also acknowledgement to Dr. Schwaber, p. 13.

among: (1) an oedipal *phase* or oedipal *period* (referring to the occurrence of certain experiences—whether normal, potentially pathogenic, or pathological—that typify a certain age; (2) an oedipal *stage* (referring to the normal set of experiences at that age); and finally (3) the Oedipus *complex* (the pathological distortion of the normal stage). (I should add at once that the latter two categories are posited independently of considerations pertaining to the frequency of occurrence.) In the context of the issues raised by the contributors to this volume, the most significant differentiation is that between the oedipal "stage" and the Oedipus "complex."

I can condense the problem we are facing by translating it into the following question: If a normal, joyfully experienced stage of self-development exists that, in harmony with psychoanalytic tradition, may be called the oedipal stage, what is the essence of this stage? And if the experiences of this normal stage can become distorted and, in this distorted form, provide the seedbed for the drive-wishes, conflicts, guilt feelings, and anxieties of the Oedipus complex, the nucleus of the oedipal neuroses, what is the essence of the "complex" in contrast to the essence of the "stage"? Furthermore, what exactly causes the deleterious transformation of a normal stage into a pathological and potentially pathogenic complex?

Traditionally, analysts have held, with Freud, that the normal oedipal stage is identical with the Oedipus complex or, stated differently, that the Oedipus complex constitutes the experiential content of a normal stage of development. Leaving aside the problems that arise when we attempt to define the "normalcy," as opposed to the frequency or even the ubiquity of an occurrence (dental caries is "ubiquitous" but not "normal"), I first emphasize again that self psychology does not consider drives or conflicts as pathological nor does it consider even intense experiences of anxiety or guilt as pathological or pathogenic per se. Three cheers for drives! Three cheers for conflicts! They are the stuff of life, part and parcel of the experiential quintessence of the healthy self. The same can be said of anxiety and guilt. The healthy self may be beset by conflicts and, derivatively, experience intense guilt and anxiety. But such experiences are not tantamount to the drives, conflicts, guilts, and anxieties of the Oedipus complex which, under certain circumstances, may in adult life lead to the symptoms of the so-called oedipal neuroses. They do not, in other words, bring about the *type* of conflict—half of which is entirely unconscious (the drive-wishes) and half of which is largely unconscious (the defenses against the drive-wishes), with only a bit of this unconscious iceberg manifest in the form of symptoms—that constitutes the nucleus of the classical transference neuroses of adult life according to Freud's beautiful, internally consistent, early formulation.

And why does self psychology believe that Freud's early theory, despite its ingenuity and intellectual coherence, is in error? The answer is clear: Once clinical observation is informed by the self psychological assertion that the self and its matrix of selfobjects are, in principle, an indivisible unit (analogous to the inseparableness of the human body and the oxygen-containing atmosphere that surrounds it), the data concerning the child's experiences do not support the old theory, but require a new one.

The question at issue is this: What, in the analyses of the transferences of our patients, is the deepest level to which we can ultimately penetrate after we have thoroughly investigated and worked through the drive-wishes, conflicts, guilts, fears, and anxieties of the Oedipus complex? Have we reached biological bedrock once we have dealt with these oedipal issues, or is their analysis followed by the emergence of a more deeply buried selfobject transference that underlies the Oedipus complex? To put it differently, do we eventually gain access to a pathogenic selfobject transference which, replicating the pathogenic experiences of childhood, reveals the object-instinctual drives (and the related conflicts, guilts, and anxieties) to be only intermediate pathogenic links leading—if the circumstances in adult life promote this development—secondarily, to the manifestations of the oedipal neuroses?

Our affirmative answer to this question—our clinical discovery of the regularity with which pathogenic self-selfobject experiences in childhood account for an Oedipus complex—suggests a return, after more than 80 years, to Freud's original seduction theory. Freud, we recall, had formulated this theory on the basis of his patients' communications only to discover, suddenly and to his intense dismay, that he had been misled and duped, had been too credulous, had had the wool pulled over his eyes.

But though we affirm the correctness of the general etiological presuppositions that underlay Freud's original seduction theory, we certainly do not advocate a return to the specific content of his early formulation. (*Actual* seduction of children by parental figures is in essence the manifestation of a much more serious kind of selfobject failure than that which leads to the pathological and, potentially, pathogenic distortion of the oedipal stage.) But we do enjoin analysts to look for and discover that basic layer of psychological truth about the past that Freud had first encountered in the stories of parental seduction told by his hysterical patients. It is well known that Freud at first totally accepted the accusations that these hysterics leveled against their parents and that he then, in an understandable *volte-face*—unfortunately, as I now add—totally rejected them.

But here I must stop. It is clearly beyond the scope of this discussion to outline, even briefly the failures of the oedipal selfobjects that bring about the Oedipus complex. Such failures transform the normal upsurge of affectionateness and assertiveness—essential attributes of the proud and joyful oedipal self—into the pathological and pathogenic drives, which we traditionally viewed as the manifestations of the final stage of normal infantile sexuality. Suffice it to say that, as with "pre-oedipal" infantile sexuality and destructive aggression, we consider the infantile sexuality and hostile-destructive aggresssion of the oedipal phase (i.e., the Oedipus complex) to be disintegration products. As such, they supervene only after the selfobjects have failed to respond to the primary affectionateness and assertiveness of the oedipal-phase self with fondness and pride because they have, on the basis of their own psychopathology, experienced (preconsciously) these emotions of their oedipal child as sexually stimulating and aggresively threatening.

II

From the examination of the oedipal period we proceed to another challenging topic that was considered by several contributors to this volume; I refer to an age-old puzzle that one might loosely characterize as the "inside-versus-outside" question. In brief, this asks whether certain phenomena (i.e., perceived data) should be assigned a position within the framework of the inner world, accessible via introspection and vicarious introspection (empathy), or whether they should be situated within the framework of the outer world, accessible via extrospection and vicarious extrospection (eyewitness accounts). Ignoring for the time being the fact that the phenomena of the outer world are themselves "endopsychic" inasmuch as extrospection depends on our sensory organs (i.e., the fact that the independent essence of any class of phenomena, whether psychic or physical, is, in principle, unknowable), I wish to focus at once on one concrete aspect of this issue that is immediately relevant to self psychology and was therefore raised, directly and indirectly, by several of the contributors. In condensed form, the question posed was whether it makes sense to speak of self-selfobject relationships as we often, and perhaps increasingly, do. On the face of it, the phrase is illogical. Selfobjects, as they arise in the transference, are inner experiences. Specifically, they are inner experiences of certain functions of others on which our analysands focus because of certain thwarted developmental needs of the self; more objectively still, they are aspects of our analysands' experiences of certain functions of people who, extrospection informs us, are physically separate from them.

I wish I could plead innocent here concerning the reproach of terminological and conceptual inconsistency, but I admit that I cannot. But although a violation of the rules of logic cannot be denied, there are extenuating circumstances. I can adduce the fact, for example, that I am not any more inconsistent in this respect than any of my analytic predecessors; there is simply no good way out of this dilemma.

Even though I have recently addressed myself to this issue in a different context,[2] I take this opportunity to comment further on this important matter. Consider, in this respect, such a well-known and basic concept of psychoanalysis as the transference. As originally defined by Freud (1900), the transference was a purely metapsychological concept, unrelated to (extrospective) social psychology. It concerned a specific dynamic interplay within the mental apparatus by which something in the System Unconscious affected something in the System Preconscious, and a kind of compromise was formed within the latter mental area. This "something," an energized structure (a drive-wish and its ideational elaboration), was transferred onto something else, another energized structure (an idea or image in the preconscious mind). The two structures were thus amalgamated to each other, the second becoming the

---

[2]I am referring to a long, essay-type letter written to my friend Robert Stolorow a few months ago, which is included in the third volume of *The Search for the Self*, currently in preparation.

carrier of the first. The manifest content of dreams was thereby designated a transference (the result of a transfer, one might say): A day residue in the preconscious was amalgamated to an unconscious infantile wish. Manifestations of the psychopathology of everyday life and symptoms of the transference neuroses were conceptualized in this same way; so also was the transference in the clinical situation. The conscious perception of and preconscious imagery about the analyst were invaded by psychic contents from the unconscious, leading to an amalgam (the clinical transference) in the System Preconscious. What a great and internally consistent theory this originally was. As all analysts realize, however, this conception of transference changed almost immediately, becoming less consistent yet, paradoxically, much more relevant to the practical needs of the psychoanalytic clinician.

There are not many analysts, I dare say, who worry greatly about the inconsistencies, the flagrant inconsistencies, involved in their daily use of the term "transference relationship." Yet, the fact is that when traditional analysts speak of transference in the clinical sense, they are invoking a term that is located in the same ambiguous never-never land between endopsychic reality and social reality as the self-psychological concept of a self-selfobject relationship. In its strict sense the term "selfobject" denotes an inner experience, especially, though by no means exclusively, an inner experience of childhood that occurs when the child's self is firming. Yet, at the same time as a self psychologically informed investigator of early development thereby gains access to the selfobject experiences of children via empathy, he is simultaneously in touch with the social realities of childhood and, qua social psychologist, he will also—and I would emphasize that he should—observe the interaction between children and parents. He thus examines not only what goes on *inside* the minds of the children and their parents—their inner experiences—but, simultaneously, what goes on *between* them (e.g., how parents dispense selfobject functions that either consolidate or weaken the self of the child, and how children, in turn, act to elicit the needed responses of parents and how they differentially react when parents provide or fail to provide what they need).

What kind of reality, inner or outer, are we reconstructing during the analysis of a transference, in particular during the analysis of a selfobject transference? A whole host of problems is raised when we ask such a seemingly simple question. I focus here only on the general question that lies behind all the specific ones. This is the question concerning the nature of scientific objectivity or—reformulated in terms that are ultimately decisive for us—the more focused question of what constitutes scientific objectivity in depth psychology.

As we know, modern physics, in particular quantum physics, has come to accept the fact that, *in principle,* no aspect of known reality can ever be independent of the observer. Observer and observed are an unbreakable unit, and what we see can never be understood without including the observer and his tools of observation as an intrinsic part of the field that is being observed. Having articulated and accepted this crucial axiom,[3] however, we can immediately go further and subdivide the kinds of reality that we observe. On the one hand, there are fields in which we need not take into account the influence exerted by the observer on what is being observed, even though we must theoretically acknowledge the existence of this influence. On the other hand, there are fields where the observer's influence on the field of observation is not only of theoretical but, indeed, of the greatest practical importance. When I look at a mountain, my physical presence, the flash of my camera, and so on alter neither the form of the mountain, the position of the mountain, nor the composition of the minerals that constitute the mountain to an appreciable, important extent; in cases like this the observer's participation in the field can be disregarded. But when I look at a subparticle, my physical presence and my means of observation can-

---

[3]Although I feel almost certain that my present remarks about objectivity in science will not be misunderstood by the scientific psychoanalyst and psychotherapist—or by the physicist for that matter—I stress, as a precautionary clarification, that when I speak of the influence of observers on the field they observe, I do *not* have in mind the well-known fact, emphasized by certain philosophers of science such as Wittgenstein and Popper, that the theories held by observers determine what they are looking for and, therefore, what they find. I *am* in the present context referring to the *direct* results of the observer's physical or psychological presence. It is the gravitational pull of the physical mass of the observer, for example, or the electromagnetic participation of his beam of light that I have in mind when I say that the observer is *in principle* necessarily part of the field that he observes. That the different theories held by different observers will significantly influence the data they gather, the configurations they perceive, is quite another matter—notwithstanding the fact that two observers holding different theories and, therefore, "seeing" different constellations may *secondarily* influence the field they observe in different ways. The latter type of difference, attributable to "influence" as I use the term, might derive from the different explorational approaches or psychological stances adopted by different observers on the basis of the different configurations yielded by their respective theories.

not be disregarded; in this case the observed includes the observer, not only in principle but in a practical and appreciable way.

Returning from physics to depth psychology, we can now, with the aid of a metaphor, reformulate the question regarding the nature of scientific objectivity in depth psychology in the following specific way: Is the analyst, as a clinician and as a scientist, a macropsychologist looking at psychological "mountains" or, to complete the analogy with modern physics, is the analyst a micropsychologist looking at psychological "subparticles"? The answer is that he may be doing either. When we observe id-impulses clashing with prohibitions, we are observing an inner world that corresponds more nearly to the world of Newtonian macrophysics; we are in that observational capacity adopting the role of macropsychologists. When, however, as in self psychologically informed psychoanalysis, we investigate the psychological structures themselves and scrutinize the particles of psychological structure that are laid down as the self forms in interaction with its selfobjects, then we are, so to say, more nearly involved in micropsychology (i.e., in a psychology that corresponds more closely to Planckian than to Newtonian physics).

We do have the theoretical outlines of normal self-development, and our observations are thus made in relation to a schema of its maturation. Still, this framework serves only as an orienting background. The main focus of our observation is directed at the minute interplay between self and selfobject. This interplay encompasses experiences of optimum selfobject responses guided by accurate empathic perceptions that enhance growth and firming of the self, along with the experiences of traumatic selfobject responses guided by faulty empathic perceptions that interfere with the laying down of the structure of the self. Can the presence of the observer here be disregarded, or is it significantly implicated in what he observes? There is no question that the observer's presence is so implicated. Seen within the framework of the self-psychological observer (i.e., within the framework of micropsychology), the observer is not a neutral screen. The psychoanalytic situation, for example—to focus now on the, for the practicing psychoanalyst, most relevant illustration of the firming of a self in its interplay with the selfobject—is characterized, via implication and direct verbalization, by the fact that, for years, one individual is in the center of another individual's attention. To be in someone else's mind—to be listened to, watched, understood, thought about, remembered—is not "neutral"; rather, it is one of the most subjectively meaningful experiences that a human being can have. Such experiences embody dimensions of a self-self-object relationship that provide self-confirmation and self-sustenance. These experiences can never be disregarded by the analyst qua therapist; the activation of such experiences during therapy must further be acknowledged by the analyst qua theorist as being, in principle, an immanent and fundamental element of both the psychoanalytic process and the psychoanalytic field. Stated in more experience-distant theoretical terms, as soon as the formation of structure becomes a central therapeutic concern, as it does in self-psychological analysis, the analyst-observer must acknowledge that therapist and patient, observer and observed, form of necessity an unfissionable unit.

III

Having hopefully clarified, in the foregoing, the problems that arise when we speak of "self-selfobject relationships," I now turn to a set of questions that concern a new area of growth for self psychology. Although these questions were touched on by Stolorow, they were brought to the fore in Wallerstein's critique of the theory of the self in the broad sense (i.e., his critique of the theory of the bipolar self). The issue raised, by Wallerstein as I understand it, is this: Even granting self psychologists the license to speak of self-selfobject relationships, does it make sense to say, as we do, that these relationships exist—indeed, that they must exist—throughout life?

I am in a peculiar situation here. Due to the fact that the evolution of my terminology lagged behind the evolution of my theories, my critics can now play out the Kohut of 1971 against the Kohut of 1977. The claims made in *The Analysis of the Self* (1971), in other words, have by now become more widely accepted—surely not by everyone, but by a good many colleagues, including those who count themselves among my critics. These critics now say that we can on the whole agree with the hypothesis that archaic selfobject transferences can be analyzed and that, by resolving them via the working-through process, formerly untapped productive potentialities of the analysand may be actualized. The message embraced by these colleagues—correctly read, but not understood in its broader meaning—is that, according to the 1971 presentation of my theory, analysis enables the analysand to get rid of something archaic and unrealistic. For the critics, this verdict is in keeping with the traditional tenet that the effect of analytic exposure of the unconscious to the light of consciousness is tantamount to the eradication of the pathogenic nucleus of the analysand's psychopathology.

Correlated to this idiosyncratically constricting interpretation of my 1971 theory, that is, correlated to the erroneous assumption that my theory of the pathogenicity of selfobject failures (reactivated in the psychoanalytic situation in *archaic* selfobject transferences only) pertained only to early (pre-oedipal) childhood or even only to infancy—was another assumption silently made by many critical colleagues. They mistakenly took for granted that my theory of the reactivation of selfobject needs in analysis and of the curative effect of the working through of these needs implied that, once the archaic selfobjects had been transmuted into self-structure, object-instinctual relationships would take the place of narcissistic ones. Colleagues making this assumption clearly failed to take into consideration that from 1966 on I postulated separate lines of development for narcissism and object love (i.e., I maintained from the outset that narcissism did not mature by turning into object love). Instead, I expressly equated such maturation with: (1) the development toward such mature forms of narcissistic expression as realistic self-esteem, the ability to be guided and sustained by realizable ideals, and the achievement of such "wholesome transformations" as humor, creativity, empathy, and wisdom (Kohut, 1966); (2) the self's progressing toward a mature attitude in relation to its selfobjects, that is, toward the acquisition of the ability to seek and find realistically available other selves who will sustain it by functioning as mirrors and ideals. I might add here that even many colleagues who, from early on, accepted my postulate of separate developmental lines failed to draw the appropriate conclusion with regard to the successful analysis of narcissistic personality disorders; they too overlooked the fact that, already in 1971, I clearly equated such therapeutic success with the maturation of "narcissism."

But I must go still further in clarifying the problem under discussion. Assuming a colleague accepts the occurrence of selfobject transferences and their analyzability; assuming also that he understands that selfobject failures occur not only in infancy and early childhood but throughout early life as the ultimate cause of psychopathology; assuming finally that he accepts the idea that, after successful analysis, archaic selfobject needs are replaced by the need for mature selfobjects—cannot this colleague still question whether we have overextended the meaning of the term "selfobject," whether our theory in fact provides for anything but selfobject relationships?

My answer is that I am much more of a drive psychologist than some of the critics of self psychology. Self psychology does not replace drive psychology any more than quantum physics replaces the physics of Newton. We are dealing with different vantage points, shifts in outlook, complementarity of perspective. Modern extrospective science is very free to employ different approaches to the explanation of external reality; modern introspective science, I am convinced, must be equally free in its domain.[4] Self psychology will continue to explain the "I's" experience of the "you" from the viewpoint of our empathic comprehension of a strong, harmonious, cohesive self that is pushed toward others by sexual and aggressive drives, a self that turns toward others experienced as independent centers of initiative differentiated from itself. Under different circumstances, however, empathic comprehension will lead us to speak of a self in various states of structural fragmentation, weakness, or disharmony—not only when its disruption is severe and protracted but also when its disturbance is only fleeting and mild. Such a self is in need of others—or, repeating what I stressed earlier, at least in need of others as "others" are apprehended by the sociopsychological observer—whom it experiences not as independent centers of initiative, but as extensions of itself that can provide needed sustenance and strength. Our mother lifted us up and held us close when we were babies and thus enabled us to merge with her calmness and strength; she was an archaic idealized selfobject. A friend puts his arm around us or understandingly touches our shoulder, and we regain composure and strength; he is a mature selfobject for us now.

Contemporary self psychology originated with my exploration of archiac self-selfobject relationships (Kohut, 1959, 1968, 1971) because the particular clinical demands of patients with serious narcissistic personality disorders drew my attention initially to the

---

[4]I do not take up here the idea, to which I have referred informally to my colleagues on a number of occasions, that certain theoretical inconsistencies are valuable and that, temporarily at least, they should be tolerated as unresolved because of the "creative" tension they generate.

need for the selfobject in its archiac stage. But though our selfobject experiences mature, there is no doubt that the archiac selfobject continues to exist in the depth of our psyche; it reverberates as an experiential undertone every time we feel sustained by the wholesome effect of a mature selfobject. Even when we feel uplifted by what I have come to call our "cultural selfobjects" (i.e., the artists, musicians, poets, novelists, and dramatists of our culture) or by an inspirational political leader, the archiac selfobject experience through which we felt "uplifted" early in life will reverberate in the unconscious and impart a sense of fullness and authenticity to what we feel.

Through these insights we have proceeded to the realization that the feeling of being within the compass of human empathy may indeed exert a beneficial, wholesome, and, under certain circumstances, "therapeutic" effect (Kohut, 1980). An existence characterized by the absence of all potential empathy is vastly more terrible than life or even death in potentially empathic surroundings. For example, to be fought, or even killed by someone who hates us is preferable to being exposed to the indifference of persecutors. The latter was the inhuman fate of millions in the Nazi concentration camps who faced extermination like vermin, not death like hated enemies. It was this experience above all, I believe, that made it so difficult for most of the survivors of concentration camps to return to a normal human existence. The prolonged exposure to a milieu that lacked all selfobject support created self-defects in at least some of the survivors, including the propensity toward profound disintegration anxiety that the mere passage of time will not cure. In such cases we are dealing not with severe traumatic neuroses, but with profound self-disorders acquired *in adult life*—a fact whose crucial significance for our understanding of the self's needs for selfobjects *throughout life* cannot be overestimated. With such patients, no spontaneous cure can be expected, and only the beneficial effects of prolonged self psychologically informed therapy will, in favorable instances, have a chance of undoing some of the damage.

Extreme situations, such as the one to which the inmates of Nazi extermination camps were exposed,[5] demonstrate with special poig-

---

[5] A group of American astronauts were subjected to a psychologically similar situation when their space capsule became damaged far away from the earth and, for a while, it was feared that the spacecraft was not under full control (cf. Kohut, 1978).

nancy that the dangers which elicit the greatest fears in people are not associated with biological death per se, but with the destruction of the self through the withdrawal of selfobject support. And what is true under exceptional conditions also holds in the ordinary course of individual existence; in general, it is not death that we fear, but the withdrawal of selfobject support in the last phase of our lives. When someone who is dying is told by a friend, "I, too, will someday have to cross the barrier that you are crossing now, and watching you and observing your courage will be an inspiration to me when I face the end of my existence," this friend functions, whether knowingly or by virtue of his spontaneous human responsiveness, as a selfobject for the dying person. And the dying person, feeling himself sustained within a functioning selfobject matrix, will end his life proudly and without undue fear, even as consciousness is fading away.

Finally, let us glance briefly at the self-selfobject relationships of the oedipal period and of adolescence. In the present context I can do little more than emphasize that a number of heretofore neglected aspects of these two important stages of self-development invite inquiry as soon as we consider the influence of the selfobject milieu on the ultimate shaping of the self that will form the center of the adult personality. Although the pathogenicity of a parent who cannot respond to the child's selfobject needs in early life may simply continue throughout the oedipal period, latency, and adolescence, the conclusion is inescapable that, in certain instances, parental selfobjects who responded appropriately during earlier phases of self-development prove unable to accommodate the needs of certain later periods, such as the oedipal period and/or adolescence. If the classical neuroses still exist—as I believe they do, however rarely they are encountered in contemporary, Western society—then we will be able to explain them fully only if we broaden our understanding of the genetics and structure of these neuroses. Specifically, we must modify our perspective on the role of drive-related conflicts in such disorders to accommodate the realization that underlying selfobject failures lead to the disintegration of the oedipal-stage self and thereby account for the expression of sexuality and aggression that typifies the Oedipus complex. Finally, I must stress that even a self whose development has been comparatively normal up to early adolescence may remain permanently incomplete as a consequence of selfobject failures experienced during this period. In particular, the adolescent's loss of an idealized selfobject of the same gender may block an important step in his subsequent self-development: the establishment, via transmuting internalization, of a self able to pursue adult sexual aims with confidence and a sense of unforced security.

IV

Having to this point focused on topics that had, implicitly or explicitly, figured in several contributions to this volume, I now turn my attention to two criticisms that were raised by Wallerstein. The first is that self psychology is monotonously uniform in its genetic explanations because it traces all forms of psychopathology back to empathy failures on the part of the patients' mothers. His second criticism pertains specifically to my recent report of "The Two Analyses of Mr. Z" (1979). My success in the second of these two analyses, Wallerstein believes, was not, as I submitted, a result of a shift in my theoretical outlook that enabled me to deal with the core of the patient's psychic disturbance. According to Wallerstein the first analysis with Mr. Z failed because it was poorly conducted, whereas the second one succeeded not because of the new theoretical orientation I had adopted, but because I had finally done what any good analyst, equipped with the conceptual instrumentarium of ego psychology, would have done from the beginning.

Are the explanations of self psychologically informed psychoanalysis indeed monotonously uniform, whereas those of traditional analysis (a comparison implied by this criticism) are multiple and varied? My answer to this accusation is, at least up to a certain point that I return to later, a clear and unambiguous "not guilty."

First of all, and this argument needs no elaboration, self psychology adds something to traditional analysis; it does not substitute for it (cf. Kohut, 1980). It can, therefore, hardly be argued that self psychology is impoverishing analysis by supplementing the traditional point of view with the vista obtained from a new vantage point. Of course, an opponent of self psychology with a sense of humor could respond that the claims of self psychology are like those of the new immigrant to the United States who boasted that if he were as rich as Rockefeller he would be richer still. When asked how he would achieve this goal, the immigrant replied that he would carry on all of Rockefeller's businesses but, in addition, open a little tobacco store on Broadway that would bring in a lot of money too. Clearly, we are obliged to show that self psychology is not the little tobacco store on Broadway of which the new immigrant speaks, but instead constitutes a significant expansion and enrichment of psychoanalysis.

Are the explanations of self psychology as uniform as some of our critics claim? I think not. To claim that they are boringly monotonous is, to my mind, like claiming that all of traditional analysis is simplistic because it explains psychopathology on the basis of conflict. Both reproaches are equally misconceived. We are dealing with different explanatory frameworks, but not with any dearth of variety within the respective frameworks. Just as traditional analysis conceptualizes endless varieties of conflict and points to endless subtleties of the conflicts that it uncovers, so self psychologically informed analysis conceptualizes endless varieties of selfobject failures that produce endless varieties of self pathology.

Rather than attempting to provide an outline of the varieties of self-selfobject failures and the corresponding varieties of resulting self-disturbances, I offer a brief illustration of the subtlety of the differentiations—or, I should rather say, of the *seeming* subtlety of the differentiations—that are involved. It is natural that upon acquaintance with a new class of phenomena one is at first able to recognize individuals only as representatives of that class. To an Oriental who has never seen Westerners, all Westerners look alike. It is only later, after having lived among Westerners, that he can differentiate between members of various nationalities, social classes, regions, urban and country folk, and the like. Eventually, he will be able to recognize many individuals effortlessly as the result of a single apperceptive closure. So also in self psychology. To the outsider, so to speak, all of our explanations may at first appear to be the same: selfobject failures of the mother. To those of us who have now worked in this field for some years, however, the differentiations have become ever so complex and variegated. We already differentiate between failures in mirroring, in idealizability, and in alter-ego presence as bringing about, variously, the fragmentation, weakness, or disharmony of the self—no less than nine options, I may add half jokingly, or even eighteen if we add to our list present-day "Schrebers" who experience the decisive selfobject failures from the side of the father. We realize, moreover, what an enormous field for further research has opened up before us, challenging us to bring further order to an almost overwhelming range of explanatory possibilities. This task of arriving at an optimum number of explanatory clusters of specific selfobject failures with their respective self pathologies still lies largely ahead of us. It was my recognition of this fact that prompted me earlier to qualify my "not guilty" plea to the accusation that the explanations of self psychology are monotonous and uniform. I submitted that self psychology was not guilty of this charge "up to a certain point." This qualification, as I hope to have now clarified, points to a need for further refinement in the classification of an optimum number—not too many, not too few—of different clusters of selfobject failures that must await our future efforts.

I now proceed to a clinical illustration that further clarifies my meaning. This illustration is drawn from the presentation of Dr. Anna Ornstein in fall 1980 at the "Symposium: Reflections on Self Psychology" in Boston. I do not wish to waste our time in praising her clear and persuasive report, but instead focus on a single, circumscribed flaw in her comprehension of the material and thus in her response to her analysand. Before doing so, however, I permit myself an aside regarding the specific data in question, because the self-psychological attitude toward the material under scrutiny—the type of dream we characterize as a "self-state dream"—has been the target of strong disapproval by some critics of self psychology.

It appears that a short passage from *The Restoration of the Self* (1977, pp. 109–110) has given rise to the erroneous claim that we are "wild" analysts who interpret the manifest content of dreams and do not listen to our patients' associations. This criticism is based on a serious misreading of my work.[6] What are the facts? They are just as I described them in 1977. In self-state dreams, I observed, free associations do not lead to layers of the mind that are more deeply unconscious, more deeply hidden than the manifest content of the dream; at best they provide us with further imagery that remains on the same level as the manifest content of the dream.

---

[6]This misreading is almost as far off the mark as the one that has given rise to the reproach that we gratify our patients by "mirroring" them and that we enjoy basking in their "idealizing" of us (cf. Kohut, 1971, pp. 260–264, where I emphasize that we do not interfere with the unfolding of selfobject transferences in order to be able to analyze them).

Thus, as a harbinger of incipient depression (i.e., before there is consciousness of a profound mood disturbance) a patient may demonstrate some marginal awareness of the impending change via dreams of empty landscapes, burned-out forests, decaying neighborhoods, and the like. Later we may well come to appreciate the fact that the depression announced in these dreams is, for example, a reaction to the analyst's going away. Moreover, the analysis may ultimately lead to the reconstruction of the genetic precursors of the analysand's sense of abandonment, including, for example, the withdrawal of a previously available selfobject following the birth of a sibling. At the moment of the harbinger dream, however, only the unconscious awareness of the impending ominous change in the state of the self is depicted, and no admonition to the patient to supply further associations to the dream elements will succeed in squeezing genuinely valid dynamic (transference) or genetic (childhood) information out of the manifest content. The only valid interpretation at this point in the analysis would therefore be: "You are getting depressed; you feel like a burned-out forest; you feel like a decaying city."

The same point can be made with regard to patients who, still consciously unaware of any mood change, announce for the first time in dreams (e.g., of an airplane out of control that wildly flies higher and higher) their anxiety lest an uncontrollable manic excitement overtake them. Again, it would be an error for the analyst to offer dynamic and genetic interpretations when such dreams occur, even though the analyst's calm reference to the precipitating trauma or to a childhood precursor of the trauma may have a beneficial (psychotherapeutic) effect at a later point in treatment (e.g., after analogous dreams have been reported and the patient has become aware of his anxiety). And it would be even worse if, after the patient has told us his dream, we gave voice to our expectation that the patient could now supply associative links to current precipitating and/or genetic-historical factors. If we, in such instances, led by our convictions about the correct path that is to be followed in analyzing a dream, thus encourage the patient to leave the manifest dream and try to approach its latent meaning, the patient will often perceive our pressure, however gently and compassionately it is applied, as an indication that we, too, have become anxious. Our most appropriate (and reassuring) response would be the simple message: "I believe you feel that you are again getting depressed (or overstimulated and out of control) and that you are anxious about that."

The same considerations, to round out this exposition, also hold for the *end* of a period of depression or of (hypo-)manic excitement. Days (or even weeks) before any mood change is noticeable (i.e., the patient is still deeply depressed or still hyperactive and excited), the patient may announce through self-state dreams the fact that he will regain his mental equilibrium. While still deeply depressed, he will dream of a snow-covered landscape with freezing and wingless gray and black birds; among these sad creatures, however, one bird will appear who flaps his wings strongly and also has a speck of color in his plumage. Correspondingly, a still overexcited, (hypo-)-manic patient may dream that, though shaky and veering a bit from side to side, the plane that he is piloting is coming in for a landing.[7]

But now I must end my discussion of self-state dreams in general and proceed to the specific dream that figures in the clinical illustration at hand. I would only express the hope, in conclusion, that future critics will cease to generalize and take into account the fact that self psychologists approach self-state dreams as a specific, circumscribed, identifiable group of phenomena. With regard to the majority of dreams, we have at no time voiced any doubt that they can indeed be deciphered only if the associative material to each of the dream elements is pursued in the traditional way.[8]

Having concluded this expository aside, let me return to Anna Ornstein's case report. I wish to focus on a single flaw in her generally exemplary presentation because I believe it is relevant to the alleged claim that self psychological interpretations are monotonous and uniform, that the flawed empathic response of the selfob-

---

[7]This analysis could be extended to show that, just as the empty and devitalized self of the depressed and the empty self of the (hypo-)manic depict their conditions through self-state dreams, so also with regard to the fragmenting self and the self that reestablishes coherence, and to the chaotic, disharmonious self and the self that reestablishes inner harmony.

[8]Although this is not the place for an extensive comparison of similarities and differences between the "Symbols in Dreams" and "Typical Dreams," which Freud (1900) presented at length in *The Interpretation of Dreams,* and the "Self-State Dreams" of Self Psychology, Freud's statement about the "two techniques of dream-interpretation" can be fruitfully consulted in the context of my own emphasis, previously stated, that, "the majority of dreams . . . can indeed be deciphered only if the associative material . . . is pursued in the traditional way."

ject is our single explanatory factor. The illustrative material culled from this case report runs as follows: At a point in the analysis when termination issues began to appear, "the patient had a dream—a self-state dream—that "there was a ship in the ocean, that the hull was seemingly all firmly put together but that, in fact, it was in great danger because all the nails and bolts that had held the parts together were gone and, furthermore, that the ship was turning over or, at least, that it was in danger of turning over." The analyst took the dream to be a self-state dream; I cannot decide with absolute certainty whether it was indeed such a dream, but I assume that the analyst, who had come to know her patient intimately, could sense the fact that the patient was describing the state of his self at this point in the treatment. The analyst thus suggested that the dream portrayed how the patient felt in relation to the recently mentioned prospect of (eventually) terminating the analysis. Concentrating on the ship-in-the-ocean image employed by the dreamer, the analyst observed that the patient was anxious about the fact that, after the end of the analysis, the safe shore of the treatment situation would no longer be in reach and that he (i.e., the patient) felt anxious and insecure on this account.

Although I believe that, as regards the dynamic precipitant of the dream, the analyst's response was on target, I do take exception to one not unimportant aspect of her interpretation. The patient's dream contained no reference to "a shore," no reference to "not reaching a shore." The nature of the patient's anxious, insecure self-state, the danger depicted in his dream, was (1) that the parts of the ship were not being held together firmly anymore, that the connecting links that had held them together (the bolts and nails) were gone, and (2) that the ship was (in danger of) turning over. In other words, the anxiety the patient felt was not—at least not at the time of the dream—focused on the loss of "the safe shore" of the analysis; it was not focused, for example, on the loss of the supportive arms of an idealized maternal selfobject. Instead, it concerned the fragmentation of the self and its lack of equilibrium, balance, uprightness in space.

The importance of such distinctions cannot be stressed enough. They do not concern shades and nuances, but rather conspicuous differences, at least for those of us who understand the specific significance of different self-states. The misunderstanding embodied in the analysts's ill-chosen metaphor was twofold: (1) It dealt with a disturbance of the self-selfobject relationship, whereas the patient was in fact preoccupied entirely with the state of his self. This is a very common misperception which, as I pointed out long ago (cf. Kohut, 1971, pp. 286–287), is often due to the analyst's reluctance to acknowledge that he has been relegated by the analysand to a position in which he is important only as a part of the analysand's self. (In our specific case the analyst had been serving as the nuts, bolts, and nails that held the patient's self together.) (2) It referred to a supposed wish or need of the patient to reach shore (it implied, in other words, that the patient was upset about the future unavailability of a harboring, sheltering selfobject), whereas the patient in fact was preoccupied entirely with disintegration, imbalance, and loss of uprightness.

Why is it so important that the analyst's understanding of the state of the analysand's self as depicted in the imagery of self-state dreams be accurate? Why, in the specific dream under scrutiny, was it not enough that the analyst supplied a dynamic referent by mentioning the termination topic? The answer is simple: Only when an analysand feels that the state of his self has been accurately understood by the selfobject analyst will he feel sufficiently secure to go further. It is one of the basic tenets of psychoanalytic self psychology as therapy (cf. Kohut, 1977, pp. 77–78) that understanding must precede explanation—indeed, that even completely accurate explanations may be useless if they have not been preceded by the establishment of a bond of accurate empathy between the analysand and the interpreting analyst.

In the specific instance at hand, only the communication of an accurate understanding of the manifest dream imagery by the analyst could have provided the emotional basis for a decisive forward move—via the emergence of further imagery about the state of the self, via the acknowledgment and the emergence of memories from childhood pertaining to early precursors of the transference dynamics in relation to the selfobjects of childhood. In response to a correctly chosen metaphor about the self-state dream, a metaphor concerning a self or body-self in danger of falling apart and losing its balance, the patient might have shared with the analyst heretofore unexpressed hypochondriacal fears about the disintegration of his body and mind; he might also have remembered similar childhood fears about his health and sanity that arose when his mother went away or became emotionally unavailable. Finally, in response to a correctly chosen metaphor, the patient might have shared with the analyst heretofore unexpressed spatial insecurities; he might have remembered traumatic childhood experiences when tentative attempts at standing, walking, running, or swimming led selfobjects to withdraw their attention or become anxious rather than to react with pride and confidence to these crucial developmental achievements.

In conclusion, then, I would emphasize that this self-state dream may have offered one more chance for analyst and analysand to grasp with new precision the nature of the selfobject's pathogenic influence on self-development. Why had the nuts, bolts, and nails of the self—O'Neill's "the grace of God is glue"—not become (via transmuting internalization) an intrinsic part of the self-structure during childhood? What was it about the nature of the selfobject's cohesion-enhancing support that necessitated the selfobject's actual presence? These are crucial questions and to answer them (e.g., via further material that may have been forthcoming after an accurate understanding of the patient's self-state was communicated through the use of an appropriate metaphor) may not only have advanced this particular analysis but added to the storehouse of scientific information that could be applied to subsequent analyses.

I believe this consideration of the interpretive subtleties elicited by a single self-state dream underscores my principal point: Far from being uniform and monotonous, self psychologically informed genetic explanations are prodigiously varied. The nine basic permutations we have outlined thus far (fragmentation, weakness, or disharmony of the self in response to a lack of mirroring, a lack of alter-ego support, or an unavailability of idealizable selfobjects) represent no more than a first crude outline of the multiplicity of self-deficiencies that derive from the multiplicity of selfobject flaws. It is challenging and exciting to contemplate the research task before us: to examine in detail the various self-states as they emerge during analysis and to correlate, via the study of the transference, specific flaws in selfobject responsiveness with specific disturbances of the self.

V

Having considered at length Wallerstein's claim that self-psychological explanations are monotonous and uniform, I now turn to his other criticism pertaining to my report of the two analyses of Mr. Z

(Kohut, 1979). Wallerstein feels that the ultimate success of Mr. Z's second analysis was not due, as I believe, to a shift in my theoretical outlook from traditional psychoanalytic theory to self psychology, but to the fact that, simply stated, the second analysis had been conducted by me with reasonable competence (i.e., in line with traditional theory and technique), whereas the first analysis had not.

Even before confronting Wallerstein's judgement concerning the two analyses of Mr. Z, I had given a good deal of thought to the position he adopts, as it has been debated by others on earlier occasions (cf. Goldberg, 1980; Ostow, 1979). You should therefore not be surprised when I immediately express my certainty that this position is essentially erroneous. Before I attempt to prove my point, however, I must briefly turn to a related issue that must be confronted before we can examine in earnest the question concerning theory change. *Expressis verbis,* the question of whether I moved to a new theory—with regard to the viewpoint of self psychology in general and with regard to the second analysis of Mr. Z in particular—implicates a larger question that has been asked a number of times. This question is whether the new theory of self psychology, if in fact there is such a theory, should be accorded the status of a new paradigm in psychoanalysis.

I must admit that I dislike the term (and the concept) of "paradigm," at least as it has come to be understood in psychoanalysis during the past 15 years or so (cf. Gitelson, 1964). It is no longer a sober, well-defined scientific concept—if, indeed, it ever was one—but a value judgment. It connotes, so to speak, a scientific batting average of .400 or more; it has undergone the kind of transformation that Wallerstein likes to characterize as "vulgarization." Even at best (i.e., even if we could cleanse the concept of the admixture of grandiosity that it has acquired), I do not believe the concept has much to recommend itself, at least not with regard to the use to which psychoanalysts have tended to put Kuhn's (1962) original formulation. Psychoanalysts have used (or abused) it in order to protect and buttress a scientific conservatism, which holds that Freud spelled out the principles that must continue to guide analytic thinking, that Freud's basic dictums define psychoanalysis, and that any major reorientation of psychoanalytic thinking is tantamount to an abandonment of the psychoanalytic paradigm and the establishment of a new science.

I have discussed these issues before (cf. Kohut, 1977, pp. 298–312) and suggested that, taking physics as a model, the definition of any branch of science, including psychoanalysis, should be open-ended. Overly precise definitions, especially when based on sup-posedly unalterable doctrine, cannot help but have a stifling effect on thought and thus on the vitality of the science that is restricted by them. I believe, in this connection, that analysts should realize that it is not specific theories that define their science, but the field of investigation (the inner life of man) as defined by their basic observational stance (introspection and empathy). The contribu-tions of both Newton and Planck, although based on completely different orienting theories, constitute physics because the field of observation (the inanimate world) and the scientist's basic attitude toward it (extrospection) remain unchanged. And the same should hold true for psychoanalysis, a science that is defined not by the specific theories formulated by Freud's ordering mind, however awe-inspiring the depth and breadth of his life work, but by the good fortune—the genius of the moment, one might say—of Breuer's and Anna O's seminal encounter. It is the basic psychoanalytic situa-tion, in other words, the situation of someone reporting his inner life while another empathically listens to the report in order to be able to explain it, that defines analysis and not the particular theory or ordering principle that the listener employs.

Having said this much, let us finally turn to the two analyses of Mr. Z. Bypassing all questions about psychoanalytic technique in general and dispensing with any defense of my personal skills as an analyst in particular, I restrict my focus to the only task that I consider significant. Specifically, I undertake to support two inter-related claims that have been rejected by my critics: the claim that I was indeed guided by a different theory during the second analysis, and furthermore, the claim that this different theory indeed allowed me to see Mr. Z's personality disorder from a vantage point that was closer to the psychological truth than the vantage point provided by the first analysis. My attempt to support these two interrelated claims is made with the aid of a single comparison between my interpretation of one specific set of data in the first analysis and my interpretation of this same material in the second analysis. My spec-imen is Mr. Z's dream of his father's return, which occurred toward the end of the first analysis and was spontaneously remembered by the patient—and reanalyzed—during the corresponding stage of the second analysis.

I need not burden my discussion with an account of clinical de-tails, but merely direct the reader to the relevant sections of the original report (1979, pp. 8–9, 22–23). Suffice it to say here that the dream in question was clearly a significant transference dream[9] and that it was correlated to crucial genetic experiences of the oedipal period. (Mr. Z's father, who had been away, leaving mother and son alone, returned when the little boy was about 5.) In the dream Mr. Z's father is depicted as loaded with gifts for the patient and trying to enter the house. The patient, however, tries desperately to keep him out, throwing his whole weight against the door, which the father is trying to open.

Leaving aside any discussion of certain shades and nuances concerning the interpretation of this dream, I believe I can safely claim, as indeed I did in my report, that when I interpreted this dream as depicting an aspect of the Oedipus complex of my patient, I was fully in harmony with the traditional outlook in which I had been trained and to which I had more or less subscribed up to that time. The father intends to intrude on the mother-son couple; his gifts are his Trojan horse. The son, for his part, feeling that the father is trying to seduce him in order to gain entrance and that once inside the house will castrate him—"I fear the Greeks even though they bring gifts"—experiences profound anxiety and mobilizes all the power at his disposal to keep the father out.

Returning to the issue at stake, I cannot accept as valid the claim that my original conceptualization of this dream from the perspective of the Oedipus complex was an unusually clumsy or erroneous move. On the contrary, I remain as convinced as ever that an overwhelming majority of my colleagues would have approached it in approximately the same way; indeed, that a large majority of analysts would do likewise even today. I would further avow that disregarding certain questions of emphasis (e.g., the question of to what extent the boy's passive homosexuality may have found expression in the dream), the explanatory framework that I invoked was fully in tune with tradition.

And what was my attitude in the second analysis? How did the fact that I had broadened my conceptual instrumentarium via the formulation of a new set of theories influence my perspective on this

---

[9]Although this particular aspect of the dream lies ouside the area of our specific present concerns I should point out that it occurred in the first analysis (and was remobilized in the second) at a juncture when termination was contemplated, that is, at a juncture when the pressure to complete the analytic task paralleled the pressure (to be discussed later) that the boy felt vis-à-vis a similar task at the age of 5.

dream, allowing me to come closer to the psychological truth than had been possible during the first analysis?

The shift in perspective that determined the focus of my empathic perceptions as I analyzed Mr. Z's dream in the second analysis was indeed a crucial one. Stated most tersely, it was a shift from macropsychology to micropsychology.[10] I had shifted, in other words, from the effort to identify psychological macrostructures in conflict, on the one hand, to the effort to identify certain specific defects in the structure of the self along with certain manifestations of the patient's activated need to acquire a strong, cohesive, and harmonious self, on the other hand. Formulated in the terms of experience-near theory, Mr. Z had been deprived of the presence of an idealizable selfobject father during an important phase of self-development in childhood. Therefore, his self was defective and in need of transmuting internalizations via prolonged exposure to innumerable small-scale disappointments in the idealized paternal selfobject (optimal frustrations). The dream under scrutiny, as I saw during the second analysis, did not depict a rival's return and fear of castration but an *embarras de richesses*—the sudden availability of an excess of identificatory opportunities. Unable to assimilate all that was now offered to him, the boy's psyche was overburdened, and he experienced the intense anxiety of a traumatic state, hopelessly trying to stem the influx of identifications that endangered the existence of his precariously established self. (It must not be forgotten, I should stress, that any self, however stunted its growth and however abnormal its form and content, is better than no self at all, and that any threat to the continued existence of even a severely defective self

---

[10]cf my earlier distinction between "macropsychology" (metaphorically speaking, psychological "mountains," e.g., id-impulses clashing with prohibitions) and "micropsychology" (metaphorically speaking, psychological "subparticles"). In the specific instance of Mr. Z, the distinction is between the predominant aim of my attention in the two analyses. In the first analysis my attention was not on the pervasive defects in the fabric of the self, but on conflicts that I saw raging between large areas of *segments* of the mental apparatus (intersystemic: hostile impulses in conflict with superego injunctions; intrasystemic: hostile impulses clashing with loving ones) or on conflicts that I saw raging betwen broad *sectors* of the mental apparatus (hostile impulses in conflict with reality or, expressed in intersystemic terms, in conflict with the ego as the agent of reality). In the second analysis, however, my predominant attention was not on gross intersystemic or intrasystemic conflicts, but on the minute but pervasive defects in the fabric of the patient's self (for a description of the process by which the particles that form the fabric of psychic structure are laid down, see Kohut, 1971, and Kohut & Seitz, 1963).

will be opposed with all the powers at the disposal of the personality.)

I would add, furthermore, that the homosexualization of Mr. Z's identificatory needs, which had undoubtedly taken place—a homosexuality with passive anal- and oral-incorporative preconscious imagery surrounded by disintegration anxiety that may at times have been tinged with a trace of paranoid suspiciousness—is, in our context, to be understood as his attempt to modulate and control the intense need for the identificatory, structural "gifts" that the father's presence now suddenly made available. The boy's attempt to block the intrusion of the father and his gifts is therefore to be understood not as a defense against castration anxiety but as a defense against the threat of loss of self, preconsciously elaborated as a closing of bodily openings into which the maleness of the father is experienced by him as wanting to intrude. The child needs the maleness; he needs the identificatory gifts. By getting them all at once, however, his precariously established self is now in danger of being destroyed, of being replaced, of being taken over wholesale by the self of another.[11]

Should we then claim, on the basis of this clinical example illustrating the direction into which our thinking has moved, that self psychology has created a new "paradigm"? I believe that this question is a matter of taste and nomenclature rather than a substantive scientific issue. Having appended this qualifier, however, I am still inclined to respond to the question in the negative. In particular, with reference to the theory change that took place between the two analyses of Mr. Z, I agree with M. Ferguson (1981), who convincingly adduced my report on "The Two Analyses of Mr. Z" as evidence

---

[11]The individual who at a developmentally decisive juncture, such as that outlined for Mr. Z at the time of his father's return, abandons his precariously established self, thus relinquishing all hope for its future strengthening and growth, lays the groundwork for a manifestly homosexual position in later life. That even in the instances the original self is retained, however disdainfully it may be disavowed, is attested to by the lifelong mourning that a perceptive observer can sense in many homosexuals (i.e., by the depressive undertones that resonate throughout the whole span of any "gay" life). It is least in evidence, though still discernible, in the active partner of the homosexual couple (whether female or male) who, in the enactment and lifelong dramatization of the incorporation of the needed selfobject of childhood, assumes the role of the endlessly giving, self-substance-providing selfobject at the same time as the partner represents his own needy childhood self (for an early description of these relationships, see Kohut, 1948).

for his own (in my words) "antiparadigm" position. Ferguson demonstrates, in support of the conception of the steps by which science
advances held by such philosophers of science as Laudan (1977) and
Feyerabend (1975), that the significance of the theory change that
took place between the two analyses of Mr. Z is most cogently defined with reference to the fact that the new theory has greater
explanatory power and broader explanatory scope than the old theory it replaces.

Still, having given expression to my agreement with the "antiparadigm" position, at least as regards psychoanalysis, and having
endorsed Ferguson's way of formulating the effect of self-psychological theory on the success of the second analysis of Mr. Z, I now feel
impelled to make an entry on the other side of the account. I feel
impelled to stress, in other words, that the significance of the forward move in the development of depth psychology embodied in the
theories of self psychology and in its whole outlook on man is insufficiently appreciated so long as one restricts one's evaluation to the
problem-solving power of its formulations. Or, to restate my view in
yet another way, the greater problem-solving ability of self psychology is, itself, an outgrowth of a shift in emphasis and perspective
that differentiates it from traditional analysis and allows us to
speak of it as a new step in psychoanalysis.

Self psychology constitutes a new step in depth psychology because its psychological observations are made against the background of a broader conception of man and his problems. It sees man
not only as "Guilty Man," a psychic organization split by conflicts
and either functioning despite them or malfunctioning because of
them, a psychic organization fueled in its activities by drives and
either breaking down under their at times excessive pressure or
withstanding the pressure and transforming the underlying energy
into adaptive action. It also sees him as "Tragic Man," an abiding
self in need of nutriment for its establishment and maintenance and
endangered by the flawed responses of selfobjects throughout life, a
self falling ill (the fragmented, enfeebled, or disharmonious self)
when the gap between the need for sustenance from selfobjects and
the actual performance with which they respond becomes too great,
or able to maintain itself courageously, despite selfobject failure, on
the basis of the sustaining responses it has experienced in the past
and the confident expectation of renewed selfobject availability in
the future.

Self psychology, further, constitutes a new step in depth psychology because, after first identifying certain dominant values by which analysts have traditionally been guided—values, I must add, which have unduly narrowed and even, at times, distorted our perception of the psychological phenomena that we observe both as therapists and as scientific investigators of the human mind—it has been able to achieve an appropriate degree of emotional detachment from them, broadening our outlook on the psychological field, and thereby rectifying some of the former distortions of our clinical perception and theoretical understanding. Among the ideals that self psychologically informed analysis no longer places at the very pinnacle of its hierarchy of values, I can mention two: (1) the ideal of courageously facing the truth; (2) the ideal of psychological independence. Both ideals, as any student of the history of ideas knows, have for a number of centuries been leading values of Western man. And psychoanalysis, via Freud's personal affinity for these values, adopted them as integral constituents of its therapeutic and scientific philosophy. Up to a point they are, of course, important and attractive values, but their relative importance as inner guides and prompters is not uniform for all people. They may be less relevant than other values to the particular kind of inner guidance needed by certain individuals. Moreover, there are also specific periods of history—our own is one of them, we believe—when the values of truth-facing and/or independence are unrelated to the dominant era-specific psychological dangers that man confronts. In such periods man must maintain his threatened psychological integrity with the aid of other, era-specific values and ideals. We believe that truth-facing should be, to express our meaning in traditional mental apparatus terms, predominantly a function of the ego and not of the superego. In this context an ideal of independence, which undoubtedly functioned as an important value for certain individuals during certain periods of history, must, in a broader psychological perspective, be evaluated as an idealistic and unrealistic abstraction. As the self psychologist sees it—and we believe that we are here in tune with the essential psychological problem of our century—the dominant positions in the value scale of modern man are occupied by those values that further the establishment and buttress the maintenance of man's creative-productive self. The peak values of modern man, in other words, are those values that guide and sustain him in the attempt to reassemble his self through an increased and guilt-free ability to find appropriate selfobjects and in the attempt to liberate his innate ability to serve—and to serve joyfully—as a selfobject for others.

But I fear that I have let myself be lured away from the main purposes of my discussion by the attraction that experience-distant, broad topics tend to exert on all of us. In reflecting thus on scientific progress and the historical change of values, however, I have not lost sight of the fact that this volume is primarily directed to those interested in the clinical application of self psychologcal theories, and it behooves me to end my discussion on a note of concreteness and sobriety. Returning, therefore, to the clinical point on which I focused earlier in the analysis of the dream of the return of Mr. Z's father, I repeat that in the first analysis my attention had been focused almost exclusively on the scrutiny of psychological macrostructures (i.e., on Mr. Z's conflicts), whereas in the second analysis the theory changes that had taken place during the interval between the analyses guided me toward the examination of microstructures (i.e., to the condition of Mr. Z's self). "What was the state of Mr. Z's self as it was reflected in the dream?" I asked myself. And then, grasping the fact that Mr. Z was not trying to keep out a dangerous competitor—a drive-object—but was trying to control the sudden, massive influx of identifications that endangered his self, I was able to assist him in the task of bringing his analysis to a successful conclusion.

REFERENCES

Ferguson, M. (1981). The two analyses of Mr. Z. *Annual of Psychoanal.* 9: 133–160.

Feyerabend, P. (1975). *Against Method: Outline of an Anarchistic Theory of Knowledge.* Atlantic Highlands, N.J.: Humanities Press.

Freud, S. (1900) The interpretation of dreams. *Standard Edition,* 4 & 5. London: Hogarth Press, 1953.

Gitelson, M. (1964). On the identity crisis in American psychoanalysis. *J. Amer. Psychoanal. Assn.* 12: 451–476.

Goldberg, A. (1980). Letter to the Editor. *Int. J. Psychoanal.* 61: 91–92.

Kohut, H. (1948). Death in Venice by Thomas Mann: A story about the disintegration of artistic sublimation. In *The Search for the Self,* Vol. I. P. Ornstein, ed. New York: Int. Univ. Press, 1978, pp. 107–130.

———(1959). Introspection, empathy and psychoanalysis: An examination of the relationship between mode of observation and theory. In *The Search for the Self,* Vol. I. P. Ornstein, ed. New York: Int. Univ. Press, 1978, pp. 205–232.

———(1966). Forms and transformations of narcissism. In *The Search for the Self,* Vol. I. P. Ornstein, ed. New York: Int. Univ. Press, 1978, pp. 427–460.

———(1968). The psychoanalytic treatment of narcissistic personality disorders. In *The Search for the Self,* Vol. I. P. Ornstein, ed. New York: Int. Univ. Press, 1978, pp. 477–509.

———(1971). *The Analysis of the Self.* New York: Int. Univ. Press.

———(1977). *The Restoration of the Self.* New York: Int. Univ. Press.

———(1978). Letter in response to lecture by Heller, E. In *Critical Inquiry,* Vol. 4. Chicago: Univ. of Chicago Press, p. 441.

———(1979). The two analyses of Mr. Z. *Int. J. Psychoanal.* 60: 3–28.

———(1980). Reflections on advances in self psychology. In *Advances in Self Psychology.* A. Goldberg, ed. New York: Int. Univ. Press, pp. 485–487; p. 510 ff.

———(in preparation). Letter to R. Stolorow. In *The Search for the Self,* Vol. III. P. Ornstein, ed. in press.

——— & Seitz, P. F. D. (1963). Concepts and theories of psychoanalysis. In *The Search for the Self,* Vol. I. P. Ornstein, ed. New York: Int. Univ. Press, 1978, pp. 337–374.

Kuhn, T. S. (1962). *The Structure of Scientific Revolutions.* Chicago: Univ. of Chicago Press.

Laudan, L. (1977). *Progress and its Problems.* Berkeley, L. A. and London: Univ. of California Press.

Ostow, M. (1979). Letter to the Editor. *Int. J. Psychoanal.* 60: 531–532.

Name Index

E

Edgecumbe, R., 192, *201*
Eissler, K. R., 26, *33*, 121, *122*, 317, *335*, 369–370, *384*
Emde, R. N., 62, 80, *82*, 119, *122*
Erikson, E. H., 19, 103, *104*, 192, *202*, 264

F

Fagan, J. F., 63, 66, 67, *82*
Ferenczi, A., 5, 26
Ferguson, M., 412–413, *415*
Feyerabend, P., 413, *415*
Fogel, A., 67, *82*
Fraiberg, S., 53, *82*
French, T. M., *335*
Freud, A., 21, 30, *33*, 240, 315, *336*, 354
Freud, S., 4, *7*, 11, 19, 22–23, 24, 26, 28, 30, 32, *33*, 37, 38, 40, *42*, 70, 120, 122, 135, 136, *147*, 152, 154, 156–157, *161*, 187, 191, 192, 198, 207, *215*, 224, 225, 226, 228, 230, 233–234, 240, 241, 242, 269, *277*, 285, 287, 288, 289, *296*, 299, 300, 306, 314, 315, 317, 322, 327, 330, 331, 334, *336*, 351, 357, 358, 359, 368, 378, 388, 389, 390, 391, 404n8, 409, 414, *415*
Frey, P., 5, *7*

G

Gedo, J., 151, *161*
Gertsman, L. J., 60, *81*
Gibson, E. J., 57, *82*
Gifford, S., 19, 20, *33*
Gill, M., 24, 240
Gitelson, M., 26, 408, *415*
Glover, E., 16, 17, 28, *33*, 113, *122*
Goffman, E., 71, *82*
Goldberg, A., 31, *33*, 127, *133*, 151, *161*, 283, 284, 286, 295, *296*, 297–312, 339, 340, 345, 356, 387, 408, *415*
Greenson, R. R., 26, 199, 328, 329, *336*, 376
Greenwood, A., 65, 66, *83*
Greundel, J. M., 71, *82*
Gunther, M. S., 266
Gutheil, T., 131, *133*

H

Haith, M. M., 59, *82*

Hartmann, H., 17, 21, 26, *33*, 120, 122, *123*, 150, 152, *161*, 198, 240, 265, *267*, 293, *296*, 298, 359
Havens, L., 131, *133*
Hendrick, I., 6, *7*, 19

J

Jacobson, E., 5, 152, *161*, 240
Jacobson, J. G., *336*

K

Kagan, J., 56, 65, 66, *82*
Kaplan, S., *48*, 85, 109, 110, *112*, 182n5, *185*, 219–222
Kardiner, A., 24, *33*
Kearsley, R. B., 56, 65, 66, *82*
Kernberg, O., 151, 152, 153, *161*, *267*, 315, 329, *336*, 354, 362–363
Klaus, M. H., 88, *104*
Klein, G., 24, *48*, 46, 47, 109, *112*, 284, 288, 289, 291, 292, *296*, 345, 346, *384*
Klein, M., 55, 69, 70, *82*
Klerman, G. L., 250, *267*
Kohut, H., 13–17, 20–21, 22, 23, 24–33, *34*, *48*, 43–44, 45, 50, 74, *82*, 85, 109, 110, 111, *112*, 113, 114, 120, 122, *123*, 127, 128, 131, 132, *133*, 135, 137, 138n1, 139, 147, *148*, 149, 151, 152, 159, 160, *161*, 163, 164, 181n4, *184*, 189, 192, 195, 201, 204, 205, 209, 211, 214, 219, 220, *222*, 224, 234–235, 236, 237, *238*, 247–249, 256, 263, *267*, 273, 287, 288, 291–295, *296*, 298, 300, 305, 313–319, 321–335, *336*, 340, 341, 346–348, 350, 351, 354, 355, 357, 358, 360, 362, 366, 367, 371, 374–377, 379, 380, 381–383, *384*, 387–416
Koslowski, B., 67, *81*
Kris, E., 26, 320, *336*
Kuhn, T. S., 243, 317, *336*, 356, 408, *416*

L

Lachmann, F., 131, *133*, 151, *161*, 289, 292, 294, 295, *296*
Lampl-deGroot, J., 201, *202*
Landan, L., 413, *416*
Lasch, C., 10, 11, 29, *34*
Lawson, K. R., 57, *82*
Levin, S., 6, *7*

Subject Index

Action, interpretation versus, 279
Action language, 290, 348, 349
Affect(s)
  drive states and, 108
  infancy, 41, 69
Affective experience, 70–79
American Psychoanalytic Association, 20, 313
Analogy, 181n4
Analytic relationship
  models of, 345
  variations in, 26
  (*see also* Empathy)
Anxiety
  disintegration anxiety, 121
  infancy, 68
  self psychology and, 388
Applied psychoanalysis, 11–12
Archaic selfobject, 346–347, 356
  relationships, 397–398
  transferences, 395–396
  (*see also* Selfobject)
Attachment, separation-individuation, 160
Attachment theory, 53–54
Attention, 107
  neurophysiology of, 96–97
Autonomy, 342

Background and foreground constructions, 166–170, 183, 193, 190–195, 205, 207

Bassinet monitor, 89
Behavior
  longitudinal study of, 100–104
  organizational perspective on, 85
  prestructuring of, 59–62
Behaviorism, 225, 229
Biorhythmicity, 90–104
Bipolar self, 128, 235
  analytic situation and, 210–211, 236
  concept of, 313, 348–350, 352
  development of, 322–323
  ego psychology and, 152
  health concept and, 205
  theoretical implications of, 153, 366–367
Borderline patients, 226
  confrontation and, 248, 262
  diagnostic considerations in, 248–249
  therapist and, 276
Boston Psychoanalytic Society and Institute, 6, 7, 20
Brain
  consciousness and, 86
  equilibrium, 96
British Object Relations School, 72

Castration anxiety, 155, 157
Causal conditions, prestructuring of, 64–65
Causal science, 25
Center for Psychosocial Studies (Chicago), 9

421